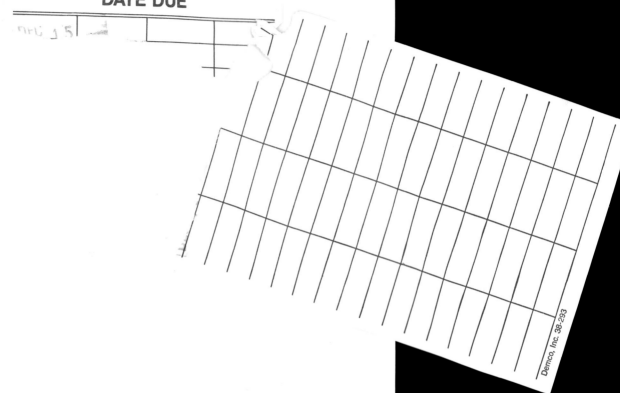

Academic Librarianship in a Transformational Age
Program, Politics, and Personnel

Academic Librarianship in a Transformational Age
Program, Politics, and Personnel

Allen B. Veaner

G. K. Hall & Co. • Boston, Massachusetts

Academic Librarianship in a Transformational Age:
Program, Politics, and Personnel

Allen B. Veaner

Selections from *The Change Masters* copyright (c) 1983 by Rosabeth Moss
Kanter. Reprinted by permission of Simon & Schuster, Inc.
Selection from *Three Degrees above Zero* by Jeremy Bernstein. Originally
appeared in the *New Yorker,* 8/20/84. Reprinted by permission of Charles
Scribner's Sons, an imprint of Macmillan Publishing Company.
Selections from ACRL statements quoted and reprinted with permission of the
American Library Association.
Selection from the *Texas Library Journal* reprinted with permission. The *Texas
Library Journal* is the quarterly journal of the Texas Library Association.
Selection from "When Executives Burn Out" reprinted by permission of *Harvard
Business Review.* Excerpt from "When Executives Burn Out" by Harry Levinson
(May-June 1981). Copyright (c) 1981 by the President and Fellows of Harvard
College; all rights reserved.

Printed on acid-free paper and bound in
the United States of America.

Library of Congress Cataloging-in-Publication Data

Veaner, Allen B., 1929-
Academic librarianship in a transformational
age : program, politics, and personnel / Allen B. Veaner.
p. cm. - (Professional librarian series)
Includes bibliographical references.
ISBN 0-8161-1866-3. - ISBN 0-8161-1875-2 (pbk.)
1. Libraries, University and college-Administration.
I. Title. II. Series.
Z675.U5V4 1989
025.1'977-dc20   89-27335
                                  CIP

To Bonnie and Julie

CONTENTS

FOREWORD

Allen Veaner's main message, which I heartily endorse, is that the greatest challenge facing academic libraries in the next decade is not funding or technology, but leadership and administrative ability. We need to develop a cadre of library leaders and administrators who are committed to making libraries more productive, more innovative, and more entrepreneurial to ensure their viability in a world where the competition for resources and markets is unrelenting. With the publication of this volume, Allen Veaner has made an important contribution to that goal.

This book is first and foremost an excellent and comprehensive treatise on academic library administration, designed to give the reader insight and instruction in the various aspects of managing the rapidly evolving academic library. But it is far more than that. It is, as the title suggests, a book about how academic libraries and their parent institutions have been and are being transformed by powerful economic, social, and technological forces during the second half of this century.

What distinguishes this book from others on library administration is that several chapters provide a perspective and context for understanding where academic libraries have come from and where they are going in the decade ahead. The first three chapters describe the transformed world of libraries, academic institutions, and administrative theory and practice, while the concluding chapter offers a perceptive look at the trends, problems, and challenges of the next decade and beyond. All four are recommended to anyone with a serious interest in the evolution and future of academic libraries. The many chapters in between offer a wealth of practical knowledge and insights for academic librarians holding or aspiring to administrative positions.

Academic Librarianship in a Transformational Age is not only informed by the author's thirty years of experience as an academic library administrator and innovator in three of the country's leading academic research libraries, it also draws upon an impressive array of scholarly sources in a variety of disciplines. Thoughtful and thought provoking, the book will take its place as a classic in the field of academic library administration.

Richard De Gennaro, Director
The New York Public Library

PREFACE

WHY ANOTHER BOOK ON LIBRARY ADMINISTRATION?

Countless books have been written on every aspect of general administration, and there are several excellent works on library administration by experienced and highly respected authors.[1] Since 1971, *University Library Administration* by Rogers and Weber has been a classic text for use in North America and the most comprehensive modern work of its kind; it is still highly valuable. Guy R. Lyle's *The Administration of the College Library* is no longer current, but is a useful reference work. More recent works by Thompson and Carr, Durey, and Stirling maintain a strong British Commonwealth focus and do not emphasize many aspects of administration that are peculiar to North America. Works by Evans and Rizzo provide the student of academic library administration with sound theoretical foundations. Stueart and Moran's *Library Management*, now in its third edition, is an excellent generic handbook aimed at all types of libraries. White has written a superb book on general library personnel administration. Readers edited by Wasserman and Bundy, Lynch, and Person offer gatherings of recent management literature from within and beyond the library profession; Miller and Rockwood, and more recently, McCabe, have edited readers on the administration of small academic libraries.

Why one more? Twenty-five years of experience with academic librarians and administrators at many levels convince me that the profession now needs a work that (1) pointedly emphasizes the persistent conflicts between a rapidly changing external world and the slowly changing world of personnel; (2) focuses on how the world of administration actually operates, as distinct from models that describe the way it ought to function; and (3) stresses everyday, realistic problems and practicalities--the kinds of issues discussed by graduate library school alumni new to administration, seasoned administrators, and library personnel officers at professional conferences and workshops and during visits to other institutions. It is not that earlier works have ignored these issues, but rather that subsequent events have amplified their impact and importance, and demanded new responses. In detail, there are four main justifications for a new work.

Technical and Social Changes

In less than a generation major social and technological changes have revolutionized the world of administration. The chief administrator is no longer an autocrat with virtually unlimited powers. Because of the impact of new tools, especially microcomputers, completely new relationships are emerging among managers, professionals, and others. Everywhere they are used, microcomputers are changing management structures, distributing information more widely, and, more important, giving professionals superb opportunities to be innovative and much more creatively independent than ever before.

Perceived Inadequacies in Socialization for Administration and Management

As Person has shown, the historically stronger focus of graduate programs in librarianship on technique and technology, rather than management and administration in the real world, has produced a generation of professional staff not ideally suited to the demands of the present or the immediate future.[2] Librarianship generally has prepared its professionals very well for service responsibilities and technical-bibliographic proficiency, but has done much less well in socializing them to leadership roles. Librarians moving into leadership and administration are sometimes surprised by their new responsibilities and the expectations of campus administrations. Some are not only unprepared for such responsibilities, but are unwilling or unable to make the transition from a vocational to an administrative way of thinking. Although many schools have modernized their curricula and alert practitioners have upgraded themselves through continuing education, administrators will still have to deal with the products of earlier programs. Unlike computer hardware and software, staff cannot readily be unplugged and replaced with updated versions.

Changes in Staff Attitudes and Expectations

Contemporary views of governance and collegiality are much different from those of a generation ago. Today's employees consciously see themselves far more as individuals than did their predecessors. The outlook, orientation, and expectations of people entering the library work force--at both the professional and support levels--have shifted from willing obedience to eagerness to maintain greater control over their work performance.

Decline of Institutional Autonomy

Compared to the 1950s, administrative actions now are governed by numerous external constraints, such as programs and legislation at state, federal, and provincial levels, and the terms of collective bargaining agreements.

This volume takes a position between the highly developed academic treatises and the management books from the business world with their ready-made solutions. The value of academic treatises in administrative science cannot be ignored, and it would be equally foolish to disregard the experience of the business world. Academic library managers and administrators can have no more powerful weapons in their intellectual armory than mastery of appropriate theoretical literature in management science and thorough familiarity with contemporary business administration.

For these reasons I have generously cited both academic and business-oriented materials, relying on readers' judgment to select what is useful and reject what is not. Successful administrators absorb the full spectrum of pertinent literature from every source, precisely because they know that "textbook" solutions do not exist and that real administration always combines theory and practice on a daily basis.

READERSHIP AND PURPOSE

The intended readership of this book is academic librarians holding or aspiring to administrative positions. One of its purposes is to help readers understand basic institutional realities and learn about certain fundamental issues and forces that are independent of methodological differences and administrative styles. My intention is to describe certain key issues, facts, and problems and to encourage librarian-administrators to develop their own solutions. Therefore this book focuses on persistent issues and forces that endure long after one technology has replaced another. A secondary purpose is to aid career development by identifying major characteristics and requirements of administrative life. Not everyone is suited to administration; some aspirants would do themselves and the profession a favor by choosing a different line of career development.

Although I offer selected practical hints on problem solution and problem avoidance, solving specific problems is not my primary focus; that administrative challenge must be tailored to the infinite variety of conditions on the campuses. By learning how to cope successfully with rapid external change and with comparatively slow institutional change, librarian-administrators can develop methodologies for inventing their own answers--surely the ultimate challenge to imaginative leadership. I have freely incorporated my own biases and views into suggestions and recommendations specific to certain problems. I have tried to avoid being anecdotal but rather have attempted to present generalities and broad principles. In the expectation that this volume is not the type one reads from cover to cover, I restate in several places the political character of administration and the necessity to form alliances and coalitions.

SCOPE AND LIMITATIONS

The subject of this book is the general function of administration in four-year colleges and universities.[3] Because a work on this topic cannot be exhaustive (administration is much too complex for that) there are significant omissions. Anyone looking for the complete how-to-do-it handbook will be disappointed. With the exception of personnel, readers will find comparatively little advice specific to the management of any single function in the academic library (e.g., automation, bibliographic instruction, branch library management, collection development, collective bargaining negotiations, measuring organizational effectiveness, reference, technical services, training, etc.) Many specialized works have been published on these topics. For general and comprehensive coverage, Rogers and Weber's book remains unequaled, despite its age.

For convenience, much of the text is illustrated from the viewpoint of a chief librarian; however, the problems, principles, and methods are similar for any level of administration. A great many of the cited works derive from medium-size and large academic libraries, but are easily adaptable to smaller institutions. The extreme size range of academic libraries makes design of a general work difficult; it is my hope that readers can adjust the contents to their specific situations.

My recommendations concerning the legal aspects of the employer-employee relationship and personnel actions are solely the suggestions and opinions of a layperson, not legal advice. Every administrator contemplating or involved in adverse personnel actions must obtain legal advice from a lawyer or the institution's staff legal counsel, or both.

In reaching for a gender-free writing style, I have striven for a middle ground, between those who would interdict all use of "he" and those who would ignore an important change in public perception and usage. I chose not to attempt the technique of equally distributing masculine and feminine pronouns. For word choice in doubtful cases, I have generally (but not always) followed

Rosalie Maggio's *The Nonsexist Word Finder* (Phoenix, Ariz: Oryx, 1987).

Although I reside in Canada, my entire administrative career has been with academic libraries in the United States. My knowledge of Canada and Canadian academic institutions is limited. Hence this work does not pretend to cover the substantial differences between the two countries with respect to culture, law, and administrative practice in higher education. Nevertheless I hope the work will prove useful in Canada and perhaps even elsewhere beyond the United States.

Between now and the year 2020 academic library administrators will deal principally with the "baby-boomer" generation, whose most productive years, according to the U.S. Bureau of the Census, will range over that period.[4] Beginning in the year 2000 North American academic library administrators will confront challenges quite different from today's, probably including the beginnings of something entirely opposite to the baby-boom phenomenon: a "shrunk generation." That coming generation is likely to face scarcity of material and personnel resources, hold reduced expectations, and harbor few illusions about the inevitability of progress. Still another book on administration will then be required. Meanwhile, I hope the present work will stimulate further research, debate, and publication on the topic, and help today's academic library administrators prepare for a very rapidly evolving future.

Notes

1. See the appendix for full citations to the works mentioned here.

2. Ruth J. Person, "The Third Culture: Managerial Socialization in the Library Setting," *Advances in Library Administration and Organization* (JAI Press) 4 (1985): 1-24.

3. In this work administration is the broad, global word; management is the narrower word.

4. Bureau of the Census, *Statistical Brief SB-1-86*, December 1986.

ACKNOWLEDGMENTS

I am pleased to acknowledge the assistance of the following persons who suggested topics and contributed ideas: Donna Arrowood (Stanford), Lynn Baird (Idaho), Joyce Ball (formerly California State, Sacramento), William K. Black (Iowa State), Shirley Bolles (Rutgers), Sheila D. Creth (Iowa), Erik de Bruijn (British Columbia), Evelyn Daniel (North Carolina), Margaret Deacon (University of California, Santa Barbara), Barbara I. Dewey (Iowa), Ruth Donovan (Nevada/Reno), Miriam Drake (Georgia Tech), Shirley Echelman (formerly Association of Research Libraries), Patricia A. Ekland (University of Victoria), Patricia Fisher (University of Denver), Karen K. Griffith (Case-Western Reserve), Ellen Hoffmann (York), Edward G. Holley (North Carolina), Judy Horn (University of California, Irvine), Darrell L. Jenkins (Southern Illinois), Larry Kahle (Nebraska), Janice Koyama (University of California, Berkeley), W. David Laird (Arizona), Hwa-Wei Lee (Ohio University), Sul Lee (Oklahoma), Thomas W. Leonhardt (Oregon), Anne Lipow (University of California, Berkeley), Kay Marie Mackenzie (Toronto), Charles Martell (California State, Sacramento), Nancy H. Marshall (William and Mary), James R. Martin (Florida State), Suzanne Massonneau (Vermont), John Mayeski (Kearney State), Barbara Moran (North Carolina), Charlotte Mudge (Toronto), Marilyn Myers (Wichita State), James G. Neal (Indiana University), Randy Olsen (Brigham Young), Marion Paris (University of Alabama), Valerie Pena

(University of Pennsylvania), Ruth J. Person (University of Missouri, St. Louis), Susan Steele (Texas A & M), Norman D. Stevens (Connecticut), Ann Stone (Duke), Suzanne S. Striedieck (Penn State), Maureen Sullivan (Yale), Don R. Swanson (GLS, Chicago), John Teskey (Alberta), John Vasi (University of California, Santa Barbara), Mary Vasilakis (Westinghouse Electric), Gisela Webb (Texas Tech), Herbert S. White (Indiana University), Jo B. Whitlatch (San Jose State), Thomas L. Wilding (MIT), Jerome Yavarkovsky (New York State Library), Irene Yeh (Stanford).

In twenty-five years of academic library administration, I learned a great deal from mentors and colleagues. I would especially single out Douglas W. Bryant, Eleanor A. Montague, Rutherford D. Rogers, Gail Ann Schlachter, and David C. Weber.

For many years I have especially benefited from the stimulating and always informative discussions of the Personnel Administrators and Staff Development Officers Discussion Group in the Association of College and Research Libraries. I owe more than I can ever repay to all the members of that dedicated group. I am equally appreciative of the many helpful contributions from ALA's Office for Library Personnel Resources and its dedicated director, Margaret Myers. Mary Jo Lynch, director of ALA's Office for Research, generously gave of her time to supply statistical data.

I am grateful to the Faculty of Library and Information Science (FLIS), University of Toronto, for permitting my unrestricted use of their superb collections. Diane Henderson, head librarian, Ellen Jones, Jean Wheeler, and the numerous student staff members of the FLIS Library gave me an enormous amount of gracious assistance.

I owe a special debt to two researchers in administrative science: the late Albert Shapero, William H. Davis Professor of American Free Enterprise, Ohio State University, author of *Managing Professional People: Understanding Creative Performance* and other studies; and Professor John W. Hunt, London School of Business. Shapero was one of the few writers who clearly understood the unique role of professionals in both the profit-making and the nonprofit sectors. Hunt has distilled years of technical research into a highly readable work, *Managing People at Work: A Manager's*

Guide to Behaviour in Organizations, that is mercifully free of jargon and aimed at the practical needs of real world managers. The debts I owe to fellow librarians--particularly the faculty in graduate schools of library and information science who have published seminal studies in academic librarianship--are too numerous for mention and too great to be be repaid.

The fictitious schools, Waverly University and Waindell College, are the respective creations of Robertson Davies and Vladimir Nabokov, writers whose works I admire and enjoy.

To Carol C. Chin, editor at G.K. Hall, I express my thanks and deep appreciation for her keen insights, critical analysis, patience, and high expectations. The efforts of India Koopman, development editor at G.K. Hall, are also appreciated. I thank Karen Sirabian, formerly of Knowledge Industry Publications, Inc., for her constant encouragement during the formative stages of this work, as well as for her very helpful critique of the finished manuscript. Sarah Jeffries meticulously copyedited the work and protected me from more errors of grammar and style than I care to admit. Especially deserving thanks are Richard De Gennaro, who gave me encouragement and wrote the foreword, and Maurice B. Line, who kindly offered valuable critical comment on chapters 1-3 and 14.

I owe the greatest debt to my beloved wife, Susan Klement, my devoted partner and severest critic, who reviewed the entire manuscript from the viewpoint of a librarian who has never worked in an academic library. Susan twice read the entire manuscript, suggested numerous substantive changes, rewrote certain portions, recommended major editorial and stylistic improvements, and prepared the comprehensive index. I owe successful completion of the work to her loyalty and patience.

CHAPTER 1

The Transformed World of Academic Librarianship

INTRODUCTION

Except for a president or chancellor, no college of university officer deals with more constituencies and external jurisdictions on a regular basis than the librarian: sponsoring agencies, government at many levels, key academic officers, professional and support staff, faculty, peer-level administrative officers, students, labor unions, local citizens, alumni, donors, foundations, publishers, other libraries, networks and consortia, vendors all over the world, local business and industry, and finally, regional, state, provincial, national, and international professional associations. Numerous constituencies, many of them inherently and perpetually in conflict, demand from the library administrator a high order of polydimensionality. Folk wisdom declares that one cannot be all things to all people, yet that is the role such a person must attempt to assume. One aim of this work is to illustrate the multifacetedness of library administration and its essentially political character, and

1

show how administrators, constituencies, and other stakeholders interact in college and university libraries.

Education is one of a nation's costliest enterprises. In fiscal 1986 the fifty states spent one-third of their total budgets – about $140 billion – on education, more than on any other single category: twice the spending on welfare, almost four times as much as on highways, and almost five times more than on health and hospitals.[1] In 1983 Canada spent $30.5 billion on education, including $8.4 billion on colleges and universities.[2] In 1985, almost 22,000 librarians and other professionals worked in 2,870 United States academic institutions that reported spending almost $2.5 billion on their libraries.[3] These staggering numbers explain, in part, why the public's insistence on efficient and effective operation of campus service agencies is so reasonable, and why effective administration of the academic enterprise is so important. In this economic context, it is also easy to see why would-be academic library administrators must become sensitive to total library costs in the face of limited resources and appreciate the urgency of developing a sense of financial accountability.

We live in a world that has become radically transformed in our own lifetimes. In administration, even greater transformation lies ahead, for in ten or twenty years more than half the management and administrative positions will be held by persons whose world view is vastly different from that held by an earlier generation of managers and employers. An overview of selected social, economic, and technological changes, an understanding of their origins, and an appreciation of what has not changed, or changed very little, are essential for those who would administer academic libraries in the final decade of the twentieth century. The first three chapters of this work (1) review changes and trends as they have influenced librarianship, (2) survey those aspects of academe that make it a unique and extraordinary workplace, and (3) analyze the character of academic library work, comparing and contrasting it with work in commerce and research and development.

Academic librarianship evolved parallel with the world of higher education and with contemporary social institutions, but never in exact synchrony. Although it is a major support element of the academic infrastructure, librarianship is naturally derivative, following rather than leading institutional development. While it is not our purpose to survey the management of academic libraries in a historical context, a brief (and highly simplified) overview covering the past half century – roughly the working lifetime of many contemporary staff – serves several purposes. It provides a useful historical background, reveals in part the directions of institutional movement and development, and illustrates why new administrative styles are required. To review the academic library, we postulate three stages of development: manorial, industrial, and transformational.

ACADEMIC LIBRARY ADMINISTRATION IN RETROSPECT

Access to scholarly libraries in the Middle Ages was governed by the structure of society and was usually confined to faculty, nobility, and clergy. Students had limited access under closely controlled conditions. As the European world emerged from the constraints of feudalism and literacy increased, libraries gradually opened up to wider circles of users, and new philosophies of management emerged. For many centuries, however, autonomy, self-sufficiency, and private ownership remained the hallmarks of libraries in the cathedrals, monasteries, royal houses, and early universities.

The Manorial Period

As recently as the 1930s the academic library was still virtually autonomous and highly self-sufficient, in some ways resembling a feudal barony, or manor house. An early example of vertical integration, a manor had everything it needed to sustain itself completely, and, for stability, a rigidly hierarchical system of governance. The lord of the manor presided over all.

If the residents of a medieval manor were to visit a North American academic library in the first half of the twentieth century, they might find many familiar operations and relationships. Indeed, even as late as the 1950s, library methods closely resembled manorial ways: on-site staff provided services almost entirely from local holdings, custom-tailoring their own bibliographic control systems. The library's mission was local access to local physical holdings for a local community. Except for a few manufactured items, such as book stacks, typewriters, telephones, and card stock for the catalog, libraries made almost everything in house: catalogs, serial records, spine labels, and local authority files. Some even had their own binderies and maintained carpentry shops to build furniture.

Academic libraries harvested the output of the great publishing houses and learned societies. Ready-made bibliographic data for current English-language imprints could be obtained from the Library of Congress, but rarely arrived quickly enough to enable libraries to support academic programs effectively; sometimes it took years for foreign imprint data to appear. Interlibrary loan was a slow and cumbersome system of resource sharing, founded more on noblesse oblige than on serious interinstitutional commitment. An enormous amount of work was done by hand. The lord of the manor, the director, was surrounded by a retinue of loyal functionaries and able workers who carried out his will. The use of the masculine pronoun is accurate; except in small colleges, few women were chief librarians. The card catalog, devised just over a century ago, focused on individual titles, complementing the nineteenth-century American social emphasis on heroic individual achievement and entrepreneurship, as well as reflecting a contemporary scientific emphasis on atomism. The centuries-old manorial model survived the first two-thirds of the twentieth century with very few changes, even though North American society had experienced radical restructuring.

The Industrial Period

For readers about to enter the twenty-first century, it is difficult to appreciate the impact of the nineteenth century's technological progress, a seemingly unending series of advances culminating in the conquest of the air three years after the turn of the century. The telegraph, telephone, railway, electric motor, gasoline engine, steamship, and high speed press brought to that era the same excitement about the future that the prospect of interplanetary travel provides for contemporary generations. By the end of the nineteenth century the concept of unlimited scientific progress built on a foundation of presumed social stability had become solidly established, but the firm social order was not to be.

Between the Civil War and World War I, American society experienced the greatest transformation in its modern history when it shifted from nineteenth-century agrarianism to twentieth-century industrialism. The quickly spreading Industrial Revolution generated a new economic and social order capped by the formation of gigantic, centralized industrial combines headed by a powerful new entrepreneurial class. This metamorphosis tore down the traditional moral order of farm and small-town life, replaced it with a corporate-business order of national and international scope, and divided society into the series of dualities we now take for granted: work-home, work-leisure, white collar-blue collar, public-private, labor-management, exempt-nonexempt.[4] Colleges and universities experienced a similar transformation, changing from classic schools for the education of gentlemen into bureaucratic minisocieties whose curricula and faculties quickly became tied to rapidly evolving specializations and the preeminence of the doctoral degree.

Social theorists of the new industrial era fostered certain structural, relational, organizational, and work values that, superimposed on the manorial model, came to govern the management of libraries as certainly as they governed the mills, mines, and factories. These values included the concepts (1) of a preordained labor-management hierarchy, (2) that laborers should improve the condition of their lives through education, and (3) that hard work, long hours, and strict economy could offset the ennui of factory or office life. These values were easily grafted onto the country's established ideals of independence and self-reliance. The American industrial engineer Frederick Winslow Taylor (1856-1915) based his system of scientific management on these values designed to breed a compliant work force by inculcating the view that orderly behavior and unquestioning obedience were indispensable virtues.

Taylor's mechanistic model for managing human behavior paralleled the Newtonian world view that dominated the nineteenth century, and held that the universe was much like a giant clockworks. The prime mover (management) took care of power and design, while the individual parts of the mechanism (labor) under direction and authority, worked together harmoniously. Such a view fit quite naturally into the "sectorized" national life described by Bellah.[5] Taylor's system called for a division of labor that accorded all decision-making power to management. Rank-and-file employees were consigned to work that was rendered brainless by design. Work was broken down to its most minute, repetitive components. In the factory, the assembly line was born.

Henri Fayol (1841-1925) was one of the pioneers of classic organizational theory. A successful French mining engineer, he developed principles of management closely akin to Taylor's basic notions. Fayol's influence on modern organizational structure has been incalculable. He essentially invented the organization chart, was one of the first to employ the term "job description," and was among the first to develop formalized management principles that could be taught. Fayol's fourteen principles of organization and management, as expressed in his own words (at least in English translation) evoke a tone that is very industrial, very paternalistic, almost military.[6] The following excerpts from the first three principles will convey the flavor[7]:

> Division of labor: The object of division of work is to produce more and better work with the same effort. The worker always on the same part, the manager concerned always with the same matters, acquire an ability, sureness, and accuracy which increase their output.
>
> Division of work . . . has been recognized as the best means of making use of individuals and groups of people.
>
> Authority: Authority is the right to give orders and the power to exact obedience.
>
> In the makeup of a good boss, personal authority is the indispensable complement of official authority.
>
> Discipline: Discipline is in essence, obedience, application, energy, behavior, and outward marks of respect observed in accordance with the standing agreements between the firm and the employees, whether these agreements have been freely debated or accepted without prior discussion, whether they be written or implicit. . . .

> General opinion is deeply convinced that discipline is absolutely essential for the smooth running of business and that without discipline no enterprise could prosper.

It is clear from these excerpts that management knows all and commands all; it is the duty of subordinates, like children, to know their places and to obey. Fayol expressed this idea by varying a proverb: "A place for everyone and everyone in his place."[8] At the turn of the century this structure was the very model of modernity and, because it was comprehensive and systematic, it quickly appealed to administrators everywhere: government bureaucracies, factories, colleges and universities, and also libraries. Insofar as library work could be made to resemble industrial work, the pattern of library organization could also parallel the factory model. Departmentation was born.[9]

Functional departmentation, akin to Kanter's "segmentalism" in the business world, is the culmination of Taylorism.[10] Mental work is broken down into ever smaller components, just as if it were mechanical work. So powerful was Fayol's concept of division of labor that Harvard's chief librarian, Keyes Metcalf, writing in 1939, could state:

> Anyone putting in full time doing a particular job learns to do it better as well as more quickly. This is just as true in a task that requires special knowledge, judgment, and training, as it is in manual labor such as the digging of ditches or making a garden.
>
> If there is no division of labor, no departmentalization, if everyone is doing a little of everything, we cannot hope to have a smooth-running organization, and the results are bound to be unsatisfactory.[11]

Classic departmentation dictates a tall hierarchy and a series of feudal baronies as the appropriate organizational style. That industrial model was doubtless effective and appropriate for precomputer days when, as Ralph Shaw pointed out, more than 90 percent of what our professionals did was actually clerical work.[12] Indeed, one might say that the Williamson Report of 1923,[13] which recommended the division of library work into professional and support components, was the tardy recognition of the extent to which library organization had come to resemble the industrial enterprise. Departmentation, a child of the Taylor-Fayol-Williamson view, has proved a lusty survivor. But forces only a generation old are causing its social age to catch up with its chronological age.

ACADEMIC LIBRARY ADMINISTRATION IN A TRANSFORMATIONAL AGE

Impact of New Technologies and Major Social Changes

Change, much of it driven by technologies developed during and after World War II, has recast the world view of people throughout North America. In comparison with the 1940s and 1950s, the world of the 1980s is hardly recognizable.

Impact of World and National Political and Economic Shifts

World War I grievously damaged the nineteenth-century idea of perpetual progress that had been established in the Industrial Revolution. War War II dealt the fatal blow to that moribund concept, while the postwar era has seen the weakening of Western hegemony itself. As European, Asian, and developing countries absorb, adapt, and refine high technologies, North America finds its manufacturing, marketing, and distribution systems threatened. Discontinuities rather than smooth evolution mark the shift. Within a decade and a half, the following disturbing changes have pummeled the economic and intellectual foundations of higher education, especially in the United States:

1. The rise of highly competitive offshore manufacturing

2. Serious declines in productivity and gross national product

3. Increasing foreign control of petrochemical resources and increasing foreign ownership of American business and real estate

4. Public awareness of the costs of combating pollution

5.   Tax revolts at both state and federal levels

6.   Visible shifts toward vocationalism in higher education and an alarming decline in the general population's literacy

7.   The transformation of the United States from creditor to debtor nation and loss of the country's position as the world's export leader

8.   The social obligations attached to caring for the ever-increasing elderly population

Some very large and long-established North American companies have become smaller or merged, some have gone out of business altogether, while others, abandoning their former monolithic style, have restructured and decentralized. In addition, the United States has been dogged by technological failures in space exploration and disillusionment with the promises of cheap, clean nuclear energy. No longer is North America a region of limitless human and natural resources and endless forward motion.[14]

Impact of Public Policy Shifts

Colleges and universities have managed to retain general, although no longer total, control over programs and curricula, but their powers of self-governance in administrative areas have declined precipitously since the end of World War II. Extensive United States government intrusion into higher education started with the administration of the GI Bill, but did not loom large until the 1960s when federally sponsored research began to underpin the budgets of the large research universities and Affirmative Action requirements radically and universally changed recruiting and promotion practices. In addition, both the U.S. and Canadian governments enacted far-reaching legislation to achieve universally improved working conditions for employees, such as broader coverage for minimum wage requirements, more comprehensive health and safety rulings, and greater security of employment. Government intervention has resulted in many very costly processes: detailed record maintenance for time-and-effort reporting; involved and expensive new styles of employment, recruiting, and termination; complex formulas for overhead reimbursement on grants and contracts; and increased overhead costs of internal procedures to ensure legal compliance.

Impact of Behavioralist School

After World War II a new generation of management theorists, the behavioralist school (led by Frederick Herzberg, Rensis Likert, Abraham Maslow, Douglas McGregor, and others) rose to prominence. Within less than a generation their humanistic and progressive outlook successfully overturned the antiseptic and materialistic view of Taylor's so-called scientific management and strongly challenged the fixity of Fayol's principles. The behavioralists strove to give full scope to human potential, regardless of an employee's location in the corporate hierarchy. Workers were no longer to be regarded as mere extensions of machines or subjected to management's omniscience. Herzberg's bimodal analysis of working conditions into hygienic and motivational factors, Maslow's familiar hierarchy of needs, and McGregor's well-known Theory X and Theory Y fit in well with a new generation's changed world outlook.[15] During the 1960s and 1970s many young professionals in librarianship saw their own situations powerfully reflected in the tenets of the behavioralist school; however, the resonance they felt collided vigorously with established hierarchical management systems and resulted in growing tensions.

Impact of Changed Student Views

The concept that higher education was the right of every United States citizen and not a privilege limited to the affluent few emerged suddenly, at the end of the Second World War when millions of ex-soldiers attended college on the GI Bill. Twenty years later, the ex-soldiers' offspring, the "baby-boom" generation, brought into the academic community new values, behavior, and beliefs that challenged the country's ideas more immediately, and often more threateningly, than television's stark views of violent happenings in remote corners of the world.

Included among the other responses to changed social conditions were new academic institutions founded in the United States after World War II, the self-styled "free universities." Flourishing during the turbulent 1960s, these were in part a reaction against an overbureaucratized system of higher education. As counterculture organizations they represented certain aspects of innovation and creativity. The counterculture outlook and the free universities both faded when the colossal economic expansion of the Great Society went into reverse, causing the political tone of the country to become more conservative and citizens to become preoccupied with earning a living in a shrinking economy.

Student views are often the earliest evidence of impending social change. The students of the 1960s promoted fresh, new, and sometimes the most thoroughly radical world views, including militant attitudes on vital international issues, and social responsibility and personal ethical behavior. Educationally and attitudinally, the current generation of employees – who not long ago were these same students – forms a labor pool far, far different from the relatively stable and compliant personnel of Williamson's day when only the offspring of the wealthy or the children of hardworking immigrants attended college.

The student revolution temporarily disordered higher education in North America, but it did not democratize or restructure its highly stratified social edifice.[16] What did it accomplish? Perhaps something of greater long-range significance: a pervasive change in curriculum, a change aided by progressive economic contraction. Since the 1960s the goals of postsecondary education have distinctly shifted from knowledge for its own sake – liberal education as a sign of culture – to a kind of coarse instrumentalism. Modern college education is geared to the job market; curricula follow rather than lead. Students study hard in the hope of finding well-paying jobs; honors programs are in fashion again. For many employees who entered the academic library work force in the 1960s, the political fervor of yesteryear's radicals has been transformed and refocused inward on mundane personnel considerations: salaries, benefits, promotions, and job security. Perhaps students of the 1960s were warned by some subtle prescience that North America would face an economic crisis in the 1980s. They demanded courses that were "relevant." So little of the curriculum in the 1960s seemed relevant to a generation reared on television. Despite the excitement of the space program, itself a television spectacular, it was hard to study either space science or the classics when one could see heads being bashed in civil rights marches and atrocities committed by military forces in distant countries.

Impact of Television

Television has exerted an especially compelling force – surpassing the power of home, religion, and public school – on this generation, the first to be reared from infancy under its full influence. In personal life, television promises romance, glamour, and success with little effort. In politics and administration it has effectively demystified those aspects of leadership that once depended on maintaining physical distance between the leaders and the led. In mass communication television has enormously enhanced the power of charisma. Both at school and at work, it has significantly reduced people's attention span, and is sometimes blamed for the decline of reading skills and a general unpreparedness for the realities of working life.[17]

It is easy to say that we have seen all this before, that generational and technological changes have always been around. This response is too facile. Such prodigious changes cannot fail to be reflected in the workplace of higher education. What made the baby-boom generation far more influential in higher education than its predecessors was the simultaneous occurrence of factors, any one of which might have brought about major social change: the universal availability of television, open access to higher education, weakening of the elitist tradition, and the decline of the nuclear family were all coupled to unprecedented, long-term prosperity through that generation's childhood and adolescence.

In comparison with their predecessors, the seventy-two million Americans and the nine million Canadians born between 1945 and 1965 took affluence for granted, and were much better educated, more self-centered, and much less pliant in the face of traditional authoritarian management styles than their parents. They also were less motivated by institutional loyalty. Most of them had never experienced hunger, cold, or lack of cash. Having never known real deprivation, they were much less interested in security than their parents had been. The baby boomers sought immediate satisfactions and were eager to replace duty with entitlement, responsibilities with rights. Focusing on what Bellah called "expressive individualism," they dedicated themselves to the achievement of Maslowian self-fulfillment and self-realization in expectation of unending affluence and unimpeded upward mobility.[18]

All these changes have had a formidable impact on the way contemporary employees, especially the younger ones, view work and the workplace. Many are not keen on authority, nor do they trust the wisdom of older heads. They do not unquestioningly accept delegation of work from a hierarchical management, but prefer partnership and participation. Their new attitudes of hostility toward authority, hierarchy, and inequality have left marks on North American society, marks that have a definite relationship to the staffing, social atmosphere, and work environment of the modern academic library.

Computer Impact on Office Productivity and Outlook

Computer technology has brought innumerable new capacities to manufacturing and industry, but in offices it has created irritating new problems for white collar workers and professionals. The conversion of much office work to long sit-down sessions with video display terminals (in some ways not much different from hours of watching television) reduces the once familiar (and valuable) social interaction among staff, introduces potential health hazards, and keeps people from talking or walking very much.[19] Some employees become so inured to working with machines that they are desocialized, almost robotic in behavior; they lose or never develop the social skills needed to get along in a group. Alienation at the computer terminal and deterioration of human skills in personal communication aggravate the difficulties of administration.

Managers and analysts complain that office productivity lags considerably behind gains in manufacturing. Why? Computer technology has destabilized traditional work systems and procedures. Computer-supported systems and procedures have become infinitely more complex, and often much more frustrating, than their old manual counterparts. Early batch systems introduced long processing delays into procedures that once functioned more or less on line in manual systems. The first computerized on-line systems overcame batch system deficiencies at the price of greatly increased complexity and competition for access to limited numbers of expensive terminals. Cheap terminals and distributed computing have not relieved these conditions because new applications keep being added to the base. Computerized systems quickly and completely transform requirements of staff training, enormously increasing their depth, duration, and cost. Training is no longer an initial orientation after which a worker becomes productive, but an expensive, continuing activity for everyone.

The Industrial Revolution imbued people with an image of the world as simple machine; the Silicon Revolution appears to have picked up where the former left off. Both revolutions tend to see technological progress as the natural, linear development of accumulated discovery and invention. Having become accustomed to the speed of the "technological fix" and its television-induced counterpart – that tough problems are magically solved in sixty minutes with four commercial breaks – few people willingly give much thought to the long range.

The Transformed Academic Library

As we enter the 1990s and prepare for the year 2000, we observe a completely transformed world in academic librarianship. Internally, many of the manorial aspects of the 1950s have all but disappeared: self-sufficiency and total autonomy have given way to cooperation and outreach, sometimes gladly embraced, sometimes accepted grudgingly, but nevertheless functional. The idea that libraries could be managed at all has come to be widely accepted, evidenced by establishment of the *Journal of Library Administration*, the *Journal of Academic Librarianship,* and *Library Personnel News*; by the changing foci of conference programs and traditional professional journals; and by the growth of continuing education offerings. There is other evidence that the concept of academic library manageability has matured: (1) for nearly twenty years the Association of Research Libraries' Office of Management Studies has served its clients creditably; (2) The American Library Association's (ALA's) Library Administration and Management Association has come to be the most rapidly growing division of ALA, with the highest percentage of conference attendance of all ALA divisions; and (3) the Association of College and Research Libraries' series of national conferences has powerfully unified the North American community of academic librarians under concepts that are clearly technology and management focused.

Acceptance of the MARC format as an international bibliographic standard has revolutionized every aspect of library service. Libraries everywhere, uniting behind the computer networks and consortia or buying bibliographic files on compact disc, enjoy rapid, virtually unlimited access to bibliographic data. Both the card catalog and its short-lived challenger, the book catalog, have given way to the increasingly popular on-line public access catalog (OPAC); even the smallest library can now acquire a turnkey microcomputer system to support many of its clerical functions and certain professionally based bibliographic ones as well. Distributed computing, having reduced the centricity of library catalogs, is also contributing to the formation of new structures and making it possible to create new patterns of resource reallocation. Through distributed computing, the library community is actually coming full circle bibliographically: from a manorial stand-alone facility through interdependency by way of the bibliographic networks, and now, back to local autonomy. Yet this regained autonomy is not a throwback to solitary independence, but a transformed concept with connectedness, linkages to a vast, continentwide, even worldwide, array of bibliographic resources and services.

In 1979 it was possible for Cline and Sinnott to state in a draft report:

> Traditionally, persons who have been attracted to the profession of librarianship have identified with the scholarly activities and tools of the profession. They frequently describe themselves as people who "love books" and label as "bookmen" those who have a

vast knowledge of both the physical properties and content of books. It is a term conveying strong and positive approbation. To be called a "bookman" is a mark of honor, and it expressed the traditional essence of the profession. But among those traditionally attracted to librarianship, there are very few who feel comfortable and enthusiastic with what is required to understand, design, and operate computer systems. The world of books and the world of computers are perceived as vastly different ones. Consequently, many academic librarians resist increasing automation activities.[20]

No one would make such a claim today. Indeed, Cline and Sinnott, in the two-year interval between draft and published version, changed the wording "very few" to read "a small, but growing, minority."[21] The ancient ideal of university or college librarian as a bookman is based on a never-to-recur model of an administrator who had a compliant, uncomplaining, and probably utterly devoted staff. That reality is extinct. Within one generation the academic library has moved from the medieval manor to a semicomputerized society. The broad age distribution of the library staff, the turbulent dynamics of student life, and the constant disruptions of new technology have interacted differentially, sometimes synergistically, sometimes destructively. Their complex and continuing interaction focuses the elements of the academic library of the late 1980s into a picture that would have been quite unrecognizable in the mid-1960s and entirely inconceivable only a decade earlier. Librarians and the library community are among the largest users of networking and integrated systems in North America. Within a decade the librarian image (as least within the profession) has gone from bookman to "byteman." Attitudinally, students have evolved from hippies to aspiring yuppies and they depend on higher education in ways that might have made their predecessors laugh. Despite the fact that much of the activism of the 1960s is now passé and the pendulum has swung to conservative behavior, some library staff members of that generation, now in middle age, still carry with them some of that era's baggage and represent outlooks that are out of phase with current realities. Administration must still contend with that unquiet decade.

SUMMARY

In the single generation after World War II academic librarianship experienced more change than in its entire previous history. Almost no bibliographic methodology in common use today would have been conceivable or recognizable in the 1950s; similarly, some modern and quite ordinary services (e.g., low-cost, volume photocopying) would not have been expected. A baby-boom generation reared on prosperity and high expectations of personal achievement graduated from college and entered the work force. At the same time as new technical developments began to ease library operations and services, and related forces were shifting economic and strategic balances worldwide, depriving the United States of its former easy hegemony and introducing Americans to some things they were not accustomed to: economic contraction and the concept of limited resources.

Notes

1. "Over One-Half of State Expenses Are for Education and Welfare," *Data User News* 22, no. 12 (December 1987):11.

2. *Canada Year Book 1988* (Ottawa: Statistics Canada, 1987), 4–1. Roughly half of Canada's education budget is spent in Ontario, the nation's most populous and prosperous province.

3. Data obtained from *Library Statistics of Colleges and Universities, 1985: National Summaries, State Summaries, Institutional Tables* (Chicago: ACRL, 1987). These data are from the U.S. Department of Education, Center for Education Statistics, and reflect information only from the 2,870 responding institutions. If data were available for the more than 5,000 academic libraries in North America, the figures would be even higher.

4. These major social changes are impressively documented by Robert N. Bellah et al. in *Habits of the Heart* (New York: Harper and Row, 1986). See esp. 42-44.

5. Ibid., 43-44.

6. Henri Fayol, *General and Industrial Management*, trans. Constance Storrs (London: Pitman, 1949), chapter 4, 19-42. Brief analyses of Fayol's fourteen principles are found in G. Edward Evans, *Management Techniques for Librarians*, 2d ed. (New York: Academic Press, 1983), 26-31, and in Robert D. Stueart and Barbara B. Moran, *Library Management*, 3d ed. (Littleton, Colo.: Libraries Unlimited, 1987), 7-9.

7. Ibid., 20-24.

8. Ibid., 36.

9. It is interesting to observe how the various parallel structures of departmentation evolved more or less contemporaneously: the assembly line in the factory, the "twigging" of academic specialties leading to the creation of semiautonomous academic departments, and the fractionation of library organization.

10. Rosabeth M. Kanter, *The Change Masters: Innovation and Entrepreneurship in the American Corporation* (New York: Simon and Schuster, 1984), 28-35.

11. Keyes D. Metcalf, "Departmental Organization in Libraries," in *Current Issues in Library Administration*, ed. Carlton B. Joeckel (Chicago: University of Chicago, 1939), 92.

12. Ralph R. Shaw, "Mechanical Storage, Handling, Retrieval and Supply of Information," *Libri* 8, no. 1 (1958): 38.

13. Charles C. Williamson, *Training for Library Service* (New York: Carnegie Corporation, 1923). Reprinted in *The Williamson Reports of 1921 and 1923* (Metuchen, N.J.: Scarecrow Press, 1971).

14. Paul Kennedy, "The (Relative) Decline of America," *Atlantic* 266 (August 1987): 29-34, and the same author's *The Rise and Fall of the Great Powers: Economic Change and Military Conflict from 1500 to 2000* (New York: Random House, 1987).

15. Theory X maintains that people are inherently lazy, dislike work, require and prefer close supervision, are mainly motivated by money, and only respond to the threat of punishment; in this system management both designs and assigns the work and makes virtually all work-related decisions. Theory Y builds on the opposite

idea – that people are naturally creative and imaginative, enjoy meaningful work, want to do a good job, and are eager to learn, accept responsibility, and fulfill their potential to the utmost. Theory Y invites widespread employee participation in decision making.

16. A superb account of the impact of the student revolution on academic library administration is David Kaser's "The Effect of the Revolution of 1969-1970 on University Library Administration," in *Academic Libraries by the Year 2000: Essays Honoring Jerrold Orne*, ed. Herbert Poole (New York: Bowker, 1977), 64-75.

17. Superbly readable accounts of television's social influence are Joshua Meyrowitz's *No Sense of Place: The Impact of Electronic Media on Social Behavior* (New York: Oxford, 1986) and Neil Postman's *Amusing Ourselves to Death: Public Discourse in the Age of Show Business* (New York: Penguin, 1986).

18. The following three titles are excellent sources for understanding the expectations of the baby-boom generation: Daniel Yankelovich, *New Rules: Searching for Self-Fulfillment in a World Turned Upside Down* (New York: Random House, 1981), esp. chapter 17, "Working Through to Reality," 187-91; Lawrence Wright, *In the New World: Growing Up with America, 1960-1984* (New York: Knopf, 1988); and Robert N. Bellah et al., *Habits of the Heart* (New York: Harper and Row, 1986), 32-35, 48-50.

19. The following three items demonstrate the tone of varied groups concerned about the impact of working with display terminals: "Warning: Office Work May be Hazardous to Your Health" (Washington, D.C.: American Federation of State, County and Municipal Employees, 1982); "Facing the Future: AFSCME's Approach to Technology" (Washington, D.C.: American Federation of State, County and Municipal Employees, Department of Research, 1983); and "VDTs – A New Social Disease?" *Harvard Medical School Health Letter* 8, no. 5 (April 1983): 1-2, 5.

20. Hugh F. Cline and Loraine T. Sinnott, from "Organizational Case Studies of Collection Development Policies and Practices" (the unpublished 1979 draft of *Building Library Collections*), 6-6.

21. Hugh F. Cline and Loraine T. Sinnott, *Building Library Collections* (Lexington, Mass.: Heath, 1981), 135.

Resources

Bell, Daniel. *The Coming of Post-Industrial Society: A Venture in Social Forecasting.* New York: Basic Books, 1973.

Bellah, Robert N., et al. *Habits of the Heart.* New York: Columbia University Press, 1985. (Also published in paperback by Harper and Row in 1986.)

Benziger, James R. *The Control Revolution: Technological and Economic Origins of the Information Society.* Cambridge: Harvard University Press, 1986.

Birdsall, William F. "Librarianship, Professionalism and Social Change." *Library Journal* 107 (1 February 1982): 223-26.

Bloom, Allan. *The Closing of the American Mind.* New York: Simon and Schuster, 1987.

Bloustein, Edward J. *The University and the Counterculture.* New Brunswick: Rutgers University Press, 1972.

Boulding, Kenneth E. "The Management of Decline." *Change* 7, no. 5 (June 1975): 8-9, 64.

Boyer, Ernest L. *College: The Undergraduate Experience in America.* New York: Harper and Row, 1988.

Bundy, Mary Lee, and Frederick J. Stielow. *Activism in American Librarianship, 1962-1973.* New York: Greenwood Press, 1987.

Carnegie Council on Policy Studies in Higher Education. *Three Thousand Futures: The Next Twenty Years for Higher Education.* San Francisco: Jossey-Bass, 1980.

"The Case for Concern about Very Low Frequency Fields from Visual Display Terminals: The Need for Further Research and Shielding of VDTs." Hamilton, Ontario: Canadian Centre for Occupational Health and Safety, 1983.

Chafe, William H. *The Unfinished Journey: America Since World War II.* New York: Oxford University Press, 1986.

The Changing System of Scholarly Communication. Washington, D.C.: Association of Research Libraries, 1986.

Cline, Hugh F., and Loraine T. Sinnott. *Building Library Collections: Policies and Practices in Academic Libraries.* Lexington, Mass.: D.C. Heath, 1981.

_____. *The Electronic Library: The Impact of Automation on Academic Libraries.* Lexington, Mass.: Heath, 1983.

_____. "The Impact of Automation on University Libraries: An Investigation." In *Solving College and Univerity Problems through Technology*, edited by Donna Davis Mebane, 333-42. Princeton: EDUCOM, 1981.

Coleman, James S., and Torsten Husén. *Becoming Adult in a Changing Society.* Paris: OECD, 1985.

The Computer Age: A Twenty-Year Review. Cambridge: MIT Press, 1979.

Cooke, Alistair. *America Observed: The Newspaper Years.* New York: Viking, 1988.

Cordell, Arthur J. *The Uneasy Eighties: The Transition to an Information Society.* Background Study, no. 53. Ottawa: Science Council of Canada, 1985.

Council on Environmental Quality and the Department of State. *The Global 2000 Report: Entering the Twenty-First Century.* 3 vols. Washington, D.C.: U.S. Government Printing Office, 1982.

Cox, Robert W. *Production, Power, and World Order: Social Forces in the Making of History.* New York: Columbia University Press, 1987.

De Gennaro, Richard. *Libraries, Technology, and the Information Marketplace.* Boston: G.K. Hall, 1987.

Dickstein, Morris. *Gates of Eden: American Culture in the Sixties.* New York: Basic Books, 1977.

Dougherty, Richard M. "A Revisionist View of Scientific Management." In *Academic Librarianship: Yesterday, Today, Tomorrow*, edited by Robert D. Stueart, 17-30. New York: Neal-Schuman, 1982.

Ellul, Jacques. *The Technological Society*. New York: Vintage, 1964.

Fayol, Henri. *General and Industrial Management*. Translated by Constance Storrs. London: Pitman, 1949.

Forester, Tom. *The Microelectronics Revolution*. Cambridge, Mass.: MIT Press, 1981.

Friedrichs, Guenter, and Adam Schaff, eds. *Microelectronics and Society: A Report to the Club of Rome*. New York: Mentor, 1983.

Gash, Debra Carol. *The Effects of Microcomputers on Organizational Roles and the Distribution of Power*. Ph.D. diss. Cornell University, 1987.

Graubard, Stephen R., and Geno A. Ballotti, eds. *The Embattled University*. New York: Braziller, 1970.

Gumpert, Gary. *Talking Tombstones and Other Tales of the Media Age*. New York: Oxford University Press, 1987.

Halberstam, David. *The Reckoning*. New York: Free Press, 1986.

Hamlin, Arthur. *The University Library in the United States: Its Origins and Development*. Philadelphia: University of Pennsylvania, 1981.

Harris, Marvin. *Why Nothing Works: The Anthropology of Daily Life*. New York: Simon and Schuster, 1987.

Harris, Philip R. *Management in Transition*. San Francisco: Jossey-Bass, 1985.

Harvard Business Review. *The Management of Technological Innovation*. Boston, 1982.

Hayes, Robert M. *Universities, Information Technology, and Academic Libraries*. Norwood, N.J.: Ablex, 1986.

Holley, Edward G. "The Land-Grant Movement and the Development of Academic Libraries." College Station: Texas A & M University Libraries, 1977.

_____. "Librarians, 1876-1976." *Library Trends* 25 (July 1976): 177-207.

Hyatt, James A., and Aurora A. Santiago. *University Libraries in Transition*. Washington, D.C.: National Association of College and University Business Officers, 1987.

Jones, Barry. "Information, Education and Human Resources Development: The Information Explosion and Its Threats." C.A. Housden Lecture. Supplement to the *Australian School Librarian* 18, no. 4 (Summer 1981): i-xv.

Jones, Landon Y. *Great Expectations: America and the Baby Boom Generation*. New York: Ballantine, 1981.

Kanter, Rosabeth M. *The Change Masters: Innovation and Entrepreneurship in the American Corporation*. New York: Simon and Schuster, 1984.

Kaser, David. "The Effect of the Revolution of 1969-1970 on University Library Administration." In *Academic Libraries by the Year 2000: Essays Honoring Jerrold Orne*, edited by Herbert Poole, 64-75. New York: Bowker, 1977.

Kettle, John. *The Big Generation*. Toronto: McClelland and Stewart, 1972.

Kuhn, Thomas S. *The Structure of Scientific Revolutions*. Chicago: University of Chicago Press, 1970.

Lamm, Richard D. *Megatraumas: America at the Year 2000*. Boston: Houghton Mifflin, 1985.

Lasch, Christopher. *The Culture of Narcissism: American Life in an Age of Diminishing Expectations*. New York: Warner, 1979.

Laxer, James. *Decline of the Superpowers: Winners and Losers in Today's Global Economy*. New York: Paragon, 1987.

McAnally, Arthur M. "Departments in University Libraries." *Library Trends* 7, no. 3 (January 1959): 448-64.

McCabe, Gerard B. "Contemporary Trends in Academic Library Administration and Organization." In *Issues in Academic Librarianship: Views and Case Studies for the 1980s and 1990s*, edited by Peter Spyers-Duran and Thomas W. Mann, Jr., 21-35. Westport, Conn.: Greenwood, 1985.

Maccoby, Michael. *The Gamesman.* New York: Simon and Schuster, 1976.

McDougall, Walter. *The Heavens and the Earth: A Political History of the Space Age.* New York: Basic Books, 1986.

McGregor, Douglas. "The Human Side of Enterprise." In *Adventures in Thought and Action*, Proceedings of the Fifth Anniversary Convocation of the MIT School of Industrial Management, June 1957, 23-30. Reprinted (in condensed form) in *Management Review* 46, no. 11 (1957): 22-28 and in his *Leadership and Motivation*.

_____. *Leadership and Motivation: Essays of Douglas McGregor.* Cambridge, Mass.: MIT Press, 1966.

Margulies, Newton. "The Myth and Magic in OD." *Business Horizons* 15 (August 1972): 77-82.

Mason, Marilyn Gell. "Trends Challenging the Library: Technological, Economic, Social, Political." In *The ALA Yearbook of Library and Information Services* vol. 11, 1-6. Chicago: ALA, 1986.

Merelman, Richard M. *Making Something of Ourselves: On Culture and Politics in the United States.* Berkeley: University of California Press, 1984.

Mesthene, Emmanuel G. *Technological Change: Its Impact on Man and Society.* New York: New American Library, 1970.

Metcalf, Keyes D. "Departmental Organization in Libraries." In *Current Issues in Library Administration*, edited by Carlton B. Joeckel, 90-110. Chicago: University of Chicago, 1939.

Meyrowitz, Joshua. *No Sense of Place: The Impact of Electronic Media on Social Behavior.* New York: Oxford University Press, 1986.

Mindell, Mark G., and William I. Gorden. *Employee Values in a Changing Society.* New York: AMACOM, 1981.

Mitchell, Arnold. *The Nine American Lifestyles: Who We Are and Where We Are Going.* New York: Macmillan, 1983.

Mitroff, Ian I. *Business NOT as Usual.* San Francisco: Jossey-Bass, 1987.

Mitroff, Ian I., and Susan Mohrman. "The Whole System Is Broke and in Desperate Need of Fixing: Notes on the Second Industrial Revolution." *International Journal of Technology Management* 1, nos. 1/2 (1986): 65-75.

Moffett, William A. "Reflections of a College Librarian Looking for Life and Redemption This Side of ARL." *College & Research Libraries* 45 (September 1984): 338-49.

Mumford, Lewis. *Technics and Civilization.* New York: Harcourt, Brace, 1963.

Nora, Simon, and Alain Minc. *The Computerization of Society.* Cambridge: MIT Press, 1980.

Ong, Walter. *Orality and Literacy: The Technologizing of the World.* New York: Methuen, 1982.

Piore, Michael J., and Charles F. Sabel. *The Second Industrial Divide: Possibilities for Prosperity.* New York: Basic Books, 1984.

Postman, Neil. *Amusing Ourselves to Death: Public Discourse in the Age of Show Business.* New York: Viking, 1985.

Provenzo, Eugene F., Jr. *Beyond the Gutenberg Galaxy: Microcomputers and the Emergence of Post-Typographic Culture.* New York: Teachers College, 1986.

Rifkin, Jeremy. *Time Wars: The Primary Conflict in Human History.* New York: Holt, 1987.

Rueschemeyer, Dietrich. *Power and the Division of Labour.* Stanford, Calif.: Stanford University Press, 1986.

Segal, Howard P. *Technological Utopianism in American Culture.* Chicago: University of Chicago Press, 1985.

Sheppard, Harold L., and Neal Q. Herrick. *Where Have All the Robots Gone? Worker Dissatisfaction in the 70s.* New York: Free Press, 1972.

Shiflett, Orvin Lee. *The Origins of American Academic Librarianship.* Norwood, N.J.: Ablex, 1981.

Smith, Anthony. "The Influence of Television." *Daedalus* 114, no. 4 (Fall 1985): 1-15.

Taylor, Frederick W. *The Principles of Scientific Management.* New York: Harper & Brothers, 1911.

Taylor, Robert S. *The Making of a Library: The Academic Library in Transition.* New York: Becker and Hayes, 1972.

Thomas, Evan. "Growing Pains at 40." *Time* 127, no. 20 (19 May 1986): 22-41.

Tiger, Lionel. *The Manufacture of Evil: Ethics, Evolution and the Industrial System.* New York: Harper and Row, 1987.

Turkle, Sherry. *The Second Self: Computers and the Human Spirit.* New York, Simon and Schuster, 1984.

Visual Display Terminals (VDTs): An Occupational Health and Safety Bibliography with Selected Annotations. Hamilton, Ontario: Canadian Centre for Occupational Health and Safety, 1983. Covering work organization, ergonomics, and other topics, this bibliography is worldwide in scope.

Williamson, Charles C. *Training for Library Service.* New York: Carnegie Corporation, 1923.

World Commission on Environment and Development. *Our Common Future.* New York: Oxford University Press, 1987.

Wright, Lawrence. *In the New World: Growing Up with America, 1960-1984.* New York: Knopf, 1988.

Yankelovitch, Daniel. *New Rules: Searching for Self-Fulfillment in a World Turned Upside Down.* New York: Random House, 1981.

CHAPTER 2

The Academic Community as Institution and Workplace

Special features dominate the academic community, making it one of the most highly stratified yet most highly desirable work environments in North America, if not the world. The academic workplace is highly political and strongly elitist, an island of exclusivity in an openly democratic society. It is a place where social mobility is tightly constrained by uniform boundary conditions. These conditions are highly consistent from campus to campus, even though institutional programs and individual beliefs and attitudes vary widely.

CAMPUS POLITICS: UNABASHED

Librarians contemplating a career in administration require a clear understanding of the political realities of academic life. In *Deaning: Middle Management in Academe,* Van Cleve Morris drew a remarkably frank, informative picture of faculty politics.[1] Politics in the public sector, although frequently scandal ridden, is much more open and undisguised than in its academic counterpart. At least public politics benefits from frequent turnover owing to the elective process. No such regular housecleaning occurs in academe, where entrenched power may rule for thirty or more years and grudges are long remembered. The old, powerful, and experienced delegate the ugly and unpleasant things to their juniors, for example, being department chair and thus having to take the heat on recommending or deciding on promotions for one's colleagues, or serving on the library committee.

So strong, however, is the public's stereotype of academe as the ivory tower and the professoriate as a service enterprise peopled by a self-sacrificing intellectual nobility, that very few laypeople ever comprehend the viciousness of academic politics. In their relentless and egotistic competition for resources, the faculty manifest bad behavior toward each other that, although refined in execution, is no less savage than that prevailing in the outside world: extreme pettiness, backstabbing, treachery, malicious destruction of colleagues' careers, one-upmanship, and dark and mean-spirited power plays. In a study of corporate leaders in high-technology firms, Michael Maccoby found that engineers and managers were far more cooperative than professors. He stated, "If corporate managers engaged in the nitpicking and down-putting common in universities, little would be created and produced. If managers treated their subordinates with the neglect and contempt common in the attitude of professors to graduate students, no one would work for them."[2] He further suggested that "the talented jungle fighter probably has a much better chance for advancement in the university than in the corporate psychostructure."[3] The worst academic politics is usually characterized by exquisite finesse. In fact, so subtle are the workings of campus infighting that at one very old and distinguished American university the saying is "When they slit your throat, you bleed internally."

CONSERVATISM AND ELITISM: UNABASHED

Few more profoundly conservative places exist than the college or university campus. It is a commonplace that the roots of modern academic institutions can be traced back almost a thousand years to the early medieval universities. Less obvious, especially to entry-level staff, are the depth, strength, and durability of conservative practice and belief in these academic establishments. Tradition is given its superficial due in the dress of commencement exercises and is symbolized by the brass plaque at the grove of trees planted by alumni decades or centuries earlier. It is similarly reflected in and on the buildings named after long-gone wealthy donors, and even in the library's bookplates and endowed book funds. Yet those are merely the ceremonial, external aspects of conservatism. Other aspects – customs, rituals, lines of demarcation of status, and taken-for-granted attitudes – reside far deeper in the institutional body and work their influences at levels that seldom reach consciousness.

Only in the possession of wealth and political power do differences between North Americans emerge as acutely, prominently, and candidly as they do in an academic organization. Within a largely democratic society the college and university environment unashamedly exhibits highly visible class distinctions: academics and nonacademics, the professoriate and everybody else, exempt staff and nonexempt, transient students and permanent employees, librarians and support staff. The dualities go on and on.[4]

Generally, the differences between the various denizens of the academic community reflect a tall pyramidal structure and, despite the student revolution of the 1960s, a firm elitism. There is no question that the faculty form the top layer of an elitist society whose layering clearly reflects academe's medieval origins. Next come administrative staff and librarians, permanent appointees sometimes perceived as occupants of a no-man's land in the academic landscape. Students form a transient population, responsive to ever-changing fads in food, dress, and sociopolitical causes. Support and clerical staffs are viewed essentially as service personnel who relieve the academics of burdensome functions: keyboard entry, photoduplication, maintaining records, answering the telephone, making appointments, administering parking and payroll, running the college bookstore, and keeping the stacks in order. Sometimes librarians are even lumped, at least conceptually, with this nonacademic side. Lingering in the shadows are the hangers-on – eternal graduate students, dropouts of all types, former spouses of faculty or students, ABDs, faculty who failed to earn tenure, and the lost or disillusioned. All make up a readily available

31

labor pool. At the bottom of the heap are the artisans and craftspeople who maintain the physical plant: groundspeople, carpenters, painters, plumbers, electricians, and others. In short, the academic community is the most complete and fully formed living survivor of medieval society, but it is most definitely not a fossil, not obsolete or even obsolescent, but strong, enduring, and powerfully influential.

Self-governance in the academic community is also a layered process, with faculty the most empowered group. Of all campus constituencies, only they have the right to select their own members. Their power is usually institutionalized in an academic senate or similar body, a unit authorized by trustees or government to run much of its own business and make many of its own rules. Senate statutes, by-laws, and regulations have the force of law and contract. The standing of the University of Chicago's Graduate Library School typifies the degree of academic autonomy in Tier 1 (Ivy League) schools. Designated by the university as a ruling body, the Graduate Library School has legislative authority over

> all matters pertaining to its own meetings, and to the admission requirements, curricula, instruction, examinations, grading, and degrees in its own School or Division, and these powers of each Faculty shall be exclusive and final. . . .[5]

Only recognized members of the body may participate in the system of academic governance and the membership is zealous to keep nonmembers out of its proceedings. The library, especially in institutions where librarians enjoy faculty status, is equally exclusive.

Regardless of size, almost all academic institutions are loose confederations of highly competitive units that happen to share physical facilities and a single administrative infrastructure. The whole community is conservative in outlook because it is highly institutionalized and wishes to preserve its enormously powerful political structures. Among complex institutions, colleges and universities maintain a highly distinctive style of organization that is perhaps closer to that of ancient religious institutions than to modern governments or industries. Clearly segmented by definition, academe is a precariously balanced hotbed of conflicting interests and warring powers – centralization and decentralization ever battling but in constant stalemate. Cohen and March coined the term "organized anarchy" to characterize the academic community and to help explain why it resists change with such remarkable effectiveness.[6]

INEQUALITY: CONSPICUOUS AND UNDISGUISED

The World of Work

Work has become the central experience in human life, displacing almost completely the earlier roles of family, village, and religion. Work, the workplace, the work force, governments, unions, and corporate bodies cannot be discussed independently as each one has a vital, legitimate stake. During the past century, new forces (e.g., collective bargaining and greatly enlarged worker participation) have reshaped the workplace from its once exclusively vertical mold into a more nearly horizontal configuration. Yet work in industrial societies remains a relationship between unequals, with the gulf between the powers of the several constituencies remaining very broad. As we move into a postindustrial era, a considerable mythology is evolving about the nature of work and its future, with increased focus on further reducing its inherent inequalities. Some futurists project an almost romantic picture of days to come, with technology removing the barriers between types of workers and converting the last of factorylike tasks to mental effort accomplished through voice-recognition systems or artificial intelligence. In this romance of the new workplace, collegiality replaces hierarchy, everybody is on a first-name basis, executive parking lots disappear, everyone dines in the plant cafeteria, and all employees come to work in shirtsleeves. How applicable are these concepts to the academic world?

Some popular books focus on building company loyalty through teamwork, thus promoting a high regard for all levels of employees. This laudable goal is far more easily realized in industry than in the academy. Company solidarity can often be built through business-sponsored social clubs, athletic teams, achievement contests, cash incentives, vacation packages, and the annual company picnic. Such corporate culture techniques can hardly be effective in academe, where strong individuality and highly personalized work methods prevail.

Attitudes and Outlook of an Educated Library Work Force

Increasingly, the industrial work force is requiring better-educated employees, a change directly attributable to the incorporation of microchips into almost every complex tool and product, especially appliances, machine tools, and automotive products. Kanter reported that four decades ago only 5 percent of America's entire work force had completed college while currently the statistic is 25 percent and rising rapidly.[7] In strong contrast to industry, whether smokestack or technology-based, an academic community by nature is *already* filled – usually overfilled – with highly educated persons, many of whom hold graduate degrees and whose life goal is not to move on but to *remain* in a college or university. If academic appointments are not available, some of these persons will choose support staff jobs or even semimenial, task-oriented work. A doctoral candidate who has finished "*all but the dissertation*" (the "A.B.D."), accustomed to the academic lifestyle, falls back into a clerical job merely to hang on as a kind of eternal graduate student. A faculty member denied tenure may elect to stay on campus as a library assistant, partly to maintain the connection, partly to continue enjoying a school's generous fringe benefits. Student and faculty spouses, often educated as well as or better than their mates, work at the school for a second paycheck or to make beneficial use of their advanced degrees. Such persons cannot be co-opted by industry borrowings (e.g., idealistic slogans, company picnics, bowling teams) to join a school's "big happy family." Often denying that they have made limited career choices, these employees are driven by deep emotions: jealousy, envy, and sometimes a conviction that they are being badly underused and even exploited. These members of the academic community, in the words of P.G. Wodehouse, may not always be disgruntled, but they are "far from being gruntled."

Impact of Staff Attitudes on Librarian-Administrtors

Of all the constituencies on campus, librarians may be the least comfortable in an openly elitist camp. Emerging from largely middle-class, liberal backgrounds, they respond ambivalently to the caste system and raw political power. Achievement of faculty status is one important response to this ambiguity; this parity provides comfort, acceptance, and feelings of achievement–of having "arrived."[8] In reality, however, teaching and research faculty rarely perceive librarians as their academic peers. In a thoroughly researched work analyzing how academic librarians came to occupy their current position in American higher education, Orvin Lee Shiflett portrayed them as still possessing "neither power nor dignity." While a full discussion of Shiflett's views is beyond the scope of this work, his conclusion that academic librarianship has "failed to establish a consistent form as a profession" and has failed to become fully defined is important, although few in the field will happily welcome it.[9]

Clerical and support staff, especially those who started working a generation or more ago, may view themselves as loyal retainers, proud to serve faculty and institution, confident that they have found a secure, responsible position in a prestigious workplace. Younger personnel may perceive themselves quite differently–as exploited or disenfranchised, actually or potentially–and show considerable interest in collective bargaining.[10]

Naisbitt and others forecast a radically changed structure for North American industry. They pictured a decline of the tall hierarchy and the machine bureaucracy, with their heritage of systematic division of labor, assembly lines, and adversarial relationship between labor and management and supposed that a parallel shift will soon permeate other sectors of work, perhaps in the public sector.[11] Certainly the labor movement has had a significant impact on the structure of academic, administrative, and support work in publicly funded institutions and, since the Cornell decision in 1970, in private institutions as well.[12] Yet unionization had a fairly superficial impact, having brought about few if any fundamental changes in the structure or function of colleges or universities.[13] The academic establishment remains largely what it was centuries ago – a strongly elitist, thoroughly undemocratic community, in spite of having taken on a few trappings of democracy, such as the formation of staff associations and various advisory bodies, and the appointment of students to boards of regents. The concept that the college or university will turn into yet another place that has been leveled remains an important ideal among some librarians reared in the baby-boomer era. This hope may be attributed to two factors: (1) a powerful public library influence on open access and freedom to read help librarians support democratic ideals, and (2) traditional aspects of curriculum in programs of graduate education reinforce the personal openness and generosity that undoubtedly attracted librarians to an intellectually based service profession. Professionals who choose academic librarianship frequently bring with them lofty ideals of human perfectability, deeply rooted feelings of egalitarianism and strong beliefs in the democratic process.[14] For junior librarians entering administrative careers, probably the most difficult reality to accept is this continuing unresolved tension between democracy and elitism. Some grudgingly come to realize that the administration of an academic library is not and cannot be a democratic process, but younger support staff, even the now aging generation of the 1960s, tend to seek or promote actions aimed at reducing the distinctions between themselves and academic personnel. These differing philosophies create continuous tensions that can flare up if leadership does not understand them or is unprepared to deal with them.

Throughout its history the academic library, like all other institutions, has employed adults of all age groups. Unlike most other institutions (except possibly the military) it remains the only conservative social institution continuously operating in the midst of a huge, transient population of young adults.[15] The student contribution to rapid change is itself mercurial, fickle, and cyclic. Nonetheless, students remain a source of constant vitality and value conflict in colleges and universities. Student attitudes and behavior, the inherent tension of their lives, and the baby-boomer phenomenon do not add to the impact of technological change but rather multiply it. The administrative challenge is to manage these discomforts and tensions so they result in creative new response rather than impotent reaction.

THE ACADEMIC WORKPLACE: FEATURES, BENEFITS, PROBLEMS

In the light of acute stratification, strong tensions, and inescapable ambiguities, a fair question is, what makes the academic library such an attractive place to work? In fact, it is a highly specialized environment with a rich, varied, and unique combination of extremely agreeable features found hardly anywhere else.[16] Almost no other employer can offer all of the following features:

- Freedom from work hazards; personal safety: By and large, academic communities are safe; employees are not extensively exposed to the industrial and environmental hazards one finds in manufacturing, chemicals, agriculture, and construction; violent crime is less common on a campus than in many other workplaces.

- High prestige: Such work is widely considered prestigious because of the public's generally deep respect for higher education, which endures despite taxpayers' revolts and waves of political conservatism.

- Geographic variety: Academic institutions exist all over North America. Employees can often choose the area that suits them: rural, small town, big city, suburban, coast, inland, mountains, desert, lakes, semitropical, and so on.

- Economic and social stability: Despite economic ups and downs, colleges and universities still represent one of the most stable and reliable institutional work environments, with excellent prospects of secure, long-term employment. Whatever financial traumas higher education experiences, they are not normally as severe as those accompanying government changes, industrial takeovers, or the vagaries of the market. For many, the academic workplace means a lifetime job with virtually no fear of termination, save for criminal activity or gross incompetence.

- Administrative informality: As a rule, workers do not have to contend with the most severely bureaucratic practices of big business and government, such as electronic surveillance of employees working at terminals, lie detectors, drug tests, loyalty oaths, and nondisclosure agreements.

- Self-governance combined with security: Academic appointees form a society in miniature and have the power to make many of their own rules and regulations, even deciding or helping to decide who is chosen for permanent membership on the faculty. They enjoy unequaled protection from arbitrary personnel actions.

- Tolerance of nonconformity: The academy is highly tolerant of political dissent and extreme varieties of lifestyle; despite its nondemocratic ways, the academy offers the freest conceivable atmosphere.

- Cultural diversity: In terms of cultures, the work environment is probably the most varied in North America: students, faculty, and employees represent an enormous range of traditions, customs, religions, nationalities, and languages.

- Humanistic environment: Insulated from business and industry's ruthless search for profits, workers experience a comparatively reduced stress level; the focus on the human side of enterprise in academe is perceived as more genuine than in commerce.

- Attractive facilities: Except for a few older, urban institutions in decaying, inner-city locations, most colleges and universities are housed in sound buildings sited on attractive, well-maintained grounds; except for very poor schools, most also offer modern facilities and equipment.

- Recreational opportunities: Many schools are located in regions renowned for recreational facilities and some are in areas that can be classified as resorts.

- Generous benefit packages: Workers typically are offered excellent benefit plans for health care, insurance, and retirement, together with vacation allowances so greatly exceeding those in business and industry that there really can be no comparison.

- Ready access to low-cost, high-quality cultural, sports, and educational activities: Unlimited opportunities exist for entertainment and self-improvement including ready access to extensive library collections. Some schools provide opportunity for degree programs and continuing education within local curricular offerings.

- Tuition remission: Some schools permit generous tuition allowances for employees and family members.

SUMMARY

Innovations such as the QWL (Quality of Work Life) movement and the formation of small, autonomous groups in factories continue to revolutionize the workplace in industry and reinforce democratic ideals.[17] No major social change, however, not even television, has turned the academic world into a democracy. The most ordinary library activities – selecting library materials, applying classification systems, inventing and imposing rules for the equitable use of a shared resource – are not conducted by popular vote. The fundamental activities remain, in an ultimate sense, those of an elitist nature performed for an elite by personnel employed in an institution whose hierarchical roots can be traced far back in history. This structure cannot be altered in a fortnight, even in an age when the cycle of change seems to be daily or hourly.

The academic community is a privileged and benevolent enclave, almost flawlessly insulated from the brutality of the real world. Both protective and protected, it is obviously superior to other clean environments, such as banks, insurance companies, and government agencies, and infinitely better than agriculture, manufacturing, or heavy industry. It is no wonder that working for a college or university is regarded so highly, despite the comparative absence of democracy and a salary scale generally lower than that in commerce.

This attractiveness also leads to some undesirable effects, however: tendencies toward paternalistic management styles; attractiveness to people more interested in security than innovation; overstability of staff, leading to stagnation and consequent great difficulty of adding new blood; ambivalence about higher education's elitism; extreme tenacity on the part of staff who, for the health of the institution, ought to be terminated; and comfort with the established order and a generally conservative attitude toward change. These are the principal concerns of the academic librarian's administrative challenge.

Notes

1. Van Cleve Morris, *Deaning: Middle Management in Academe* (Urbana: University of Illinois, 1981). See esp. chapter 3, "The Faculty and Its Politics."

2. Michael Maccoby, *The Gamesman*, 209.

3. Ibid.

4. See esp. Bellah, *Habits of the Heart*, 43-44, on the general "sectorization" of American life.

5. University of Chicago, *Articles of Incorporation: Bylaws, Statutes, Trustees and Officers*, 1 July 1985, 25-26.

6. Michael D. Cohen and James G. March, *Leadership and Ambiguity*, 2d ed. (Boston: Harvard Business School, 1986), 2-4, 195-229. See also Dwight R. Ladd, "Myths and Realities of University Governance," *College & Research Libraries* 36, no. 2 (March 1975): 97-105.

7. Rosabeth M. Kanter, *The Change Masters: Innovation and Entrepreneurship in the American Corporation* (New York: Simon and Schuster, 1984), 56.

8. In publicly funded colleges and universities in the United States librarians have been highly successful in invading the faculty preserve and establishing themselves, at least in terms of rank, academic expectations, and review procedures, as fully parallel with the teaching and research elite. Even so, there is some evidence that

librarians are showing decreasing interest in faculty status and more in collective bargaining. See two articles by Thomas English, "Librarian Status in Eighty-Nine U.S. Academic Institutions of the Association of Research Libraries," *College & Research Libraries* 44 (May 1983): 199-222, and "Administrators' Views of Library Personnel Status," *College & Research Libraries* 45 (May 1984): 89-195. Also noteworthy is the 1983 vote among over 600 University of California librarians, a group having academic but nonfaculty status, to join a union.

9. Orvin Lee Shiflett, *Origins of American Academic Librarianship* (Norwood, N.J.: Ablex, 1981), 275-77.

10. A 1988 vote of library technical staff at Harvard University to join a union is indicative.

11. John Naisbitt, *Megatrends: Ten New Directions Transforming Our Lives* (New York: Warner, 1984).

12. In 1970 the National Labor Relations Board, a federal agency, ruling in a case at Cornell University, declared its jurisdiction over employer-employee relations in private universities.

13. James M. Kusack, *Unions for Academic Library Support Staff: Impact on Workers and the Workplace* (Westport, Conn.: Greenwood Press, 1986).

14. Librarians' idealism is highly visible at membership and council meetings of the American Library Association, where concerns for the freedom to read, and other liberties we take for granted, extend to the whole world through passionately supported resolutions and debates.

15. Even though some high school students are already young adults, here we include only persons who have completed secondary education.

16. For stark and sometimes heartbreakingly authentic portrayals of the nonacademic working world, three titles are recommended: Barbara Garson's *All the Livelong Day: The Meaning and Demeaning of Work* (Harmondsworth: Penguin, 1983), the same

author's *The Electronic Sweatshop: How Computers Are Transforming the Office of the Future into the Factory of the Past* (New York: Simon and Schuster, 1988), and Studs Terkel's revealing documentary, *Working* (New York: Avon, 1975).

17. Enthusiasm for QWL is not unanimous. Some labor leaders cynically view it as a big business method to manipulate workers into a continuing subordinate role in the workplace.

Resources

Adams, Hazard. *The Academic Tribes.* 2d ed. Urbana: University of Illinois Press, 1978.

Armour, Richard. *The Academic Bestiary.* New York: William Morrow, 1974.

Austin, Ann E., and Zelda F. Gamson. *Academic Workplace: New Demands, Heightened Tensions.* ASHE Report, 83-10. Washington, D.C.: Association for the Study of Higher Education, 1983.

Birnbaum, Robert. *How Colleges Work.* San Francisco: Jossey-Bass, 1988.

Bok, Derek. *Higher Learning.* Cambridge: Harvard University Press, 1986.

Bryant, Douglas W. "The Role of University Libraries in Higher Education." In *University and Research Libraries in Japan and the United States,* edited by Thomas R. Buckman et al., 19-25. Chicago: American Library Association, 1972.

Carrigan, Dennis P. "The Political Economy of the Academic Library." *College & Research Libraries* 49, no. 4 (July 1988): 325-31.

Deneef, A. Leigh, Craufurd D. Goodwin, and Ellen Stern McCrate. *The Academic's Handbook.* Durham: Duke University Press, 1988.

Dorion, Raynald. *Quality of Working Life: Adapting to a Changing World.* Ottawa: Labour Canada, 1981.

Euwema, Ben. "Academic Tensions." *Educational Record* 42 (1961):187-93. Reprinted in *Reader in the Academic Library*, edited by Michael M. Reynolds, 54-59. Washington: Microcard Editions, 1970.

Farber, Evan and Ruth Walling, eds. *The Academic Library: Essays in Honor of Guy R. Lyle*. Metuchen, N.J.: Scarecrow Press, 1974.

Forth, Stuart. "Myths and Realities: The Politics of Library Administration." University of Michigan, Graduate School of Library Science, 1981.

Giamatti, A. Bartlett. *A Free and Ordered Space: The Real World of the University*. New York: W.W. Norton, 1988.

Heller, Celia S., ed. *Structured Social Inequality: A Reader in Comparative Social Stratification*. New York: Macmillan, 1969.

Howard, Robert. *Brave New Workplace*. New York: Viking Press, 1985. Penguin reprint 1987.

Ladd, Dwight R. "Myths and Realities of University Governance." *College & Research Libraries* 36, no. 2 (March 1975): 97-105.

Lapham, Lewis. *Money and Class in America: Notes and Observations on the American Character*. New York: Weidenfeld, 1987.

Lipset, Seymour Martin, and Everett C. Ladd, Jr. "College Generations–From the 1930s to the 1960s." *Public Interest*, no. 25 (Summer 1971): 99-113.

Martell, Charles. "Myths, Schooling and the Practice of Librarianship." *College & Research Libraries* 45, no. 5 (September 1984): 374-82.

Martin, Josef (pseud.). *To Rise Above Principle: The Memoirs of an Unreconstructed Dean*. Urbana: University of Illinois Press, 1988.

Miller, William and D. Stephen Rockwood, eds. *College Librarianship*. Metuchen, N.J.: Scarecrow Press, 1981.

Morris, Van Cleve. *Deaning: Middle Management in Academe*. Urbana: University of Illinois Press, 1981.

O'Neil, Robert M. "The University Administrator's View of the University Library." In *Priorities for Academic Libraries*, edited by Thomas J. Galvin and Beverly Lynch. San Francisco: Jossey-Bass, 1982. Also published in *New Directions for Higher Education* 39 (September 1982): 5-12.

Orne, Jerrold. "Future Academic Library Administration – Whither or Whether." In *The Academic Library: Essays in Honor of Guy R. Lyle*, edited by Evan Ira Farber and Ruth Walling, 82-95. Metuchen, N.J.: Scarecrow Press, 1974.

Policies of the Board of Trustees. Albany: State University of New York, Office of the Chancellor, 1981.

Pye, A. Kenneth. "University Governance and Autonomy – Who Decides What in the University." In *The Academic's Handbook*, edited by A. Leigh Deneef et al. Durham: Duke University Press, 1988.

Rothstein, Samuel. "Professional Staff in Canadian University Libraries." *Library Journal* 111, no. 18 (1 November 1986): 31-34.

Shiflett, Orvin Lee. *Origins of American Academic Librarianship*. Norwood, N.J.: Ablex, 1981.

Touraine, Alain. *The Academic System in American Society*. New York: McGraw-Hill, 1974.

CHAPTER 3

Administrative Theories, Business Paradigms, and Work in the Academic Library

A man is not idle because he is absorbed in thought. There is a visible labour and there is an invisible labour.

—Victor Hugo, *Les Miserables*

This chapter addresses the varieties of work and staff in academic libraries. Before doing that, however, it is necessary to review some theories of administration because of their intimate relationship to work and workers.

SOURCES OF ADMINISTRATIVE THEORY

Like most organizations and professions, librarianship depends on researchers in behavioral science and organizational theory for its paradigms. It is difficult to read any works on library administration without running across the names of social scientists whose fame is worldwide. This volume is no exception. Why the profession has evolved very little of its own administrative theory is not hard to understand. We are no different from other underfunded service agencies; perforce we all are natural borrowers and adapters. Besides, our fund allocators have given us, the practitioners, a mandate for action, not resources for organizational research. North American library administrators readily borrow any technique that they think will help their programs and clients.[1] But there are hazards in borrowing other people's ideas. Theories emerge in rapidly developing cycles and it is confusing to keep jumping from one to another. In addition, it is easy to develop blind loyalty to one theory and believe it is the only sure fix. Despite the dislocations induced, constant movement among theories may not be bad in itself as long as we recognize what we are doing, use current concepts to best advantage, keep looking for new ones, try not to impose someone else's total package onto librarianship, and, respecting human judgment, intuition and experience, take the best ideas from each model and adjust them to reality. In the absence of perfect theory, situational responses and seasoned judgment have great validity, a point De Gennaro made colorfully and vigorously in a classic paper.[2]

The virtually hegemonic theories of Maslow, McGregor, Herzberg, and others of the behavioralist school have enormously influenced modern administrative styles, just as the models of their predecessors, Frederick Taylor, Max Weber, and Henri Fayol, did in earlier times. Students and critics of administration now some distance away from the behavioralist school are beginning to look on the early work in the human potential movement with caution and scepticism. In a survey of ten administrative and behavioral theories, Bottomley was highly critical of the approach. Etzioni, a structuralist and prominent scholar of organizational theory, was just as critical, viewing some elements as overly simplistic. Hunt suggested that Maslow's hierarchy of needs is popular because it fits in well with organizational life, not because it can be verified empirically; in Hunt's opinion, some 60 percent of the work force is much more concerned with relationships outside the work environment than with work-focused achievement, power, or self-fulfillment, as maintained by the behavioralists. Orne alleged that the behavioralists make unwarranted assumptions about the uniformity of motivation and other human attributes. Yankelovich viewed the

Maslovian outlook as self-centeredness gone wild, the very peak of existentialist theory. In a devastating critique of the behavioralists, Maccoby characterized their views as misleading, mechanistic, unwittingly supportive of hierarchy, excessively bipolar, and failing to deal with the richness and ambiguities of human behavior.[3] To these critiques we add our own view that the behavioralist doctrine is based on ideas of universality, a presupposed uniformity of human character, and continuous economic progress–all concepts now open to serious question.

In practical librarianship the yawning gap between administrative theory and the real world of work remains deep and wide. In my experience of fifteen accreditation visits over twenty years to graduate schools of library and information science, I heard a continuous refrain whenever the visiting team interviewed alumni: the schools ought to have given us a sounder foundation in administration and management. Although curricula in the graduate schools are slowly and continuously improving, incumbent administrators cannot wait for the next generation of better-educated students or for the latest administrative theories. They have to do their work today and do it with the resources at hand, including, of course, all the staff they have, regardless of when they were hired or what may be their personal histories, outlooks, attitudes, skills, and abilities.

In an important monograph, Rehman exhaustively analyzed how management theory is communicated in programs of graduate education in librarianship.[4] His study pointed out that research in management is moving toward theories of far greater complexity than those of the behavioralist school. Yet Rehman noted that classic and behaviorist theories are taught the most and that graduate schools are giving comparatively little notice to new developments. Surely this is cause for concern. Rehman's inventory of management topics that are excluded (not extensively covered or minimally treated in library school) is striking and would seem to demand immediate examination.[5] Evidence that the schools are beginning to reexamine education for administration and management is the list of curriculum changes foreseen by major library school deans.[6] One dean observed that curricular goals are demonstrating a consistent "shift of emphasis from how to why, from techniques to philosophy, from doing to thinking, from accepting to questioning. . . ."[7]

THE FOLKLORE OF ADMINISTRATION

In the preface we alluded to Person's critical views on education and socialization to the profession.[8] Proof of her contentions is evident in the folklore and administrative proverbs cherished by every bureaucratic organization, the myths that form convenient pegs on which everyone from top management down can hang action or inaction, decision or indecision. The myths of library administration are little different from those of any other kind of administration, and some common ones are worthy of discussion.[9]

The Administration Does Not Want Change

The myth: The administration "does not want us to rock the boat." This familiar refrain is usually strongest among the lower echelons of a hierarchical structure but may even be heard from middle levels of administration. The view reflects lack of both training and commitment. It is popular among staff who are uninterested in change or unwilling to try it, even when the change is obviously beneficial to the organization or potentially to themselves. They find it convenient to "delegate up," attributing their own attitudes to administration as a means of sanctifying their ultraconservative behavior. When both middle management and subordinate staff believe this myth, they can successfully torpedo virtually every effort to change the organization. In another, less agreeable aspect to this item of folklore, conservative elements may promote the desirability of maintaining the status quo in the hope that a weak administration will, out of fear or anxiety, accept it. Thus the opponents of change indirectly protect their established ways. Strengthening this myth is the human tendency to think in binary terms, that is, either-or, success-or-disaster.

The reality: The business of administration is deliberate intervention designed to foster change, not to ensure rock-solid stability or a totally harmonious work environment. Stability and harmony deny the possibility of constructive disagreement and the introduction of orderly change. Good administrators spend much of their time thinking up, or inspiring staff to think up, new ways of doing things and new activities. They try to sell constructive ways to "rock the boat." They also perform a constructive, educational role by bringing continuity into problem-solving, and helping people realize that problems usually have a range of possible solutions, that not everything is black or white, go or no-go.

Good sales work is a prerequisite for any initiative. As the chief administrator, you must know the circumstances from all angles, obtain essential resources, get support from the campus administration, and seek the advice and counsel of appropriate staff. If you are careful to avoid changes that appear to be capricious, too expensive, too frequent, or not immediately beneficial to an important constituency, you may taste some success. Tact, diplomacy, practicality, and a clear prospect of immediate benefit can help convince staff that the administration does indeed encourage shipping some water for the sake of improvement.

Universities Cannot Be Managed

The myth: Business management principles do not apply to the academic world; there is no so-called "bottom line."

The reality: First, although an antimanagement bias is built into higher education, responsible administrative officers work very hard to govern that which seems by definition to be uncontrollable. In addition, colleges and universities attend to bottom lines assiduously: they continually track alumni contributions, alumni achievements, athletic victories, research grants, enrolments, degrees granted, endowment income, and state and provincial appropriations. Although they are not businesses in any conventional sense, they must pay the same bills as any other organization and be run with the same attention to cost-effectiveness, just as if they were profit-oriented concerns. Hence every employee has a responsibility to help manage resources efficiently.

Power Is Dysfunctional and Inappropriate in a Collegial Setup

The myth: Power is negative, oppressive, coercive, and corrupt and represents a cruel authoritarianism.

The reality: Power is neutral, neither inherently good nor evil but merely a motive force, the capacity to get something done. Only power can acquire the resources necessary for change. While exercised personally, it is not a personal instrument. Academic administration requires strong professional leadership and ability to persuade organizations and individuals to interact constructively. Formal bureaucratic structures convey goal-oriented power, whereas camaraderie and the "buddy system" produce arbitrary, unpredictable outcomes.

49

The myth: Power is concentrated in the hands of a few administrators.

The reality: Power is diffuse; every employee and every unit has some. Department heads and middle managers have much more power than top administrators because they are in direct contact with rank and file employees who do the work. People at the working level, regardless of their place in the employment spectrum, have *real* power *because they know their work and are performing it.* They also can engage in slow-downs, "work-to-rule," and sabotage, weapons far more powerful than anything an administration can muster. Administrators' main powers derive from their ritual "blessings," through which they transmit and allocate resources to programs, and from their responsibility to view an operation as an organic whole instead of a set of independent parts. The right to judge performance and mete out reward and punishment is an added source of administrative power.

The myth: Managers are autocratic, bossy dictators.

The reality: It is extremely difficult to get managers to manage at all, to take risks and make decisions. Many managers have finely tuned their capacity to slide away from administrative responsibility, avoiding it altogether or delegating it up to the top.

Achievement of the Highest Rank by All Employees Is the Ultimate Goal of All Personnel Systems

The myth: Staff development for nonexempts is promotion; eventually everyone rises to the top slot in the organization's job or position classification scheme. If this myth actually functioned, there would at some point be no subordinates. The myth probably reflects a rejection of the inherent duality of employment in academe. It is particularly cherished by nonexempt staff who are reluctant to accept the concept of job classification, and long to hop onto a perpetual up escalator.

The reality: Some people are not going anywhere, do not want to go anywhere, and will stay where they are. Others move to intermediate levels, some rise to the top, and some leave. Regular workshops conducted by the campus personnel office can help nonexempt staff learn how the job classification system works. Much more difficult is convincing nonexempt staff that to advance, they may have to take a different library job, a position in another unit of the school, or even a job in another organization.[10]

The myth: Support staff with advanced degrees should be hired into high classifications. Because the nature of the work implies the need for highly intelligent employees and because an academic library's labor pool normally includes highly educated people, applicants may expect special consideration on rank and salary. Requests may come from recent immigrants unfamiliar with North American job classification practice or affirmative action programs. Faculty spouses may also expect special treatment.

The reality: Job classification schemes for support staff classify work, not people.

The myth: Successful scholars or top bibliographic experts can and should become successful administrators.

The reality: Some can, but most scholars are soloists, not group workers. Scholars and bibliographers are sometimes unable to shift from their "vocational" pursuits to the different reality of management responsibility. They prefer to maintain focus on their intellectual interests, whereas leaders must be able to shift their agendas rapidly and deal with ambiguity. When scholars become deans, not only does their academic work suffer but their colleagues may turn against them.

Organization Charts Are Indispensible Management Tools

The myth: In each organizational unit there is a definable structure and an optimal span of control.

The reality: Staff quality is the sole determinant of both span of control and organizational structure. With first-rate people, structure can be flexible and the span of control per manager very broad – up to fifty persons, according to Shapero.[11] With a problem employee it is effectively reduced to one, because the manager must not only "cover" for that person but also devise and administer a remedial program for that person or, failing that, move for termination or transfer.

The Proverbs of Academe Are Dependable

The myths: Faculty work for the university; a small library is a poor library; the library is the "heart of the university."

The realities: Faculty are not team players – they work for themselves; as for library materials, access – not holdings – is the game; students and faculty, not the library, are the heart of the school.

These myths and proverbs inhibit creativity, originality and movement in administration. A different view of administration is needed.

REACHING FOR DEFINITIONS OF ADMINISTRATION

A generation ago it was comparatively easy to define administration. Whatever the environment, administration meant control. Even in control-intensive business and industry, however, the emphasis has gradually shifted to consensus. Consensus is emerging rapidly and nearly universally as a principal method for moving programs forward in many types of organizations. Developing consensus as an administrative tool means learning to have an impact in the absence of direct control. In comparison with business management, academic administration, because it deals with a very large professional population, has always tended less toward control and more toward a specific type of consensus, collegiality. While the move to consensus is constantly growing, the change does not mean democratic processes are at work in administration – far from it – but it does signify a substantive stylistic shift in how organizational power and authority are used.

Handbooks of administrative science and dictionaries are good sources of formal definitions for administration. We prefer unconventional definitions based on paradox, because *paradox is the kernel of administrative reality.* The following informal definitions lay out somewhat starkly the dissonance, contradiction, and ambiguity that are an inherent part of any administrative career:

> Administration is the unequal allocation of insufficient resources in a consultative but undemocratic style.

> Administration is an organizational mechanism for the simultaneous creation and maintenance of inequality and equity.

> Administration means having a powerful, enduring impact without exercising direct managerial control.

> Administration is making decisions that are necessary but that not everyone will like.

When I taught workshops on academic library administration, students of library science, including some experienced administrators, usually heard these definitions with silence and dismay. Asked beforehand to articulate their own definitions of administration, most composed noble and appealing statements, replete with sentiments pointing to high intellectual duties and a mission of elevated responsibilities. Their views revealed the deep sense of justice and desire to achieve fairness and equity that characterize the philosophy and motivation of many library science students and young librarians.

One of the main functions of administration is certainly to achieve a kind of justice, but justice circumscribed more by institutional constraints than by constitutional principles or grand social axioms. New or junior administrators typically experience difficulty with a bureaucracy's impersonality. They may confound their immediate, personal views of justice with the mandates of institutional necessity, wishing to impose the former upon the latter. As institutional goals are usually founded on quite different, long-range perspectives, the resulting conflict can lead to administrative impotence, mental confusion, constant clashes with superiors, and emotional exhaustion. In brief, some incumbent and potential library managers fail to understand their role as *agents* of institutional authority or program. Such internal, emotional struggles and difficulties relate to what Litterer and Person called the "third culture"-management, which lies between C.P. Snow's two cultures, science and humanities.[12] Person asserted, correctly in my view, that librarianship lacks a formal method for adequately socializing its managers:

> There is no widely accepted program of study for individuals who must assume managerial responsibility in libraries, nor are there clearly defined paths within library organizations that provide a structured means of socialization. Compounding this problem is the lack of a widely accepted body of knowledge about what a library manager actually *does*. Most librarians who assume a managerial role have received little structured preparation or guidance for that role.[13]

This statement helps explain demonstrable weaknesses in library management: the persistent search for democracy and equality, the failure to distinguish the rhetoric of behavioral theory from administrative realpolitik, and the inability to be decisive in tough situations.

That administrative decisions derive from processes that are essentially undemocratic and rarely deal in fairness tears at the fabric of much of our education and tradition, and is accepted only reluctantly or grudgingly by those whose orientation and traditions are strongly liberal. Some members of the profession can never submit themselves to a concept that seems to strike at the heart of democratic process. They cannot be successful administrators.

As for equity, the several parts of any organization always receive differing degrees of support from the resource allocation authorities. Each does not get its fair share of space, staffing, money, equipment, or other resources. Of course, when an administration allocates resources, it rationalizes its decisions to accord with the organization's putative mission, goals, and objectives. Invariably, however, the allocations follow the organization's real priorities; inevitably such decisions invoke judgments that spell inequity. Consider the example of a business that installs a computerized data management system. It is much more likely that the system's first use will serve the information flow that directly affects the manufacture and sale of the company's products rather than some internal function, say, control of personnel records. This does not mean that personnel records are unimportant, merely that management has decided that external functions are more economically and politically sensitive. Similar factors govern decisions to allocate academic library resources. Historically, this is one reason that circulation was automated long before cataloging, despite the obviously logical argument that an ideal circulation system should be based on a master record containing the full bibliographic data that follow-on systems would need.

It is in procedures affecting employees' working conditions that an administration must be especially careful to maintain equity. Organizations whose work reflects employment duality must maintain both equity and inequality concurrently. That is, they must administer different job classification and pay plans for exempt and nonexempt staff. The two plans must provide different work assignments to each category, in observance of the federally prescribed separation between such employees.

KANTER'S DUAL CONSTRUCTS: SEGMENTALISM AND INTEGRATION

Analysis of business structures and leadership styles by Kanter and others has urged corporate America to adopt a new organizational paradigm: an "integrative" rather than "segmental" approach to structure and function.[14] The differences between traditional and emerging organizational structures is put dramatically and forcefully in Kanter's tabulation of the assumptions behind the two styles (Table 3-1).[15]

Table 3-1. Difference between Organizational Styles

Traditional Organization Design Factors (1890s-1920s)	Emerging Organization Design Factors (1960s-1980s)
Uneducated, unskilled temporary workers	Educated, sophisticated career employees
Simple and physical tasks	Complex and intellectual tasks
Mechanical technology	Electronic and biological technologies
Mechanistic views, direct cause and effect	Organic views, multiple causes and effects
Stable markets and supplies	Fluid markets and supplies
Sharp distinctions between workers and managers	Overlap between workers and managers

For industry, Kanter's model is well founded. Indeed, much of the renaissance of manufacturing in the United States is directly or indirectly attributable to its implementation; but does it have anything to do with academic librarianship? In criticizing the application to business of a social experiment conducted at a summer camp, Kanter properly rejoined, "But that was summer camp, not a corporation."[16] In attempting to borrow again from industry, as we have consistently done in the past, our considered response to our own question should be, "But that is manufacturing; this is the academic world."

Funders in the public sector persist in regarding higher education as a business and expect administrators to run colleges and universities – and their libraries – as if they were just that. This forces library leaders to talk in one way to obtain resources and in another to administer the funds they receive, a dichotomy that will strike no library administrator as unusual. Translating the characteristics of academic life into the world of work requires administrators to reconcile the two approaches, understanding where business and academe are conjoint and where they are disjoint. Table 3-2 shows why it is so difficult to graft business paradigms onto the problems of academic administration.

Table 3-2. Characteristics of the Worlds of Business and Academe

Business	Academe
Highly integrated processes.	Anarchic, highly personalized, jumbled processes; disorderly.
Strong attempts to rationalize not yet integrated processes.	Weak attempt to rationalize even conflicting processes.
Management provides central, strongly coordinated direction, with unified program.	Management provides vague direction, with little program unity; self-governance.
Tendency towards hierarchical organizational style; some experimentation with other styles.	Mixed organizational structure with islands of autonomy supported by a hierarchical infrastructure.
Outputs generally countable, with strong focus on bottom line or profits.	Main outputs intangible; quality and outcomes difficult to quantify; no profit.
Product and/or service orientation.	Service orientation.
Strong professional R&D component.	Weak R&D component but highly professionalized staff.
High-pressure environment.	High-pressure environment.
Few professionals; many operatives.	Vast number of professionals; large number of operatives.

Success measured in part by failure of competitors.	Success does not require competitors to fail.
Heavy use of deterministic, algorithmic processes; focus on the known, knowable, predictable.	Major emphasis on uncertain variables of human interactions; heuristics; many unknowns.
Wide age range of employees, with some young companies having very youthful staff.	Many older professionals; wide age range of other employees.
Highly specific job descriptions	Vague statements for professionals
Work is highly specifiable; usually there is a best way.	Work uncertain, ill-defined; no two people do it alike; there is no best way.

It is clear from the table that managers and personnel experts who universalize their approach to human resources by applying office, factory, or industrial management methods to academic libraries fail to understand that the academic workplace is far more complex than any business. *Productivity models, performance criteria, and management styles drawn from business and industry have very little applicability in the world of scholarship, and it is essential that academic librarians not be seduced by their mechanical, deterministic attractiveness.*[17] De Gennaro's devastating critiques of business management methods in librarianship warn against their uncritical adoption.[18] Colleges and universities cannot import wholesale every new technique and structure from the business world; were they to do so, higher education as we know it would cease to exist. Certainly the leaders of academe want their institutions to evolve, adapt, and change, but in a controlled manner, at least as controlled as is possible within the framework of organized anarchy.[19]

Many of the anecdotes in Kanter's work relate to new companies whose employees are comparatively young, for example, the fictional Chipco, where everyone is under 30, an age distribution impossible to imagine in academe.[20] It is equally impossible for higher education to surrender an organizational structure based on specialization, differentiation, and status differences and become a "parallel organization" where ". . . workers and managers are involved in more egalitarian teams, where status distinctions are leveled and all struggle together for a joint solution."[21] Because academe intends to remain strongly "segmentalist," we have to distinguish carefully which views, attitudes, techniques, models, and structures can and cannot be transferred to it from commerce. In reviewing eligible constructs, the first obvious principle is that academe is not going to give up its ancient social triad: faculty, students, everybody else. Correspondingly, academic librarianship as a major support arm of faculty and curriculum cannot give up its duality: librarians and everybody else. In personnel administration, the profession is forced to remain somewhat Janus-faced, looking in two opposite directions at the same time.

Despite the decision to remain "segmentalist," academic institutions and the people who work in them would still like to have all the benefits of integrative approaches: flexibility, opportunities for personal and organization development, empowerment, stimuli to innovation and creativity, enthusiastic teamwork, and capacity to initiate and respond to change. How to accomplish this while maintaining the stratification of academic society is a major challenge.

Although Kanter was severely critical of hierarchy, it is important to note that she did not argue for dumping it. She concluded that a forward-looking organization really needs two administrative styles: a traditional hierarchy for doing what it must do in the way it already knows how, and a second aggressively entrepreneurial innovative structure, overlaid on the first, for coping with the unknown.[22] What this means, in effect, is that new organizational paradigms do not necessarily invalidate old ones; rather both paradigms coexist with different mixes of responsibility, method, and attitude, plus altered distributions of power and interrelationships. This conclusion is highly constructive because it does not present an either-or choice for organizational renewal and reformation.

LIBRARY WORK COMPARED TO AND DISTINGUISHED FROM INDUSTRIAL WORK

Industry has inputs, outputs, materials, a labor force, and energy sources to drive the engines of production. Traditionally, the production apparatus has been managed through a strongly hierarchical system. In relation to production itself, there are two major types of industrial work: factories and continuous processing plants.[23] Factory assembly lines aim to produce many of the same or similar objects, whether cheeseburgers, computer chips or underwear, with a maximum of efficiency. By definition, the tasks are highly repetitive; the procedures comparatively fixed, and the routines firmly established. Some room – but not much – is available for inventiveness, and there may be minor variations in routine, for example, turning out different car models on the same line. Continuous processing (oil refining, pipeline transmission, chemical manufacture, electricity generation, bulk food processing) is quite different in that rapid, independent judgment must frequently be invoked to keep it functioning safely or economically. Such plants are normally highly automated, however, and employ only a small number of specially trained operators capable of understanding the messages conveyed by meters, gauges, or other signaling devices, and making the correct decisions immediately. Neither factory nor processing plant resembles the academic library.

A library too depends on energy, facilities, materials, labor, and administration, but its most significant output, the work of its professional staff, differs from an industrial product in two vital ways. First, it is as intangible as the bits and bytes that course through a computer's circuitry. Second, it is almost entirely customized for an ever-changing clientele – people do not come back for more of the same information as they return to the supermarket for more cornflakes. In essence, professional library work is a form of scholarly communication; the printed, displayed, or spoken output is merely the codable, recordable, and communicable result of cerebral processes. Catalogs and bibliographies are, in a manner of speaking, merely side effects, by-products. Only a library's materials handling work (collating journals, labeling and pocketing books, reshelving, keyboarding) is repetitive enough to warrant designation as "production" and hence require a staff of operatives. Even there, the operatives are frequently required to make judgments based on highly complex rules and procedures.

In the manorial and industrial periods when librarians performed huge amounts of clerical work, libraries might indeed have looked like bibliographic factories. But even then, there was never any mass production in libraries, nor is there any today. In the academic library almost no work is done twice. From the humblest stack-maintenance job to the director's strategic planning work, almost every activity has some element of the creative or unique. In its work spectrum, the modern academic library is neither factory nor job shop but something in between. Its intellectual work is customized: collection development and cataloging are tailored to clients' real or anticipated needs; reference and research assistance are specifically demand driven and call for the highest levels of ingenuity and inventiveness. Librarians are much more than mere gatekeepers; they are truly "information navigators" and "information transformers." They spend nearly all their time repackaging, reorganizing, and reprocessing information and data, using their broad and varied knowledge and their cerebral skills to change one kind of information into another. The human is an information-processing animal, and librarians are the most expert of all such animals.

LIBRARY WORK COMPARED TO R & D

The management literature of commerce, when not geared to the factory, sometimes points to the special problems of administering research and development establishments. Even Shapero, who focused strongly on the general characteristics of professionals, placed most of his emphasis on professionals working in R & D. While we hope that practicing librarians will always undertake research and publication, hardly any library funds a position that is exclusively research. The R & D paradigm for managing professionals is thus a poor fit simply because librarians must work in a highly structured environment; they cannot enjoy the loose or nonexistent tether of a laboratory scientist. The following excerpt from an interview with Arno Penzias, Director of Research at AT&T Bell Labs is telling:

> The few competitors we have, who hire people as good as we do, do not do as well as we do because they manage too closely. There is too much short-term management. One of the things that people are constantly amazed at in this place is just how little short-term management there really is, just how little short-term management I get. People don't believe that nobody tells me what to do on a daily, weekly, or even a monthly basis. Occasionally I get a little bit of "fatherly" advice, but in the past year I do not think I have spent as much as four hours with my boss, discussing how I should be doing my job. Instead we focus on our long-range objectives.[24]

One hopes that academic librarians do not also spend four hours each year talking with their bosses about *how* to do their work, but that they spend many hours throughout the year considering daily and short-range problems and that they discuss long-range plans at appropriate intervals.

Laboratory researchers enjoy great freedom of choice in projects, rarely being told to go out and invent something; but librarians work under much tighter constraint. Their activities emerge from programs whose directions cannot be changed overnight, constructs with fairly specific educational and research goals and objectives set by a powerful external force, the faculty, whose demands must frequently be met on short notice. Even more demanding is the high-volume traffic from students who also cannot be put off with the excuse that librarians are busy with other responsibilities.

WHO AND WHAT ARE ACADEMIC LIBRARIANS?

Understanding librarians' work as intellectual, abstract, developmental, experimental, and managerial is the key to establishing the professional character of their responsibilities. The forte of all librarians is not static, objective knowledge but *process knowledge*, the capacity to work out problems that are not neat, not well formed; in other words exactly the types of problem faced by an administrator. Shapero succinctly characterized why process knowledge is the critical characteristic of professionals:

> The information required on the job is never available in neat and ready form. The problems are messy, the deadlines are changeable and abrupt. Several problems must be dealt with simultaneously, and the criteria for evaluation are vague and changing.[25]

Kanter's inventory of the incentives for initiative shows a remarkable fit to Shapero's concept:

> . . . incentives for initiative derive from situations in which *job charters are broad; assignments are ambiguous, nonroutine, and change directed; job territories are intersecting,* . . . and *local autonomy is strong* enough that actors can go ahead with large chunks of action without waiting for higher-level approval.[26]

In discussing how information technology enters the workplace successfully, Schement cited four aspects of professionalism closely related to those listed by Kanter and Shapero[27]:

1. The degree to which the members of an occupation control the content and scheduling of their own work

2. The political consciousness and organization of the members of the occupation

3. The attachment [that] members of the occupational group have to values of either innovation or tradition in the definition of their roles

4. The extent to which the occupation offers emotional or affective satisfaction to the members, or those that are served by it

It would be impossible to administer any kind of academic library service without a clear idea of who we are and what our mission is. Hence, it is essential to articulate clearly to others – especially funders – how the process knowledge described by these authors fits into a work scheme and becomes translated into professional responsibilities. Professional associations in both the United States and Canada have developed position statements outlining the responsibilities and mandates of academic librarians.

In the United States, the Association of College and Research Libraries (ACRL) had for many years striven to help academic librarians achieve faculty status. To that end, in 1971 and 1972 ACRL issued statements focusing primarily on faculty status but only secondarily on who and what academic librarians might be if they lacked that status. In 1988 the Canadian Association of College and University Libraries (CACUL), a unit of the Canadian Library Association (CLA), released a statement that defines the role and responsibilities of academic librarians independent of faculty status. Below are pertinent excerpts from ACRL statements and the entire CACUL/CLA statement[28]:

The ACRL Statements of 1971 and 1972

The academic librarian makes a unique and important contribution to American higher education. He bears central responsibility for developing college and university library collections, for extending bibliographical control over these collections, for instructing students (both formally in the classroom and informally in the library), and advising faculty and scholars in the use of these collections. He provides a variety of information services to the college or university community, ranging from answers to specific questions to the compilation of extensive bibliographies. He provides library and information services to the community at large, including federal, state, and local government agencies, business firms and other organizations, and private citizens. Through his own research into the information process and through bibliographical and other studies, he adds to the sum of knowledge in the field of library practice and information science. Through membership and participation in library and scholarly organizations, he works to improve the practice of academic librarianship, bibliography, and information service.

Without the librarian, the quality of teaching, research, and public service in our colleges and universities would deteriorate seriously and programs in many disciplines could no longer be performed. His contribution is intellectual in nature and is the product of considerable formal education, including professional training at the graduate level. . . .[29]

In 1972 the ACRL membership approved a Joint Statement on Faculty Status of College and University Librarians, which included the following paragraph:

> Librarians perform a teaching and research role inasmuch as they instruct students formally and informally and advise and assist faculty in their scholarly pursuits. Librarians are also themselves involved in the research function; many conduct research in their own professional interests and in the discharge of their duties.[30]

The CACUL/CLA Statement of 1988 on the Role of College and University Librarians

College and university librarians play an integral role in the educational process of their institutions by their contributions to the pursuit, dissemination and structuring of knowledge and understanding. They combine specialized knowledge of the theoretical base of library and information science, management skills, and competence in subject disciplines in providing services which are central to the educational functions of their institutions.

College and university librarians deal on a day-to-day basis with a broad clientele, whose needs, age range and literacy skills vary considerably. The role of the librarians in non-degree-granting institutions emphasizes the instructional process and involvement with the varied user groups. The role of the librarian in degree-granting institutions may emphasize academic competence and involvement in the research processes. While the individual and institutional emphasis on these activities may vary, college and university librarians share a common role.

Library resources and library services have a direct impact on the quality and character of education in colleges and universities. Librarians contribute to the instructional and research functions of their institutions by the exercise of their professional knowledge and/or their competence in subject disciplines. They function as facilitators, instructors and communicators in making information available to the college and university community, and integrating library services with teaching and/or research programs and priorities.

Librarians' responsibilities are diverse and may include the development and evaluation of library resources collections, the provision of subject specialized reference services, the acquisition, bibliographic control, storage and preservation of library/ resource collections, the management of human and material library resources, the development and implementation of a variety of library systems, and the provision of instruction in the exploitation of in-house resources or other resource networks. College and university librarians are administrators, scholars, teachers, bibliographic experts or a combination of the above.

Librarians share with faculty in the creative, intellectual and administrative goals of their institutions. They participate in the governance of their institutions as members of governing body committees, members of faculty and campus committees, and members of library committees. Librarians contribute to the intellectual, scholarly and community functions of their institutions by upholding intellectual freedom, by pursuing independent education and self-development activities, by undertaking research in library science or other disciplines, and by participating in college, university and professional associations.[31]

Other Views on Who and What Librarians Are

Both the ACRL and CLA/CACUL positions are congruent with a similar statement prepared by the author on commission from a major academic library:

An academic librarian is a professional who has selected the life of the mind as a career. An academic librarian is a creative partner to faculty, researchers, and students. Based upon the fact that "librarianship requires exacting preparation and that librarians perform functions vital to the well-being of the University," Paul H. Buck, University Librarian at Harvard, 1955-1964, unambiguously emphasized the intellectual focus of the profession in explaining Harvard's new library personnel program in 1958: ". . . the Library's professional staff is a group within the University fully as professional as the teaching faculty and entitled to comparable perquisites."[32] Academic librarians contribute to a university's intellectual work by linking their informational and organizational skills to all levels of the academic community. Fundamentally, academic librarians are problem solvers, system designers, service managers, and communicators; they create, build, maintain, manage and improve an information infrastructure that makes possible the conduct of effective teaching, learning and research.

As professionals, librarians contribute to the formation of their own goals and objectives within the constraints of a school's mission, goals and objectives and within the context of the library program determined by campus administration and head librarian.

Taylor suggested the broad definition for the new professional to be "the design, operation, and management of systems and services for the creation, organization, movement, and use of messages relevant to the needs of any defined group of people."[33]

In summary, the work of academic librarians encompasses the widest range of professional goals, duties, and responsibilities: faculty colleague in the educational process, manager, planner, system designer, leader and supervisor, mediator, contract negotiator, resource allocator, writer, speaker, fund raiser, researcher, teacher, research colleague of the client, subject expert, database searcher, collection builder, budget analyst, proposal writer, statistician, consultant, telecommunications expert, and entrepreneur.[34]

STRATA OF EMPLOYEES IN ACADEMIC LIBRARIES

The span of work in libraries, ranging from the highest intellectual challenges to workaday routine, naturally demands a spectrum of employment characterized more by discontinuities than smooth transitions. The continuity-discontinuity issue has a long and not very even history, and has held back librarians' status for many decades.[35] The bipolar division of work into professional and support levels, prevalent in almost all modern libraries, is most acutely, and sometimes most uncomfortably, observable in academic libraries for three reasons: (1) higher education is inherently elitist and segmental; (2) librarians are usually faculty members or academic appointees; and (3) many nonlibrarians in support staff positions are drawn from a labor pool that is the most highly educated in history, and the contrast between their educational achievements and their work responsibilities is painfully apparent. These factors, plus those detailed in chapter 2, result in a work environment of continuous unresolved conflict among all levels of library workers.

Owing to wide variations in personnel practice among privately and publicly supported institutions in the United States and Canada, the work force in academic libraries is not easily categorized. The most highly visible distinction in the United States is whether librarians are faculty or nonfaculty members; the prevalence of those with faculty status is greater in state-supported than in private schools.[36] In discussing the work of librarians and support staff, we will deal only with the generic aspects of their activities, not specific details of assignments.

Another way of classifying employees is by legal status. Employees in academic libraries generally fall into one of four categories classed as exempt or nonexempt: professionals, support staff, students, and volunteers.[37] Full-time or part-time assistants, part-time students, and volunteers are nonexempt.[38] Depending on jurisdiction, institution, and contract terms, professionals are designated variously: librarians, exempt staff, managerial-technical staff, professional-administrative, nonfaculty academics, or faculty. Support staff are typically called paraprofessionals, classified staff, library assistants, library associates, library technicians, clericals, or civil service employees. (The word "nonprofessional," now widely recognized as demeaning, is rapidly falling out of use to designate support staff.) Other than the designations "casual" and "hourly," there is not much specialized vocabulary to cover students and volunteers.

Wages, hours, working conditions, legal status, career development paths, and benefits for exempt and nonexempt personnel are vastly dissimilar. Nowhere in the academic world do laws and contracts make themselves felt more forcefully than in the recognition and implementation of differing rules and regulations for the strata of campus employees. The legislative basis for maintaining a distinction between the work of librarians and support staff is Title VII of the Equal Pay Act of 1963, which requires payment of the same wages to all persons performing work that is the same or *almost* the same. To ensure observance of applicable labor laws, regulations, and collective agreements, as well as institutional policies, and to protect schools and themselves from lawsuits, administrators must understand, appreciate, and enforce all legal and contractual distinctions among these strata.[39] Persistent violation of the distinctions between librarians and support staff decidedly damages staff morale and may result in potentially serious legal challenges.

Except when new labor rules and fresh staff definitions are being formulated (an infrequent occurrence) librarians' opinions about employee classification are not normally sought. Other than at bargaining sessions connected with collective agreements, librarians generally have no voice at all in the formation of the laws, regulations, rules and agreements governing employment, unless they are asked by a legislative body to testify. Librarian-managers are agents of the institution, however, and are required to accept and implement personnel regulations whether or not they personally approve of them.

DUALITY OF EMPLOYMENT IN LIBRARIES

Despite strong social shifts since the 1960s, movements away from control-centered management styles, and a growing focus on individual motivation and teamwork, duality continues as the most visible and enduring structural aspect of employment in the academic library. As mentioned in chapter 1, Williamson, in his 1923 report, was the first to articulate clearly the differences between librarians and support staff.[40] The distinction is probably a natural product of higher education's hierarchical traditions, however, an instance of a profession's maturing within the context of the established professoriate. Duality in librarianship, as an inherent aspect of academe, would probably have evolved without the Williamson report.

The concept of duality is so uncomfortable for some people that they prefer to reject it outright. Some writers even refuse to use the word "subordinate" in describing employer-employee relationships, on the ground that it is just as dehumanizing as "nonprofessional" – as if subordinacy implied intellectual or personal inferiority. We see little purpose in ignoring duality in a work envi-

ronment in which stratification is staring one in the face every moment of every working day. Pretending that it does not exist is like
ignoring conflict: the pretense does not cause either to go away.[41] It
is far better in academic librarianship to be candid about duality and
accept it. White put the matter neatly and succinctly: "We must distinguish between what paraprofessionals *can* do and what they must
not be allowed to do."[42]

Duality is among the greatest challenges to academic library
administration. It pits the two major personnel components against
each other and makes cooperative enterprise difficult to establish or
maintain. Library assistants tend to see librarians as remote from
"real" operations. They resent the flexibility built into librarians'
contracts; despite the M.L.S. as a bona fide occupational
qualification, they resent the existence of a privileged employment
enclave at a time when there are many more highly educated
applicants than available openings.[43] Faculty status worsens the
situation, as librarians are even further removed from their service
points, contributing to the work of faculty or schoolwide
committees. Support staff often do not understand *why* librarians
are attending planning sessions instead of working at their desks,
failing to see the developmental character of modern librarianship
or appreciate the programmatic responsibilities of librarians. No
wonder it is difficult to talk about establishing a unified team along
industrial or sports lines.

Kanter deplored the effects of hard-line stratification in industry
because it promotes "segmentalism," an organizational style similar
to departmentation.[44] But, as we have said several times, the
academy is not a commercial enterprise and stratification is an
inherent part of college and university structures. In the search for
professionalism, Cline and Sinnott suggested that academic
librarians may be squandering their energies arguing over their
professional status vis-á-vis both faculty and support staff.[45] For the
external world this claim may be valid, but because librarians are
required to manage support staff, most of whom are highly
educated, they must focus on their own status and professionalism.[46]
It is impossible to ignore a duality that is built into the way all
segments of staff interrelate in an academic library. One major
library organization is so open about duality that it provides cash

awards to incumbents who recruit new staff, the award for exempt personnel being double that for nonexempt. If the colleges and universities of the future ever do away with the centuries-old caste system, future administrations can deal with the challenge of creating new kinds of relationships between people, just as society has always done. We do not see duality weakening in higher education; in fact, the continuing evolution of bibliographic technology and the elitist character of higher education are likely to strengthen the differences between the two groups.

POSITION AND JOB

In library personnel practice, the main distinction between professionals (exempt) and support (nonexempt) staff centers on the difference between two words that are often used interchangeably: position and job.

Position

A position is a node of power and influence over the organization's program in that it represents the opportunity to make choices and decisions that influence the direction in which the organization moves. The occupant of a position has the professional education, experience, and potential to decide how to spend an institution's money and other resources in significant ways.

Position is a generic concept implying a structure in which career advancement is the joint product of the incumbent's capacities and achievements and the organization's requirements. Professional appointees have access to developmental opportunities quite different from those available to personnel in lower-echelon jobs. Through a dual track system they can advance independent of administrative responsibility and become eligible for promotion almost entirely on the basis of professional growth, expertise, and achievement. In Bardwick's concept, those in professional positions by definition face early "structural plateauing" but need never worry about suffering from "content plateauing" or facing powerlessness.[47] The possibility for advancement is inherent in the position; actual advancement depends on the achievements of the incumbent.

In addition, line workers in a professional bureaucracy exercise substantial discretion in identifying and selecting the work to be done, help devise the system for appraisal of their own performance, and exert some limited influence on institutional programs. Peer judgment, mutual consultation, codetermination of the library program, plus a capacity to deal with ambiguous forces or unexpected outcomes all define the professional position.

Because the work of professionals is task indeterminate, unlike clerical and support work, authority over these individuals is by definition diffuse: there is no need for them to be subject to the highly directed, task-specific authority characteristic of Fayol's machine bureaucracy or production-oriented systems.

A professional is not hired to "do a job" but to be and become a certain kind of person. By definition and in accordance with United States labor law, a professional is an exempt employee,[48] that is, someone hired to work *without regard to countable output and without regard to putting in any specific number of hours.* Normally, it is a condition of employment that exempt personnel work on-site at least during the institution's ordinary work week, usually from thirty-five to forty hours.[49] Although no compensation is received for overtime,[50] salaries cannot be docked if exempt personnel work less than forty hours. The work might include long hours in attendance at professional conferences, evenings and weekends spent reading relevant materials, staying late at the office for important meetings with colleagues, travel time to and from business meetings, and time outside the office developing proposals or refining research projects, all without additional monetary compensation or equivalent time off. Professionalism is a life of commitment, not of hours counted or output units produced.

Job

Job is a construct altogether different from position. It is much more specific than position, being tied to definite, usually assigned responsibilities. Those in a job also have a chance for advancement, but only within the constraints of a specific set of tasks. The job is external to the person and is associated entirely with the character of the work to be performed.

In the United States jobs are almost always nonexempt, that is, subject to compensation for authorized overtime.[51] Personnel are hired as support staff to carry out specific, well-defined tasks whose extent, nature, and detail have generally been determined (or approved) by the professional staff who supervise them. Normally, an organization's job classification and pay plan rank nonexempt jobs from simple to complex, assigning to each a salary commensurate within that ranking or level of responsibility. The plan also provides career development steps in recognition of service, longevity, and growth of expertise. The fact that an employee reaches the top of the salary scale for a given job, or has been employed for a very long time, however, is not generally a basis for promotion.[52] In addition, no matter how complex the assignment, no job ever carries with it programmatic responsibilities or the power to change the organization's direction. Advancement up the job ladder is possible only by the employee's moving on to a different, more complex, and better-paid job. If professional staff in supervisory positions fail to accept these constraints or are careless in the discharge of their administrative responsibilities, they destroy morale and establish grounds for support staff to file grievances – consequences that damage the library's program, consume disproportionate amounts of administrative time, and, finally, invite costly litigation.

Many so-called routine tasks in an information organization are repetitive and boring yet at the same time require a very high degree of attention, alertness, and perception. Applying property marks or spine labels raises questions and requires judgment. Do the end papers contain a map that must not be covered by a book plate? Is there a volume number on the spine that must not be obscured? How should a compact disc be property-marked? Preservation microfilming and photocopying academic materials present perhaps the clearest examples of work that is at once routine and boring, and requires the utmost attention to detail. Other attention-demanding work includes sorting and delivering mail, accurately reshelving library materials, keyboarding and proofing bibliographic or order entry data, and updating files in transaction-oriented systems (e.g., serials check-in, charge out of library materials).

The need for personnel to perform some of these repetitive tasks will decline with technological development. This is perhaps fortunate, as such work, although critical, offers little opportunity for job enrichment after the initial learning. The jobs also are characterized by both high stress and high turnover.

Few support staff in academic libraries, especially those who are highly educated, are content to carry out these kinds of responsibilities year after year. Occasionally, however, one finds employees who prefer closely limited work and are willing to stay in dead-ended jobs for a long time. Not only do some people resist job enrichment, but not all jobs can be enriched.[53] In such instances it is essential that management and labor reach a common understanding of the consequences of choosing such a job. Management should carefully explain the nature of the work, articulate the risks of technological displacement, and offer options for future development, including retraining.

THE HEART OF THE DUALITY PROBLEM

The main deficiency in the administration of clerical or support work in academic libraries is that the profession has failed to create or foster true career development opportunities for the non-academic staff, especially those who are highly educated. Most of the focus is on librarians. We hire entry-level librarians for their potential, and the bulk of our development effort is aimed at them. What do we do for growing cadre of workers on whose shoulders falls much of the genuine labor in library work? Support staff also seek careers and they can be just as committed as the best professionals. We remain ambivalent about these individuals, relying on their loyalty to support an indispensable element of our work but not pushing them hard enough to look elsewhere for their own advancement. They, in turn, resent the dualities and detest the snobbery inherent in the academic workplace, perceiving that they are "victims of paternalistic and authoritarian management."[54] It is no wonder that support staff have become discontent, many joining unions in order to gain improved salaries, status, and working conditions.

There is another side to this vexing problem: some nonacademic staff contribute equally, or possibly more, to their own predicament by refusing absolutely to look beyond the library. Whatever the disadvantages of and complaints about the work, the comfort and stability of the job are powerful influences, often strong enough in themselves to inhibit support staff from ever looking anywhere else or undertaking self-improvement to build up their qualifications for higher levels of employment. Like the librarians, many support staff would like to have "careers" (meaning unlimited promotion opportunity) in the library. Unfortunately, this is rarely possible at either level of work. Until administrations really grapple with this aspect of duality, tensions between nonacademic staff and professionals will continue, perhaps reaching a permanent adversarial stance, no matter how attractive the working conditions.

A secondary deficiency relates to the impact of elitism on employees. The academy is a world of widely varying privileges in which the tendency is to value people differentially: the higher up you are in the hierarchy (the closer you get to the professoriate) the better you are as human being. This translates into professorial arrogance. When it rubs off onto ourselves and we look down on support staff, we discredit ourselves and our profession. Such a view is not only a gross violation of common human decency but fails to acknowledge that, while the library might function for some weeks without librarians, it would collapse in an instant without support staff.

Is duality forever? Perhaps not. It is an inheritance from an industrial society and may no longer be appropriate to an information society. In the next century technology may drive a radical restructuring of work in the information field and eradicate the problem. Until that happens, librarian-administrators are bound to observe all the legal distinctions duality imposes. Where there is no option, there is neither preference nor decision.

ANALYZING WORK IN THE ACADEMIC LIBRARY

In any environment the analysis of work is an extraordinarily complex subject. To sharpen the focus of our concept of duality in the academic library, we shall discuss briefly two major methods for analyzing work: functional job analysis (FJA) and factor analysis.

Job Analysis

Functional job analysis, pioneered in the 1950s by Sidney A. Fine when he directed research at the United State Employment Service, has been highly influential in the evolution of job-classification and pay plans. It eventually became the foundation of the third edition of *Dictionary of Occupational Titles* (1965). Much of the methodology in the FJA system is derived from social welfare work, which involves a great deal of interviewing, filling out of forms, and counseling. It categorizes work in accordance with whether an employee is working with data, people, or things; it is concerned only with what the worker does, not with the results achieved. The method explicitly and formally separates action from process:

> A task statement requires a concrete, explicit *action verb*. Verbs which point to a process (such as *develops, prepares, interviews, counsels, evaluates,* and *assesses*) should be avoided or used only to designate broad *processes, methods,* or *techniques* which are then broken down into explicit, discrete action verbs.[55]

An example refers to a social worker interviewing a client (people work: asking questions), taking down data (data work: transcribing responses onto a form), and then typing the results onto a standard form (thing work: operating a typewriter). It is immediately apparent that this separation of thinking from doing is inappropriate to academic librarianship where, we contend, all professional activities come together as an inseparable gestalt.

Interactive computerized information systems did not exist in the 1950s, but their development has changed the way professionals work with data, people, and equipment (no doubt in the social welfare field also). Functional job analysis is surely an extraordinarily useful tool for understanding factory and office work because it concentrates on visible operations. It is completely inapplicable to analysis of the professoriate, research and development work, or librarianship, however, because a professional's process work cannot be disaggregated into convenient units.[56] In short, job analysis is a better tool for describing nonexempt work than for characterizing exempt work.

Campus personnel professionals rely on job analysis as their prime tool, yet it is the very thing that often makes it hard for them to understand what goes on in an academic library and comprehend why librarians are different from support staff and why both differ from clerks and typists. This circumstance alone requires librarian administrators to maintain close peer relationships with campus personnel administrators. (For further discussion on this topic, see the section on dealing with the campus personnel office's bureaucracy in chapter 8.)

Factor Analysis

The well-known Hay system is an analytic compensation-design tool that attempts to overcome the deficiencies of classic functional job analysis. It is designed to evaluate work content (not adequacy of performance) in order to derive compensation levels that will be perceived as just throughout an organization. Expressly designed to analyze exempt work, chiefly that done by executives and professionals (but not making the distinction we postulate between position and job), the Hay system employs factor analysis. Four principles govern the system:

1. The most significant aspects of work are the knowledge required to do it, the type of thinking required for problem solving, responsibilities assigned, and the work environment.

2. Jobs can be ranked in order of importance to the sponsoring organization, and the "distances" between jobs can be determined.

3. Factors appear in patterns that relate to certain types of work.

4. Job evaluation relates to the requirements of the job itself, not to the skills, background, or current pay of the incumbent.

To translate these principles into practical terms, the system analyzes professional and executive work in accordance with three major factors[57]: (1) the know-how required to do the work, (2) the level of problem-solving responsibility, and (3) the extent of accountability for actions, decisions, and consequences. An instrument, the guide chart-profile, is used to assign points and develop a score for each executive or professional slot in an organization.[58]

Know-How

Three dimensions make up the total knowledge and skill needed (it does not matter how they are acquired): (1) knowledge of practical procedures and techniques appropriate to the work or occupation; (2) "planning, organizing, coordinating, integrating, staffing, directing and/or controlling the activities and resources associated with an organizational unit or function, in order to produce the results expected of that unit or function"[59]; and (3) face-to-face skills for interpersonal relationships.

Problem Solving

Problem solving has two dimensions: (1) the environment in which the problem solving and thinking take place and (2) its degree of challenge or difficulty. It involves the nature of analysis, reasoning, evaluation, judgment, hypothesis formation, and the drawing of inferences and reaching of conclusions.

Accountability

This is one's answerability for actions: consequences. Its three dimensions, in rank order, are: (1) the executive or professional's freedom to act, (2) the extent and depth of an individual's direct impact on results, and (3) the magnitude and scope of the function or unit. This last dimension is sometimes expressed as the dollar value of revenues or expenses in the operations for which the professional is responsible.

To achieve the goal of compensation patterns that will be perceived as fair and reasonable, work is analyzed, benchmarks are established, and jobs are ranked by a committee broadly representative of staff and line employees in the organization. This part of the work is typically a team effort, the aim being for the organization to "own" the results, believe in them and thus ensure wide acceptance.

A guide chart-profile method is used to implement the Hay system. A typical chart might postulate many different intensity levels for each category. For example, know-how could be illustrated by postulating seven levels of expertise, ranked in descending order: technical-specialized mastery; seasoned technical-specialized; basic technical-specialized; advanced vocational; vocational; elementary vocational; and basic. The lowest rank would involve work at a strictly operational level governed by fixed guidelines; the highest would be associated with in-depth knowledge, expertise that is both industrywide and internationally renowned. For problem solving, levels might be abstractly defined, generally defined, broadly defined, clearly defined, standardized, semiroutine, and strict routine. In accountability, eight work levels might be ranked in descending order: strategic guidance; broad guidance; oriented direction; directed; generally regulated; standardized; controlled; and prescribed.

A complex system of numerical weights and points is used to derive a total score, which might run from a low of 20 to a high in the mid-300s. The Hay point system is claimed to be independent of extraneous factors such as gender, personality, and job tenure. One obvious benefit is that it gets away from oral tradition or emotional investment for ranking positions. Disagreement exists about the impact of this and similar point systems if administered confidentially. Yet if the system's criteria are made public, some personnel officers fear that employees will attempt to structure their own responsibilities to "make points." On the other hand, if details of the system are kept secret, staff morale may suffer as if employees perceive that their work – and consequent job classification – is being measured by an invisible hand.

The Hay system functions very well in large organizations and has withstood critical review in judicial proceedings, administrative hearings, and arbitration cases. One of its doubtful aspects, which perhaps is important for the small college library or small branch in a large system, is that it tends not to acknowledge the full scope of the complexity factor in one-person operations. The Hay system apportions greater credit to those who do a greater absolute amount of specialized work and thus, seemingly, puts managers of one-person libraries at a disadvantage.

Factor analysis and point systems may be especially useful instruments for analyzing executive work in large, bureaucratic service organizations, such as insurance companies or government agencies. They are surely superior to industrial-style job analysis. Whether they are applicable to professionals in academe, especially those who operate in a collegial system, is controversial. Point systems inevitably create perceptions that some jobs are more important than others, a concept that is already rampant in the elitist academic environment. Yet who is more "important" when the college heating system breaks down: the professor or the steamfitter? Is it fruitful to suggest that professional librarians are more important than those who check in journals or maintain the stacks? As stated above, the probability is high that a library could function without librarians for quite a while, but would fail at once if the support staff quit or went on strike.

It is enough that we must contend with the stresses of employment duality; point systems may worsen existing antagonisms. As with many aspects of administration, there is no perfect method of analyzing library work. In general, broad and flexible guidelines are superior to closely detailed, prescriptive approaches.

IMPACT OF STRESS AND BURNOUT IN LIBRARY WORK

The literature of administration devotes considerable space to the burnout problems of professionals, often to the point of ignoring the exhaustion and frustration that can overcome support staff. A study by the U.S. National Institute of Occupational Safety and Health (NIOSH) indicated that far more people at the bottom suffer stress and hypertension than those at the top. The reason seems obvious: the greater the power, the less the stress, and vice versa. Powerlessness is a direct cause of stress and is easily translated into passive aggression. Therefore, in an academic library, we might expect fairly high, continuous stress levels among filers, terminal operators, reshelvers, circulation counter staff, and check-in clerks.

That reference librarians regularly suffer stress from facing an unending stream of clients at peak periods is well known. In contrast, we might expect stress among professionals in technical services to occur in spurts, perhaps when revised cataloging codes or new automation systems are introduced, while the upper echelons of management would experience the least amount. A major difference, of course, is that when stress comes to the administrator, it can be present in very intense bursts of some duration. Cyclic stress may itself generate further stress.

SUMMARY

Librarianship is mental work done by professionals. Because there is almost no production work and little pure research, personnel-management systems derived from business, manufacturing, or research and development have little relevance to the profession. Most of librarianship's output is intangible, and few management techniques from the business paradigm apply to it. Employment in academic libraries is nevertheless governed by federal legislation in much the same way as other sectors of the economy; no special treatment is accorded to libraries because they are a "social good" or involve mental work.

Employment duality closely follows the stratified social structures of higher education, and is expected to endure as long as higher education retains its elitist character. Federal legislation contains specific tests to determine whether employees are exempt or nonexempt, although some judgment is always involved. The chief determinant is work content and actual duties, not job or position title, and not even job or position description. The duties under consideration must actually be performed, not merely assigned. Hence, it is vital that library administrators and supervisors know precisely what their employees are actually doing, which may not be the same as the contents of the description. Regardless of their personal views and opinions, managers are charged with protecting a school's interests by fulfilling all legal requirements of the employer-employee relationship.

Notes

1. By contrast, in their *An Introduction to University Library Administration*, 4th ed. (London: Bingley, 1987), 63, Thompson and Carr rather pointedly state, "The application to library staff management of the principles of business theory–especially of American origin–has so far, mercifully, been quite limited in United Kingdom universities."

2. Richard De Gennaro, "Theory vs Practice in Library Management," *Library Journal* 108, no. 13 (July 1983): 1318-21.

3. Specific critiques of behavioralist theory and the human potential movement may be found in the following: (a) Michael H. Bottomley, *Personnel Management* (Plymouth: Macdonald and Evans, 1983), esp. chapter 2, 12-23, "Job Satisfaction and Motivation," which briefly surveys ten theories, ranging from F. W. Taylor to E. E. Lawler and L. W. Porter. (b) Amitai Etzioni, *Modern Organizations*, (Englewood Cliffs, N.J.: Prentice-Hall, 1964), esp. chapter 4, "From Human Relations to the Structuralists." (c) John W. Hunt, *Managing People at Work: A Manager's Guide to Behaviour in Organizations* (London: McGraw-Hill, 1979), 5ff. (d) Jerrold Orne, "Future Academic Library Administration: Whither or Whether," in *The Academic Library: Essays in Honor of Guy R. Lyle*, ed. Evan Ira Farber and Ruth Walling (Metuchen, N.J.: Scarecrow Press, 1974), 82-95, esp. 86-87. (e) Michael Maccoby, *The Gamesman: The New Corporate Leaders* (New York: Simon and Schuster, 1976), esp. chapter 8, "The Psychology of Development," 210-33. (f) James Michalko, "Management by Objectives and the Academic Library: A Critical Overview," *Library Quarterly* 45 (July 1975): 235-52. (g) Henri Savall, *Work and People: An Economic Evaluation of Job-Enrichment* (Oxford: Oxford University Press, 1981), esp. chapter 1, "The Problem of Job Design," 13-59. (h) Daniel Yankelovich, *New Rules: Searching for Self-Fulfillment in a World Turned Upside Down* (New York: Random House, 1981), esp.

chapter 23, "Getting Off Maslow's Escalator," 234-43. (i) Frances FitzGerald, *Cities on a Hill: A Journey through Contemporary American Cultures* (New York: Simon and Schuster, 1986), 280-86.

4. Sajjad ur Rehman, *Management Theory and Library Education* (New York: Greenwood, 1987), esp. 86-87, 117-18.

5. Ibid., esp. 86ff.

6. "Changes in Library Education: The Deans Reply," *Special Libraries* 77 (Fall 1986): 217-25.

7. Ann Schabas, in "Changes in Library Education: The Deans Reply," *Special Libraries* 77 (Fall 1986): 224.

8. Ruth J. Person, "The Third Culture: Managerial Socialization in the Library Setting," *Advances in Library Administration and Organization* (JAI Press) 4 (1985): 1-24.

9. For some of the material in this section I am indebted to Miriam Drake's presentation, "Power and Politics in Your Organization," at the annual conference of the Special Libraries Association, Anaheim, 10 June 1987.

10. It is easy to get into a no-win situation here because classified staff can interpret sincere staff development motivation as rejection, especially if it means working outside the library.

11. Albert Shapero, *Managing Professional People: Understanding Creative Performance* (New York: Free Press, 1985), 7.

12. Joseph A. Litterer, *An Introduction to Management* (New York: Wiley, 1978), 9.

13. Ruth J. Person, "The Third Culture," esp. 3.

14. Rosabeth M. Kanter, *The Change Masters: Innovation and Entrepreneurship in the American Corporation* (New York: Simon and Schuster, 1984).

15. Ibid., 42-43.

16. Ibid., 261.

17. For further discussion of this important topic, see chapter 8, which deals with the campus personnel office's bureaucracy.

18. See Richard De Gennaro's "Library Administration and New Management Systems," *Library Journal* 103, no. 22 (December 15, 1978): 2477-82, and his "Theory vs Practice in Library Management," *Library Journal* 108, no. 13 (July 1983): 1318-21.

19. Michael D. Cohen and James G. March, *Leadership and Ambiguity: The American College President*, 2d ed., (Boston: Harvard Business School Press, 1986).

20. Kanter, *Change Masters*, 133.

21. Ibid., 203.

22. Ibid., 205.

23. There are, of course, other types of industrial work, such as mining and farming, which at various stages involve neither factories nor continuous processing plants, but these additional categories are not essential to the point we are making.

24. Arno Penzias, quoted in Jeremy Bernstein, *Three Degrees above Zero: Bell Labs in the Information Age* (New York: Charles Scribner's Sons, 1984), 232. Published originally in the *New Yorker* 60 (20 August 1984), 68, 70.

25. Albert Shapero, *Managing Professional People* (New York: Free Press, 1985), 28.

26. Kanter, *Change Masters*, 143, emphasis in the original.

27. Jorge Reina Schement et al., "Social Forces Affecting the Success of Introducing Information Technology into the Workplace," in *Proceedings of the 48th ASIS Annual Meeting* 22 (1985): 278-83.

28. Excerpts include only those statements explicitly outlining the role of academic librarians; omitted are the arguments aimed at justifying faculty status.

29. "Standards for Faculty Status for College and University Librarians," adopted by ACRL, 26 June 1971, *College & Research Libraries News* 35, no. 3 (May 1974): 112-13. Reprinted in *Academic Status: Statements and Resources* (Chicago: Association of College and Research Libraries, 1988), 9.

30. "Joint Statement on Faculty Status of College and University Librarians," *College & Research Libraries News* 35, no. 2 (February 1974): 26.

31. Prepared by the Canadian Association of College and University Libraries, Academic Status Committee, published in *Feliciter* 34, no. 10 (8 October 1988), 8.

32. Paul Buck, *Libraries and Universities: Addresses and Reports* (Cambridge: Harvard University Press, 1964), 95-96.

33. Robert S. Taylor, "Reminiscing About the Future: Professional Education and the Information Environment," *Library Journal* 104 (15 September 1979): 1871-75.

34. Adapted from Allen B. Veaner, "Librarians: The Next Generation," *Library Journal* 103, no. 6 (1 April 1984): 623. The view of librarians as professionals and intellectuals developed powerfully after World War II. Much of the prior emphasis on education for library science focused on the concept that librarians were technicians who to some extent needed protection from excessive intellectual stimulation. See especially chapter 4, "The Professionalization of Academic Librarianship," in Orvin Lee Shiflett's *Origins of American Academic Librarianship* (Norwood, N.J.: Ablex, 1981).

35. See the following two articles for further discussion on employment strata in libraries: Allen B. Veaner, "Continuity or Discontinuity: A Persistent Personnel Issue in Academic Librarianship," in *Advances in Library Administration and Organization* 1 (1982): 1-20, and Richard Rubin, "A Critical Examination of the 1927 *Proposed Classifications and Compensation Plan for Library Positions* by the American Library Association," *Library Quarterly* 57, no. 4 (October 1987): 400-25.

36. The history, specific advantages, disadvantages, and administrative aspects of faculty versus nonfaculty status are thoroughly covered in the published literature. Current research and discussion on faculty status are amply covered in the *Journal of Academic Librarianship* and *College and Research Libraries*, while a historical overview is in Virgil Massman's *Faculty Status for*

Librarians (Metuchen, N.J.: Scarecrow Press, 1972). A summary of ACRL positions, standards and guidelines on faculty status is in *Academic Status: Statements and Resources* (Chicago: ACRL, 1988). A survey of the literature of faculty status is contained in Fred Batt's "Faculty Status for Academic Librarians: Justified or Just a Farce?" in *Issues in Academic Librarianship*, ed. Peter Spyers-Duran and Thomas W. Mann, Jr. (Westport, Conn.: Greenwood Press, 1985), 115-88. Also available are sixteen articles of mainly historical interest in Robert B. Downs' ACRL monograph, *The Status of American College and University Librarians* (Chicago: ALA, 1958).

37. Some libraries have three rather than two strata of employees: professional, supportive (or library associate), and clerical; education is sometimes the criterion for distinguishing them, with graduate degrees a prerequisite for the first, college for the second, and high school for the third. Whether there are two or three levels, however, does not change the distribution of programmatic responsibilities, which remain the exclusive prerogative of librarians.

38. Strictly speaking, volunteers are not employees, as they commonly receive neither wages nor benefits.

39. See especially 29 USC 152(12)(a) 1976, which defines the distinction between exempt and nonexempt staff. Other major legislation affecting employment is listed in the chapter on recruiting.

40. Charles C. Williamson, *Training for Library Service* (New York: Carnegie Corporation, 1923), 136.

41. In his critique of a human relations school training film, Amitai Etzioni makes the similar point that differences in economic interests and power positions cannot "be communicated away" by clever media presentations. See his *Modern Organizations* (Englewood Cliffs, N.J.: Prentice-Hall, 1964), 44.

42. Herbert S. White, remarks at the ASIS Conference, Las Vegas, 1985. (Cited with the author's permission.)

43. Richard M. Dougherty, "Personnel Needs for Librarianship's Uncertain Future," in *Academic Libraries by the Year 2000: Essays*

Honoring Jerrold Orne, ed. Herbert Poole (New York: Bowker, 1977), 112-13. See also Veaner, "Continuity ior Discontinuity," 1-20.

44. Rosabeth M. Kanter, *The Change Masters*, esp. chapter 7.

45. Hugh F. Cline and Loraine T. Sinnott, *The Electronic Library: The Impact of Automation in Academic Libraries* (Lexington, Mass.: Lexington, 1983), 157.

46. William Joseph Reeves, in *Librarians as Professionals: The Occupation's Impact on Library Work Arrangements* (Lexington, Mass.: D.C. Heath, 1980), concludes that librarianship remains an occupation that has been unable to establish itself as a true profession. His argument is directed to the external world, however, and for our purposes is irrelevant for the same reason Cline and Sinnott's is: librarians must *manage* resources, whether they wish to or not, and that requirement establishes a professional status within the work environment.

47. Judith Bardwick, *The Plateauing Trap* (New York: Bantam: 1988), 82.

48. The word "exempt" means that the so-designated employee is exempted from government regulations requiring that others (i.e., nonexempt personnel) be paid for all work in excess of 40 hours weekly. The exempt-nonexempt distinction does not arise (in a legal sense) when the work week is less than forty hours. See 29 USC 152(12)(a) 1976; see also section 213a, which lists eleven categories of personnel exempt from the requirement of overtime pay. Canada implements a similar, legislatively based distinction.

49. Correspondingly, in most institutions, exempt employees cannot bank time (by working a fictitious overtime) to accumulate additional time for extended vacations. In short, overtime does not exist for exempt employees.

50. Overtime is not to be confused with compensatory time, which is merely a rearrangement of schedule for personnel who work evenings or weekends.

51. In large libraries, some very high-level technical positions may be filled by nonlibrarians, for example, the head of circulation

in a major branch. If the position meets established criteria, the school may designate the position as exempt.

52. There could be exceptions to this principle if a collective bargaining agreement so provides.

53. Frederick Herzberg, "One More Time: How Do You Motivate Employees?" *Harvard Business Review* 46, no. 1 (January-February 1968): 53-62. Holley, in "The Magic of Library Administration," *Texas Library Journal*, 52 (May 1976): 60, reported that one of his graduate students concluded that "a dull, boring job is still likely to be a dull, boring job. . . . "

54. James M. Kusack, *Unions for Academic Library Support Staff* (New York: Greenwood Press, 1986), 86. See also Hugh F. Cline and Loraine T. Sinnott, *The Electronic Library: The Impact of Automation in Academic Libraries* (Lexington, Mass.: Lexington, 1983), 156-57.

55. Sidney A. Fine and Wretha W. Wiley, *An Introduction to Functional Job Analysis* (Kalamazoo, Mich.: W. E. Upjohn Institute for Employment Research, 1971), 10-11.

56. Albert Shapero, *Managing Professional People*, xii-xviii, 28, and elsewhere. For a completely different view of the value of job analysis and the Fine/Wiley methodology in academic librarianship, see Forest C. Benedict and Paul M. Gherman, "Implementing an Integrated Personnel System," *Journal of Academic Librarianship* 6, no. 4 (September 1980): 210-14. See also Virginia S. Hill and Tom G. Watson's "Job Analysis: Process and Benefits," *Advances in Library Administration and Organization* 3 (1984): 209-19. Hill and Watson concede that job analysis is better suited to routine work having a tangible outcome than to professional service work.

57. There is a fourth factor relating to work under physically hazardous or unpleasant conditions that is normally not included when the system is used to analyze work that is strictly white collar.

58. For a full explication of the Hay method see Alvin O. Bellak, "The Hay Guide Chart-Profile Method of Job Evaluation," *Handbook of Wage and Salary Administration*, 2d ed. (New York: McGraw-Hill, 1984), and the earlier presentation by Charles W. G.

Van Horn, "The Hay Guide Chart-Profile Method," in *Handbook of Wage and Salary Administration*, 1st ed., ed. Milton L. Rock (New York: McGraw-Hill, 1972), 286-97.

59. Adapted from "Job Evaluation Using The Hay Method," a booklet issued by Hay Management Consultants, n.d.

Resources

Abell, Millicent D. "The Changing Role of the Academic Librarian: Drift and Mastery." *College & Research Libraries* 40 (March 1979): 154-64.

Abell, Millicent D., and Jacqueline M. Coolman. "Professionalism and Productivity: Keys to the Future of Academic Library and Information Services." In *Priorities for Academic Libraries*, 71-87, edited by Thomas J. Galvin and Beverly P. Lynch (San Francisco: Jossey-Bass, 1982),.

Arroba, T., and K. James. *Pressure at Work: A Survival Guide.* Toronto, McGraw-Hill Ryerson, 1987.

Bellak, Alvin O. "The Hay Guide Chart-Profile Method of Job Evaluation." Prepared for *Handbook of Wage and Salary Administration*, 2d ed. (New York: McGraw-Hill, 1984).

Bold, Rudolph. "Librarian Burn-Out." *Library Journal* 107 (1 November 1982): 2048-51.

Bottomley, Michael H. *Personnel Management.* Estover, Plymouth: Macdonald and Evans, 1983.

Boyd, Craig. *Technostress: The Human Cost of the Computer Revolution.* Reading, Mass.: Addison-Wesley, 1984.

Brockman, John R. *Academic Library Management Research: An Evaluative Review.* Loughborough: Centre for Library and Information Management, Department of Library and Information Studies, Loughborough University, 1984.

Canadian Association of College and University Libraries. *Position Classification and Principles of Academic Status in Canadian*

University Libraries. Ottawa: Canadian Library Association, 1969.

Canelas, Dale B. "Position Classification in Libraries and an Introduction to the Library Education and Personnel Utilization Policy." Unpublished paper presented at the ALA Conference, Detroit, June 1977.

Cherniss, Cary. *Staff Burnout: Job Stress in the Human Services.* Los Angeles: Sage, 1980.

Cherniss, Cary, E. Egnatios and S. Wacker. "Job Stress and Career Development in New Public Professional." *Professional Psychology* 7, no. 4 (1976): 428-36.

Clemons, Bonnie. "Career Ladders for Support Staff in University Libraries." Ph.D. diss., Florida State University, 1983.

Creth, Sheila. "Personnel Planning, Job Analysis, and Job Evaluation with Special Reference to Academic Libraries." *Advances in Librarianship* 12 (1982): 47-97.

Edelwich, Jerry, with Archie Brodsky. *Burn-out: Stages of Disillusionment in the Helping Professions.* New York: Human Sciences Press, 1980.

Estabrook, Leigh. "Labor and Librarians: The Divisiveness of Professionalism." *Library Journal* 106 (January 1981): 125-27.

Etzioni, Amitai. *A Comparative Analysis of Complex Organizations: On Power, Involvement, and Their Correlates.* Rev. and enl. New York: Free Press, 1975.

Evans, Charles W. "The Evolution of Paraprofessional Library Employees." *Advances in Librarianship* 9 (1979): 64-102.

Fine, Sidney A., and Wretha W. Wiley. *An Introduction to Functional Job Analysis.* Kalamazoo, Mich.: W. E. Upjohn Institute for Employment Research, 1971.

Focus: The Wage and Hour Law and Exempt/Non-Exempt Employees. Englewood Cliffs, N.J.: Prentice-Hall, in press.

Freudenberger, Herbert J. *Burn Out: The High Cost of High Achievement.* Garden City, N.Y.: Anchor, 1980.

Gael, S. *Job Analysis: A Guide to Assessing Work Activities.* San Francisco: Jossey-Bass, 1983.

Ginzberg, Eli. *Understanding Human Resources.* Lanham, Md.: University Press of America, 1985.

Hack, Mary, John W. Jones, and Tina Roose. "Occupational Burnout Among Librarians." *Drexel Library Quarterly* 20 (Spring 1984): 46-72.

Handbook of Wage and Salary Administration. 2d ed. New York: McGraw-Hill, 1984.

Herzberg, Frederick. *The Managerial Choice: To Be Efficient and to Be Human.* Homewood, Ill.: Dow Jones-Irwin, 1976.

_____. *The Motivation to Work.* New York: Wiley, 1959.

_____. *Work and the Nature of Man.* Cleveland, Ohio: World, 1966.

Hill, Virginia S., and Tom G. Watson. "Job Analysis: Process and Benefits." *Advances in Library Administration and Organization* 3 (1984): 209-19.

Holley, Edward G. "Defining the Academic Librarian." *College & Research Libraries* 46 (November 1985): 462-68.

Holley, Robert P. "Academic Librarianship: Intersection of Multiple Worlds." *Journal of Library Administration* 9, no. 3 (1988): 111-17.

Howard, Helen. "Organization Theory and Its Applications to Research in Librarianship." *Library Trends* 32, no. 4 (Spring 1984): 477-93.

_____. "Personnel Administration in Libraries." *Argus* 11, nos. 3/4 (May-August 1982): 85-90.

Hunt, H. Allen, and Timothy L. Hunt. *Clerical Employment and Technological Change.* Kalamazoo, Mich.: W. E. Upjohn Institute for Employment Research, 1986.

Job Analysis in ARL Libraries. Washington, D.C.: Association of Research Libraries/Office of Management Studies, 1987.

Kaplan, Louis. "On the Road to Participative Management: The American Academic Library, 1934-1970." *Libri* 38, no. 4 (1988): 314-20.

Kleingartner, Archie, and Carolyn S. Anderson. *Human Resource Management in High Technology Firms.* Lexington, Mass.: Lexington Books, 1987.

Klingner, Donald E. "When the Traditional Job Description Is Not Enough." *Personnel Journal* 58 (April 1979): 243-48.

Kusack, James M. *Unions for Academic Library Support Staff.* New York: Greenwood Press, 1986.

Lawrence, Paul R., and Jay W. Lorsch. *Organization and Environment: Managing Differentiation and Integration.* Rev. ed. Boston: Harvard Business School Press, 1986.

Leitko, Thomas A., and David Szczerbacki. "Why Traditional OD Strategies Fail in Professional Bureaucracies." *Organizational Dynamics* 15, no. 3 (Winter 1987): 52-64.

Levinson, Harry. "When Executives Burn Out." *Harvard Business Review* 59 (May-June 1981): 72-81. Reprinted in Eliza G. C. Collins, ed., *The Executive Dilemma: Handling People Problems at Work* (New York: John Wiley & Sons, 1985), 61-71.

McCormick, Ernest J. *Job Analysis: Methods and Applications.* New York: AMACOM, 1979.

Maher, John R. *New Perspectives in Job Enrichment.* New York: Van Nostrand Reinhold, 1971.

Management Law Newsletter. Minneapolis: Great Way Publishing. Monthly.

Martell, Charles. "Administration: Which Way – Traditional Practice or Modern Theory?" *College & Research Libraries* 33, no. 2 (March 1972): 104-12.

_____. "Automation, Quality of Work Life, and Middle Managers." Paper presented at meeting of ALA/LAMA/Systems and Services Section/Management Practices Committee, New York ALA Conference, 1986.

_____. "Myths, Schooling and the Practice of Librarianship." *College & Research Libraries* 45, no. 5 (September 1984): 374-82.

Maslach, Christina. "Burned Out." *Human Behavior* 5, no. 9 (September 1976): 16-22.

Melendez, Winifred Albizu, and Rafael M. de Guzman. *Burnout: The New Academic Disease.* ASHE Report 83-9. Washington, D.C.: Association for the Study of Higher Education, 1983.

Miles, Raymond E. *Theories of Management: Implications for Organizational Behavior and Development.* New York: McGraw-Hill, 1975.

Morgan, Gareth. *Images of Organizations.* Beverly Hills: Sage, 1986.

Nauratil, Marcia J. *The Alienated Librarian.* Wesport, Conn.: Greenwood Press, 1989.

Ozaki, Hiroko. *The Role of Professional and Non-Professional Staff in Libraries, with an Emphasis on the Division of Their Duties in the Cataloging Unit: A Select Bibliography.* Ottawa: National Library of Canada, Library Documentation Centre, July 1981.

Personnel Classification Schemes. Washington, D.C.: Association of Research Libraries/Office of Management Studies, 1978.

Pines, Ayala M., and Elliot Aronson. *Burnout: From Tedium to Personal Growth.* New York: Free Press, 1981.

Pines, Ayala M., and D. Dafry. "Occupational Tedium in the Services." *Social Work* 23 (November 1978): 506-8.

Reeves, William Joseph. *Librarians as Professionals: The Occupation's Impact on Library Work Arrangements.* Lexington Mass.: D.C. Heath, 1980.

Ricking, Myrl, and Robert E. Booth. *Personnel Utilization in Libraries—A Systems Approach.* Chicago: American Library Association, 1974.

Rogers, Everett M., and Judith K. Larson. *Silicon Valley Fever: Growth of High-Technology Culture.* New York: Basic Books, 1986.

Savall, Henri. *Work and People: An Economic Evaluation of Job Enrichment.* New York: Oxford University Press, 1981.

Shapero, Albert. *Managing Professional People: Understanding Creative Performance.* New York: Free Press, 1985.

Sheppard, Harold L., and Neal Q. Herrick. *Where Have All the Robots Gone? Worker Dissatisfaction in the 70s.* New York: Free Press, 1972.

Shera, Jesse H. *The Foundations of Education for Librarianship.* New York: Becker and Hayes, 1972.

Smith, Nathan M., Nancy E. Birch, and Maurice P. Marchant. "Stress, Distress and Burnout: a Survey of Public Reference Librarians." *Public Libraries* 23 (Fall 1984): 83-85.

Spaniol, LeRoy, and Jennifer J. Caputo. *Professional Burn-Out: A Personal Survival Kit.* Lexington, Mass: Human Services Associates, 1979.

Treiman, Donald J. *Job Evaluation: An Analytic Review.* Interim report to the Equal Employment Opportunity Commission. Staff paper prepared for the committee on Occupational Classification and Analysis, Assembly of Behavioral and Social Sciences, National Research Council. Washington, D.C.: National Academy of Sciences, 1979.

Treiman, Donald J., and H. I. Hartmann. *Women, Work, and Wages—Equal Pay for Jobs of Equal Value.* Washington, D.C.: National Academy Press, 1981.

Tunley, Malcolm. *Library Structures and Staffing Systems.* London: Library Association, 1979.

Van Horn, Charles W.G. "The Hay Guide-Chart Profile Method." In *Handbook of Wage and Salary Administration*, edited by Milton L. Rock, 286-97. New York: McGraw-Hill, 1972.

Van Rijn, Paul. *Job Analysis for Selection: An Overview*. Washington, D.C.: U.S. Office of Personnel Management, Staffing Services Group, 1979.

Welch, I. David. *Beyond Burnout: How to Enjoy Your Job Again when You've Just About Had Enough*. Englewood Cliffs, N.J.: Prentice-Hall, 1982.

Westin, Alan F., et al. *The Changing Workplace: A Guide to Managing the People, Organizational and Regulatory Aspects of Office Technology*. White Plains, N.Y.: Knowledge Industry Publications, 1985.

White, Herbert S. *Library Personnel Management*. White Plains, N.Y.: Knowledge Industry Publications, 1985.

Woodsworth, Anne. "Getting Off the Library Merry-Go-Round: McAnally and Downs Revisited." *Library Journal* 114, no. 8 (1 May 1989): 35-38.

Yankelovich, Daniel. *New Rules: Searching for Self-Fulfillment in a World Turned Upside Down*. New York: Random House, 1981.

Zuboff, Shoshana. "New Worlds of Computer-Mediated Work." *Harvard Business Review* 60, no. 5 (September-October 1982): 142-52.

CHAPTER 4

Managing Your Inheritances: Critical Aspects of Startup for the New Administrator

Everything you require for the first day's operations you will inherit: staff, collections, physical facilities, campus administration, local policies and procedures, calendar, budget, faculty, and students. You also inherit the entire gestalt of the previous administration, a society in miniature with its successful programs, its excellence, and its influential friends, more or less balanced or offset by its vested interests, inequities, injustices, and enemies. Your secretary will likely be your predecessor's, as will your office. If you are fortunate, you may get some new office furniture. You will arrive in the midst of complex mechanisms already in place and functioning to varying degrees of efficiency. In every sense you will be the interloper, the threat to a variety of formal and informal establishments and power structures.

THE ESTABLISHMENT

Machiavelli's familiar cautions on imposing a new order of things on the establishment have become worn; perhaps of greater value and certainly of greater interest is the following advice he offered the new administrator:

> . . . the reformer has enemies in all those who profit by the older order, and only lukewarm defenders in all those who would profit by the new order, this lukewarmness arising partly from fear of their adversaries who have the laws in their favor; and partly from the incredulity of mankind, who do not truly believe in anything new until they have had actual experience of it. Thus it arises that on every opportunity for attacking the reformer, his opponents do so with zeal of partisans, the others only defend him half-heartedly, so that between them he runs great danger. It is necessary, however, in order to investigate thoroughly this question, to examine whether these innovators are independent, or whether they depend upon others, that is to say, whether in order to carry out their designs they have to entreat or are able to compel. In the first case they invariably succeed ill, and accomplish nothing; but when they can depend on their own strength and are able to use force, they rarely fail.[1]

The late twentieth-century newcomer to administration is at a triple disadvantage: new, lacking allies, and with a minimal capacity to apply "force." The new administrator's "tokens" are not ammunition but rather a fount of goodwill, a status devoid of old political debts, and a capacity for doing and accomplishing through persuasion. These tokens are created by the blessings of the search panel and the campus administration. Force is a very peculiar and paradoxical attribute of administration. Conventional thinking suggests that might begets might, or at least suppresses revolt. But in a bureaucracy, might is the very power that, when invoked, diminishes itself, driving the administrator out of power immediately and decisively. Bureaucratic power, like nuclear deterrent, is useful only if it is not used.

THE FIRST WEEKS

The designation of an administrator's early time in office as a honeymoon is somewhat of an exaggeration. For the staff and the various constituencies it is a time of testing the new leadership; it is a time of hope that inequities will be removed and injustices righted, and fear that the new administrator will upset certain well-tuned and long-set policies, procedures, and habits.

The first several weeks in a position of leadership are a critical period in both institutional history and your personal career development. Long before you arrived on campus – probably during the interview process – you will have examined the library's broad mission and suggested, perhaps pushed for, any major changes of direction you deemed necessary. That was the best time to sell campus administrators on any major institutional shifts that might cost more than the regular budget could bear. Now is the time to follow up and start the program revision process. Task forces, committees, break-out sessions, commissions, open discussions, consultants – any technique that stimulates thought and action can be used. The point is not to lose the momentum imparted by your appointment.

If during your early tenure you initiate little action on program review or revision, staff at all levels will likely perceive you as a passive person, interested only in a caretakership. Your early actions (or inactions) will set a tone and, if the tone is not right, it may take months or even years to alter the initial perceptions and emotions held by the staff. Your main challenge is to influence staff and market your ideas, not impose them.

Aside from the creative work in program review, which is both demanding and exhilarating, you will face challenges that range from the mundane to the exhausting. You learn your way around an unfamiliar campus and make yourself highly visible to your administrative peers. You acquaint yourself thoroughly with the details of the institution's major policies and procedures in finance and personnel. You quickly pick up information about campus politics: who are the powerful, the influential, who is in disrepute or out of favor. Finally, you examine with great care the current reports on staff performance; the higher the rank and the closer to your own position, the greater the care and attention you must give to the documentation.

An institution's administrative history strongly influences staff attitudes and expectations. Where the administration has been loose, the tendency is greater for staff to assert rights than to focus on responsibilities. The longer the former administration has been in power, the more difficult it will be to change. Thus it would be a grievous error to suppose that you can mandate change even when it is obviously needed and universally desired. You will have to prove to your staff that they will find an advantage in adaptation. They must perceive a payoff; tangible, observable benefits must be realized within a real time frame. You should be forthright and direct in indicating what you expect, equally forthright in providing appropriate rewards, and above all, capable of securing the resources staff need to fulfill your expectations. There must be no hidden agendas, nothing left unclear or ambiguous, nor any suggestion that caprice governs the administration's decisions. What you want to achieve you must sell, so that the achievement is everyone's, not yours.

You will inherit some people who entered the profession many years ago when expectations for both performance and career goals differed radically from contemporary standards. Some will have adapted smoothly, others not. Some will be utterly devoted to the vocational aspects of librarianship and may be frightened of the idea of taking responsibility for supervision or decision making, having long ago virtually ceased to function creatively. Others, never losing a chance to enlarge their horizons, will be extraordinarily energetic and original. Those who plateaued a long time ago can be counted on to react with little but cynicism to every initiative. Differential adaptation, possibly coupled to salary differences between recent hires and long-tenured staff, creates dissonance, something you have been hired to cope with.

Whatever grand designs you may have conceived for making the library a paragon of advanced performance, the most important initial responsibility is simply to maintain established systems. Nothing destroys a library administrator faster than disruption or breakdown of services clients are long accustomed to and regularly expect. Unhappy faculty, staff, and students can form very strong, demanding, and dangerous coalitions. Naturally, you will have your own ideas about programs and priorities, but you should not summarily dismiss your predecessor's program. Evaluate it carefully; chances are the staff has contributed to it and the campus administration has blessed it to some extent. A good first priority is to complete any unfinished elements that you judge to have substantial merit.

If reorganization is on your agenda, however, it is better to begin it fairly soon. The longer you wait, the more staff assumes that you approve the arrangements prevailing when you arrived, and the harder it becomes to change later. In addition, the bigger the organization, the longer it takes to learn enough about it to be certain that a change is justified. On the other hand, some administrators impose change whether it is needed or not, as a political act to place their personal stamp on the institution. No one can prescribe which is the wiser course; you must make your own decisions and take the attendant risks.

Your first weeks at the post may see you reading far into the night the library's criteria for advancement and promotion, details of the school's technical regulations on leave without pay, annual reports, and budget statements. For a change of pace you can be reading the evaluation documents of both professional and support staff for the current and several preceding years. But read you must.

EARLY DEALINGS WITH THE CAMPUS ADMINISTRATION

It is a given that managers must be able to motivate and mobilize their subordinates. It is even more important that they be able to mobilize their superiors. The only managers who will realize programs successfully are those who can win resources from their superiors by (1) arguing their cases convincingly and (2) developing excellent collegial and social relationships. The second may well outweigh the first. It is from these people that you must get resources and it is to them that you must market the library, plugging the services that benefit the powerful constituencies and making the library visible as a service provider rather than a consumer of funds. All this means playing a very good game of politics. (See chapter 6 for more detail on this subject.)

EARLY DEALINGS WITH STAFF

With or without initiatives from the new administration, during the first weeks delegations from various staff constituencies may approach the front office with inventories of problems to be solved. Special pleadings may accompany these approaches. All representations will partly reveal the natural rivalries and jealousies that exist in any complex workplace. Sessions with small groups will afford insights into the personalities of those who lead the informal organization or seek to protect vested interests. As an outcome of such conferences, you will doubtless acquire some loyal enthusiasts in the first few weeks or months. You may also acquire enemies, persons whose habits you have disrupted, whose advances you reject, or to whom you are unwilling to grant favors.

Approaches from delegations can be a danger signal, indicating that the new leadership is not demonstrating initiative to seek out information on actual and potential trouble spots immediately. Your program of research, study, and reading into institutional policies and the history of performance appraisals for key staff (and others) must not interfere with your responsibility to communicate effectively. You should be reaching out to the employees early, not waiting for them to come to you. Administrators who start moving among the employees – all employees, not just professional staff – almost as soon as they arrive will learn about hot spots long before they burst into flame.

Moving among the employees, or "management by walking around" will take time away from your study of institutional documentation and reading of the mass of mail that comes to every library administrator. Such movement affords an unsurpassed opportunity to learn employees' names, as well as facts about their personal lives. An administrator who understands the staff's human problems will be all the stronger and more capable for that knowledge. The interest must be sincere, however; staff quickly see through artifice and will not respect anyone whose approach looks manipulative.

GAMES PEOPLE PLAY

Gamesmanship, an inherent aspect of every bureaucratic environment, cannot be escaped in academe. In business, the gamesman-leader employs the techniques of behavioral science to mold employees into a winning team; individual goals are submerged, as in sports. The academic community, however, resists every business paradigm: how can one build a team when by definition independent professionals are bent on advancing their own special interests and responsibilities?

Nor can a library administrator's gamesmanship be modeled after the old-fashioned, paternalistic owner-entrepreneur. Librarian-administrators do not own their libraries and cannot do what they please, but are obliged to support institutional goals or give up their positions. In this sense they are much closer to modern corporate managers, having very little freedom to implement personal philosophies.

Any resemblance between corporate culture and the academy ends at this point, because academics' self-governance and rights of program codetermination have few counterparts in the business world.[2] It is unlikely that any library administrator could successfully apply the corporate gamesmanship strategies and team-development techniques described by Maccoby; even an attempt would guarantee failure. *The challenge in academe is not to build a team but to develop a style of cooperative independence, uniting diverse interests into the achievement of common goals without destroying or weakening opportunity for individual growth and development.* This is a vastly more difficult challenge than team building. Even so, academe still has its own style of gamesmanship.[3]

Beyond the challenge of gamesmanship at the institutional and corporate levels lie the private, irrational games individuals play, the kind so well described by Eric Berne[4] and other transactionalists. Social scientists have devised many interpretive models to explain the behavior of troubled and troublesome people. Beneath overt behavior lies a "vast interpersonal underworld," suggested Schutz, and it is from this invisible and not so rational world that games emerge.[5] Zaleznik developed behavioral models to help administrators comprehend difficult people, analyze their games, and figure out how to cope.[6] Many of the most annoying games that "difficult people" play can be better understood by a careful study of Zaleznik's paper and Berne's *Games People Play*.

Yet to seasoned administrators behavioral models often appear somewhat mechanistic and all-inclusive, claiming to explain almost anything and everything. Like business paradigms, some easily acquire a dated look; no sooner does one identify a model than the behavior begins to defy it. At best these constructs can only help us understand that human behavior is boundless in its variety and motivation.

Another hazard is that these models may encourage us to enter realms where we really lack competence. Just as we do not want the campus psychiatrist to play library administrator, we should be careful not to play psychiatrist.

"Difficult Person" Game

Most employees are hard-working, dedicated people who want to perform well. The heaviest challenges come from a small minority who dedicate their lives not to work but to private, interpersonal games. From their viewpoint the best games are those that consume as much administrative time as possible. Some of these difficult people willfully, deliberately, and consciously frustrate, demoralize, and stress others, putting them into no-win situations. Rarely is their response unconscious; they have carefully worked out which buttons you respond to most actively and are willing, even eager, to use you as a live video game for which no coins are required.

Having adopted a maladaptive lifestyle, they use relatively fixed strategies. Difficult people usually like to control a social situation, directly or indirectly; *being controlled is what they find intolerable.* They may try to intimidate, bait, bluff, rattle, charm, or trap you into a game of "heads-I-win-tails-you-lose." Physical responses may include finger pointing, staring, and refusing to take a seat. Verbal responses may include certain entrapment techniques, such as telling an ethnic or off-color joke with the intent of getting you to reciprocate, and then later using your response against you. One of their specialties is trying to force you to lose your cool, but it is important never to raise your voice in dealing with employees, regardless of how provocative the situation.[7]

"Gotcha" Game

"Gotcha" requires highly skilled players who are content to remain invisible. The players combine contradictory qualities: exceptional brilliance, legalistic mentality, pettiness, frustration with lack of power, extreme patience and persistence, and no lack of cheek. The basic aim is to catch the boss in violation of the school's regulations, or better yet, some state, provincial, or federal regulation or law. Because persons who play "gotcha" spend hours exhaustively searching and studying these legalities, they are sometimes, but not always, marginal performers. As no one can possibly keep on top of every agency rule, these players ultimately discover an area in which you have failed. They do not confront you with their findings but clandestinely go to your boss, peer staff, subordinates, or the media. "Gotcha" players rarely take any credit for their findings; they are usually content to work anonymously.

There is no way to eliminate these people from the administrative battlefield. The best precaution is to abide carefully by established rules; here is where the long hours of study of campus regulations pay off. But the rules are becoming more complex, not simpler, and as your responsibilities broaden, you will have to rely on trusted staff officers, campus peers, and colleagues, to keep you sufficiently informed so as not to lose this particular game.

Credibility Game

Some people are professional exegetes, always seeing dark, hidden messages in even the most direct, explicit statements. They expend a great deal of energy trying to explain to themselves and others what their bosses "really" meant. They attribute to messages meanings never intended or question the reality of policy decisions. Players view themselves as expert communicators and interpreters. Their method of play is to ask the questions, "What does it really mean? How much can I get away with before a policy is really invoked?"

The credibility game is a fairly routine method of testing whether an administration has any teeth.

Amateur Lawyer Game

Amateur lawyers are similar to the "gotcha" players except they play in the open. They will either confront you directly or tell co-workers all the things that you cannot do because:

- You do not have the authority to do it.

- It is illegal – against state, provincial, federal regulations.

- It is contrary to college or university policy; see the campus Policy and Procedure Manual, section so-and-so.

"It's Not in My Job Description"

This is a favorite game of "lifers" (people who have retired on the job but still report to work). Lifers resemble "knife-edgers," the people who reliably turn in a barely acceptable performance; they measure their responses to the work environment carefully, always leaving on time or earlier and never venturing into any responsibility outside their job or position descriptions. They are usually intelligent, capable, and loyal people who know their work very well. Years of administrative neglect, rigidity, or deprivation of opportunity to contribute to the organization, or even be heard, have probably contributed to the lifer mentality.

While it is easy to ignore or dismiss them, it would be a great waste of talent. Given the right stimulus, opportunity, and recognition, lifers may make surprising turnarounds. It is up to the leadership, not to these personnel, to restore their initiative. The successful transformation of lifers into active, productive staff members provides a satisfying reward for everyone.

A final comment on this game emphasizes a point made earlier: because all work emerges from an institution's program, the school, not an individual, "owns" job and position descriptions. There is a difference between an assigned responsibility and a commitment. Loyalty to a position may come from years of experience, but not even the passage of time conveys possession. Commitment is something altogether different from possession, a deeper quality implying a capacity to change and a dedication beyond one's immediate, specific responsibilities. It is commitment, not ownership, that leads to growth, development, and change in both job and position descriptions.

End Run

The larger and more decentralized the library, the more tempting the end run. Of course, classic organization theory rules that end runs are illegal–people are not supposed to go behind the boss's back to another level of the organization without a by-your-leave. But classic organization theory is poorly geared to the academy, where end runs are a normal part of life. A much better strategy than trying to eliminate end runs is keeping your own linkages with faculty and peer administrators strong and healthy. In other words, play a good game of "head 'em off at the pass."

Management's Games

It might be supposed from the discussion thus far that most troublesome games originate from lowest-level staff. To make that assumption maligns the people who really operate the library and are actually doing something helpful, productive, and constructive. In fact, games are played even by managers and supervisors, who have some special diversions open only to their ranks. The worst of the managerial games are in the area of decision making. White provided a rather sad but highly realistic inventory of the how-to-make-sure-that-I-never-get-blamed-for-a-decision game: inaction (on the grounds of the "no time to study your proposal"), invisibility (door closed, never available for an appointment), creation of phony obstacles (called by White the "Yes, but . . ." game), instinctive rejection of all new ideas, passing the buck (a variation of "it's-not-in-my-job-description"), and ultimately, total abdication.[8]

REVIEWING YOUR OWN DUTIES AND RESPONSIBILITIES

Do not be surprised if the institutionally furnished statement of duties and responsibilities for the chief librarian's position is outdated, inadequate, or both. If an academic library has run smoothly for some years, chances are the position description will have changed little. Sometimes the campus administration does not really have a clear idea of what a chief librarian's duties and responsibilities are. In that case, you will do everyone a favor by preparing a new draft for consideration by the officer(s) to whom you report. It would be particularly advantageous to make such a suggestion part of the negotiations for the position. After all, such a description will likely contain statements relating to performance expectations, and it will be to your advantage to participate in its formulation.

There is another reason for chief librarians to contribute to the construction of their own position descriptions as early as possible: no matter how small the institution, any number of people will be ready and willing to define your administrative duties for you. Most especially, and a means of self-protection and preservation of the status quo, some are quite anxious to define the limits of your responsibilities in a restrictive way. You will be viewed variously – figurehead (no real authority), window dressing (no real authority), high-class gopher (fetcher of money to maintain the status quo), Mr. or Ms. Outside (glad-hander with rich donors), advocate of some special interest in the organization (say, to benefit professional staff rather than support staff) – but not invariably as someone with the power and authority to work on changing established ways.

Of the many roles you play, none is exclusive. Sometimes you are a figurehead; the role is not to be denigrated. The chief librarian (or any library administrator) fulfills many symbolic duties, conducts important rites, and invokes blessings, all indispensable functions in the social life of the academic community. Being a figurehead from time to time does not relieve you of performing your other duties and responsibilities, however. Even in small organizations power abhors a vacuum: if administration does not exercise leadership, the defaulted responsibility is quickly distributed to an ever-ready corps of power brokers in the informal organization whose goals and objectives may show little congruence with those of the institution.

BUILDING YOUR OWN PROFESSIONAL IMAGE

Modern media experts stress the extent to which perception takes precedence over reality, a condition made possible by the overwhelming dominance of television in day-to-day communication. Intellectually, we may deplore the notion of leader as someone who plays a role or otherwise manipulates our perceptions of and responses to the real world. Administrators cannot ignore image, role playing, or body language in themselves or others, however. The impressions they make in the first few weeks may contribute lastingly to the images they convey throughout their tenure.

Personal image is a significant theme in perception. It consists of your dress, basic physical appearance, and how you communicate. Even office facilities complement it, as they influence the way your listeners perceive you and your message. For executives, control of personal image is an indispensable element in effective communication, self-presentation, and projection of professionalism. In both the United States and Canada consulting firms do a thriving business helping executives use body language to build a suitable image.

Dress and Appearance

In older novels and films the popular image of the male in higher education is the pipe-smoking academic wearing a tweed jacket or cardigan long past its prime, and a pair of loafers. Today's image probably replaces tweed and loafers with jeans and running shoes. Women professionals in academic administration are still such a comparative novelty that few stereotypes exist for their appearance. The idea persists, however, that casual clothing is the accepted order of things. The truth is that as much variety of apparel obtains in the academic workplace as anywhere else.

Standards for dress obviously vary according to season, region, and local custom. In factories, where work and social structures are becoming more horizontal, managers are giving up their coats, ties, and white collars for more casual apparel in an effort to buttress team concepts. The academic environment is much too sophisticated for this approach, which staff would see as an obvious gimmick. Therefore, despite the current popularity of casual dress on campus, it is a mistake to think it a sign of egalitarianism. Casual dress is sometimes defended on the theory that it reduces the distance between management and employees, eases communication, and enhances the concept of a team of equals. Academe is *not* Kanter's fictitious Chipco, all of whose employees are young. Formal togs donned only for an appraisal interview will not eradicate the "buddy" image that casual dress attempts to create, and if worn infrequently, signal clearly that "something is up."

The appropriate apparel is one among several symbols of authority unashamedly displayed by those with administrative powers and responsibilities. The right clothes also protect the integrity of your position as an administrator, in that you will not be parading about as someone you are not.

None of this means that men will never take off their ties and jackets in the workplace or that a women cannot wear a tasteful pants suit. The rules for dress cannot conform to a fixed code or uniform, but should always be based on common sense. In the final analysis, conservative dress is always more helpful than harmful to an administrator.

Voice

Because everyone from the custodial staff to one's immediate deputies is present, an all-staff meeting is usually the library administrator's most demanding public speaking challenge. Conflict contributes to a hostile atmosphere in an open meeting. When it arises, it is vital to keep cool and respond with evident self-control. Males and females equally may need to unlearn some of the behavior to which they have been socialized. Men may have to tone down aggressiveness, and talk more slowly and deliberately. Women may have to increase their assertiveness, giving up anything that might signal "cuteness," weakness, or uncertainty, such as excessive smiling, overflorid figures of speech, or an unbusinesslike stance at the podium. Direct, forceful communication is a benefit to everyone.

Eye Contact

In Western society averting the eyes is taken to signal guilt, nervousness, fear, or humility.[9] Staring at people is equally a barrier to good communication. Good eye contact is a valuable quality that is easily acquired.

The Role of Touch

The acceptability of touching varies widely among cultures. Touch ranges from the simple handshake to a pat on the shoulder, pulling the other person's body toward oneself, and, in rare instances in North America, hugging. In North America an administrator should be very cautious about touching another person, even in jest. It is an extremely delicate, highly personal act that may work in one direction only: from the superior to the subordinate. To some people it emphasizes and strongly reinforces an existing power relationship, a fact that may not be welcomed by subordinates.

Touching is often misinterpreted by the one who is touched and by those who witness it. Depending on jurisdiction and local regulations, an unwanted touch by another person could be construed as assault or battery and cause for charges to be filed. Touching a person of the opposite sex, whether in public or private, during business hours could result in charges of sexual harassment, which the courts have defined as creating a work environment that is hostile, offensive or intimidating. In general it is best to avoid touching in public and to consider very judiciously whether to employ it at all. In private offices it is best to avoid it altogether; fate has a way of suddenly transforming private quarters into public space.

If an employee cries during a performance appraisal or in any similar emotionally charged context, be extraordinarily cautious not to touch him or her. Do not even extend a hand or otherwise reach out in a gesture of comfort.[10] Someone may be trying to set you up for a charge of sexual harassment or assault. The one best and simplest rule about touch is *don't!*

ESTABLISHING PREFERRED OFFICE ROUTINES

Your office staff not only controls the communication channels, files, furniture, work methods, and layout that existed before you came, but they possess a tremendous depth of historical knowledge that you depend on in the initial stages. Yet you cannot expect a staff unaccustomed to your style and work habits always to greet you with enthusiasm. Mostly, your arrival is a disruption to their established routines, even though conditions prior to your arrival may have been so bad that any change brings a sigh of relief.

Office employees are generally loyal, hard working, devoted, and deeply knowledgeable. Meet with them frequently, especially at the beginning. Explain your own preferences immediately: how you want your letters formatted and the phone answered; whether the office is to be covered during the lunch hour and how; who will be responsible for locking up and security. The first few weeks, as you learn the building, the institution, and the staff, is a good time to consider reviewing the job descriptions of office personnel. You must do this at least to learn what tasks are assigned to whom.

Processing the Administration's Mail

The administrative suite or "front office" is the nerve center of the library, the crossover and switching point where all (or nearly all, you hope) important communications intersect and from which they are routed. Even in a small academic library the amount of mail entering the front office is much too large for the head librarian to process alone. Someone, even if it is only a student assistant, must help sort and route it. Most people have little idea how much printed communication comes to librarians. Therefore the first task is to winnow the wheat from the chaff: forward the misdirected book and journal invoices to your accounting clerk, get rid of the promotional flyers for material you already have on standing order, send the misaddressed journals to the check-in clerk, and so on.

Of course, in a small library you might find yourself opening your own mail during exam time when students are in short supply. As the staff grows beyond a few persons, however, you will have to delegate that responsibility. Mail sorting is a sensitive and vital position – sensitive in that the sorter may see confidential personnel material, vital in that your capacity to act is often dependent on that person's judgment of what is important enough to warrant your direct attention.

An administrator's mail is not public, organizational property; there is no collegiality about it. Sharing it with other employees is not just bad manners; it is a serious breach of confidentiality. In some organizations that kind of behavior is cause for immediate dismissal. If you can trace leaks of sensitive information or consistent instances of bad judgment to the person who handles your mail, you will probably want to make an immediate change. If you are lucky enough to inherit a person who is both trustworthy and sensible, count your blessings.

MANAGING ADMINISTRATIVE TRAVEL

In most academic libraries the principal burden of travel related to major policy decisions and regional or national issues continues to fall on the head librarian. In cases where the chief acts in an official capacity (e.g., is the library's voting delegate in a membership body, such as a regional network), it is impossible to delegate the trip.

Two constituencies may not appreciate the chief librarian's (or any librarian's) need for travel. The first and more important of these is the campus administration itself, and the second is the staff. The administration will take note of the increased demands travel is placing on the budget and probably will not understand the justification without thorough orientation and education from the head librarian. The staff at large, especially some old-timers for whom interinstitutional collaboration and networking may still seem intrusive, could look on librarians' business travel either as a boondoggle or the glamorous realm of a privileged few.

To forestall problems with the campus administration, carefully prepare the case for travel. Examples from peer institutions may be useful. An oral presentation is probably more effective than a written one as it reduces the amount of hard data that a budget analyst might be asked to review. The less to review, the less the likelihood that reasons will be found to deny support. An even better arrangement, usually workable only in United States private schools, is to have the travel budget residing unobtrusively in the director's discretionary fund.

Travel is one of the items typically cut during a budget crisis, so it is not desirable to give it high visibility in the first place. If local budget report forms do not analyze travel costs, it is best not to solicit a new report. An administrative assistant can use a spreadsheet program to assemble the necessary data for your own information.

Beyond the required expense reports you submit to the controller's office, keep a careful personal log of your trips and keep well informed on the business travel of colleagues in other institutions. Because others, undelegated and on their own initiative, will keep track of your travel, you could unexpectedly find reports reaching the campus administration that you are "away" frequently, "not in your office," or "not on the job." Responsibility for your business travel is too important to leave to others by default. Maintain your own accurate, current justification, and make sure that for each major trip your boss understands exactly why you are away and that your trip has full support. Leave nothing to chance.

There are two extreme approaches to the administrator's business travel: one is to keep it under wraps as much as possible and the other is to publicize it openly. The latter is far preferable as an offset to unfounded criticism. Actually, the first approach is impractical, as it is virtually impossible to maintain secrecy about travel, even in private institutions. Besides, part of your responsibility is to educate your staff on the benefits of your contacts with the entire community, and to encourage appropriate outreach by others. In addition, when appropriate, widely distribute copies of the agenda in advance. As soon as you return, report the significance of the trip for the library or the profession; this can be done orally or by means of a short report for the library bulletin.

KEEPING FILES AND DATA SECURE

Your Office

An obvious caution is to key separately any office with sensitive records, especially your own, and have the door equipped with a heavy-duty, commercial-grade lockset. If fire regulations permit, the door should open inward so that the bolt cannot be slipped with a knife or credit card, or the pins removed from the hinges. If the door opens out, the bolt area should be protected by an astragal.

The library is often the largest and most complex building on campus, even in a small college, and it must remain open or partially open far longer than any classroom or administrative space. An inventory of locking doors produces a surprisingly large number of access points subject to varying degree of control. Fortunately, it is now possible to automate almost every aspect of key control conveniently through the office microcomputer and rid oneself of cumbersome manual control systems.[11]

No matter how sophisticated the control system, it is advisable to change critically important locks at random intervals, even if there is no apparent cause for concern. It is extremely naive to base a records security program on the "do not duplicate" warning. The smallest college is a microcosm, with innumerable linkages on a personal level that an administrator may not suspect. Staff friendships make it quite possible, indeed highly likely, for unauthorized keys to circulate.

It is impossible to specify a frequency of change; that will vary in accordance with local conditions. It is suggested that no critical access point remain with the same key for more than two or three years. If an employee with access to confidential records has been terminated for cause, change the locks immediately. While changing locks is expensive, it is far less costly than the damage that can rarely be undone when confidential information is leaked through the combination of an administrator's carelessness and a disgruntled employee's desire for revenge.

PERSONALIZING ADMINISTRATIVE GOALS

Without a vision of the future and hope for change, few would willingly enter the difficult and frustrating world of administration. First-time administrators, and even seasoned leaders going into more challenging positions, may be tempted to see the outline of their future achievements with an altogether too powerful magnifying glass. You are dealing with an organism whose corporate culture was established long before you arrived. Just how you will start to interact with the human element (the stuff of administration) is unpredictable and unknown. The temptation to formulate overambitious goals for yourself or for your institution is inviting, and one always has the visible evidence of a predecessor's failure or shortcomings. It is easy to convince yourself that you will not make similar mistakes. To be sure, you will not; you will make your own.

It is unlikely that any academic library leader will be able to command or commandeer really vast resources. That has not been the pattern of the recent past and there is little prospect of change in the immediate future. Establish limited goals that are local, realistic, and achievable. Deliver obvious, tangible, and visible – and preferably immediate – benefits to your most powerful constituencies, the faculty and staff. Long-range goals may have to wait, especially if they have a utopian component. You have to prove your ability to fulfill some simple, valuable goal, one that will have wide acceptance, before you can aim at a lofty target. For example, you might find it valuable to campaign with selected faculty to acquire some specialized database services on compact disc to benefit directly their most keen interests. Obviously you would not start by articulating the goal of converting an entire retrospective college library collection to laser disc.

The advice not to try solving all the library's problems at once sounds transparently obvious, but it is a good idea to keep reminding yourself that you are just one human being, whether your staff is competent and supportive or otherwise. Administration that deals with the most variable entity of all – the human being – sometimes confronts problems that cannot be solved. Pick the solvable ones.

SUMMARY

Because a lasting tone is set in the early weeks of a new administration, it is important that it accord as much as possible with what you want. Many established forces and interests within the informal organization have their own agendas for tone and aura, even ideas about programs that may not accord with yours or with institutional mission, goals, and objectives. Each force has its own powers and influences and each plays against the other in battles that are real, although the blood is figurative.

In the United States the politics of library administration are typically American: powers are divided; pluralism and factionalism prevail enough so that only rarely can one party impose its will on the other. How well you can unify the competing factions and get them to support your possibly threatening new ideas is a major test of your administrative talent. The early weeks are the time to become acquainted with the major powers on campus, make treaties and forge alliances, study and analyze, stir and inspire but not openly threaten, ask rather than tell, learn rather than teach, and collaborate – quite literally, work together – to form new initiatives with prospects of quick payoff. Rapid payoff enhances credibility; credibility increases the value of the remaining tokens that came with your appointment and enable you to keep moving the program forward. Recognize your limitations and do not allow your position or your ambition to go to your head. An appropriate professional image is always an enhancement to administration. Finally, an important continuing aspect of the chief librarian's position is the responsibility always to enhance the elitist character of the parent institution, never to tear it down. Whatever your private thoughts about democracy, you will not find much of it in academe.

Notes

1. N. Machiavelli, *The Prince*, trans. Luigi Ricci, rev. E. R. P. Vincent (London: Oxford University Press, 1935).

2. A few corporate think tanks and R & D facilities offer campuslike facilities and freedoms, but corporate managers generally are driven by company goals, not personal ones.

3. Excellent accounts of how the academic game is played are found in Van Cleve Morris's *Deaning: Middle Management in Academe* (Urbana: University of Illinois Press, 1981) and in A. Leigh Deneef et al., *The Academic's Handbook* (Durham, N.C.: Duke University Press, 1988).

4. Eric Berne, *Games People Play* (New York: Grove Press, 1967).

5. William C. Schutz, "The Interpersonal Underworld," in *The Executive Dilemma*, ed. Eliza G. C. Collins (New York: John Wiley & Sons, 1985), 521-42; see esp. p. 542. Reprinted from the *Harvard Business Review* 36, no. 4 (July-August 1958): 123-35. Schutz is the originator of the well-known FIRO-B (Fundamental Interpersonal Relations Orientation = Behavior) analytic instrument.

6. Abraham Zaleznik, "The Dynamics of Subordinacy," *Harvard Business Review*, 1965. Reprinted in Eliza G. C. Collins, ed., *The Executive Dilemma: Handling People Problems at Work* (New York: John Wiley & Sons, 1985), 92-111.

7. To portray the ideal administrator, Van Cleve Morris coined the term *coolth*, as an antonym to *warmth*, meaning cool-headedness, distance, detachment. See his *Deaning*, 22.

8. Herbert S. White, *Library Personnel Management* (White Plains, N.Y.: Knowledge Industry Publications, 1985), 78-82.

9. In some cultures outside North America a lot of eye contact may connote disrespect; you may have to adjust your style for visiting foreigners or employees from other cultures.

10. When an employee cries, extending a box of tissues is probably an acceptable gesture with minimal risk.

11. An example is the Grandmaster system, offered by Facilitrac, 325 East Southern Ave., Suite 11, Tempe, AZ 85282.

Resources

Bennis, Warren. "The Sociology of Institutions or, Who Sank the Yellow Submarine?" *Psychology Today* 6, no. 6 (November 1972): 112-20.

Berne, Eric. *Games People Play.* New York: Grove Press, 1967.

Bixler, Susan. *The Professional Image.* New York: Putnam Publishing Group, 1985.

Bramson, Robert M. *Coping with Difficult People.* New York: Anchor/Doubleday, 1981. (Also available in six audio cassettes).

Broadwell, Martin M. *The New Supervisor.* 3d ed. Reading, Mass.: Addison-Wesley, 1984.

Cawood, Diana. *Assertiveness for Managers: Learning Effective Skills for Managing People.* Seattle, Wash.: Self-Counsel Press, 1988.

Cohen, Michael D., and James G. March. *Leadership and Ambiguity: The American College President,* 2d ed. Boston: Harvard Business School Press, 1986.

Detz, Joan. *How to Write and Give a Speech.* New York: St. Martin's Press, 1984.

Ekman, Paul. *Telling Lies: Clues to Deceit in Marketplace, Politics, and Marriage.* New York: W. W. Norton, 1985.

Gabarro, John J. *The Dynamics of Taking Charge.* Boston: Harvard Business School Press, 1987.

Josefowitz, Natasha, and Herman Gadon. *Fitting In: How to Get a Good Start in Your New Job.* Reading, Mass.: Addison-Wesley, 1988.

Kellogg, Rebecca. "Beliefs and Realities: Libraries and Librarians from a Non-library Administrator's Point of View." *College & Research Libraries News* 47, no. 8 (September 1986): 492-96.

Keltner, Vicki, and Mike Holsey. *The Success Image: A Guide for the Better-Dressed Businesswoman.* Houston: Gulf, 1982.

Kenny, Michael. *Presenting Yourself.* New York: John Wiley & Sons, 1982.

Koontz, Harold, and Cyril O'Donnell. *Essentials of Management*, 4th ed. New York: McGraw-Hill, 1986.

Levinson, Harry. *Ready, Fire, Aim: Avoiding Management by Impulse.* Compiled by Janet E. Levinson. Cambridge, Mass.: Levinson Institute, 1986.

Levitt, Mortimer. *The Executive Look: How to Get It, how to Keep It.* New York: Athenaeum Press, 1983.

Lurie, Allison. *The Language of Clothes.* New York: Vintage Press, 1983.

Maccoby, Michael. *The Leader.* New York: Random House, 1981.

Mambert, W. A. *Effective Presentation.* 2d ed. New York: John Wiley & Sons, 1984.

Morein, P. Grady, and H. Lea Wells. *Strategies and Tactics for Enhancing the Role and Position of the Library within the College or University.* Chicago: ACRL, 1981.

Morris, Van Cleve. *Deaning: Middle Management in Academe.* Urbana: University of Illinois Press, 1981.

Osgood, Charles. *Professionally Speaking.* New York: Simon and Schuster, 1986.

Peck, Stephen Rogers. *Atlas of Facial Expression.* New York: Oxford University Press, 1987.

Rogers, Everett M. *Diffusion of Innovations.* 3d ed. New York: Free Press, 1983.

Sashkin, Marshall, and William C. Morris. *Experiencing Management.* Reading, Mass.: Addison-Wesley, 1987.

Smith, Terry C. *Making Successful Presentations: A Self-Teaching Guide.* New York: John Wiley & Sons, 1984.

Transvision. *The Silent Communicator.* Fort Collins, Colo., 1987. Videotape, 45 minutes. Includes handbook.

Turk, Christopher. *Effective Speaking: Communicating in Speech.* New York: Methuen, 1985.

Webb, Susan L. *Sexual Harassment . . . Shades of Gray: Guidelines for Managers, Supervisors, and Employees.* Seattle, Wash.: Pacific Resource Development Group, 1989. Five videotapes plus manuals.

Wells, Theodora. *Keeping Your Cool Under Fire: Communicating Non-Defensively.* New York: McGraw-Hill, 1980.

Wolfgang, Aaron. *Nonverbal Behavior: Applications and Cultural Implications.* Orlando, Fla.: Academic Press, 1979.

_____. *Nonverbal Behavior: Perspectives, Applications, and Intercultural Insights.* Lewiston, N.Y.: Hogrefe International, 1984.

CHAPTER 5

The Administrative Challenge

POWER, CONTROL, AND AUTHORITY

Power

Unfortunately, power enjoys a poor reputation in professions whose members identify with liberal roots. Yet it is a central concept in all organizational management, the feature of administration that enables an institution to cope with externally imposed contingencies. Without power and authority it would be impossible to weld together groups of diversely motivated, highly independent people to get something done in an organized and efficient manner. Without that coordinating element, every member of an organization would go off in an independent direction, academics more so than any other group.

Although it is impossible to uncouple power from politics, the most common fault in library administration is not being political enough. People who see power as evil and manipulative or who take a moralistic, judgmental view of it disarm themselves so thoroughly that they cannot accomplish anything. Actually, their distaste merely reveals an incapacity to deal with the dynamics of leadership and the vagaries of institutional politics. Hence the wish to exercise power must be regarded as a positive attribute of the highest importance. According to Hunt, it is one of the best predictors of managerial success.[1]

A special difficulty in library administration is the tendency, especially among middle managers, to exercise power, or wish to exercise it, without willingly accepting the associated responsibilities. This condition is not, of course, peculiar to librarianship but does emerge frequently in our profession because of our weak socialization in politics and power. At all levels of management or administration, the main requirement is to buy into responsibility without the option to abdicate or be evasive when the heat is on.

Authority

Authority is the right, legitimized by an organization, to exercise power. A person can have a great deal of authority and very little power. Every administrative position carries with it limitations of power and authority; none has total independence or autonomy. Understanding these limits is part of the art of administration, and depends on a person's quality of judgment as well as the specifics of institutional politics.

Certain groups, such as sports teams, enjoy being controlled by a strongly focused power. Academics do not constitute a team, however. Because management models are frequently drawn from industry, traditional administrators sometimes imagine they wield great power over their staff. In the folklore of business administration the boss does indeed look like a plenipotentiary. But the person who flaunts authority for its own sake is stationed at the lowest levels on the ladder (e.g., the hotel clerk who denies accommodation to a person trying to check in a few hours later than scheduled). If you are similarly exhilarated by wielding authority, count it as a danger sign. In educational bureaucracies, where the spread of personality types is wide, a few timid people may easily be manipulated by a martinetlike supervisor, but few experienced academics show even mild anxiety before peers or superiors.

Control

The word "control" can conjure up all manner of Orwellian or totalitarian styles of decision making. The sense in which an administrator controls an academic library relates mainly to program, and even there, control is closely limited by institutional mission and broadly shared with professional staff through consultation, consensus and persuasion. Administrators do have the responsibility to decide which program elements receive more resources and which less, and the final decisions are not going to please all who compete for support.

Sharing Power and Authority

Power is of two kinds: formal and informal. Real power, as we said earlier, is distributed, not centralized. It exists in the informal organization, not in the boxes on the organization chart. Ultimately, it is the front-line staff – those facing the clients and their support personnel – who implement the informal power structure and make or break the organization. Their collective will determines whether and how well the organization functions. Regardless of organization size, staff are willing, even eager, to participate in both the informal and informal power structures. Encouraging participation not only takes some of the heat off the administrator, but it reduces the natural competitive intensity for the chief's own position.

As an organization makes the transition from a strongly hierarchical, paternalistic style to one of shared power and responsibility, employees sometimes send ambivalent messages: give us a share of the power, but please do not give us a share of the accountability that goes with it. Staff may justifiably complain if the chief librarian makes all the decisions, but at the same time appreciate the convenience that they need not take any share of blame for a failure. Wittingly or unwittingly, even when a program is expressly designed to bring about a transition from centralized to decentralized administration, some staff may actually work hard to perpetuate the former style, mourning the loss of their old means of exculpating themselves from responsibility. Where risk avoidance is the habit, inertia rules.

The Role of Advice

Administrators usually like to consult widely before deciding on important questions. From time to time, however, an issue arises that is so vital to an administrator's fundamental strategic goals that it may be necessary to make a decision alone or even contrary to advice. The point about advice is fairly simple: never ask for it unless you absolutely intend to take it into consideration. If your mind is already made up, it is not required, and if you request it under such terms, staff readily perceive the charade. No amount of consultation or advice relieves the chief librarian from the responsibility to decide.[2]

When advice is genuinely sought, be sure that staff understand exactly and precisely that advice is just that. Distinguish it unambiguously from decision making and leave no confusion in anyone's mind. Try to select issues amenable to a series of choices and request the advisors to provide a series of responses. This helps to offset tendencies toward yes and no responses, and also enhances the concept of consensus.

Merely because some major administrative decisions are made nondemocratically does not mean the absence of consultation or solicitation of advice. Middle managers are superb sources of advice, since they know intimately the potential consequences of change. They should not be allowed the luxury of a cop-out or be permitted to contend that they are merely "mouthpieces" of the administration. Such a view reflects organizational stagnation and indicates that there has been little delegation of authority and responsibility. Probably all the decision power has heretofore been reserved for top management, and middle managers have never been asked to analyze problems, define options, and make some real choices. An organization top-heavy with authority will most likely be lethargic and reactive at all levels, with all but unimportant decisions delegated to the top. The effect is to strip middle managers of any authority and responsibility and deprive them of imagination and the motivation to innovate. They will naturally look to the top for all important decisions while grumbling about those they do not like.

MAKING DECISIONS

Institutional Decision Making

All critical campus-level decisions (the really important ones that consume, demand, or divert substantial resources) are invariably reached by a strictly political process, a point powerfully articulated in a classic paper by De Gennaro.[3] Unfortunately, with very few exceptions, academic library administrators are virtually held incommunicado from the arenas where persons in the major positions exercise their political powers. Worsening an already bad situtation, junior administrators rely on rationality, convincing themselves that "if only the upper echelons understood how vital such-and-such a program is . . .," they would be compelled to support it. Those who can make the decision may indeed know and care, or may know and not care, or not know and not care. Upper-level administrators operate in a maelstrom of prevailing and countervailing political pressures from many sides. It is not surprising that the library is not a very powerful force in this vortex and cannot go it alone, certainly not on rationality. Those contending for resources must be aware of existing pressures before deciding in which direction to proceed. Often that direction coincides with the political vectors of the strongest factions influencing or controlling resources. Occasionally, it parallels the desired course of a library program. How frequently those choices can be managed to coincide with what is beneficial to the library program is an ultimate measure of a librarian's administrative skills in forming coalitions and building political support on campus.

Classified staff in institutions have a meaningful role in decision making only if the institution at large or a bargaining contract provides for one on a systematic basis. Because many support staff are on the firing line and have direct knowledge of a decision's impact, they can make valuable contributions to many broad practical issues, such as layoff procedures, holiday closings, methods for responding to sexual harassment charges, issues of comparable worth, smoking in the workplace, and work-sharing as a method of dealing with budget cuts. Basically, these concerns do not involve input to programmatic decisions, which are always reserved for academic staff. The implementation of participative decision making requires considerable care in design, particularly in spelling out the eligible areas and devising the mechanisms to collect the input. Participation works best when its limits are known and everyone understands the rules. When organizations do not make clear where participation is encouraged and will truly be welcomed, staff quickly become cynical, disillusioned, and alienated, recognizing that the participation is merely cosmetic.

Because campus politics takes place in real time, there is almost no way alumni can assist the library with its political crises on campus. The few who are loyal are mostly people who remember the library as a study haven during exam week. If one can build relationships with the right alumni, however, positive support is achievable.

It is ironic that program merit plays a dubious role in academe. Indeed, it will be inimical to success, possibly even dangerous to one's survival in administration, to suppose for a moment that proposals for resource allocation will be reviewed, treated, and decided on through reasonable processes, or that a proposal's clear, evident merit will inevitably result in a supportive decision. Obviously, this does not mean that one can throw merit and reason to the winds. What it does mean is that one's reason must be used to build a well-argued case founded on a sound understanding of the political nature of decision-making.

In academic libraries power, authority, and responsibility interact to produce decisions in much the same way as they do in the public sector. The same political processes operate. Few decisions follow the chain of command, although many of the dissidents of the 1960s thought they did. Business, industry, and education employ a broad spectrum of processes, all the way from no consultation to lengthy public hearings. Unfortunately, the librarians for whom politics is a dirty word inherit a Weltanschauung that fails to appreciate political realities. Whether strengthened by education and training in logical and ruly processes, such as interpretation of cataloging codes, classification, or development of search strategies, or perhaps encouraged through some predisposition of personality, new or junior administrators in librarianship sometimes exhibit an outlook reflective of a world that operates systematically, with the best decisions wisely arrived at through rational processes. A world founded on such naivete exists only in the mind and is not often found on campus, where disorderly infighting is the norm. That kind of apolitical, wholly rational world view is not a suitable platform from which to launch a campaign to get new resources or redirect existing ones. Nor is it a suitable base on which to build an administrative career.[4] To influence major campus decisions significantly, library administrators require a voting seat on the school's policy council so that they too can participate in the infighting.[5]

Given the attitudes to which many librarians are socialized, it is no wonder that decision making inside the library can be a problem. Uncertainty, the natural co-conspirator with indecision, wreaks havoc on staff morale, eventually damaging the program. As in performance appraisal, a straight answer, even if it is not the preferred one, is better than no answer.

A decision does not always have to be top quality to be satisfactory or acceptable. Nor need it always involve consultation and consensus. If librarianship's traditional quest for perfectionism in bibliography is transferred to the political process, the results are predictably disastrous: unable to surrender the delights of research and investigation, the naive administrator dawdles with all the possibilities, perhaps appointing a study committee to put together a report. Unfortunately, in academic administration just as elsewhere, choices sometimes have to be made quickly and decisively. Opportunity and emergency both require fast response, not studied contemplation. When a pipe breaks or a bomb threat is received is not the time to appoint a committee to form a disaster response plan. Base budget money may suddenly be withdrawn; grant money may equally suddenly become available and a go/no-go decision is needed in a day or two, possibly within an hour or two. In every such instance, the main thing is simply to make a decision very quickly.

The collegial setup of professional staff imposes an additional requirement seldom found in other administrative environments. It is not enough for managers to make decisions. They must explain them in a reasonable manner. Professionals and support staff may not always agree, but all appreciate a full understanding of why a certain path was taken and another ignored. Caprice or the appearance of caprice damages leadership and is not long tolerated.

An effective organization draws appropriately upon *all* of its professional staff to analyze its problems and formulate quality decisions. Especially among middle managers, it requires the will to analyze problems, propose solutions, make decisions, and agree to be held accountable for the results, whether successful or not. But this construct does not function if the middle managers are unwilling or unable to strike out on their own and take some of the risks.

"Crisis Management" and Intuitive Decision Making

General administration consists almost entirely of dealing with the unexpected. The principle of "no surprises" simply does not hold in day-to-day activity. Yet almost all constituencies regularly and severely criticize administrations and administrators for operating from one crisis to another, as if complex institutions and their even more complex and varied human constituents could be adjusted the way an automobile engine is tuned.

Crisis management in academe is the norm, not something to be avoided or discredited. Few if any techniques from business and industry, however, are transferable to the campus. The reason is that colleges and universities are not that orderly. In fact, that is an understatement. The style of administering organized anarchy[6] is perforce empirical, experimental, and situational. It leans much more heavily on a leader's intuitive powers than on analysis and the abstractions of administrative theory. Yet because of the historical North American tendency to stress systems and rationality, intuitive decision making has come to be devalued. The rise of management-information systems and computerized decision models, the development of spreadsheets and other "what if" techniques, and general reliance on microcomputer software for decision support systems could lead to another round of imitating business and industry's predilection for deterministic decision making – a sort of updated nineteenth-century style.[7]

DELEGATING TO OTHERS

It is always possible to delegate authority, but never responsibility. That always rests with the manager. We usually think of delegation as vertical and unidirectional, from the boss to the subordinate, and binary, either something is delegated or it is not. In real organizations delegation is always multidirectional and multidimensional. Even Fayol's classic bureaucracy provided for horizontal communication between equivalent administrative levels.[8] Lateral or diagonal delegation is simply part of the normal informal communication that occurs in every healthy organization. Without it, activity comes to a standstill, choked on the organization chart's bureaucratic flow. In modern organizations, delegation ranges along a continuum, with the possibility of an explicit, direct order at one extreme and self-delegation of duties and responsibilities in support of institutional goals and objectives at the other. In matrix-style organizations, delegation may occur in extremely diffuse patterns.

Enemies of Delegation

Delegation without authority is empty. Before delegating think carefully whether you are willing to permit work to be done without your direct oversight or review. Too much review, especially of professionals, breeds apathy, dependency, and passive resistance, and destroys motivation.

Those who follow the principle of never delegating to anybody who can do it as well as they can effectively create zero delegation. In other words, perfectionism is also the enemy of delegation. It is just possible that others really will *not* do the work as well as you, but it suffices if they can do it well enough. One more enemy to which librarians are especially susceptible is reluctance to surrender the vocational aspect of work for the more abstract, seemingly less productive managerial responsibility. Finally, effective delegation requires timely action: it does little good to delegate after some critical time has elapsed.

Undelegatable Duties

Depending on the institution, academic library administrators and librarians hold certain responsibilities that cannot be delegated. The inherent duality of the profession reserves programmatic responsibilities exclusively for professional staff. (The concept of programmatic responsibilities is discussed at length in chapter 7.)

MANAGING CONFLICT

People sometimes pretend that conflict can be humanized out of existence. It cannot. While almost all organizations have some degree of conflict, academic libraries are made to order for it to flourish. Given intelligent, semi-independent appointees in a professional bureaucracy that purports to operate in a collegial manner, a well-educated support staff with limited career potential, and the top brains among faculty and students, conflict is not sporadic but chronic, inevitable, and far more intense than in industry. Depending on local circumstances, such as size, history, location, and bureaucratic traditions, conflict resolution can demand from one-fourth to one-half of an administrator's time budget.[9] In extreme cases, the fraction can rise to as high as 80 or 90 percent. Rarely does conflict erupt on a grand scale, however. Skirmishes are won or lost, and stalemates also occur.

Conflicts arise from many sources, more often connected with value than fact. Professionals show a duality of their own in dividing their loyalty between the profession and the institution, they resist regulation and supervision. They sometimes put personal standards above institutional standards or see their status within their peer group as outweighing a library's mission. Conflicts emerge from personal regimes (see below), cultural differences among people, personality clashes, inherent resistance to any change of working environment, contention over limited resources, and disagreement over mission, goals, and objectives.

Tenure and departmentation are especially productive of conflict in the discipline-oriented academic world. Infighting is often exciting to faculty, making research and instruction interesting, even bringing in funding. While intellectual conflict can be a wellspring of originality, persistent argument over policies and procedures in a service organization is more enervating than creative.

Schmidt and Tannenbaum postulated five stages in the development of conflict: (1) anticipation, (2) conscious awareness of tensions, (3) public discussion of issues, (4) open dispute, and (5) war, with opposing camps committed to a win-lose mentality.[10] In recommending a variety of approaches to resolution, they affirmed that denial or avoidance is the worst response. Pretending that nothing is happening merely stalls all progress and ensures that no new ideas ever emerge. Other techniques are repression and diversion; hardly different from denial, they merely postpone the inevitable outburst. Some managers elect a third technique, encouragement of open conflict in the hope of reaching agreement; others go for the so-called highest technique, direct problem solving. Actually, however, a leader might invoke any one of the techniques depending on circumstances. Each response has a cost. Keen managers analyze the emotional and administrative investment demanded by each, possibly even mixing responses.

Despite the rich dissonance in academe, every administration must speak with a single voice in policy and procedure. Acting as trustees for the parent institution's goals and objectives, managers exercise fiduciary responsibilities. They are not free under the claim of academic freedom to permit their personal views to interfere with their duty and obligation. Dissent among them is a special case of conflict that touches on constitutional protection and due process, but is also related to the administrator's requirement to "buy in" (see chapter 12). Dissent before resolution is commendable, but after a policy decision has been promulgated it is damaging. Does "buy in" mean that dissent must be silenced? Yes, in the sense that administration implies agency, loyalty, and a single voice. No, in the professional sense. Open discussion, the normal consultative process that contributes to a decision in the first place, is appropriate before a solution has been selected. Afterward, and most useful for airing professional differences, dissenters can analyze and publish their views through articles or speeches in which the topic is researched and discussed generically, and completely divorced from a specific instance, person, or institution.

Resolving Disputes

Whether an institution relies on in-house, collegial discussion and grievance procedures or the more adversarial collective bargaining approach, disputes often go far beyond the inconveniences of the personal regime. Faculty and librarians alike argue over program content, performance appraisal, budget allocations, space assignments, computer operating systems, the ethics of business-sponsored research, land usage, construction projects, relations with townspeople, and too many other topics to name. But disagreements on personnel decisions are always the nastiest to deal with. When built-in methods to resolve them fail, the parties can invoke outside intervention such as litigation or binding arbitration.

Binding arbitration, the usual mechanism included in collective bargaining, relies heavily on labor relations practice, a fact that breeds some suspicion because it is hard to find arbitration personnel acceptably expert in academic issues. An appeal to outside arbitration is really a signal that internal resolution methods are either inadequate or have broken down. Some schools are now moving in the direction of alternative dispute resolution (ADR), which has spawned a variety of publications and services. In 1988 the Bureau of National Affairs began to issue *Alternative Dispute Resolution Reporter,* a biweekly newsletter on ADR. Other resources include *Negotiation Journal,* the Society of Professionals in Dispute Resolution, the National Institute for Dispute Resolution, and a variety of commercial organizations, (e.g., The Conflict Clinic, Inc., Haynes Mediation Associates). In a valuable review of a new handbook on ADR, Douglas raised the question whether faculty are even equipped to manage this technique, or whether they would have to bring in professional negotiators or conciliators, a move that would not only be costly but also might be tantamount to binding arbitration.[11] Whatever the fate of ADR, it is clear that dispute resolution will become more and more complex, driven in part by tenure, readiness to litigate, the high cost of litigation, the tight job market, and an uncertain economic future for North America.

COPING WITH RIVALRY FOR POWER

Coordinating the work of a complex service organization is sometimes compared to conducting a symphony orchestra. Of the many flaws in this comparison, the main one is the assumption that perfect organizational harmony is the norm. An organization of independent professionals can no more perform like an orchestra than they can play like a football team. Nor is harmony an attainable internal goal, except possibly in small college libraries, where staff might, like a chamber music group, function with remarkable accord. Most large musical organizations have conductors, but the simile does not hold in librarianship, and the comparison is not only imperfect but misleading.

Musical groups work with a score whose content is decided by the composer, not the performers. The style of the performance is determined by a conductor who is in a position of absolute command of the orchestra, and who issues decrees that are inarguable and unappealable.[12] Although there cannot be a predetermined score in academic librarianship, the library's program is the analog, but with this difference: unlike a musical composition, the score is, in part, created by the players themselves, for the professional staff is charged with contributing to its creation. Preparing the program is a joint responsibility. Chief librarians coordinate both the composition of the score and its performance, and this is the main sense in which they might be viewed as conductors. There is also an unquestionable element of glamour about the position of chief librarian, and in this aspect, too, the comparison with the conductor of a symphony orchestra has some validity.

Within any group of highly qualified professionals some people may be as capable of administering the unit as the chief, for example, an in-house candidate who was not chosen for the top post. Such a contender might actually be relieved at not getting the position and prove highly supportive of the winner; or the individual could harbor resentments damaging to the unity and strength of the administration. But once a chief has been appointed, it is up to him or her to find ways to use creatively and positively the talents of potential rivals rather than have their energies squandered in internal power struggles or a proliferation of destructive attitudes. Even if elected like a department chair, the chief librarian is not a first among equals no matter how collegial the setup, at least not while in power. Players who cannot make themselves subordinate to the leader should be content with secondary or tertiary positions, or realize that they must go elsewhere to test their leadership talents fully.

New or newly promoted library administrators will constantly be tested, mostly by subordinate constituencies, to determine whether they are in charge of their programs. This testing is one aspect of the final exam each administrator takes every day. While flunking the test a few times may not lead to prompt dismissal or reassignment, frequent failure is not conducive to long-term survival.

ROLE OF MISSION, GOALS, AND OBJECTIVES

Classic theory holds that an organization does not focus its energies without a well-articulated statement of mission, goals, and objectives.[13] Even when these are clearly defined, an organization does not always extract top performance from experienced staff. We all know of institutions that function remarkably well with hardly any notice paid to mission, goals, and objectives.

Despite the countless person-hours organizations and leaders invest in debating and preparing elegantly formulated aims, and without denigrating the validity of their efforts, the results rarely enter into the day-to-day, hour-by-hour operation of the library. Mission, goals, and objectives exert their power (1) on significant occasions, such as interviewing and hiring, disciplining or terminating, establishing a new program, and kicking off a fund-raising campaign; (2) at scheduled events, for example, performance appraisals and all-staff meetings; and (3) in times of emergency. They are absolutely required as an institution's foundation, but in day-to-day affairs, the ideals serve more to prevent chaos than to unify. Thus, we should dispose at once of the notion that such grand abstractions, however internally consistent and philosophically attractive, exert directive influence on every administrative action or library activity; they do not. Successful organizations are strongly goal oriented and invariably have well articulated statements of mission, goals and objectives, but rarely do they follow them undeviatingly.

As an organized anarchy, academe is a vortex of conflicting and competing entities, many parts of which can be neither fully known nor defined. There is a strong likelihood that the members of an academic community will not behave terribly rationally. Contributing to this uncertainty is the fact that very large group of near-autonomous professionals (faculty, research fellows, senior administrators, librarians) cannot be directed like a phalanx to realize of some abstract goal envisioned by a chief executive. Depending on whose interests are at risk, academics can easily find reasons why any particular mission or goal is inimical to progress. Sometimes an exciting new research opportunity emerges that is not exactly congruent with stated goals; in fact, it could be in serious conflict. This explains, in part, the tendency to express mission, goals, and objectives in a fairly nebulous way: to make sure that the organization can change direction almost, but not quite, at will. Thus do these aims contribute to keeping the anarchy organized.

Academics may acknowledge the general validity of an institution's broad, abstract goals, but they have their own goals too, and it is to these that they give their prime energies. For a faculty member, it may be putting out a new edition of a book, publishing a scholarly paper to obtain some points for the reward system, acquiring a research grant, or competing with another faculty member's bid for research money. For a senior administrator it may be securing a major government grant or contract so that the overhead income can contribute to the operating budget. A librarian's goals might include closing the card catalog through a full retrospective conversion project, enlarging the program of bibliographic instruction, or initiating a preservation program.

College and university professionals, like people everywhere, have mundane, personal goals that compete with grand, programmatic visions: tonight's dinner menu, the bathroom renovation project, getting home early enough to attend the theatre, and on and on. Clear-minded administrators acknowledge the validity of these goals and respect them.

GOALS IN CONFLICT

The Personal Regime

It would be ridiculous to do battle against personal goals; everyone has them, even administrators. Of much greater interest is the personal regime, in which employees institutionalize their own goals by restructuring work to accord with the needs of their private agendas. Private agendas may be partially related or even totally unrelated to the library's program. White stated that ". . . since individuals personalize their decisions they have no trouble in unifying personal and organizational objectives, usually by adjusting the latter to fit the former."[14] The result is strong dissonance between institutional and individual goals.

White suggested that these "adjustments" occur "innocently and usually without awareness."[15] This is not always the case. Personal regimes sometimes emerge from conscious decisions made by strong-willed people and they thrive for various reasons: excessive diffusion of authority, ignoring accountability, weak peer pressure, weak or abdicated leadership, lack of supervision, inadequate communication, and poorly articulated mission, goals and objectives.

Personal regimes can be adopted by not only individuals but also by groups, whose members are capable of displacing an institution's mission with their own priorities. This condition sometimes prevails in libraries with strong traditions of departmentation. Both types of regimes tend to flourish where there is some physical isolation, from the administrative center, the constituencies the group serves, or peers, such as a branch library, a technical processing unit occupying rental quarters distant from the user community, or even a reference librarian with an office far removed from everyone else's.

These regimes range from fairly simple conflicts (a cataloger's low output attributable to perfectionistic mentality versus an administrator's policy to get the books on the shelves quickly for the users) to major battles (which bibliographic utility to join, or whether it is permissible for a professional to spend very large amounts of time on creative publication projects that benefit the librarian more than the library). The following is a typical case, involving a long-term appointee in a cataloging department.

Edward and the Arid Lands Bibliography

Edward enjoys local renown for work of very high quality, but his productivity has always been low. Given his fifteen years of experience cataloging science materials and his education with two master's degrees in appropriate fields and all but the dissertation in desert botanical studies, this seems puzzling. In consultation with his department head and him, you all agree there is a problem. In conference all concur that his work load, heretofore half on cataloging and half on selection, will be adjusted to three-quarters cataloging and one-quarter selection; after all, there is little point in acquiring new material while the backlog keeps growing. After six months you note a barely perceptible improvement in Ed's productivity. Then a mailing from a publisher, which ought to have gone to your collection development officer, reaches your desk. The mailing announces the imminent publication of a comprehensive four-volume bibliography of arid land studies prepared by Edward. You now realize that for years Ed has been subsidizing his bibliographic publication work at the expense of the duties and responsibilities for which the university hired him.

Many questions are raised in this example: how could Ed's bibliographic work remain unknown to management for so long a period? Why did he never alert his department head and the administration about it, and thus turn it into a plus for his school and himself? What is the impact of his activity on peers who performed their contract duties assiduously? Does the school have a policy on outside commitments? If so, did Edward violate it? Is he to be disciplined for his creativity? Clearly, dealing with the personal regime is not a simple issue.

One need observe only a few professionals to see enormous differences of value, style, and priority as they interact with the impersonal institution. Conflict is inherent in this relationship exactly because professionals are not operatives who mechanically carry out assignments in accordance with designated procedures. It is impossible, and possibly undesirable, to eliminate from an organization everyone who has a private agenda. Besides, tenure and the conservative nature of academe are very protective of personal regimes. Unless it can be demonstrably established that the persons responsible for conflict are systematically tearing away at the heart of the program and wholly displacing organizational goals with private goals, an administration should try very hard to redirect conflict energy into constructive work. Still, however, judgment must be invoked. If the deviation from an established program is clearly counterproductive or is destroying the library's program capacity, it must be halted or redirected. It might take years of patient reorientation and reeducation, plus some turnover or even termination for cause, to right the course of a program gone awry because of a professional's misguided personal regime.

Do personal regimes among professional staff signal a failure of the collegial process in program formation as well as a failure in performance appraisal? Not necessarily. Unchecked and unexamined ones (like Ed's) can distort a library's mission, goals, and objectives by threatening management's responsibility and prerogative to decide what work will be done. When this happens a constant struggle arises between the rights and duties of the several parties. It would be wrong to dismiss personal regimes out of hand, however. It is always possible that they could prove of incalculable value and result in a major programmatic shift. For example, instead of working comparatively secretly, Ed might have proposed a university-sponsored publication project with himself as editor. One historical example of an eventual programmatic shift was the work of people in the mid-1960s who were often accused of wasting time and money trying to apply computers to librarianship.

Personal regimes are not confined to professional staff. Among support staff, they are more likely to evolve vigorously among the less educated than among those with advanced education. The advent of automation, with its rapidly and radically altered procedures, has had great shock impact on support staff in the loyal retainer category. Such old-timers view newcomers as upstarts and will not be happy about giving up procedures to which they have dedicated much of their working lives. A persistent lack of supervision, abdication of management responsibility, inadequate communication and consultation, and a failed performance appraisal system contribute to the evolution of personal regimes in any group. With support staff it is somewhat simpler – although not necessarily any easier – to correct the situation; one may have to appoint a new supervisor.

PLANNING

Planning in academe has a daunting array of possibilities. Sited at the focus of conflict, the administration is the center where the forces of all divergent interests meet. Every-day management in academe functions at some kind of emergency level. We search in vain for systematic and businesslike planning to replace putting out fires. We assume, indeed demand, that managers expect the unexpected and be prepared to deal with emergencies: strikes, power failures, natural disasters, sudden changes in employee behavior, absence of key employees. In the words of Peter Drucker, ". . . as every executive knows, nothing ever goes right. The unexpected always happens – the unexpected is indeed the only thing one can confidently expect."[16]

We accept that planning in an organized anarchy cannot proceed in accordance with some facile formula. Strategic planning makes sense only in the context of institutional planning, but long-range planning in academic institutions is itself often vague, outdated, not infrequently late, and beset with uncertainties and politics.[17]

To what extent is planning practical? In an environment where the planner controls almost nothing, strategic or even short-range planning is somewhat of a bad joke. To plan in the absence of ability to control, suggested Cronin, is yet another administrative paradox:

> In the public sector, the forces which govern establishment levels are often effectively outside the control of those who would wish to institute new working methods and relationships. Practically, the pursuit of excellence may as often be hindered by the existence of over-arching structural constraints as by organisational inertia or individual apathy.[18]

Identical constraints operate in higher education. Yet some works on library financial planning have an unwarranted air of rationality about them. Both writers and working librarians make reasonable but quite unrealistic assumptions: (1) that a proper, well-reasoned budget request will produce the desired funding, (2) that the campus administration is clear about its goals and objectives, and (3) that library budgets are flexible enough to permit rapid realignment to fit programmatic requirements.

One or all of these assumptions may be false, and the third is absolutely dangerous. If libraries could realign the budget every year, discharge the unproductive staff, eliminate programs that are financially unsound, and establish a budget from a zero base, what glorious powers of reallocation we would possess! Planning must proceed in an atmosphere of political and personnel reality, however, not as if it were immune from faculty pressures, tenure, and civil service regulations, collective bargaining agreements, and budget reductions. An additional impediment is that many senior librarian-administrators have not benefited from the management instruction provided by newer library school curricula. They may lack training in systematic budget planning, resist acquiring the expertise, or even wish to slough off the responsibility onto the chief librarian or planning officer.

We cannot control publishing output, enrolments, or the macro-economy. It is no longer even possible to have much control over personnel or count on retirement as a source of new staff. Steven Muller, President of Johns Hopkins University, speaking at the 1981 Academic Libraries Frontiers Conference, observed, "We are living in a revolution and it wasn't planned. The next twenty years aren't going to be planned either."[19] Still, we plan, for failure to do so is to put the library boat adrift in stormy seas.

Simulation games or role playing exercises may help the planning process. To be effective, such activity would have to be ongoing, yet there is risk that continuous role playing will become tiresome and artificial and, ironically, leave one unprepared for a real emergency.

Strategic Planning

Strategic or long-range planning is an informed process for selecting the most desirable outcome among a series of identified futures and choosing the right mechanisms to achieve the preferred future. It employs formal steps, each with an output – usually a report – and a set of feedback loops to each preceding step or report. Steps normally include context identification, situation assessment, analysis, synthesis of alternatives, selection of a main direction, refinement and extension, and completion of a final report. Uneasiness and skepticism commonly go along with any long-range planning, but real nervousness does not set in until an administration indicates that some action might be forthcoming. At that point all the vested interests look into the plan's threat to their own turf and begin to raise objections as to why it will not work or should not be implemented.

The time scale for a major planning effort has to be controlled closely. A project should probably not last longer than six months. After that long, enthusiasm and interest dissipate and the plan begins to look more and more abstract and distant. An enormous time investment also may breed resentment. People know they are evaluated on their work output and measurable (or at least noticeable) accomplishments. They suspect that few points will be awarded for participating in planning work so, after a while, they see these responsibilities as competing for their time to do that for which they will be held accountable.

Who does planning? Is it a broad-based activity? Among top managers of large consortia there is little sentiment for democratic process in this area. Rowland C.W. Brown, former president and chief executive officer of OCLC, offered an interesting perspective on strategic planning: "To me, [strategic planning] is not a governance function nor is it a particularly democratic function. It is a searching process that realistically assesses all kinds of contingencies and competitive developments in a disciplined way."[20] The American Library Association (ALA), choosing a combined top down-bottom up approach, hired a professional consultant-facilitator to develop its strategic planning process.[21] A professional facilitator is accustomed to dealing with many types of organizations and is sufficiently aloof not to become too closely involved with program elements or attempt to take over the selection of goals and priorities.

Among the techniques ALA used in its planning process was to survey leading professionals on four topics:

1. List the top five issues the library and information profession will be facing five years from now.

2. List the top five organizational issues ALA will be facing five years from now.

3. Imagine that ALA is everything you think it should be five years from now. Then describe the five major services members will be getting.

4. Imagine that ALA is everything you think it should be five years from now. Then describe the five major achievements of the association at that time.

Few academic libraries will be able to afford a consultant or professional facilitator to help implement a strategic planning process. But the ALA process has been very well documented and local staff can undertake a similar in-house exercise on an appropriate scale.[22]

In a brief conspectus of the strategic planning process, Riggs, university librarian of Arizona State University, maintained that the process strategic planning is different from other administrative activities, such as resource allocation or redeployment, and requires distinctive techniques.[23] A primary distinction is that strategic planning is not driven by annual cycles or budgetary constraints. It is a top-down method, contrary to current administrative philosophies, but some balance is needed. Staff at all levels should be invited to contribute, or at least respond, to an administration's broad views of the future, for without grass-roots support no strategic plan can ever become a practical instrument. Whatever the staff involvement, the chief librarian plays the dominant leadership role and takes care not to delegate this responsibility to a planning officer or other subordinate.

Obstacles and Frustrations in Strategic Planning

Methodical planning on any time scale has been rare in academic libraries for a number of reasons. Traditionally, libraries have been structured around notions of sureness, dependability, and steady-state operations growing at a more or less predictable rate. In the past there was not much focus on risks or potential failures, very little asking "what if" questions. Dealing with a variety of possible future events, some of them radical, is comparatively new in librarianship. In addition, planning implies change, which, owing to its threatening character, tends to stiffen staff resistance if not galvanize it. Even in a collegial environment it is difficult to bring up new ideas within one's own group since some of the people in the group may be rivals, not friends.

Libraries have relied more on intuitive planning than on scientific approaches, tending to mistrust the latter. The perception that professional judgment is superior to scientific management has frequently put librarians into a reactive mode when dealing with scientifically trained persons, giving credence to the folklore that humanistic organizations are too complex to be managed. Libraries have also looked on each new technological development as a passing phase in the historic panorama of scientific advance, and perceived that they survived, or at least outlived, earlier changes without elaborate planning schemes. Libraries often operate at the limit of their budgets, barely covering current operations. They have not enjoyed the luxury of planning, since proposed expenditures always seemed to be swamped by the immediate responsibility of "getting work done." Nor can librarians plan the future of their libraries autonomously. Invariably the parent institutions have other prevailing priorities; also, library needs fall far below the strongly articulated interests of powerful faculty. Much of the time libraries are kept in the dark about vital academic issues, sometimes deliberately but more often through simple oversight, a fact that sometimes serves as an excuse for *not* planning. In reality, these oversights merely signify how poorly librarians have played the game of campus politics so that they have become not worthy of consideration when it comes to the grand scheme of things.

With some notable exceptions, academic institutions are notorious for procrastination. State and provincial funding authorities play havoc with planning by arbitrarily withholding money or not appropriating it on time. How can you plan when the budget call or necessary related information comes to you at the last minute? The output of strategic planning is often vague, abstract, disorganized; at other times it seems to be too slick, too handsomely packaged, or too prescriptive. In either case, the result seems far removed from the staff's daily burdens.

Finally, rapidly changing technology inhibits planning more than a few years ahead.

Another factor in lack of enthusiasm for planning is that it goes against our North American traditions of laissez faire. Specifically, the United States library community frequently exhibits a positive distaste for any kind of concerted planning, perceiving it as a threat to individual freedom even at the institutional level. For these reasons a great deal of library planning has necessarily been more reactive and crisis driven than systematic. Still, none of these factors has inhibited American libraries from developing and implementing the greatest and most effective schemes for library cooperation anywhere in the world.

Lack of an early warning system in the library profession is increasingly drawing some administrators to look at decision support systems in the hope of reducing the factor of surprise. Academic libraries have conducted no large-scale experiments with such systems to date. Decision support systems seem not to acknowledge that many administrative problems cannot be solved by fact or logic but require values and judgments. Planning models are often filled with algorithms, calculations, and probabilities. At the opposite extreme are proverb-based models leaning on moralistic injunctions: plan your work, then work your plan; waste not, want not; run a tight ship; implement your organization chart. It all sounds so systematic, but life is characterized by ambiguity, contradiction, uncertainty, and messiness. Random events play immensely powerful roles in administration. Some employees respond to this reality by refusing to contribute to any kind of planning. This is convenient when things go wrong, as there is always someone else to blame.

One final caution on strategic planning: do not expect too much of it. Its main benefit is not the resulting plan but the process that stimulates everyone to think beyond the immediate future, to realize that change is no less real merely because we do not readily perceive it daily. That a grand plan may look a little ridiculous five years hence does not excuse us from the responsibility to think that far ahead.

Kanter even suggested that the age of strategic planning may have come and gone, because planning is a constant, not something that goes in jerks.[24] She also pointed out that it has many symbolic and ritualistic aspects, serving to bring together leaders and other forces so that the entire organization develops a capacity to change.[25] A good plan contains the seeds of its own modification, or even abandonment, as circumstances change. No doubt this is what Shapero meant when he pointed out the paradox of planning: "Organizations and individuals that plan do better than those that don't, *but* they never follow their plan."[26]

DEVELOPING AN ADMINISTRATIVE STYLE

As indicated in chapter 3, administrative styles in librarianship have historically echoed external developments. Because colleges and universities are uniquely dissimilar in their administrative affairs, they generate highly situational administrative styles. Obviously there can be no ideal. Since Evans and Rizzo have already covered many aspects of this topic comprehensively,[27] we comment here on only three styles: one obsolete, another in vogue, and a third much discussed.

Authoritarian-Paternalistic Styles

Despite the disrepute that surrounds the conventional, authoritarian-paternalistic style, and the occasional denial that it exists, Marchant and Sager indicated that this highly traditional approach is still quite common:

> The normal management style in today's American university libraries is authoritarian, characterized by a director who makes decisions regulating the library but usually allows staff reaction before formalizing them.[28]

> The teaching of library administration in library schools has been done largely with books that assume an authoritarian approach.[29]

> Most management systems are designed on the assumption that the individual worker cannot be trusted.[30]

145

Paternalism tends to be found where there has been little turnover in leadership. Evidence of its presence includes persistent unwillingness of professional staff to be responsible for themselves. They look to the administration to provide opportunity for development and movement. These individuals seem not to realize that professionals are responsible for themselves, and can and must create their own opportunities. Of course, the staff and administration who are stuck in pattern of behavior have worked out a symbiotic modus vivendi, each feeding on the other.

Management by Walking Around

Management by walking around (MBWA) has much to commend it. You gain presence and visibility. Also on the positive side, it serves as an antidote to corporate isolation. In an organization of any size it is a great way to establish personal warmth, learn people's names, and overcome cold bureaucracy. Properly used, MBWA can help an administrator pick up first-hand information on what is really going on in the organization.

It carries hazards and losses, too. Some staff may interpret your presence as disguised surveillance; others may expect you to pay regular visits of a more or less social character; then there is always the nonstop talker. Another hazard of MBWA is that it can become merely a perfunctory walk-through. If that happens, the information-seeking aspect is lost. Employees who perceive that you are not really footing it about to learn something about them and their problems will simply tell you that everything is fine, just to get you off their turf, because they know the conversation will not achieve anything.

Your time for social visits is really quite limited. Cultivating them perpetuates whatever "buddy image" a paternalistic style of administration may have imprinted on the institution. It may convey to some people that they exercise more influence over the boss than is really the case. In institutions making the transition from a family style of administration to a more formalized one, chiefs who are not regular visitors will be missed and their absence criticized.

Walking around can deprive you of the time you need for nurturing your contacts with campus peers and faculty, for keeping up with your phone calls and written communications, and for thinking and planning. In a large library, a daily regimen of MBWA might mean that you do little strategic work. In a small library, MBWA is the de facto modus operandi anyhow; you see almost everyone almost all the time.

Like many other management techniques or catchphrases borrowed from industry, MBWA must be used in accordance with local conditions and the size of the institution. Probably when the total staff exceeds fifty or so persons, it becomes impossible to see every employee daily. Yet the chief librarian of even the largest library should not be someone who is seen by all levels of employees only at the annual staff picnic or all-staff meeting. One's style for knowing staff and being known by them cannot be dictated by a convenient formula.

Japanese Management Style(s)

Several features of Japanese management may be useful in an academic library. The main one, fostering cooperation in place of an adversarial labor-management relationship, essentially reflects the collegial style that already functions in a well-managed academic library.[31] Others include the formation of small work groups and the provision of incentives for the further development of employees' skills. Nonprofit institutions, however, generally lack the capacity for financing incentive techniques.[32] One technique likely to be unworkable in a college or university is large-scale consensus meetings designed to provide program direction. Another is a flattening of the supervisor-subordinate relationship substantial enough to dilute the inherently elitist character of higher education, and most especially any action to eliminate or water down the distinctions between major classes of employees – faculty, administrators, librarians, and support staff.

Some important cautions arise when considering importing Japanese management styles into the library: much of the evidence about the effectiveness of quality circles, which are highly developed in Japanese industry, has come from the manufacturing sector whose employees traditionally enjoyed lifetime employment. In addition, the North American traditions of job analysis and procedure manuals are not established in Japan. Boundaries between jobs are loose and vague in Japanese industry and, claims one writer, Japanese workers "perform their duties regardless of how their jobs are defined in the manuals."[33] Finally, there is not yet any evidence that Japanese management style has done anything to enhance the relatively low status of librarians in any sector of that country's society. Despite decades of valuable U.S.-Japan exchanges of ideas in librarianship, Japanese academic librarians are still generally treated as low-level clerical workers, little appreciated and hardly noticed by the professoriate and government officials.[34] It remains to be seen whether the country's style is a passing fad or whether any of it can be transferred to academe. Meanwhile, as with any other innovation, the manager must assess the merits of that style and consider what parts of it may be used appropriately.

SUMMARY

Some people readily admit they have neither the desire for an unpredictable life nor the talent to survive the unsteady pulls and pushes that govern the life of the administration. Others, unaware of their unsuitability, may try to venture into a role charged with uncertainty and contradiction: leadership and control, not the same thing, although each may be demanded according to circumstances; staff development versus accomplishing the library's work, frequently in conflict; participation in decision making and making decisions, easily confused but not equivalent. There are times when you must be stubborn and unreasonable. It helps if you are a street fighter.

What is the attraction of this role? The opportunity to change organizations often largely governed by inertia, to place a personal and enduring imprint on a bureaucracy, to help other human beings develop to their full potential make administration irresistibly challenging.

Formulistic approaches are symptoms of a search for principles that are at least long lasting if not completely stable. They treat administration as if it were a fixed body of knowledge, a set of received axioms, and therefore a transmittable skill. But it is a field that is never the same from one day to the next. Academic library administration is an interactive process that is constantly reinvented, sometimes even on an hourly basis. This ever changing, elusive atmosphere can be troubling for those who do not live easily with uncertainty and ambiguity, or who are uncomfortable with dissonance and conflict. It is not a responsibility for those who seek and enjoy a high degree of regularity, reliability, and dependability in the work place, or whose life goals are dominated by a desire for perfectability, or who want a safe path in career development.[35]

Successful administrators possess many of the same qualities as successful entrepreneurs: a high need for achievement, a strong locus of control or belief in the power of one's own influence, willingness to take risks, and a capacity to see ambiguity as opportunity rather than threat.[36] They do not mind unstructured or ill-structured situations. Success in administration demands the utmost in flexibility, openness to new ideas, decisiveness in action, capacity to tolerate uncertainty, loyalty to the institution and, above all, a caring attitude toward human beings.

I emphasize that it is not my purpose to convey a cynical view of administration but rather to portray this essential activity in a realistic, unromantic way. Few types of academic work comprehend such a wide range of pain and pleasure, or involve enormous emotional swings whose intensity easily equals or surpasses the physical demands. Only the highest levels of stamina and stability enable administrators to cope with the work's demands and not lose either their health or their sanity.

Notes

1. John W. Hunt, *Managing People at Work: A Manager's Guide to Behaviour in Organizations* (London: McGraw-Hill, 1979), 12.

2. James Thompson and Reg Carr, in *An Introduction to University Library Administration*, 4th ed. (London: Bingley, 1987), 43, make the same point: "It still has to be made plain to library staff, however, that such [participatory] channels of discussion and communication do not diminish the [chief] librarian's ultimate responsibility for decision making."

3. Richard De Gennaro, "Library Administration and New Management Systems," *Library Journal* 103, no. 22 (15 December 1978): 2477-82.

4. Realistic, accurate pictures of the politics of academic administration are found in the following works: Stuart Forth's "Myths and Realities: The Politics of Library Administration," (Ann Arbor, Mich.: University of Michigan, Graduate School of Library Science, 1981); Van Cleve Morris's *Deaning: Middle Management in Academe* (Urbana: University of Illinois Press, 1981); and Michael D. Cohen and James G. March's *Leadership and Ambiguity*, 2d ed. (Boston: Harvard Business School Press, 1986).

5. Cf. Dennis Carrigan, "The Political Economy of the Academic Library," *College and Research Libraries* 49, no. 4 (July 1988): 325-31.

6. Michael D. Cohen and James G. March, *Leadership and Ambiguity*, 2d ed. (Boston: Harvard Business School Press, 1986). See esp. 2-4, 195-229.

7. The dramatic stock market crash of October 1987, blamed on programmed trading, may be an example of undue reliance on algorithmic processes in place of judgment.

8. Fayol ran a horizontal line across the pyramid of hierarchy and called it a "gangplank" that managers of equal rank could use for horizontal communication.

9. Gordon L. Lippitt, "Can Conflict Resolution Be Win/Win?" *School Administrator* 40 (1983): 20-21.

10. Warren H. Schmidt and Robert Tannenbaum, "Management of Differences," *Harvard Business Review* 36, no. 6 (1960): 107-15. Reprinted in *Executive Dilemma*, 506-20.

11. Joel M. Douglas, review of Jane McCarthy, Irving Ladimer, and Josef Sirefman's *Managing Faculty Disputes* (San Francisco: Jossey-Bass, 1984), in *Arbitration Journal* 41, no. 2 (June 1986): 63-65.

12. In a brilliant essay in *Crowds and Power* (New York: Farrar Straus Giroux, 1984), 394-96, Elias Canetti succinctly encapsulated the spirit and power of orchestra conductors in a way that should

leave no doubt about the inappropriateness of comparing them with library directors.

13. In this work a goal is a desired organizational outcome, an objective is one or more actions, measurable or time oriented, designed to reach the goal. Priorities determine how resources are deployed to achieve the goals. Mission is the unified articulation of all the goals, objectives, and priorities set within a total institutional context.

14. Herbert S. White, "How to Cope with an Incompetent Supervisor," *Canadian Library Journal* 44, no. 6 (December 1987): 381.

15. Ibid.

16. Peter F. Drucker, *The Effective Executive* (New York: Harper and Row, 1985), 103.

17. Because of the vagaries of state and provincial politics, the environment for long-range planning is worst in publicly financed universities.

18. Blaise Cronin, "Excellence Under the Microscope," *Aslib Proceedings* 39, no. 1 (January 1987): 28.

19. Steven Muller, "Future Changes in Academic Programs and Structures," in *Universities, Information Technology and Libraries: The Next Twenty Years*, ed. Robert M. Hayes (Norwood, N.J.: Ablex, 1986), 68.

20. OCLC, Inc., "Strategic Planning," (Dublin, Ohio: OCLC, 1985).

21. The ALA hired Glenn H. Tecker, 31 Perry Drive, Trenton, NJ 08628, (609)771-0086.

22. See M. E. L. Jacob's *Planning in OCLC Member Libraries* (Dublin, Ohio: OCLC, 1988); Charles R. McClure's "Library Planning: A Status Report," in the 1986 *ALA Yearbook of Library and Information Service* (Chicago: ALA, 1986), 9-10, 12-13; and the same author's "Management Information for Library Decision Making," *Advances in Librarianship* 15 (1984): 2-47.

23. Donald E. Riggs, "Strategic Planning: What Library Managers Need to Know," ALA/LAMA *Newsletter* 12, no. 1 (January 1986): 1-2, 4.

24. Rosabeth M. Kanter, *The Change Masters: Innovation and Entrepreneurship in the American Corporation* (New York: Simon and Schuster, 1983), 41.

25. Ibid., 296ff.

26. Albert Shapero, *Managing Professional People: Understanding Creative Performance* (New York: Free Press, 1985), 118-19.

27. John R. Rizzo, *Management for Librarians: Fundamentals and Issues* (Westport, Conn.: Greenwood Press, 1980), and G. Edward Evans, *Management Techniques for Librarians*, 2d ed. (New York: Academic Press, 1983).

28. Maurice Marchant, *Participative Management in Academic Libraries* (Westport, Conn.: Greenwood Press, 1977), 1.

29. Ibid.

30. Donald J. Sager, *Participatory Management in Libraries* (Metuchen, N.J.: Scarecrow Press, 1982), 111.

31. See Jon Alston, *The American Samurai: Blending American and Japanese Management Practice* (New York: Walter de Gruyter, 1986), and Hideo Ishida's "Transferability of Japanese Human Resource Management Abroad," *Human Resource Management* 25, no. 1 (Spring 1986): 103-20. One of a few works on Japanese management style that has been translated into English is *Manager Revolution! A Guide to Survival in Today's Changing Workplace* (Stamford, Conn.: Productivity Press, 1985), by Yoshio Hatakeyama, president of the Japan Management Association. Hatakeyama's work appears to focus entirely on the manufacturing sector and contains relatively little that applies to the management of higher education. A critique of Japanese management style is George S. Odiorne's "The Trouble with Japanese Management Systems," *Business Horizons* 27 (July-August 1984): 17-23.

32. A few institutions do provide incentives in the form of cash awards or additional days of vacation. In general, however, incentive practice in the nonprofit sector is unenlightened.

33. Hideo Ishida, "Transferability of Japanese Resource Management Abroad," *Human Resource Management* 25, no. 1 (1986): 103-20.

34. Theodore F. Welch, *Toshokan: Libraries in Japanese Society* (Chicago: ALA, 1976).

35. A good orientation piece for new or prospective managers is "You'll Manage: Becoming a Boss" (Chicago: Library Administration and Management Association, Middle Management Discussion Group, 1980).

36. Thomas M. Begley and David Boyd, "Pyschological Characteristics Associated with Performance in Entrepreneurial Firms and Smaller Businesses," *Journal of Business Venturing* 2, no.1 (Winter 1987): 79-83.

Resources

Advances in Library Administration and Organization. Greenwich, Conn.: JAI Press, annual.

American Library Association, Office for Library Personnel Resources. "Administering Staff Cutbacks: Planning and Implementing a Reduction in Force." Chicago, 1983.

American Media. *Stress: You're in Control.* West Des Moines, Iowa. Videotape. 23 minutes.

Armstrong, Michael. *A Handbook of Management Techniques.* New York: Nichols, 1986.

_____. *A Handbook of Personnel Management Practice.* 3d ed. New York: Nichols, 1988.

_____. *How to Be an Even Better Manager.* New York: Nichols, 1988.

Beach, Dale S. *Personnel: The Management of People at Work.* 5th ed. New York: Macmillan, 1985.

Berle, Adolf A. *Power*. New York: Harcourt, Brace, World, 1969.

Bird, Malcolm. *There Is a Better Way to Manage*. New York: Nichols, 1985.

Blake, Robert R., and Jane S. Mouton. *The Managerial Grid III*. Houston: Gulf Press, 1985.

Blau, Peter M., and Marshall W. Meyer. *Bureaucracy in Modern Society*. 2d ed. New York: Random House, 1971.

Block, Peter. *The Empowered Manager: Positive Political Skills at Work*. San Francisco: Jossey-Bass, 1987.

Boyatzis, Richard E. *The Competent Manager: A Model for Effective Performance*. New York: Wiley-Interscience, 1982.

Bradford, David L., and Allan R. Cohen. *Managing for Excellence*. New York: Wiley, 1984.

Broadwell, Martin M. *The New Supervisor*. 3d ed. Reading, Mass.: Addison-Wesley, 1984.

Brophy, Peter. *Management Information and Decision Support Systems in Libraries*. Brookfield, Vt.: Gower, 1986.

Brown, Nancy A., and Jerry Malone. "The Bases and Uses of Power in a University Library." *Library Administration and Management* 2 (June 1988): 141-44.

Brown, William R. *Academic Politics*. University: University of Alabama, 1982.

Buck, V. E. *Working Under Pressure*. Bradford, U.K.: MCB University Press, 1972.

Bunge, Charles. "Stress in the Library." *Library Journal* 112 (15 September 1987): 47-51.

Cargill, Jennifer, and Gisela M. Webb. *Managing Libraries in Transition*. Phoenix, Ariz.: Oryx, 1987.

Cleveland, Harlan. *The Education of Administrators for Higher Education*. Urbana: University of Illinois, 1977.

Cohen, Herb. *You Can Negotiate Anything*. Secaucus, N.J.: Lyle Stuart, 1980.

Cohen, Michael D., and James G. March. *Leadership and Ambiguity*. 2d ed. Boston: Harvard Business School Press, 1986.

Collins, Eliza G. C., ed. *The Executive Dilemma: Handling People Problems at Work*. New York: John Wiley & Sons, 1985.

Darling, John R., and E. Dale Cluff. "Social Styles and the Art of Managing Up." *Journal of Academic Librarianship* 12, no. 6 (January 1987): 350-55.

Detweiler, Mary Jo. "Planning – More Than Process." *Library Journal* 108 (1 January 1983): 23-26.

Dionne, Richard J. *Review of the Formulation and Use of Objectives in Academic and Research Libraries*. Washington, D.C.: Association of Research Libraries/Office of Management Studies, 1974.

Downs, Robert B. "The Role of the Academic Librarian: 1876-1976." *College and Research Libraries* 37 (November 1976): 491-502.

Dreyfus, Hubert L., and Stuart E. Dreyfus. *Mind over Machine: The Power of Human Intuition and Expertise in the Era of the Computer*. New York: Free Press, 1988.

Drucker, Peter F. *Management: Tasks, Responsibilities, Practices*. New York: Harper and Row, 1974.

Eilon, Samuel. *Management Assertions and Aversions*. Oxford: Pergamon Press, 1985.

Engel, Herbert M. *How to Delegate: A Guide to Getting Things Done*. Houston: Gulf Publishing Co., 1983.

Ensor, Pat, et al. "Strategic Planning in an Academic Library." *Library Administration and Management* 2, no. 3 (June 1988): 145-50.

Euster, Joanne. *The Academic Library Director: Management Activities and Effectiveness*. New York: Greenwood Press, 1988.

Evans, G. Edward. *Management Techniques for Librarians*. 2d ed. New York: Academic Press, 1983.

Famularo, Joseph J., ed. *Handbook of Human Resources Administration*. 2d ed. New York: McGraw-Hill, 1986.

Fisher, Roger. *Getting to Yes: Negotiating Agreement Without Giving In*. New York: Penguin, 1983.

Flamholtz, Eric G., and Yvonne Randle. *The Inner Game of Management: How to Make the Transition to a Managerial Role*. New York: AMACOM, 1987.

Forth, Stuart. "Myths and Realities: The Politics of Library Administration." Ann Arbor: University of Michigan, Graduate School of Library Science, 1981.

Gardner, Jeffrey J. *Resource Notebook on Planning*. Washington, D.C.: Association of Research Libraries/Office of Management Studies, 1979.

Giesecke, Joan, and Kent Hendrickson. "Interactive Planning in an Ever-Changing Environment." In *Building on the First Century*, Proceedings of the Fifth National Conference of the Association of College and Research Libraries, Cincinnati, Ohio, 8 April 1989, edited by Janice C. Fennell, 71-77. Chicago: ACRL, 1989.

Goldberg, Robert L. "A Library Planning Model – Some Theory and How It Works." *Drexel Library Quarterly* 21, no. 4 (Fall 1985): 92-114.

Goulding, D., et al. *Power, Control and Bureaucracy*. Bradford, U.K.: MCB University Press, 1978.

Gundry, Lisa Karin. "Critical Incidents in Organizational Cultures: The Enculturation of Newcomers in Organizations." Ph.D. diss. Northwestern University, 1987.

Hall, H. Palmer, Jr. "Personnel Administration in the College Library." In *College Librarianship*, edited by William Miller and D. Stephen Rockwood, 79-86. Metuchen, N.J.: Scarecrow Press, 1981.

Hardesty, Larry, Jamie Hastreiter, and David Henderson. "Development of College Library Mission Statements." *Journal of Library Administration* 9, no. 3 (1988): 11-27.

_____, comps. *Mission Statements for College Libraries*. Chicago: Association of College and Research Libraries, 1985.

Hasegawa, Keitaro. *Japanese-Style Management: An Insider's Analysis*. Tokyo: Kodansha, 1986.

Hunt, John W. *Managing People at Work*. 2d ed. New York: McGraw-Hill, 1988.

Hyatt, James A., and Aurora A. Santiago. *University Libraries in Transition*. Washington, D.C.: National Association of College and University Business Officers, 1987.

Ianconetti, Joan, and Patrick O'Hare. *First-Time Manager*. New York: Macmillan, 1985.

Ishida, Hideo. "Transferability of Japanese Human Resource Management Abroad." *Human Resource Management* 25, no. 1 (Spring 1986): 103-20.

Jandt, Fred E. *Win-Win Negotiating: Turning Conflict into Agreement*. New York: Wiley, 1985.

Jones, Noragh, and Peter Jordan. *Staff Management in Library and Information Work*. Brookfield, Vt.: Gower, 1987.

Kakabadse, Andrew. *The Politics of Management*. New York: Nichols, 1984.

Kaser, David. "A Dialectic for Planning in Academic Libraries." In *The Academic Library: Essays in Honor of Guy R. Lyle*, edited by Eva Ira Farber and Ruth Walling, 96-104. Metuchen, N.J.: Scarecrow Press, 1974.

Keller, George. *Academic Strategy: The Management Revolution in American Higher Education*. Baltimore, Md.: Johns Hopkins, 1983.

Kellogg, Rebecca. "Beliefs and Realities: Libraries and Librarians from a Non-library Administrator's Point of View." *College & Research Libraries News* 47, no. 8 (September 1986): 492-96.

Kerr, Clark. *The Administration of Higher Education in an Era of Change and Conflict.* Urbana: University of Illinois, 1972.

Kohl, David F., ed. *Administration, Personnel, Buildings, and Equipment.* Santa Barbara, Calif.: ABC-CLIO, 1987.

Koontz, Harold, and Heinz Weihrich. *Management.* 9th ed. New York: McGraw-Hill, 1988.

Kopelman, Richard. *Managing Productivity in Organizations.* New York: McGraw-Hill, 1987.

Lee, Susan A. "Conflict and Ambiguity in the Role of the Academic Library Director." *College & Research Libraries* 38 (September 1977): 396-403.

Leitko, Thomas A., and David Szczerbacki. "Why Traditional OD Strategies Fail in Professional Bureaucracies." *Organizational Dynamics* 15, no. 3 (Winter 1987): 52-64.

Leung, Shirley W. "Coping with Stress: A Technical Services Perspective." *Journal of Library Administration* 5 (1984): 1-19.

Levinson, Harry. *Psychological Man.* Cambridge, Mass.: Levinson Institute, 1976.

Library Administration and Management Association. "SOS: Survival of Supervisors." Chicago, 1981.

Library Administration and Management Association, Middle Management Discussion Group. "You'll Manage: Becoming a Boss." Chicago, 1980.

_____. "You'll Manage: Becoming a Boss. A Bibliography." Chicago, 1980.

Lieberman, Ernest D. *Unfit to Manage! How Mis-Management Endangers America and What Working People Can Do About It.* New York: McGraw-Hill, 1988.

Lynch, Beverly P. "The Role of Middle Managers in Libraries." *Advances in Librarianship* 6 (1976): 253-77.

———, ed. *Management Strategies for Libraries: A Basic Reader.* New York: Neal-Schuman, 1985.

McCabe, Gerard B. *The Smaller Academic Library: A Management Handbook.* Westport, Conn.: Greenwood Press, 1988.

McCarthy, Jane, Irving Ladimer, and Josef P. Sirefman. *Managing Faculty Disputes.* San Francisco: Jossey-Bass, 1984.

Maccoby, Michael. *The Leader.* New York: Random House, 1981.

MacCrimmon, Kenneth R., and Donald A. Ehrenburg, with W. T. Stanbury. *Taking Risks: The Management of Uncertainty.* New York: Free Press, 1986.

McLean, Alan A. *Work Stress.* Reading, Mass.: Addison-Wesley, 1979.

McClure, Charles R. "Library Planning: A Status Report." In *The ALA Yearbook of Library and Information Services*, vol. 11, 7-16, esp. 12. Chicago: ALA, 1986.

McGregor, Douglas. *Leadership and Motivation: Essays.* Cambridge: MIT Press, 1983.

McKenney, James L., and Peter G.W. Keen. "How Managers' Minds Work." *Harvard Business Review* 52, no. 3 (May-June 1974): 79-90.

Maidment, Robert. *Robert's Rules of Disorder: A Guide to Mismanagement.* Gretna, La.: Pelican, 1976.

March, James G. *How We Talk and How We Act: Administrative Theory and Administrative Life.* Urbana: University of Illinois, 1980.

Martell, Charles. "Automation, Quality of Work Life, and Middle Managers." Paper prepared for ALA/LAMA/Systems and Services Section/Management Practices Committee, New York ALA Conference, 1986.

Martin, Murray S. *Personnel Management in Academic Libraries.* Greenwich, Conn.: JAI Press, 1981.

Meharabian, Albert. *Silent Messages.* Belmont, Calif.: Wadsworth, 1981.

Mesthene, Emmanuel G. *Technological Change: Its Impact on Man and Society.* New York: New American Library, 1970.

Metz, Paul. "The Role of the Academic Library Director." *Journal of Academic Librarianship* 5 (July 1979): 148-52.

Mintzberg, Henry. "The Manager's Job: Folklore and Fact." *Harvard Business Review* 53 (July-August 1975): 49-61.

Morris, Van Cleve. *Deaning: Middle Management in Academe.* Urbana: University of Illinois, 1981.

Myers, Donald W. *Human Resources Management: Principles and Practice.* Chicago: Commerce Clearinghouse, 1986.

Nierenberg, Gerald I. *The Art of Negotiating.* New York: Pocket Books, 1984.

Odiorne, George S. *How Managers Make Things Happen.* 2d ed. Englewood Cliffs, N.J.: Prentice-Hall, 1982.

_____. *MBO II: A System of Managerial Leadership for the 80s.* Belmont, Calif.: Lake, 1979.

_____. "The Trouble with Japanese Management Systems." *Business Horizons* 27 (July-August 1984): 17-23.

Peters, Thomas. *Thriving on Chaos: Handbook for a Management Revolution.* New York: Knopf, 1988.

Peters, Thomas, and Robert Waterman. *In Search of Excellence.* New York: Warner Books, 1982.

Porter, Jack Nusan, and Ruth Taplin. *Conflict and Conflict Resolution: A Sociological Introduction with Updated Bibliography and Theory Section.* Lanham, Md.: University Press of America, 1987.

Reinharth, Leon, et al. *The Practice of Planning: Strategic, Administrative and Operational.* New York: Van Nostrand Reinhold, 1981.

Reitz, H. Joseph. *Behavior in Organizations.* 3d ed. Homewood, Ill.: Dow Jones-Irwin, 1987.

Rizzo, John R. *Management for Librarians: Fundamentals and Issues.* Westport, Conn.: Greenwood Press, 1980.

Roberts, Stephen. "Planning for Change–Impacts on Structures and Procedures." In *The Impact of New Technology on the Management of Libraries*, 9-30. Loughborough: Centre for Library and Information Management, Department of Library and Information Studies, 1982.

Rogers, Rutherford D., and David C. Weber. *University Library Administration.* New York: Wilson, 1971.

Rooks, Dana C. *Motivating Today's Library Staff: A Management Guide.* Phoenix, Ariz.: Oryx, 1988.

Rosenbach, William E., and Robert L. Taylor. *Leadership: Challenges and Opportunities.* New York: Nichols, 1988.

Rothschild, William E. *Putting It All Together: A Guide to Strategic Thinking.* New York: AMACOM, 1976.

Runyon, Robert S. "Strategic Planning for Technological Change in Academic Libraries." In *Issues in Academic Librarianship: Views and Case Studies for the 1980s and 1990s*, edited by Peter Spyers-Duran and Thomas W. Mann, Jr., 36-51. Westport, Conn.: Greenwood Press, 1985.

Sashkin, Marshall, and William C. Morris. *Experiencing Management.* Reading, Mass.: Addison-Wesley, 1987.

Scarpello, Vida Gulbinas, and James Ledvinka. *Peronnel/Human Resource Management.* Boston: PWS-Kent, 1988.

Shapero, Albert. *Managing Professional People: Understanding Creative Performance.* New York: Free Press, 1985.

Simon, Herbert A. *Administrative Behavior: A Study of the Decision-Making Processes in Administrative Organization*. 3d ed. New York: Free Press, 1976.

Smith, Kenwyn, and David N. Berg. *Paradoxes of Group Life: Understanding Conflict, Paralysis and Movement in Group Dynamics*. San Francisco: Jossey-Bass, 1987.

Stueart, Robert D., and Barbara B. Moran. *Library Management*. 3d ed. Littleton, Colo.: Libraries Unlimited, 1987.

Sullivan, Maureen. *Librarians as Supervisors*. Workbook for ACRL Continuing Education Course CE 101. Chicago: ACRL, 1982.

Thompson, James, and Reg Carr. *An Introduction to University Library Administration*. 4th ed. London: Bingley, 1987.

Trow, Martin A. *The University Presidency: Comparative Reflections on Leadership*. Urbana: University of Illinois, 1984.

Virgo, Julie A.C. *Principles of Strategic Planning in the Library Environment*. Chicago: ACRL, n.d.

Vroom, Victor H. and Edward L. Deci, eds. *Management and Motivation: Selected Readings*. Harmondsworth: Penguin, 1970.

Walton, Richard E. *Managing Conflict: Interpersonal Dialogue and Third Party Roles*. 2d ed. Reading, Mass.: Addison-Wesley, 1987.

Wasserman, Paul, and Mary Lee Bundy, eds. *Reader in Library Administration*. Washington: Microcard Editions, 1968.

Webster, Duane E. "Managing the College and University Library." In *Current Concepts in Library Management*, edited by Martha Boaz, 83-95. Littleton, Colo.: Libraries Unlimited, 1979.

_____. "Planning Aids for the University Library Director." Washington, D.C.: Association of Research Libraries/Office of Management Services, 1971.

White, Herbert S. *Library Personnel Management*. White Plains, N.Y.: Knowledge Industry Publications, 1985.

White, James. *Successful Supervision*. 2d ed. New York: McGraw-Hill, 1988.

Wishnie, H. A., and J. Nevis-Oleson. *Working with the Impulsive Person*. New York: Plenum, 1979.

Yavit, Boris, and William H. Newman. *Strategy in Action*. New York: Free Press, 1982.

Zaleznik, Abraham. "Managers and Leaders: Are They Different?" *Harvard Business Review* 55, no. 3 (May-June 1977): 67-78.

Zaltman, Gerald, ed. *Management Principles for Nonprofit Agencies and Organizations*. New York: AMACOM, 1979.

CHAPTER 6

Program, Governance, Communication, and Finance

SCOPE AND ISSUES

In most academic libraries governance comprises at least eight issues: (1) program formulation (this chapter); (2) policy formation (this chapter); (3) defining the professional staff's ranks, steps, duties, and responsibilities, and promotion, merit, appointment, retention criteria (chapter 7); (4) defining the professional staff's performance-appraisal system (chapter 9); (5) defining staff development at all levels (chapter 11); (6) understanding, detailing, and administering wages, hours, and working conditions for classified staff (chapter 3); (7) defining and administering the library's internal and external communication systems (this chapter); and (8) developing financial support (this chapter). We view these topics as inseparable, founded on the political character of the academic library and its parent institution.

The conventional vocabulary of administration is ill suited to a self-governing entity. There can be no militarylike command and control system in an academic bureaucracy. Even the words "administration" and "management" are troublesome. For some, administration connotes the mindless application of rules and regulations in a machine bureaucracy, while management invokes the image of direct, organizational control usual in commerce or industry. Both words imply a definitely pyramidal structure, and convey unity of command and the other usual aspects of Fayol's bureaucracy.[1] Tight control systems are intended to maintain consistency and uniformity; they are designed deliberately to discourage innovation and deviation from a prescribed norm. While the academic library resembles other social structures, it has certain aspects completely in opposition to business and government bureaucracies.

An academic library is the confluence of several organizational streams and therefore presents a spectrum of work environments. It hosts several different organizational structures and management styles concurrently; as in a complex symphony, a number of themes are playing simultaneously. One major theme is surely duality, with its split of the work force into exempt and nonexempt staff (see chapter 3). Related to that is the internal duality among professionals themselves, who divide their loyalties between the profession and their employer. Student employees are normally in a work situation closely resembling the production environment of an office or factory. Similarly, nonexempt clerical and support staff, who are typically involved in task-oriented work and follow established procedures, operate in a definitely hierarchical structure with a distinct line of command. Even those in the highest levels of support, senior employees charged with broad responsibilities, possibly exempt, and exercising comparatively great freedom of judgment, fit into a vertical reporting structure. The concerns of support groups normally crystallize about wages, hours, and working conditions, typically the issues covered in a collective bargaining agreement. It is generally appropriate to use the word "manage" in connection with nonexempt staff and student employees.

The scope and coverage of governance issues are directly influenced by the different allocations of powers between library officers and academic staff as a collegial body. Details are spelled out in various ways: library charter, academic personnel policy handbook, set of by-laws, constitution, sometimes even a collective agreement. Operational aspects generally function through bureauratic processes, such as committees and forums commonly paralleling an academic senate or academic department. Governance always goes far beyond the specific duties and responsibilities for which librarians have been hired. *In an ultimate sense, it means the capacity and the responsibility to change the institution itself.* A college or university normally expects its librarians to participate in the full panoply of governance responsibilities. The first element is program. To indicate that librarians play a special, exclusive governance role in the academic library's program, we have devised the term "programmatic responsibilities."

THE ACADEMIC LIBRARY PROGRAM

A program is a mental construct, directive in character and emerging from an institution's mission, goals, and objectives, that determines what an institution spends its money on, who is authorized to spend that money, and how it may be spent. A program is an exclusive locus of power. Its control is so central and so vital that it is never a point of negotiation in collective bargaining and only rarely a matter of contention with sponsoring authorities. Authorization to develop, change, or administer a program is carefully allocated. In curriculum, the chief program officers are deans, department chairs, curriculum or educational policy committee, and the provost or vice president for academic affairs. In library affairs the chief librarian is the principal program officer and all librarians in concert – the library faculty – act as a collegial body in forming the program. As the teaching and research faculty exercise their power through their exclusive control over curriculum, admission standards, and degree requirements, the library faculty similarly control the library program as an instrument of support for instruction, research, and community service. The chief librarian's vision to the long range, together with the professional staff's experience, knowledge, graduate education, and commitment, bring the program from concept to realization.

Because it is the corpus of activities representing approved policy and resource allocation decisions, the chief librarian and no one else is accountable to the community at large through the campus bureaucracy. Although the program may serve an entire community (and beyond) and be developed collectively, accountability for its effective implementation links directly and bureaucratically to only one campus officer. The situation is much the same in the larger scale of things, where a campus administration controls the money and faculty control the curriculum. Because of these divisions of power, responsibility, and accountability, program can become a battleground if the chief librarian and professional staff hold significantly different visions.

Not all programs emerge from staff or chief librarians' initiatives. Entire programs or parts of them may be imposed, such as: when a school starts a new academic program or cuts back an existing one; when government order or legislation mandates changes in personnel policy and procedure; when the library gets more money for a new program; or when the campus redistributes or reallocates its own resources to begin one activity at the expense of another that must then be halted or reduced. Even the publication of a revised cataloging code or a change in the MARC format imposes a program change from the outside.

When we say that academic librarians have, inter alia, programmatic responsibility, we mean that they contribute directly to the formation of policies, priorities, procedures, and resource allocation decisions, all the actions that add up to the library's program. Thus such responsibility carries with it the power to change the direction of the organization, which is exactly a governance function. Next to actual service on behalf of their clientele, academic librarians have no more important function. It takes a proactive, creative, imaginative individual to help build the program. The capability and motivation for making such a contribution are usually distributed unequally, just as other talents are. Not every librarian will have the capacity or the desire to carry out that part of the total professional responsibility, but all should have the opportunity to contribute.

Codetermination, the concept of collegial responsibility for program, is comparatively recent and can be traced, in part, to the influence of the Association of Research Libraries' management review and analysis program.[2] Not long ago, in the heyday of departmentation, librarians were largely expected to stay within the limits of their prescribed work and leave the program to the central administration. A generation or more ago the program was formulated virtually as a personal decision of the chief librarian, perhaps aided by a tight cluster of trusted aides and a few influential faculty and administrators. An example of this style, taken from a text on academic library administration, is as follows:

> It is the [chief] librarian alone who can plot the optimum development of the library, because no one else, can possess all the available pieces of relevant information and interpret this information in library terms.[3]

Even a modest-sized academic library is vastly more complex to administer than were some large university libraries of the 1950s. With the present degree of complexity and more on the way, it is impossible for chief librarians to construct a program single-handedly. Those who think they can are overestimating their own talents and risking alienation of their organizations' best minds.

Librarians whose institutions are making the transition from paternalistic and strongly hierarchical management styles to modern, group-oriented, multidimensional approaches commonly lack practice in codetermination and are sometimes reluctant to take on programmatic responsibilities. Tradition may have imbued them with the tendency to confine their work to strictly management-defined tasks rather than assume responsibility for constructs beyond their own career specialties. They must also overcome fear of failure. Professionals who want to influence their own development and earn greater rewards must establish, sell, and defend their own initiatives and proposals.

Program: An Exclusive, Nondelegatable Responsibility

We emphasize repeatedly that responsibility for the library program is an exclusive prerogative that cannot be delegated to nonacademic staff. Without such authority the professionalism of librarians is seriously diminished. It does not mean, however, that librarians act alone, without consulting staff officers, faculty, students, campus administration, support staff, or other constituencies. It does mean that there is but one locus of control for program: the professional staff.

Role of Support Staff in Program Formulation

Support staff in an academic library typically possess a remarkable range of talents, education, experience, and knowledge, and most certainly do not lack the capacity to generate ideas. Their role in program formulation cannot be the same as the librarians', however, because (1) their task-oriented work tends to impart a narrow, institution-specific or procedure-specific focus and (2) their general lack of exposure to broad professional issues does not give them a sound basis for program formulation.[4] But there is an even more important and vital reason for giving them a different role: their work does not carry professional responsibilities. In fact, in the matter of program formulation it is a substantial error of administrative judgment to treat the support staff equally with the professional staff, a practice that is sometimes done out of well-intentioned but misguided staff development. If such equality is assumed, the result is thorough confusion as to who librarians are and what they do, plus an invitation to grievances (even lawsuits) leading to salary adjustments, reclassifications, or changes in appointment status of support staff.[5] Ultimately, such confusion destroys the profession.

The role of these personnel in program formulation is straightforward but indirect. Their advice and counsel is obtained through the administrative line by normal channels of communication and supervision. Their contribution is solicited, digested, and synthesized by the professional staff and the chief librarian, who meld it and all other input into a gestalt. This pattern can be effective in libraries of any size, whether the organizational structure is a tightly knit hierarchy or a loose and collegial group.

Role of Other Professionals in Program Formulation

In fulfilment of their programmatic responsibilities, librarians are frequently involved with professionals in many other areas, such as data processing, financial planning, personnel, computer programming and systems design, and other services on the campus. In general, these relationships are advisory, with librarians maintaining the prime responsibilities for the library and its services. Normally, these advisory relationships are political rather than social in character.

Developing the Program

In more affluent times it was reasonable to approach program development by asking, "what do we want?" An approach driven by mission, goals, objectives, and financial constraints generates a different set of primary questions. (1) What do we need? (2) What will it cost? and (3) Can we afford it? Helping to answer these are additional related questions. (4) Should we spend more money on activity x if we can get it? (5) Should we redirect any of our existing commitments to new programs? (6) Will we terminate an activity? At a still more basic level are the questions: (7) What is the problem? (8) Why is it a problem? and (9) What are the consequences if nothing is done?

Developing Alternative Program Proposals

To help professional staff develop high-quality program proposals, chief librarians keep in close touch with the general world of higher education; watch state, regional, provincial, and local politics very closely; and acquire and share essential information.[6] How have the institution's program and curriculum changed? In campus politics, whose stars are rising, whose declining? What new funds have arrived? What budget cuts have been prescribed by the central administration? How are current conditions interacting with the library's long-range plan from several years back? How are demographic and economic changes affecting enrolment and the employment pool? What is happening to support for higher education in state and provincial legislatures?

Professional staff's contribution to program formation requires flexibility of mind, a capacity to develop and focus on alternatives, an appreciation of trade-offs, tolerance for error, and willingness

171

Table 6-1. Work Sheet for Program Initiative: Summary of Required Resources

Resource Type	Prof'l Staff	Support Staff	Student Staff	Sq. Feet Needed	Total Costs	Lifetime	Cost per Yr	Notes
Personnel								
Equipment capital cost								
Space								
Alterations								
Collection dev.								
Equipment maint. cost								
Freight, taxes								
Installation								
Training								
Supplies								
Services purchased								
Totals:								

occasionally to accept some uncertainty and messiness in outcomes. But because librarians are often socialized to a perfectionistic tradition, they are sometimes ill equipped to cope with situations that do not provide all of the desired answers. Some may not be accustomed to dealing with trade-offs and compromises or have not accepted that the era of easy money is gone. A problem rarely submits to a single answer, yet even professional staff sometimes propose a single fix that overlooks variables not under the library's complete control (e.g., money, space, personnel slots). Invariably, choices and trade-offs are involved in program development. To illustrate, an industrial parallel is useful: a computer system vendor might offer a customer speed, accuracy, and low cost, and say "pick any two." Administrators have to educate staff to understand that many factors – some of them contradictory and incompatible, as in the industry example – contribute to program design. Not everything will be technically possible, neat and tidy, and economically affordable, or function effectively in the work environment.

Costing Program Alternatives

A program planning work sheet can encourage librarians to develop fully their responsibilities as planners, designers and administrators. It helps analyze a problem by enumerating all the resources that a proposal requires. Table 6-1 is an example of a work sheet that can be tailored to suit a particular library's circumstances. When submitted to an administrative officer, to back up the text of a proposal, it provides a preliminary analysis and saves the embarrassment of proposals returned for lack of detail. Its use also indicates that an administration expects its professionals to perform their own problem analysis from the outset and not delegate up.

What to Expect of Professionals in Fulfilling Programmatic Responsibilities

The first obvious expectation is initiative – the formation of original concepts, new ideas, proposals for action. If an employee constantly comes to you for new work or the next assignment, you may well question whether he or she truly understands professionalism. Such an individual should be coming to management with ideas and projects, not requests to leaders to use their initiative to provide enough work.[7] The real professional offers fully developed, well articulated proposals, not just "great ideas" that the boss or a deputy is expected to flesh out. An administrator has a right to expect at least the following in a professional's proposal:

1. Background and history

   a. Why do we have a problem?

   b. How have other institutions responded to similar challenges?

   c. What advice have colleagues in other institutions offered?

2. What activity is currently going on or not going on?

3. Why is current activity absent, deficient? Why is change needed?

4. What is the political impact?

   a. What constituency benefits from the change and why?

   b. What constituency might be damaged?

   c. Who is likely to win if battle ensues?

5. What could be altered without adding resources and still result in an improvement? Can an activity be:

   a. Dropped?

   b. Transferred to another unit?

   c. Scaled up or down?

   d. Reorganized to achieve the same or better result with fewer resources?

6. What impact would change have on resources? Consider factors such as:

   a. Professional FTE

   b. Support FTE

c.   Space

d.   Cost of facility alterations/renovations

e.   Cost of supplies, equipment, service contracts

f.   Cost of new or different services purchased

g.   Savings in various resource categories

Librarians who answer these questions at least supply the administration with a foundation for further analysis and ultimate action. It is in this sense that they have the opportunity to behave as truly modern professionals and be part of the next generation I have described elsewhere.[8]

Program Evaluation and Review

The meaning of program review varies according to context. The concept has several origins: routine, healthy self-examination driven by the desire for excellence; known or sudden drastic change in financial resources; sudden staff changes; arrival of a new president or chancellor; major shift in academic focus; new library building proposals; and introduction of expensive, large-scale technical change, such as, installation of a stand-alone computer to support all the library's database functions. Such a review has a dark side, too: if the institution wants to jettison a program or an administrator, it can be a euphemism for a high-class witch hunt.

A program review originating outside the library can be both comprehensive and threatening. The best strategy is preemptive: the library initiates its own review long before anyone in the central administration thinks about doing one. To minimize the inherent risks, whether library initiated or external, administrators must take care that the review is not perceived as trespassing on the central administration's turf. A simple preventive (and good practice) is to establish a tradition of comprehensive self-study, so the whole process almost has an air of routine. The chief librarian has to be reasonably sure of program quality and effectiveness, as well as loyalty from campus allies and general satisfaction, especially from faculty. It makes no sense to start a review that will predictably end in a disaster. While there is no handy formula for determining whether and when to initiate this kind of self-study, a visit from a regional accrediting body provides a convenient opportunity for a dry run on a modest scale, especially if the visiting team intends to study library resources and services. If cleverly handled, accreditation can be turned to one's advantage. A report from these neutral outsiders pointing out deficiencies in the library program can often accomplish what the chief librarian cannot do alone: put the campus administration on high alert. Sometimes the result is substantial new resources, sometimes a new chief librarian, sometimes both.

Retreats are a special kind of program review. They are usually devoted to a thorough examination of some very broad topic, perhaps long-range program planning for the next five years or a critical survey of the preceding five years. Typically retreats are held off campus, deliberately so to provide a fresh environment. Generally they are semiformal, with a broad agenda and perhaps even position papers by senior staff. Breaks provide opportunity for relaxation, athletic activity, and conversation. A recorder takes notes of principal discussion points and conclusions, and the chief librarian prepares a summary of the results.

Retreats are expensive, not only because of the investment in staff time but also because of the cost of meals, rented facilities, and, if the site is at some distance, transportation. They are excellent for building esprit de corps, however, and encouraging staff to see the library as an organic whole.[9] They are easiest to manage for large libraries because department heads and senior administration can put others in temporary charge of operations and the larger schools can afford the costs. A small library could schedule one when service demand is low; a middle-size library would have to decide who attends and who does not, to be sure that service points are covered. These problems are minor, however; retreats can be held on weekends or between semesters.

Control of Preliminary Program Reviews

Whatever we may think or say about program, mission, goals and objectives, they are rarely the most salient issues in people's minds. Since retrenchment began to loom as a dominant concern for all employees, their real question has been, "Am I still going to have work?" It is always being asked but becomes a real attention-grabber only at budget preparation time or, in publicly financed schools, when the politicians begin to meddle with support funds. How does one respond to the campus administration's mandate to start thinking about a budget cut? One option is to air the matter at once, risking some panic among staff. Another is for the chief librarian and the cabinet to hammer out preliminary ideas and priorities in camera. The risk of the latter approach is a charge that the administration is operating in secrecy. Generally, panic is better; people can cope with unpleasant knowns far better than they can deal with mystery. It is best to involve the staff early and widely. Bear in mind, however, that from time to time the campus administration, for reasons that may not be communicated to you, will order a confidential review. When this happens you may try convincing campus officials that a confidential approach is ill advised. If you fail, the library administration will have to present its own analysis, with alternatives, costs, and consequences, and take the heat if word leaks out to staff, as it frequently does.

PROFESSIONAL AUTONOMY AND ADVANCEMENT

Autonomy

One of the most vexatious aspects of goal conflict centers on motivation among professional staff: how do they develop themselves while still serving the needs of the institution? One extreme would have them carrying out only whatever duties and responsibilities had been designated by management, a clear contradiction of what defines a professional. At the opposite end they would be totally autonomous, reporting to no one, with no supervisors, and being accountable only to the profession. As is usual with extremes, neither one is tenable.

We are accustomed to the idea of physicians, lawyers, and architects as autonomous. Some academic librarians draw parallels with these other professionals and see themselves as completely independent agents. Even in those highly individualistic professions, however, professional practice is becoming much too complex and expensive for one-person firms. Architects need expensive CADCAM software, doctors need costly electronic diagnostic instruments, and lawyers require access to legal databases. All must have a full range of technological support, including computers, advanced telecommunications, facsimile equipment, and the like. In response to these business needs, clinics and similar professional collaboratives have been formed. The parallel of autonomy from these professions, while seductively attractive, is not realistic.

Several nonfinancial factors distinguish librarians from other professionals. Government licensure is a major one. Virtually nowhere in North America are librarians licensed by a government to an exclusive claim to practice their profession, as are doctors, lawyers, and engineers. (A rare exception is Canada's Quebec province, where only members of the provincewide Corporation of Professional Librarians may claim the title "professional librarian."[10]) Within academe there are three additional, even more important, constraints to full autonomy. First, almost never can librarians freely choose their clients; they must take all comers. Second, since almost all institutionwide programmatic decisions reflect directions determined by faculty and central administration, rare are the individual librarians who are free to create an independent service program. Unlike faculty members, they cannot write their own tickets.[11] Finally, like the doctors in a clinic, academic librarians are so dependent on shared facilities and resources that no one alone could provide the broad services clients demand. Everyone, even the highest ranking or the especially qualified, is accountable to someone.

Librarians occupy a middle ground, like corporate managers. In the words of Schement, "They experience both independence and subordination . . . because they are also charged with operationalizing directives from higher decision levels, they must conform to decisions made above them. Depending upon the culture of the organization, these middle managers/professionals may experience a work environment close to that of independent professionals, or that of subordinate workers."[12] Collegial governance and peer pressure act as conciliating and balancing mechanisms, providing coordinated independence. Academic librarians cannot be autonomous because the library program does not exist for itself. Their work must be coordinated by a higher authority, remain within a budget, conform to stated institutional mission and goals, implement authorized programs, observe legal requirements and, for economy's sake if for no other reason, follow national and international standards.[13]

Advancement

Advancement is closely related to constrained autonomy. A professional appointee advances in rank not only because of capacities and achievements but also by assuming greater and greater levels of responsibility and accountability. Be careful with the verb "assume." Academic librarians are not freelancers. Assuming higher and higher levels of responsibility does not mean that they choose their work completely independently. Their duties and responsibilities, like those of all other institutional employees, are governed by an institutional context, not by criteria from their private world. In this respect librarianship is quite different from professions in which individual practitioners enjoy substantial autonomy in choice of specialization or research interest, and even select their own clients.

FORMING LIBRARY POLICY

Impact of National and International Standards

A world of policy is predetermined for academic libraries. Many library policies are set within the context of standards based on cooperation on a worldwide scale: national and international bibliographic standards (e.g., MARC format, ISBN, ISBD), cataloging codes, classification systems, network communication protocols, and interinstitutional cooperative agreements. The policy aspects of these agreements are negotiated at levels far beyond an individual library. On a global level international bodies, such as the International Federation of Library Associations and the International Organization for Standardization, national professional associations, and national libraries, are the players. On a national scale, cooperatives and membership groups, such as the Online Computer Library Center (OCLC) and the Research Libraries Group (RLG), require the observance of standards as conditions of membership. Individual librarians may argue about Library of Congress classification decisions and subject headings, but no one argues about the value of the MARC format as a major tool of library policy or the validity of networking as an instrument for realizing academic library programs. Modern standards are accepted by institutions and the profession because of their instrumental value, not as an outcome of philosophical debate.

Role of the Library Cabinet

Local library policies emerge from several sources. Many are formed by collaborative effort and consensus, following initiatives from leadership or professional staff. Others derive from changes imposed by the central administration, such as a new program being established or an old one dismantled. As everyone knows, some policies also exist for no reason other than "we have always done it this way." Organizational size is of comparatively little moment in determining the focus of local policy making. The working environment is sufficiently complex, even in a small library, that widely based advice and counsel are indispensable to high-quality decisions. Organizational style also is of small consequence: whether the academic library is organized into a traditional hierarchy, a college, or a loosely knit group, both chief librarian and organization need a broad base of input for decision making. A cabinet or council is the primary mechanism for arriving at major policy decisions.

In a small college library the cabinet might consist of all professionals and could also include support staff as observers or contributors. As size increases and it becomes less practical to involve the entire professional staff directly, cabinet membership tends to shrink to the chief librarian and the principal, most senior personnel. In a matrix structure, the cabinet includes team or project heads, together with the top manager; in a traditional hierarchy it is the department heads.

Typically, parallel bodies within major subunits assist in administering groups, projects, and departments. Support staff contribute to policy decisions in the same manner as with program formulation: they work through the administrative line but do not formally take programmatic responsibilities.

Getting Advice

To share information more effectively and solicit advice from a wider base, some libraries have, in addition to the policy-making body, one or more standing advisory groups. Whatever the basis, it is important that everyone understand the difference between advice and decision making. A written charge or mandate helps convey to advisory groups their purposes and their limits.

Separate the solicitation of counsel on program content from the search for advice on working conditions. For example, concerns about nighttime safety for staff at a remote parking lot should be discussed differently from a program-related proposal to change staffing or hours at a service point. A collective bargaining contract normally mandates a specific advisory method or negotiating process on proposals affecting wages, hours, and working conditions.

The formation of advisory groups not already authorized by approved charters or agreements may require review by the parent institution. Legal counsel should analyze any proposed charter or by-laws to ensure that they are not in conflict with government legislation, campus regulations, collective bargaining terms, or existing agreements. Both unions and parent institutions may feel nervous about the formation of groups purporting to represent the interests of a specific constituency on campus.

Committees are well suited to the collegial atmosphere of higher education and are valuable elements of governance. The ideal committee has a few highly motivated, knowledgeable members determined to analyze a problem and prepare a menu of solutions or recommendations for the administration to consider. It is bad administration to use a committee to defer a decision beyond a reasonable time in the hope that endless discussion will cause an issue to go away or that dissension will prove a problem to be unsolvable. Factors weakening the value of a committee include an unclear charge, lack of resources, a weak leader, inability to meet deadlines, and the notion that each constituency must be represented. The effective use of committees is covered in many standard works and textbooks.

Acquiring Broad Input on Nonprogrammatic Issues

We like to imagine that mission, goals, and objectives fill every administrator's mind, but a lot of the job consists of dealing with much less grandiose yet equally important nonprogrammatic issues that affect the quality of life for all employees, especially the nonexempt staff. Examples of such issues include safety and health; traffic congestion and parking; smoking, and food and drink in the workplace; getting supplies without going through some bureaucratic nightmare; and personal use of the telephone and photocopier. Generally, the least effective mechanism for resolving these problems is going through the chain of command, since it merely invokes the bureaucracy. The bureaucracy itself is often the problem in nonprogrammatic areas.

Although not many industrial techniques are transferable to libraries, one proved semiformal method may help them cope with nonprogrammatic irritants and the nuisance of bureaucracy. This is the management advisory group (MAG).[14] A MAG is an elected body from which supervisors and managers are excluded. Membership is drawn from broad constituencies but does not represent any specific one, since that would likely be disallowed by a collective agreement or foster competition with a union. Election to a MAG, however, is not broad based; once the group gets started, membership thereafter is determined by vote. The terms of membership are brief, usually three months, with the privilege of one renewal coupled to the prohibition of returning before some substantial time has elapsed. Advantages of this arrangement are reasonably rapid turnover and prevention of the group's turning into an exclusive, self-perpetuating power center. The MAG elects its own chairpersons, meets regularly, usually with the chief executive officer, and publishes its agendas and minutes widely. It gives employees a direct, formal pipeline to management without the annoyance of end runs or fears that communication will be hindered by managers or supervisors. Because the latter know that employees have direct access to top management and can get immediate responses on nonprogrammatic matters, they are less inclined to be careless or overbearing. The MAGs were designed to function in an industrial setting. Their effectiveness in the highly sectorized academic world is unknown at this time, but experiments may be worthwhile.

Conducting the Cabinet's Business

Normally the chief administrator decides on the frequency of cabinet meetings; it would be hard to operate even a small library without having them at least once a week. A dependable schedule gives some order to academic work life, which at best is haphazard and lacks the comparative regularity of commerce. The essential ability to convene ad hoc sessions whenever any member senses that an important issue demands early discussion should not be abused; an excess of such meetings suggests a lack of real planning and unpreparedness for coping with change.

Depending on the size and complexity of the library, it may not be necessary to convene meetings of all cabinet members all the time. Pick the appropriate attendees. To avoid slighting others, Drucker suggested notifying the noninvitees of the subject under discussion, asking them to use their own judgment about attending, and guaranteeing an early written summary of the decisions reached.[15]

Need for a Single Voice

An administration must speak with a single voice on all policy matters. In this sense, the decisions of a cabinet are like those of government. They are not the personal conclusions of the leader but reflect a consensus. Once a decision is reached by the cabinet and the chief librarian, all members must support it, even if it was not reached unanimously. Few things are as disruptive to administration as open dissension or multiple messages on policy issues. Even if a member of the cabinet disagrees strongly with the group's conclusion, it would be a serious breach of protocol to air the difference publicly or fail to support a policy decision.

COMMUNICATION

A hierarchical system, supposedly characterized by systematic, bureaucratic processes, in practice lends itself poorly to effective bidirectional communication. In large organizations, especially those set up with departmentation, appropriate secondary dissemination of information tends to be unsatisfactory. Uneven patterns of distribution are inevitable; different unit heads make different judgments about who should know how much about what. In groups of any size, one major impediment to good communication is the assumption of some that others are psychic, a system guaranteed to fail.

Theoretically, everyone in an organization agrees about the desirability of good communication but few acknowledge how many obstacles formal structure puts in the way. In fact, both management and staff always practice selective dissemination of information. Kenneth Boulding maintained that organizations act like filters, distorting and transforming information so that when it finally does reach top administrators it is too abstract to be truly useful, and may even be corrupted and perverted.[16] He suggested that it is often in the interest of lower level staff to "adjust" or withhold information from executives. After all, personnel at the working level lack the executive's power and can exert little direct influence on top management. Withholding information is a way for the unempowered to exercise some power. Yet in any organization these are the only people who have a true picture of what is really going on.

It can be argued that rank and file ensure organizational stability by metering and filtering information, which, if it did reach the administration unedited, might tempt management to change programs and activities. Workers also use information to protect themselves from punishment for inefficiency, or at least minimize management's interference with implementation of the institution's reward system. By withholding or adjusting the quality and amount of information, they can exercise considerable control over management decisions, even to the point of ensuring that leaders make poor decisions for want of accurate information. Thus all staff levels in an organization contribute to both the flow and the stoppage of information. In an organized anarchy these conditions are perhaps more acute than in any other kind of institution.

Withholding Communication

Rank-and-file staff are not the only ones who withhold information; leaders do it all the time. Obviously, they cannot freely disseminate personal data about staff, and in some schools salary information is a tightly guarded secret. It is in the areas of program and policy that staff become resentful when information is withheld, so there must be very good reasons for silence. Usually these involve expense, lack of need to know, and uncertainty.

Desire to Limit Direct Expenses

Communication consumes expensive supplies and services. In small organizations it is practical to share information by circulating documents, but in large ones this method is impractical; an important document inevitably is stuck on somebody's desk. Regardless of an organization's size, master copies of vital documents must be kept close at hand for consultation and reference by accountable administrators. The alternative, widespread copying and distribution, is generally too costly. Even if affordable the practice is wasteful; many copies end up unread or consigned to the wastebasket. However unfavorable may be the economics of photocopying for spreading the word, the broadcast distribution of information by electronic mail imposes an even greater drain on the budget: kilocharacter transmission or connect-time charges, or both, can quickly rack up significant costs.[17] A cheap and convenient way to provide open access to public documents is simply to keep a loan copy in the office or at the reference desk.

There is a substantial spread of interest and motivation among the staff to read various documents. Although some nonmanagerial staff are initially drawn to reports and documents out of curiosity, they may soon perceive the whole process as a yawning bore and quickly lose interest. Some managers deliberately exploit boredom and disinterest by inundating staff with communications in the hope of warding off charges of insufficient communication or proving how complex administration really is. People see through these manipulations fairly quickly.

Need to Know

Euster put the communication dilemma nicely: ". . . management generally underestimates staff's desire to be informed and staff generally overestimates its own need to be informed."[18] But not everyone needs to know everything. Even if nonconfidential material is readily available, management may not want every level of staff to spend time reading it, since that time is lost to production or service. Controlling communication, by whatever device, does arouse suspicion that the administration is withholding something exciting. In organizations with large numbers of professionals and highly educated support staff, people do not care to have their news managed, however. Hence need to know, like almost everything else in administration, is a judgment call.

Desire to Avoid Uncertainty

Uncertainty covers timing, possible inaccuracy, sensitive policy discussion in its formative stages, and anything potentially embarrassing, personally or institutionally. Unrestricted sharing of information can be just as upsetting to staff and clientele as withholding it. The larger the organization, the greater the difficulty.

Premature disclosure of uncertain "information" breeds unnecessary anxiety and stress. In the normal course of its work, the cabinet subjects an administration's own program initiatives to searching examination. If an idea turns out to be poor, impractical, or wrong, it can be buried at once. Unseasonable sharing of flawed preliminary concepts gives an administration a reputation for poor judgment. Discussions among staff about what *might* happen usually produce nothing but high anxiety, interfere with morale, and cause staff to distrust the administration. The greater the number of people and the greater the disparity of their job levels, the more interpretations and opinions will be aired. It simply does not make sense to bring every idea discussed by an administration out into the open.

Some sensitive topics must remain confidential, forever or temporarily. Areas in which sharing is inadvisable, even if possible, include the following:

- Topics deemed confidential by campus administration, regardless of your personal opinions about them

- Proposed actions having significant but unresolved legal or financial implications for the library or the school, such as the terms and details of bids and contracts for hardware, software, or services; the particulars of any settlements of grievance claims or arbitration; and the terms of certain gift acceptance negotiations

- Proposals that might raise expectations that cannot be fulfilled, such as discussions with the president's office about the remote possibility of air conditioning the library

In publicly supported institutions people sometimes claim every deliberation of an administrative body is open to public scrutiny, and therefore communication signifies unlimited access to information. That may be the case with elected bodies, such as city councils and legislatures, but as pointed out in chapter 2, like it or not, the academic library is not a democracy. In every type and size of academic institution, public or private, deans, directors and library administrators make many decisions in camera; it is the way academe operates, or rather tries to operate.[19] What to share and what to withhold is, in the end, a judgment call that must be appreciated in the context that secrecy is nearly impossible in higher education; colleges and universities leak like sieves.

Formal Communication of Policy Decisions

An exhaustive account of cabinet deliberations, with a record of detailed discussion, is generally a waste of effort; the main interest is in the decisions. Overdetailed reports can be counterproductive, and even damaging to the unity of the administration if they record acrimonious debate or sharp philosophical differences among members. Always make clear to staff that these reports will never communicate anything of a confidential nature.

Communicate cabinet decisions clearly and promptly to the entire staff. Even in small libraries, cabinet meetings are likely to take place regularly, so staff will know when they occur and will expect some word of the actions taken. An effective system is to publish regular, succinct notes announcing the nature of the decisions and a brief summary of the reasoning behind them. The chief librarian should always prepare these brief notes personally. Report in simple, declarative sentences and distribute the information immediately after the meeting, preferably the same day but certainly not more than twenty-four hours afterward. Posting the notes on a bulletin board provides easy access and is cheaper than making many copies. In large libraries, department heads should see to further internal distribution. Figure 6-1, a sample for the library of the fictitious Waverly University, illustrates the type of informative notes useful for all staff.

Figure 6-1. Sample Cabinet Meeting Notes

Waverly University Library
Notes from Cabinet Meeting

17 February 19XX

Present: Chief librarian, deputy chief librarian, head of circulation and reference, head of administrative and technical services, chair of cabinet advisory committee

In today's meeting the librarian's cabinet made the following decisions:

1. In support of a recommendation from the professional travel advisory committee, approved a grant of $200 from the professional development fund to assist Harry Symonds' attendance at the conference of the Music Library Association.

2. Concluded that it would not be possible to provide an additional telephone in the science branch this year because the supply and service budget is already overspent. Agreed to review the matter again, if requested, near the beginning of the next budget call.

3. Concurred with a recommendation from the cabinet advisory committee that the pathway behind the library leading to Lot D needs better lighting. The chief librarian has already set up an appointment with the head of campus security to press this case.

4. Received with thanks the report of the committee to study turnkey laser disc systems for local access to several commercial database services in biology and science. Returned the report for further work as it lacked detail on installation costs and continuing costs of equipment service contracts. If the missing information can be supplied within ten work days, the cabinet can recommend its selection to the purchasing department in time for action before unexpended equipment funds revert to the Provost's office.

5. Heard a report from the head of circulation and reference that some students from nearby Waindell College were intimidating our students and taking over study space to the extent that Waverly students could not get seats. Agreed that the two chief librarians should discuss the issue when they see each other at next week's meeting of the state committee on intercollegiate library cooperation. The cabinet and the chief librarian agreed that the best approach would be some kind of joint agreement between Waverly and Waindell. The chief librarian agreed to discuss this idea with her counterpart at Waindell. If there is agreement, the respective department heads will be asked to draft a joint proposal for review by both chief librarians and their cabinets.

6. Canceled next week's meeting. The chief librarian and head of reference will both be away on business. The

former meets with the state committee on intercollegiate library cooperation and the latter is taking a three-day course on the interactive search system (ISS) which goes on stream this spring as a new service of the Regional Bibliographic Network to which we subscribe. The ISS will give our users subject access to the holdings of all libraries in our region, including Waindell, as well as selected public and special libraries.

Marybeth Allison
Chief Librarian

The All-Staff Meeting

Meetings of the entire staff are powerful instruments of communication. They are good opportunities for the chief librarian (and other administrators) to provide a state-of-the-library report so that everyone hears the same message at the same time. Regular meetings afford an opportunity to report on problems and achievements, rearticulate goals and objectives, and reaffirm fundamental policy decisions. A follow-up summary of major points, published in the library bulletin, forms a permanent record. Some administrators tape the all-staff meeting for future reference and to inform those who were unable to attend. In large libraries these meetings might occur quarterly, but perhaps as frequently as twice a week during a budget crisis; in small libraries, they can almost be in continuous session. Lack of regular, scheduled all-staff meetings simply indicates an uncaring administration unwilling to share information.

In medium-size and large libraries, such meetings are of little use for problem solving, but they can alert the administration to staff concerns the leadership may be unaware of or has ignored. Administrators have to be ready to hear these comments and understand that the expressed concerns of the staff are theirs too. Openness, friendliness, and collegiality help to combat unidirectional bias and provide information to personnel at all levels.

The most uncomfortable all-staff meeting is the one convened solely to deal with emergencies that have cropped up because of poor planning. On the other hand, emergency meetings arising from uncontrolled events (e.g., fire, flood) often galvanize people into a unified, responsive force. This unity normally dissipates once the emergency is over.

Informal Communication: The Grapevine

The oldest and most natural communication system, the grapevine, is inexpensive, practical and enjoyable. The quality of communication, though variable, is usually high enough to be generally reliable. It should not be the only system, however. If there is little or no formal routine communication from the front office, an ever-present underground readily manufactures its own communiqués.

The Informational Meeting

Because informational meetings are mainly concerned with one-way communication, they can be very brief if you set a concluding time, confine announcements to the subject, shorten the meeting if there is little to report. Cancel the meeting before invitees convene, if there is nothing to report. Resist the temptation to turn the informational meeting into a discussion or policy decision session. It is almost always impossible to reach policy decisions without advance study, and the really difficult decisions may require a carefully prepared position paper.

The Discussion Meeting

Problem solving and critical reviews of initiatives and proposals dominate discussion meetings. Some topics may require several sessions. Everyone's attention must be concentrated on the business at hand. Aids to effective discussion meetings are as follows:

- Ask the presenter to control the meeting.

- Make the presenter responsible for preparing the necessary documents or transparencies in advance.

- In consultation with the presenter, fix a duration for the meeting.

- Distribute an agenda with the prepared documents.

- Instruct office staff to avoid interrupting the session except for emergencies.

- Provide refreshments.

If more debate is needed, fix the time for the next session before concluding the current one. Of course, if closure is reached before the end of a discussion meeting, the format can change to an action meeting.

The Action Decision Meeting

Action decision meetings are designed to reach closure on issues up for debate. The best time to schedule such a meeting is when people are at their peak energy levels, which generally is the morning. Assign one person responsibility in advance to analyze specified problems. That individual should prepare and distribute well ahead of time all documents essential to the session and lead discussion toward closure. He or she must stick firmly to the agenda. Agree on and record precisely what decisions or recommendations the group reaches.

Chief librarians normally chair action decision sessions and are personally responsible for composing the communiqués distributed to staff. When they have plans to be away, they can judge the gravity of the agenda and decide whether an acting head can proceed. It is advantageous from time to time to delegate the preparation and chairing of the meeting to an associate; it helps to build up that person's confidence and experience.

Miscellaneous Meetings

Ad hoc sessions and meetings that occur spontaneously are a great strength of collegial groups and loosely structured organizations. Some libraries use late Friday afternoon or early Monday morning, as a convenient time to review the week's events.

Meetings in General

If the response to a call for a meeting is a groan, something is awry with the way meetings are organized and conducted. The most miserable aspects of meetings are excess length and lack of control, both of which make attendees feel frustrated and impotent. In each instance, the convener is the responsible party. Structure contributes to controlling duration, and firmness (without dictatorial behavior) helps to discourage grandstanding or aggression.[20]

A single session can simply be broken up into sequential parts, with the rules of conduct modified according to each purpose. When different functions are addressed at one sitting, attendees are on notice and business moves along at a reasonable pace.

One key to effective meetings is to recognize that they exist for the conduct of business. If there is no important matter to conduct, do not have a meeting. The inherently pleasant social atmosphere of a gathering may encourage people to meet anyhow and just talk, on the theory that something important is bound to turn up. Resist the temptation. Everyone in the library has something important to do, and it is much better to go about doing it than to relax around a conference table. Unstructured and free-wheeling bull sessions do have their place, however. They can stimulate new ideas precisely because they are unconstrained by protocols and agendas. To make them constructive and keep them from eating into the workday, schedule them during the lunch hour or after regular work hours. Food and drink generate conviviality, and a relaxed atmosphere outside the office promotes openness.

An effective way to turn any kind of business meeting into a mindless free-for-all is to permit people to introduce unrelated topics. Few matters are so urgent that they require immediate resolution or cannot wait for prior analysis, reporting, discussion and planning. Make it clear that informational and problem-solving sessions are separate.

WRITTEN COMMUNICATION: PLUSES AND MINUSES

How much to put in writing depends greatly on institutional style and on existing circumstances. Obviously, certain essentials must be written, for example, goals and objectives, major policies, priorities, performance appraisals, personnel records, and annual reports.

If an institution has operated very informally, with too few decisions put into writing, a new administration will certainly wish to formalize basic policies. Under those conditions, well-done memos on appropriate subjects are effective. They must be few in quantity and free of bureaucratic verbiage. Writing policy memos is a challenge. No one should expect to succeed on the first try, nor without a great deal of consultation, feedback from colleagues, and help from experts.[21]

Formal, written communication on policy issues has an inescapably confrontational aspect. Memos are often chosen as a means to avoid genuine communication. They also substitute for action, decision, risk taking, and accountability.[22] People who are skilled at opting out of their responsibilities often show a great talent for composing (and broadcasting) long, detailed, "cover-your-ass" memos. An avalanche of these documents produces frustration and wastes keyboarding time and supplies. When employees generate excess memos some type of mediation should be undertaken to restore open, direct communication. In performance appraisal, however, a dearth of substantive, written communication generally does more harm than good.

Staff bulletins and newsletters are the normal medium for communicating policy issues and news of library business interspersed with staff news and social events. Their uses are practically unlimited. Editing them affords a good opportunity for staff development, if financial resources permit. During the turbulent 1960s some newsletters were given over to voicing personal views on library operations or facilitating communication between various segments of the staff. Newsletters have now become almost invariably the formal voice of administration.[23]

Communication and Cultural Diversity

Despite the general sophistication of academic communities, the enrolment of foreign students, and the presence of faculty from abroad, higher education is not always free of ethnocentrism or other biases. A clear understanding of cultural variations, customs, upbringing, and experience minimizes discomfort and misunderstanding and reduces the chance of embarrassing or humiliating any member of the community. Books, workshops, and video training aids to sensitize managers and co-workers to cultural diversity are readily available.[24] Staff in large metropolitan areas and those in remote, less populated zones would benefit from them equally. In the former case, they help the many ethnic groups understand each other better; in the latter, employees learn to understand and appreciate new, unfamiliar ways and interrelate harmoniously.

FUNDING THE PROGRAM:
THE MYTHOLOGY OF RESOURCE ALLOCATION

It would be wonderful if the variety of budget analysis and presentation methods (zero-based budgeting, program budgeting, line item, enrolment formulas, standards, empirical data on library usage, formulas relating to degree programs) actually produced the desired budget. In an important paper given at the 1984 national ACRL conference, John Vasi established that library budgets are hardly ever determined on either a rational basis or from quantifiable data. Even formulas, when they exist, may not be followed.[25] Vasi's survey of ten ARL member libraries (public and private, wealthy and underfunded) revealed that none employed a formal budget-justification method, nor did any actually obtain a budget that bore any relationship to quantitative data. He found that by far the strongest determinant of library fiscal support was history—the previous year's allocation adjusted for inflation. Further investigations led him to conclude that (1) higher education is unable to document its library needs convincingly, (2) there is no demonstrable evidence that the quality of education in the product (alumni) is any worse because of poor rather than excellent library support, and (3) libraries of the rich institutions get richer and the poor get poorer.

The study clearly indicates the complexity, thoroughly political character, and irrational aspects of higher education. If the budget-setting reality in ten large research libraries, which probably have the trained staff and analytic tools to prepare complex budget documents, is not very rational or reasonable, can one assume that it will be more so in other libraries? How, then, does one obtain resources? The first prerequisite is to recognize that political realities are the heart of the allocation process. In this respect, three truisms prevail.

About Money

Regardless of its financial condition, and despite what administrators say, an institution always has the funds to do what it wants to do. At the same time that the authorities are denying support for book funds or a new circulation system, they may be authorizing an expensive and luxurious office redecoration for the president, or remodeling laboratories for prestigious scholars. Herbert S. White coined a phrase for this phenomenon: "In the absence of money there is always money."[26]

About Mission, Goals, and Objectives

What precisely does an institution want to do? Whatever those in charge decide. Even though institutional officers always say that resources are allocated in accordance with mission, goals, and objectives, it does not take much looking to note that they are really delegated in accordance with internal political decisions. Sometimes they are distributed by processes that are far from rational, or bear little or no relationship to demonstrable merit.

Although campus administrators perfunctorily "pledge allegiance" to the library, when financial stress hits, library staff members will find themselves in competition with collection development or database access, and the entire library will be contending with other academic units.

Monies are provided to operate the library system not because the library "deserves" the funds, is the "heart" of the institution, or is a "good" thing, but because failure to allocate minimal operating funds is likely to evoke a storm of unpleasant pressures and counterpressures from powerful groups of faculty or even students. In the United States, regional accrediting agencies also figure in ensuring a reasonable budget for the library. Institutions do not like to jeopardize their accreditation status for fear of losing students, faculty, tax support, and grant money. In brief, library services must be indispensable, not merely good or highly desirable.

About Chutzpah

Fight vigorously for large sums. Humility and shyness get you exactly nowhere in the budget process. It is always much easier for campus authorities to decide between spending $17,000 and $18,000 than to decide between spending no dollars and $1,000; it would be even easier for them to decide between $50,000 and $250,000. The bigger the number, the fewer the decisions. It is to no one's advantage to try making the library one of the bargain services on campus. Everyone knows the library costs a lot of money, and if you try to make it seem cheaper than it really is or ought to be, some people will decide that the library was merely cheating the funders all along. Library administrators are much better off convincing their fund allocators that their services are valuable because they are necessary and because they provide a genuine payoff to their clients.

Role of Program Merit in Resource Allocation

Colleges and universities are awash with excellent, well-conceived program ideas, and not a few ill-conceived ones. People can and will propound well-justified, rational sounding arguments aimed at convincing the allocators that *their* program should be financed through the zero-sum game, that is, at the expense of some other academic unit's support. Those wanting to wrest dollars from the institution's limited pool never hesitate to use this tactic. The library's rivals will unhesitatingly tell the campus administration that their program is more important than yours, even suggesting that funds deserve to be transferred from your unit to theirs. They will make excellent use of the image of the library as a "sink for money." In the years ahead, as resources for higher education become tighter, and more expensive new technologies have to be installed in all campus departments, expect to see the game played ever more roughly.

Does merit have a place in the argument for funds? Absolutely. When blended with appropriate political alliances, it can exert powerful and persuasive, even conclusive, arguments. On its own, however, without the political coalition, merit can be a strategy of failure.

Second to merit come goodness and fairness. It is a misery that so many librarians are socialized to base program proposals on magnificent ideals. It is naive to believe that because the library represents a good on campus, it certainly deserves its fair share of available resources. You will soon discover that, as with love and war, all is fair in resource allocation. The struggle for resources is a form of warfare – refined, elevated, spiritual, and spirited – but complete with battles, secret intrigues, sometimes unholy alliances, and odd coalitions. You must play the same games as the other players, except that you must outplay them.

Role of Political Alliances and Coalitions in Resource Allocation

We reaffirm that the basic strategy for obtaining library resources is identical to that for getting almost any limited resource people compete for: political knowledge and political alliances. On campus, a library administrator must sense the strengths and directions of the various academic forces and know which programs are in the ascendancy and which in decline. Off campus, especially in publicly funded schools, knowledge of the higher education policies and priorities of the appropriate state or provincial agency is essential.[27] When chief librarians have assessed the forces for strength, penetration, influence, and endurance, they can begin to build proper alliances with faculty and administrators. The well-constructed political alliance will do more to put a program into place than all the intellectual merit in the world; correspondingly, an alliance with a loser is a guarantee of failure.

Library staff are almost always driven by an appreciation of program merit and logic, and frequently insulated from college and university realpolitik (sometimes by their own choice). Therefore they do not always understand, appreciate, or even accept the political intensity of academe. They can easily become disillusioned and cynical about campus politics. As De Gennaro wisely emphasized, staff participation and advice can be useful, but may contribute comparatively little to the ultimate decision process because ". . . critical strategy decisions involve a world outside the library and must usually be made by the director and his chief associates. Staff committees can give good advice on such matters, but they simply do not have the information, the knowledge, or the perspective required to make those decisions – and they cannot take responsibility for the results."[28] Compounding the politics is the fact that the pool of information on which decisions are based is not the common property of the entire community, nor can it be made so. Hence, staff input is always of limited value.

While Lowell Martin lamented that librarians seem to lack an administrative mind-set, one could argue that one reason for this is that previous library school programs did not focus strongly enough on management politics.[29] In fact, some schools have not even been sufficiently astute politically to ensure their own survival. Marion Paris's research on four that closed indicated that their faculties were generally perceived as socially and thus politically isolated from other faculty, and therefore unable to win the battle for pedagogical turf.[30] If faculty cannot manage their own political survival, how can they convey political skills to their students?

Among the obviously effective and appropriate methods for forming alliances are the following:

- Make regular, frequent, personal calls on influential department chairs and faculty members; build strong bridges.

- Quickly remove bureaucratic obstacles between the library system and its most influential users – the faculty.

- Try to keep the library neutral territory; avoid taking sides in other people's battles.

- Maintain a careful balance of library support among academic departments.

- Participate vigorously in the work of campus committees (presuming you are on the right committees in the first place; see below).

- Be visible and be heard at meetings of the academic senate or similar governing body.

- Get together with faculty and administrators on a social basis.

- Set up or help to organize academic events based on school and library strengths, such as lectures, readings, or concerts relating to programs and collections.

Does this sound clubby and locker-roomish? Definitely. In the words of Kellogg, "Pushy, manipulative, aggressive and–perish the thought–political, good!"[31] All can play the game, and it is essential to remember that the formation of political alliances is a game. As Sullivan stated pointedly, alliances are transient, convenient, and not to be confounded with lasting friendships.[32]

Service on school committees is highly productive for developing political influence. Committee slots that are good for this purpose include search panels, deans' councils, and bodies set up to advise on major policy issues (e.g., raising outside money, allocating land usage) or determining policies affecting student life. Membership on committees to designate nominees for awards is also helpful. Perhaps the best faculty committee a librarian could serve on is the one charged to develop the school's academic plans and policies. Unfortunately, this is the body librarians are least likely to be invited to join, so all the more reason to press the matter. An opportunity to influence policy is always superior to one that merely involves service. Beware of assignment as committee secretary, as that responsibility effectively puts its holder out of action. Leave it for a junior faculty member whose career is just getting started.

Facing the Competition for Budget Support

In the discipline-oriented academic world, competition for money is as open and intense as in business, but with these differences: market forces operate more subtly as professors sell their programs to the administration; the nature of offerings to the clientele (papers to journals and courses to students) changes more slowly; the competitors are largely in the same location. Academic fragmentation encourages an extremely narrow focus on budgeting.

Each department sees itself as standing alone, and ultimately each faculty member views himself or herself as representing the most vital force in academic life.

Competition for money visibly divides itself among the major areas of humanities, social sciences, and "hard" sciences. That the latter two have traditionally been able to bring in significantly more grant money than the former automatically gives them a powerful claim on resources. The work of social scientists depends heavily on data collection and analysis, while that of physical scientists centers on laboratory equipment and expensive computers. This tends to leave the humanists, traditionally the strongest library supporters, at a clear disadvantage. Faculty infighting over campus dollars is directly related to discipline and focuses on a variety of campus units, especially service agencies seen as unproductive overhead, such as the controller's office or the purchasing department.

Even though all faculty members depend on publication for the reward system, they do not exempt the library budget from attack. Depending on discipline, powerful faculty members may select various targets: staffing (why do you need so many people?), acquisitions (we should spend less on books and more on microcomputers for our offices and departments), travel (the librarians ought to travel less, stick to their work, and be readily available to help us and our students), services (we need more PCs, modems, and connect time to search databases directly in the departments rather than in the library), centralization (we should redirect central library funds to convert our reading rooms into a regular departmental library where our users would be free from library bureaucracy), and so on. Even the campus sports establishment is better insulated from internal attack on its budget than the library; the very intangibility of a library's service weakens its defensive capacity. In a thorough and comprehensive analysis, Shiflett pointed out that both academic administrators and faculty rarely perceive either the library or librarians as central to the development of American higher education. Many such attitudes continue to flourish, foster an adversarial stance from some faculty, and make budget defense among the severest challenges a library administrator faces.[33]

Faculty are not the only source of competition. It has been eminently clear from decades of technological advance that emergent forces would one day be in a position to challenge strongly the library's supremacy as the main campus purveyor of information.[34] The world of computer databases and software has been inexorably looming as a threatening rival to the oldest and most familiar central information agency in colleges and universities. It is uncertain whether one or the other, or some new, third force representing a combination of the two, will emerge as the controller of information in higher education.

Yet within the tumult of these developments, the parent institution spends real dollars to pay for the vital products and services the library provides. The chief officers of academic institutions may at heart be professors, but while they wear their administrative hats they behave as businesspeople. In that capacity they feel entitled to efficient, cost-effective services. Here is the business paradox of academe: *the library is not a business, but must be run as if it were.*

Within a cash-conscious environment the library administration that continues to operate on the simple historical expectation of continuously greater funding could be in for some shocks. Going to the campus administration as supplicants for a monetary increment based on last year's budget is tantamount to asking for a gift.

Modern library service differs from that of a generation ago not just in degeree but also in kind. Contemporary services consume very expensive resources – hardware, telecommunications, commercial database services – and massive quantities of cheap resources, such as paper for printing and photocopying. All these costs are escalating rapidly, and the demand for costly services (e.g., fax, digital communication networks) never stops. Few of the new services displace old ones, and even if they did, the total costs of the new quickly outrace any savings realized from dropping obsolete processes.

In addition, libraries continue to be very personnel intensive, a burden that in no way has been relieved by technology. In fact, the exact opposite has occurred: we need more highly educated staff who demand better pay. To suppose that libraries can continue to be financed in accordance with traditional patterns indicated in the

Vasi study is daydreaming. The resources will go to the cleverest constituencies, to those who both make the most rational sounding arguments and play the best politics. Neither analytical nor political skill alone will suffice.

SOURCES OF BUDGET-PLANNING INFORMATION

A library director or planning officer rarely has the relevant information immediately at hand for intelligent budget planning. The library commonly is left out of key program decisions at the very highest levels of administration or acquires information too late for effective planning. The information available also may be so scattered and wide ranging that it is impossible to absorb it well enough to synthesize its significance within a reasonable time. In short, there is either too little information or too little time, or both. We lack and cannot easily acquire the all-encompassing view that Cronin called "synoptic vision."[35] We go ahead in spite of these problems.

Budget-Preparation Methods and Schedules

Each parent institution has its own long-established rules, procedures, and schedules for determining each unit's budget. Deadlines, forms, and styles of submission may be governed by tradition or, in the case of public-supported institutions, statutory regulation. In some jurisdictions political interference from the legislature is routine. Various schemes for constructing budgets come and go and have their own life cycles, proponents, and handbooks. Budget techniques are so diverse and shift about so much that there is little point in attempting here to provide specific guidance.[36] Rather the focus is on concerns common to all types of institutions, plus advice and cautions of a general character. Knowledge of business administration and your previous management experience will be of inestimable help in learning the budget-preparation process at your school. Orientation sessions with campus budget-planning officers, controller's staff, and business office are a good education, and can be particularly effective if you have built a sound peer relationship with these officers.

Responding to the Institution's Budget Call

Because academic libraries are in a period of chronic budget deficiency and will remain there for the foreseeable future, budget planning no longer follows the more or less regular schedule one expected in the past. Norman Stevens maintained that budget planning is ". . . an ongoing process of negotiation where the library constantly seeks to improve its funding or defend what it already has. The notion of making formal budget requests that are granted and then become the sole basis for the year's operation just doesn't seem to exist much any more. The skills needed are different and much time is involved."[37]

This is the message library administrators must put across to staff. But despite national level evidence of major economic shifts, it is difficult to convince staff that budget crises are real. People disbelieve; they still tend to think that private schools are infinitely rich or that anxiety about votes will keep politicians from cutting funds for publicly financed schools. The conservative, stable atmosphere of academe fosters this attitude. Yet the reality of the contraction in support for higher education has been clear for some time. In 1978-79, ARL libraries were spending 91 percent more for materials than ten years earlier, yet adding 22 percent fewer books and coping with personnel costs that increased by 106 percent. More recently, among non-ARL libraries, salaries went up only 2 percent while total staff remained the same over a two-year interval.[38] Despite these figures, in the late 1980s, schools' marketing efforts toward students seem to be crowned with unusual success, as young people realize they must have higher education to advance in an increasingly technological society. Without strong political coalitions, however, the library cannot translate student recruiting success into more operating funds.

Higher education not only derives significant income from its business investments but also aims to prepare students for a rapidly changing business and professional environment. On both these grounds citizens are increasingly demanding closer financial accountability from academic managers and administrators. In general, however, librarians tend to be insensitive to operating costs for several reasons: (1) fiscal planning and responsibility have heretofore been concentrated at the top of the management pyramid, (2) except in collection development, librarians have not been socialized to fiscal accountability, (3) librarians and library staff have tended to view institutions as possessing infinite resources, and (4) before distributed computing, there could be no real-time analytic and reporting mechanism for the library's financial affairs. Our profession has no history of fiscal accountability as an expectation.

Other factors indicate why managing the library's response to the institution's internal call for budget proposals can be difficult. Staff work done by subordinates whose frame of reference is narrow often lacks the balance and wide-angle view that must govern the chief librarian's budget justifications. This is normal but does require adjustments.

In the small library having, say, ten or fewer staff members, probably you will prepare the entire budget proposal yourself after appropriate consultation with employees. Beyond this number you will doubtless arrange for systematic written input from your principal colleagues. When the library staff approaches fifty, you might require considerable staff assistance at budget preparation time, and when the figure reaches one hundred, it is likely that the procedures are so involuted and time consuming that you will require permanent assistance throughout the year. Of course, these numbers are arbitrary, mere suggestions. The points where different degrees of assistance are required vary widely according to the type and structure of institution and the complexity of the process.

With fifty or more regular employees, the chief librarian or other designated staff officer should prepare a clear, systematic public presentation providing an overview of the entire budget. It is beneficial to put such an overview into the institution's total context, so that the library does not see itself as an isolated entity, or as one having more independence than could ever be the case. Flip charts or transparencies give everyone the same information; hard copies help people study the possibilities later. Whatever size the library, although not all can make the decisions, all can contribute to discussion of key issues.

Editing Staff Input to the Budget Process

While staff input to the budget process is both necessary and desirable, editing it is virtually mandatory. Because of the long-established pattern of functional departmentation in academic libraries, middle managers tend to fill their budget proposals with specialized vocabulary and arguments related to problems of bibliographic control, network protocols, changes in the cataloging code, or computer system maintenance. Outside reviewers will hardly ever be able to understand or interpret documents that focus on such highly technical considerations, especially if they incorporate bibliographic jargon. Your budget proposal has a much better chance of success if you digest technical input and recast it into broad terms. *Because the actual decision on how much money you receive may be made by staff officers who rarely or never use the library, the advantage will always be to those who communicate their needs with such clarity that the least informed layperson will understand at once what is being requested and why it is essential.* Arguments that strike home immediately are far more effective than high-sounding intellectual platitudes or operational technicalities.

You must be able to condense your entire document into a short, hard-hitting executive summary. It is then possible that a high-level academic administrator will actually read part of it and pass it on with a favorable notation to a staff analyst for further work on the main document. If the summary successfully sets a tone for acceptance and for action, congratulate yourself, even if you do not get everything what you want.

Translating and Adjusting Staff Input

Two components to a budget request contribute significant impact to the document: hard data and details of the consequences of failing to meet the request.

Make effective use of numbers. Translate source data into something readers can understand *immediately*. For example, suppose your serials unit subscribes to 10,000 titles and you know from your library's statistics that this means checking in 100,000 separate issues each year. Reporting the need to process 100,000 separate issues each year. Reporting the need to process 100,000 items a year is not likely to have much impact. Budget analysts read the newspapers and watch television. They are accustomed to seeing gigantic numbers in connection with government data, and they handle large figures anyhow in their daily work at the school. Your impressive 100,000 might just be dismissed as an insignificant quantity. But since there are roughly 2,000 hours in a work year, you could report that the average check-in work load requires your staff to check in 50 items an hour, or almost one a minute every working day. The one-a-minute processing work load is something that analysts can identify with; they need have no other specific knowledge of internal library operations.

If one a minute is impressive, so many per second may have even greater impact. If you are dealing with any transaction-intensive data involving numerous complex steps, count the steps and multiply by the number of transactions. For example, if circulation procedures require your staff to carry out 7 operations for each loan transaction and 3 for each return, an annual volume of 300,000 items translates into 3,000,000 separate actions. Still, in these days of inflation, even 3,000,000 may not sound like much. However, a typical work year contains just over 7,000,000 seconds. Knocking off a conservative 1,000,000 seconds for sick leave, vacation, breaks, and other absences, you find that your circulation staff, on the average, must do one thing every 2 seconds just to keep the operation moving. During peak periods they might have to hustle the rate up to one item per second. This example does not even take into account the extra steps required for processing reserves, overdues, recalls, replacements for lost and missing volumes, and so forth. A realistic rate might be much, much greater than one item per second at peak times.

The figure of seven million seconds can be immensely helpful in developing a striking example for anyone involved in the decision process. Its impact will be far greater than any emotional appeal. An added advantage is its absolute honesty: no one will be able to challenge your numbers, except at the risk of proposing the discontinuance of some essential service. In that case, even doubters may approve your well-argued case because they do not want to stumble into a political thicket by taking on the faculty. If you still sense trouble, you can summon your second line of defense: enumerating the consequences of not meeting your request.

Point out what will or will not occur if the library does not get the money. Here too, it is essential to avoid anything of an abstract or quasi-intellectual character. Take political action. Counsel with the faculty library committee, deans, department heads – anyone with influence, taking care to remember that in a pinch they will put their own interests first. Determine the negative impact of a denial on faculty or students and translate that into some practical terms that an informed layperson will comprehend at once. For example, arguments for two typical situations might go something like the following:

Situation 1: If we are unable to restore the authorized strength of the staff that handles our incoming journals and magazines [do not use the technical expression "serials"], faculty and students will be denied access to the latest issues; this will produce an immediate and severely negative impact on both instruction and research. Our current work is already backlogged four weeks because of the hiring freeze. More than 2,000 current issues of journals – about a month's intake – are stacked up waiting to be checked in. The situation is so acute that in the past month faculty complaints have gone from the normal one or two a week to over fifty a week, and the faculty library committee is threatening to report the matter to the senate and vice president of the school.

Situation 2: A year and a half ago we warned of the consequences if our antiquated automated circulation system was not replaced within twelve to fifteen months. Within the past six weeks breakdowns of the old system have occurred almost daily. The equipment is so old that service personnel are no longer familiar with it nor can they understand its documentation. Parts are no longer available but have to cannibalized from spares. We can no longer manage our collections properly; dozens of times each week we face the embarrassment of being unable to report on the whereabouts of specific books our students and faculty need. Already this is interfering seriously with the school's programs of instruction and research. We cannot put books on reserve with any kind of reliability. We cannot go back to a manual system – that setup was dismantled several years ago. Even the old forms we used to have are no longer available from the supplier, and the old equipment was discarded when we automated. Trying to put up a manual system again would involve wasted training plus some additional, new positions to cope with the increased volume. (Circulation volume has gone up 50 percent since automation.) Some students are already writing complaints to their parents, and our suggestion box is beginning to overflow, not with suggestions but with poison-pen notes. Now the president of the student association wants the student newspaper to interview me for a feature article on the subject. He is also thinking of inviting one of the legislators to the campus to look at the situation.

In such critical budget situations you would never or rarely use memos as your principal means of arguing your case. Face-to-face discussion with your boss is far more productive, especially if there is threat of a legislator's intervention. You still must put your arguments into a soundly reasoned written presentation, however, because in a bureaucracy, even the person who approves your oral presentation has to pass on a decision to others for action. If you are persuasive, if your arguments are already well documented, and if you succeed, you are ready for the follow-up on the spot: simply ask your boss to initial approval of your written case and forward it for action. A functionary in the campus administration can do the rest. If you have nothing in writing, you will have lost valuable time and initiative, and during the delay another contender for funds can come between you and that functionary.

BUILDING FACULTY RELATIONSHIPS
IN SUPPORT OF PROGRAMS

No matter how strong an image a president or chancellor projects, the faculty is the prime focus of political power in every school. Like other constituents on campus, faculty members are political animals – only far more powerful. Protected by tenure and endowed with significant political powers by a school's charter, board of governors, or collective agreement, they are without question the most formidable force on campus. The faculty see the school as equivalent to themselves. They can create new programs and revise curricula, expel students or award scholarships, dismiss deans and discipline colleagues, even oust presidents or chancellors. They can also start the actions leading to termination of library administrators. Stuart Forth succinctly and eloquently articulated the influence of faculty on the library as "weak friends . . . but strong enemies."[39]

A. Michael Spence, dean of the faculty of arts and sciences at Harvard University, and his predecessor, Henry Rosovsky, in the course of Harvard's $300 million campaign in the mid-1980s, both indicated the centrality of faculty. Asked what he would do with $10 million, Spence replied:

> Well, I have a fairly simple answer. I would use it to recruit absolutely first class faculty for the University, both tenured and junior level. Aside from that, I don't have any areas at the moment that I would like to single out. . . . I think with $10 million over and above what's required to proceed on our present course, faculty recruitment would be my top priority.[40]

Rosovsky was equally pointed:

> If the faculty is first-rate, everything else will fall into place.[41]

> The ultimate determinant of Harvard's quality, reputation, and capacity to render service to its students, the country and even the world is the quality of its faculty. I've said this often. The faculty determines everything else.[42]

Similar considerations prevail in all institutions of higher education, regardless of size, wealth, age, or prestige.

Faculty members are celebrities on campus, in the community, in the nation, and sometimes in the world. Partly because of their elevated status, and partly because of their talents and achievements, their basic human qualities and characteristics may easily become exaggerated. Whatever the gamut of attitude, philosophy, motivation, and emotion among ordinary people, among faculty it is deeper, more intense, and more colorful, not because of inherent differences but because the academic workplace is set up explicitly to foster such differences. Tenure is in part a society's grant of freedom to people it deems very special. This fosters an extraordinarily broad mix of human response and output: on the one hand, intellectual excellence, creativity, incredible energy, and originality; on the other, laziness, lack of integrity, and occasionally, venality. These extremes of behavior are indulged in within a structure that affords extraordinary protection from political interference.

In addition to being powerful, faculty can be divisive and selfish. Whatever they may claim to the contrary, they work more for themselves or their discipline, than for the school. In their relationships with administrators they are generally suspicious and mistrusting, sure that money and resource decisions will be dictated more by bureaucratic habit or administrative convenience than by scholarly merit. Their rivalries and collegial style of governance make it nearly impossible for a school to create a solidly unified academic program, hard to establish consistent institutional goals and objectives, and difficult to determine priorities when budget cuts must be made.[43] Faculty may control academic program, but campus administration controls the budget; the library, right in the middle, is squeezed from both sides. With these two powerful constituencies exercising so much muscle, the possibilities for systematic, rational decision making are fairly remote.

Faculty members are not likely to care how many titles or volumes the library has amassed unless a large fraction of them supports their discipline. Some will be happier if the collection is actually distorted so that their interests are supported at the expense of some other professors. A faculty member may express outrage at what you have spent to support another field of study – if you have been foolish enough to release that information. Others will hound you and cozy up to collection development librarians in search of special favors and extra consideration for purchase of expensive collections.[44] Typically the pushy ones represent two extremes: the young, energetic assistant professors desperate for tenure, and the tenured "stars" who are driven to continuing creativity by a need to be in the forefront of achievement and an urgency to justify their continuing appeals for research support. Some who are especially acquisitive will attempt to raise money to buy those special resources. In the course of doing this they may make themselves personae non gratae with the campus development office. When that occurs, the chief librarian must keep out of the struggle. There are times when it is advantageous to be at a loss for words and this is one of them. Remember, however, that when the faculty raise money for library purchases, they are not doing it for the library – they are usually doing it for themselves.

Depending on its membership, the faculty library committee can be a useful ally (or strong enemy, as Forth suggested) in fiscal battles with the administration and with inflation. Involving them in such matters requires a great deal of finesse, as one obviously does not want to convey any impression that the reins of library control have been passed to them. Still, it is helpful and sometimes necessary to seek their advice on a range of financial questions, from how to spend new appropriations to how to distribute budget cuts. If faculty are asked only for help in cutting subscriptions or book purchases, they earn only brickbats. Work out ways for them to get credits, too.

Faculty advice is also valuable in selected programmatic areas, such as deciding which database to subscribe to or which compact disc systems should be purchased or leased for local use. Because they are a conservative lot, they must be amply consulted – and convinced – on global issues, such as closing the catalog and matters having a direct impact on their habits relating to instruction or research.

Personal attention flatters faculty. A head librarian who takes time out to show faculty members major features of an online public access catalog or explain how an automated interlibrary loan service speeds up access makes a lot of points and gains an important ally. Of course it always works better if you give your attention to the most influential. This is not manipulation; this is one of the things you are paid to do.

Faculty generally perceive library administrators not as scholars or vital academic policy makers but as technicians.[45] They have little interest in knowing or learning the technical details of a library's inner workings, but prefer to take the service for granted. Their generally self-centered views on the function and purpose of the library were probably expressed for all time by a biology professor complaining about delayed access to scholarly materials: ". . . the scientist's needs are simple, he just wants to be able to read the article that interests him immediately."[46]

The Faculty Club

In keeping with the generally elitist pattern of higher education in North America, many schools, especially the larger ones, have faculty clubs. The club is a social center for the campus power brokers. Important issues may be debated in committee meetings, but they are often negotiated and resolved in the club. Within a rank-conscious group, the faculty club exercises a limited leveling influence; it is an environment that permits and encourages free intercourse equally among its members. As forum for informal communication with faculty and high level administration, it is unequaled. A chief librarian who holds a rank equivalent to dean is usually automatically eligible for membership. Similarly, librarians with faculty status normally are eligible. Although the value of the club will probably be greatest for the chief librarian, all librarians can benefit from regular use of the facilities. The simple act of being seen frequently in the company of teaching and research faculty enhances the academic character of librarianship and increases the status of its members.

BUILDING PEER RELATIONSHIPS
IN SUPPORT OF PROGRAMS

Regardless of school size, all top and middle level administrators can benefit from quality social and professional relationships with peers if only to maintain their own effectiveness on campus. Peers include a variety of academic and nonacademic officers: the controller, head of physical plant and facilities management, campus personnel head, chief security officer, fire marshall, Affirmative Action officer, registrar, academic program planning officer, deans and department heads, financial planning officer, budget analysis officer, chief research officer, head of purchasing department, campus development officer, staff legal counsel, and director of computer center. Nonacademic peers maintain vital current operations (payroll, messenger, delivery and mail services, elevators, telecommunications) that in the short run can be far more important to the community as a whole than the library.

BUILDING EXTERNAL RELATIONSHIPS
IN SUPPORT OF PROGRAMS

Lay Support Groups: Friends, Affiliates, Associates

Well-developed local community support groups can not only raise funds for the library but also provide political support at many levels for both private and public universities. Whether active, retired, or semiretired, businesspeople, professionals, book lovers, and cultured people in general enjoy an affiliation with an academic library. Like any other group giving voluntarily of their time and resources, they like to be catered to and they certainly deserve special attention. The following recommendations, specifically geared to organizing a friends group in an academic library, are an expansion of a brief checklist prepared by Venable Lawson, Robert Oram, and Robert Runyon for Friends of Libraries USA.

1. Coordinate at the local level. First, gain support of the development officer and chief administrators of the parent institution. Be sure to present your case in a way that does not suggest that the library might become a powerful rival for funds. Second, seek advice and assistance from the school's legal counsel for setting up the group's charter, managing its funds, and assuring tax-exempt status. In some state-supported schools bureaucratic regulations may make it very difficult to establish an income center outside normal control channels; it may be necessary to set up an off-campus, nonprofit organization or foundation.

2. Appoint a member of the professional staff as key liaison person; allocate to this person enough time and resources so the position can be effective.

3. Set up a steering committee drawn from interested persons among faculty, library staff, alumni, students, and community leaders.

4. Clearly define the mission, goals and objectives of the support group. Choose program goals in areas in which needs or benefits are greatest or where budgeted support might be difficult to obtain. Examples include preservation, purchase of rare books and manuscripts, support for professional development connected with research or publication, and small-scale renovation or remodeling. Concentrate on areas having broad public appeal; a reclassification project and money to support staff travel are not good candidates. Develop a constitution and by-laws appropriate to the mission. This step is important for building a group that works for the library rather than for itself. A support group unchecked by a firm mission statement and strong leadership can easily become a law unto itself, trying to override or compete with library goals.

5. Establish dues, membership, benefits, and privileges (e.g., access to library collections, discounts on college and university publications). Take great care to ensure that members understand clearly that collections are primarily for students and faculty, and that access to the general public is limited. Outsiders who try to place equal claims on library materials will turn out to be enemies, not friends. At the same time, cut through ordinary bureaucratic regulations to make sure that members' privileges really are privileges, and make sure staff do not treat them as intruders.

6. Promote membership as a tax benefit to the donors, to the extent permitted by federal, state, and provincial laws.

7. Develop a good-looking brochure with first-rate graphics. Obtain the best designer you can afford. With some luck or energetic persuasion, you may even be able to find a professional willing to donate design services. Avoid junky-looking, amateurly produced brochures, and do not be carried away by the wonders of desk-top publishing. Thompson's *Friends of College Libraries* contains excellent

samples of invitations to membership and events, acknowledgments, program brochures, and newsletters.[47] Other noteworthy examples are the distinguished designs used by the University of North Carolina at Chapel Hill for its Friends of the Library, and by Stanford University for its associates group.

8. Build a mailing list of potential members. Advertise in appropriate media; report forthcoming meetings to campus and municipal newspapers, and public service radio stations and television channels. Enlist assistance from the campus development office. Determine whether the membership prefers that the list not be shared with other fund-raising organizations.

9. Prepare a budget. The budget must go beyond the usual costs of printing and mailing; include extraordinary costs required for every support group: speakers' fees, rental space for meetings, catering, publicity photographs, rental of audiovisual equipment, and taping and possibly transcription and publication of talks given by distinguished guests.

10. Develop programs relating to the library's strengths but also appropriate to the interests of informed, educated lay people. Some faculty may be willing to give illustrated lectures without charge; others may require honoraria. Accounts about the acquisition of special collections can be dramatic and interesting. Dinner or luncheon meetings often attract members. Be sure that the program chairperson is someone comfortable with public speaking, and organized and knowledgeable about preparing physical setups for meetings.[48] Bear in mind that many potential members may be elderly or infirm; arrange parking, buses, or escort services and select easily accessible meeting sites. A public address system will help attendees whose hearing is impaired. Here is where building and maintaining your peer contacts with campus police and security can have a good payoff.

11. Include library staff in the membership campaign; make them a part of the action.

12. Affiliate the group with Friends of Libraries USA or other appropriate organization.

Exhibits

Exhibits are an important and useful means of communication to the library's clientele and lay support groups; However, administrators sometimes regard them as an expensive nuisance. Space, exhibit cases, signage, insurance, security, and preparation time all consume resources normally seen as sorely needed for other program elements judged more productive or more responsive to immediate pressures. Exhibits offer opportunity for staff to apply imagination and creativity, however, and total absence of them shortchanges the professional staff who lose a valuable opportunity for personal development. The public also loses by not being exposed to the richness of the school's collections and the breadth of its services. The profession suffers because an opportunity to illustrate and enhance the academic status of librarians is lost.

Exhibits are a central policy concern. The power to set them up is the power to communicate to the outside world. As with the library bulletin and press releases, exhibits represent the voice of the library administration, and in a wider sense, the voice of the campus administration. Setting them up should never be delegated to any groups outside the library but always confined to the cabinet or a committee reporting to the administration. It is essential to control exhibits thoughtfully by carefully worked-out policies and procedures.

A policy must be established to protect the library and its clients from propaganda or communication that serves no legitimate library or academic purpose. Unmanaged exhibits set up without authorization or appropriate controls can cause seriously inflammatory outbursts in the community, especially if they involve political, social, or religious controversy. The Association of Research Libraries issues a guide kit for managing exhibits; like many ARL publications, it is adaptable to almost any size library.[49]

SUMMARY

Many governance aspects of academic librarianship are predetermined by national and international standards; precedent; collective agreements; federal, state, or provincial laws; and local campus policy. Individually and as a group, librarians lack the broad autonomy of teaching and research faculty. The authority system in a professional bureaucracy is comparatively dispersed, with many of the powers of administration – aspects of the reward system, authority and responsibility for program formulation, and authority to spend money – distributed among the membership. Lines of authority and responsibility are often ambiguous and the whole system has the appearance of organized anarchy. Organizational coherence, such as it is, emerges from professional commitments; shared philosophies; clearly articulated mission, goals, and objectives; and strong, dedicated leaders who have, and who effectively communicate, a strategic vision. The main zones of self-governance cover library program and personnel. The summation of major policy decisions, a program is an exclusive locus of power reserved to the school's academic and professional staff. A library's academic staff carries the exclusive responsibility for developing and administering the content of programs supporting instruction and research. Ideally, programs are codetermined by campus administration, faculty, chief librarian, and library professional staff; advice is sought from other constituencies as appropriate. Because of the mix of academic and support staff, communication within an academic library is a complex, multidirectional process blending formal and informal methods very liberally, yet centralizing substantial authority and accountability within a few administrative officers. Effective decision making is a precarious art because both management and staff withhold information in the normal tension and competition that permeate the workplace. Other aspects of self-governance include the right and responsibility to help define the character of library work, develop job and position descriptions, participate in the performance-appraisal process, establish ranks and steps, and promote staff development. In personnel, higher education is becoming increasingly sensitive to cultural diversity and equal treatment for employees of both sexes.

Resource allocation is strongly competitive and almost totally political. Success is highly dependent on powerful, well-organized coalitions. Merit plays a secondary, but not unimportant, role. It is almost always necessary for the chief librarian or library budget officer to recast staff input into a form that is brief and salient enough for quick action by campus decision makers. Both public and private academic institutions are competing aggressively for private funds to supplement income from state or provincial appropriations or endowments; the process for entry into the private fund arena is chiefly political.

Notes

1. See G. Edward Evans, *Management Techniques for Librarians*, 2d ed. (New York: Academic Press, 1983), 28-31, for a summary of Fayol's 14 principles, the essence of classical bureaucracy. Fayol's full text is reprinted in D. S. Pugh's *Organization Theory: Selected Readings*, 2d ed. (Harmondsworth: Penguin, 1984), 135-56.

2. There was a great flurry of MRAP activity in the early days of the program, but even under the best circumstances, such a program was expensive and sometimes exhausting. As a formal ARL/OMS-operated program, MRAP is currently inactive. In fact, the MRAP program as a whole may now be outdated, having served its purpose to stimulate institutional self-examination. Still, ARL reports frequent requests for segments of the process and MRAP elements themselves have found their way into new aids, such as the ARL Leadership Development Program (LDP). For further information on and critique of MRAP, see Edward R. Johnson and Stuart H. Mann, *Organization Development for Academic Libraries: An Evaluation of the Management Review and Analysis Program* (Westport, Conn.: Greenwood Press, 1980), and H. William Axford, "Academic Library Management Studies: From Games to Leadership," *Advances in Librarianship* 10 (1980): 39-61.

3. James Thompson and Reg Carr, *An Introduction to University Library Administration*, 3d ed. (London: Bingley, 1979), 30-31. It is of special interest to note that this statement does not appear in the fourth edition of Thompson and Carr's book.

4. That the same duality prevails in British university libraries is clear from Thompson and Carr, 59: "Library assistants are not employed, or paid, to carry out duties beyond what can be straightforwardly defined in purely routine terms."

5. The United States Labor Management Relations Act (29 USC 152(12)(a), 1976, provides the legal basis for not delegating programmatic duties: responsibilities of exempt and nonexempt staff cannot be interchanged.

6. In the United States, subscriptions to the *Chronicle of Higher Education* and *Change* are worthwhile investments for maintaining currency at the national level.

7. Responding to an open discussion about initiatives at an ALA conference, Herbert S. White once pointed out that sometimes when the administration does come up with an initiative and the staff reviews it, their response is: "We don't like this initiative; please bring us another one!" (Quoted with the author's permission.)

8. Allen B. Veaner, "Librarians – The Next Generation," *Library Journal* 109, no. 6 (April 1, 1984): 623-25.

9. See E. Dale Cluff and Gisela Webb, "Staff Retreats in ACRL Libraries," *College and Research Libraries News* 49, no. 8 (September 1988): 517-21, for an excellent preliminary analysis of retreats. In reviewing the literature of the 1970s, Cluff and Webb found nothing on retreats. Probably this is because retreats are viewed as internal program reviews specific to one institution.

10. Quebec legislation provides that anyone not a member of the Corporation of Professional Librarians who uses the title "librarian" shall be liable to a fine. In the United States, school librarians form another kind of exception in that school boards often require them to be credentialed teachers. Their licensure comes from their teacher education, not from librarianship.

11. Even faculty members are not totally autonomous in significant areas. A faculty member wishing to institute a new course normally needs the approval of a departmental or school curriculum

committee and a top administrator to approve the additional resources.

12. Jorge Reina Schement et al., "Social Forces Affecting the Success of Introducing Information Technology into the Workplace," *Proceedings of the 48th ASIS Annual Meeting* (White Plains, N.Y.: Knowledge Industry Publications, 1985), 279.

13. Cf. Joseph A. Raelin, *The Clash of Cultures: Managers and Professionals* (Boston: Harvard Business School Press, 1986).

14. The MAG concept originated with Versatec (now a Xerox subsidiary) and is fully described in "It's Not Lonely Upstairs," an interview with the company's founder, published in *Harvard Business Review* 60, no. 6 (1980): 111-30.

15. Peter F. Drucker, *The Effective Executive* (New York: Harper and Row, 1985), 39.

16. Kenneth Boulding, "Learning by Simplifying: How to Turn Data Into Knowledge," in *The Science and Praxis of Complexity: Contributions to the Symposium Held at Montpellier, France, 9-11 May 1984*, ed. S. Aida et al. (Tokyo: United Nations University, 1985), 25-34.

17. Some people will argue that it doesn't cost anything to use a local E-mail system. This is the same as saying that photocopying costs should not be allocated among users. Complex communication systems always need metering or pricing to limit their use. As more and more computer applications permeate academe, more cost centers will be established. Each of these centers is likely to have its own budget, and E-mail will certainly be included. Since real dollars must be found to pay for these systems, it is inevitable that chargebacks will be applied to all users.

18. Joanne R. Euster, *Changing Patterns in Internal Communication in Large Academic Libraries* Occasional Paper no. 6 (Washington, D.C.: ARL/OMS, 1981), 6.

19. Institutional confidentiality is not unlimited; in civil cases, opposing counsel may demand copies of evidential documents.

20. Two superb videos are available as training aids for the conduct of meetings: *Meetings, Bloody Meetings*, written by John Cleese and Antony Jay is 30 minutes and comes with a booklet, *How to Run a Meeting*. *More Bloody Meetings* is a 27-minute video written by Antony Jay. Both videos are distributed by Video Arts, Northbrook, Ill.

21. For developing internal memos, a handbook by Susan Z. Diamond, *Preparing Administrative Manuals* (New York: AMACOM, 1981), provides excellent guidance, as does John S. Fielden's article, "What Do You Mean, You Don't Like My Style?" *Harvard Business Review* 60, no. 3 (May-June 1982): 128-38. Fielden's guide to composing memos, while geared mostly to the drafting of material for the boss's signature, nevertheless offers very valuable guidance for preparing any documentation. Three works that will assist in avoiding sexist language are Dale Spender's *Manmade Language* (London: Routledge and Kegan Paul, 1980); Rosalie Maggio's *The Non-Sexist Word Finder: A Dictionary of Gender-Free Usage* (Phoenix, Ariz.: Oryx, 1987); and Casey Miller and Kate Swift's *The Handbook of Nonsexist Writing* (New York: Lippincott and Crowell, 1980).

22. Fayol, *General and Industrial Management*, 40-41.

23. An overview of the considerations in issuing library newsletters is Sylverna Ford's "The Library Newsletter: Is It for You?" *College & Research Libraries News* 49, no. 10 (November 1988): 678-82. *Resources: CMU Libraries' News*, available from Carnegie Mellon University Libraries, is another source of guidance.

24. Copeland Griggs Productions of San Francisco has produced a three-part video, *Valuing Diversity* (San Francisco: Copeland Griggs Productions, 1987), designed expressly to help managers and employees work together wherever there are differences of culture, language, religion, lifestyle, or physical ability. The three parts are "Managing Differences," "Diversity at Work," and "Communicating Across Cultures." A superb handbook designed for American businesspeople working abroad is Philip R. Harris and Robert T. Moran's *Managing Cultural Differences*, 2d ed. (Houston: Gulf

Publishing Co., 1987). The Harris-Moran handbook provides in-depth insights into the manners, mores, and acceptable nuances of social interaction for people from nearly every country in the world. It also covers Hispanic, black, and Native American microcultures in the United States. A work intended to help professionals not born in the United States cope with communication problems is Gregory A. Barnes's *Communication Skills for the Foreign-Born Professional* (Philadelphia: ISI, 1982). Robert Abramms-Mezoff, a consultant on cultural diversity, conducts workshops on cultural diversity; contact ODT Associates, Box 134, Amherst, MA 01004, (413)549-1293.

25. John Vasi, "How Academic Library Budgets Are Really Determined," in *Academic Libraries: Myths and Realities* (Chicago: ACRL, 1984), 343-45. The detailed study on which this paper is based was published as *Budget Allocation Systems for Research Libraries* (Washington, D.C.: Association of Research Libraries, Office of Management Studies, 1983).

26. Remarks at an ALA conference; used with the author's permission.

27. Vicki L. Gregory, "State Coordination of Higher Education in Academic Libaries," *College & Research Libraries* 49, no. 4 (July 1988): 315-24.

28. Richard De Gennaro, "Library Administration and New Management Systems," *Library Journal* 103, no. 22 (15 December 1978): 2480.

29. Lowell Martin, *Organizational Structure of Libraries,* 134.

30. Marion Paris, "The Hazards of Being Separate," remarks presented at the Chicago ALISE Conference, 16 January 1987 (typescript). See also her *Library School Closings: Four Case Studies* (Metuchen, N.J.: Scarecrow Press, 1988).

31. Rebecca Kellogg, "Beliefs and Realities: Libraries and Librarians from a Non-library Administrator's Point of View," *College & Research Libraries News* 47, no. 8 (September 1986): 492-96.

32. Peggy Sullivan, "Faculty Participation in University Policy: The Pleasures and the Perils," *Journal of Education for Library and Information Science* 29, no. 2 (Fall 1988): 113-20.

33. Orvin Lee Shiflett's *Origins of American Academic Librarianship* (Norwood, N.J.: Ablex, 1981) is the premier source for an understanding of the role and place of the library and librarians in U.S. academic libraries. John Caldwell, in an examination of the histories of twenty-eight midwestern colleges, all published in the twentieth century, also demolished the "heart of the college" cliché. In none of the histories was the library's role portrayed as central or important. See his "Perceptions of the Academic Library: Midwestern College Libraries as They Have Been Depicted in College Histories," in *Academic Libraries: Myths and Realities*, Proceedings of the Third National Conference of the ACRL, Seattle, 4-7 April 1984 (Chicago: ACRL, 1984), 301-7. Among the thirty-one authors were five college presidents, four other officers, and nineteen professors.

34. For a dramatic sketch of this threat, see the paper by Howard Resnikoff, "The Information Technologies and Institutions of Higher Learning," in *Universities, Information Technology, and Academic Libraries*, ed. Robert M. Hayes (Norwood, N.J.: Ablex, 1986), 77-133.

35. Blaise Cronin, "Disjointed Incrementalism and 1990," *ASLIB Proceedings* 37, nos. 11/12 (November/December 1985): 421-36.

36. Works by Brian Alley and Jennifer Cargill, Ann Prentice and Stephen A. Roberts provide excellent assistance at the detailed level; see resource list at the end of this chapter.

37. Norman Stevens, personal communication.

39. *ACRL University Library Statistics 1985-1986 and 1986 "100 Libraries" Statistical Survey* (Chicago, 1987), ii.

39. Stuart Forth, *Myths and Realities: The Politics of Library Administration* (Ann Arbor: University of Michigan School of Library Science, 1981), 19.

40. "Dean Spence Offers 'Forecast' of Future Challenges Facing Harvard," *Harvard Campaign Report*, December 1984, 4.

41. "Fund Supports Young Scientists," *Harvard Campaign Report*, Summer 1984, 3.

42. "Faculty Support: Henry Rosovsky Discusses Its Vital Importance," *Harvard Campaign Report*, final issue (May 1985): 12.

43. The nature of the battles waged within academe are accurately portrayed in Dwight R. Ladd's "Myths and Realities of University Governance," *College & Research Libraries* 36, no. 2 (March 1975): 97-105.

44. Librarians, in turn, often play faculty and library administration against each other, not only in collection development but also in connection with performance appraisal.

45. Julian Boyd, when librarian at Princeton, described this attitude bluntly and succinctly: "According to this view, held by too many presidents and by most scholars, librarians are technicians, far below the rank of policy-makers. They are to keep the machinery going, to chart its mileage per gallon, to change its tires, and to keep it ready-fueled, but not to touch the steering wheel." See his "The Librarian Reports to the President," *Proceedings Reports, and Addresses, 1950* (Southern University Conference, Birmingham, 11-12 April 1950), 106.

46. D. W. Ewer, "A Biologist's Reflections on Libraries and Library Service," *South African Libraries* 29, no. 2 (October 1961): 53-56, 74.

47. Ronette K. H. Thompson, comp., *Friends of College Libraries* (Chicago: ACRL/College Libraries Section/College Library Information Packet Committee, 1987).

48. It is easy to ruin the impact of a slide show if the chair does not know where light switches and electric outlets are, has not foreseen the need for extension cords, projector tables, and spare projector bulbs, does not know how to set up and operate equipment, etc.

49. Association of Research Libraries, Office of Management Studies, *Exhibits in ARL Libraries* (Washington, D.C., 1986).

Resources

Ackerman, Page. "Governance and Academic Libraries." *Library Research* 2, no. 1 (Spring 1980/81): 3-28.

ACRL. *Governance in the Academic Library*. Chicago, 1981. Videotape.

Alley, Brian, and Jennifer Cargill. *Keeping Track of What You Spend: The Librarian's Guide to Simple Bookkeeping*. New York: Oryx, 1982.

American Library Association. *ACRL Statistics and "100 Libraries" Statistical Survey*. Chicago, annual.

Association of Research Libraries. *ARL Statistics*. Washington, D.C., annual.

Axford, H. William. "The Interrelations of Structure, Governance and Effective Resource Utilization in Academic Libraries." *Library Trends* 23, no. 4 (April 1975): 557-71.

Boulding, Kenneth. "Learning by Simplifying: How to Turn Data into Knowledge." In *The Science and Praxis of Complexity: Contributions to the Symposium Held at Montpellier, France, 9-11 May 1984*, edited by S. Aida et al., 25-34. Tokyo: United Nations University, 1985.

Bradley, Jana, and Larry Bradley. *Improving Written Communication in Libraries*. Chicago: American Library Association, 1988.

Brown, Nancy A. "Academic Libraries: An Operational Model for Participation." *Canadian Library Journal* 36 (August 1979): 201-207.

_____. "Managing the Coexistence of Hierarchical and Collegial Governance Structures." *College & Research Libraries* 46 (November 1985): 478-82.

Burckel, Nicholas C. "Participatory Management in Academic Libraries: A Review." *College & Research Libraries* 45 (January 1984): 25-34.

Casagrande, Dianne O., and Roger D. Casagrande. *Oral Communication in Technical Professions and Business*. Belmont, Calif.: Wadsworth, 1986.

Chen, Ching-chih. *Zero-base Budgeting in Library Management: A Manual for Librarians*. New York: Neal-Schuman, 1980.

Cleese, John, and Antony Jay. *Meetings, Bloody Meetings*. Distributed by Video Arts, Northbrook, Ill. Videotape, 30 minutes. Includes booklet, *How to Run a Meeting*.

Cleveland, Harlan. *The Education of Administrators for Higher Education*. Urbana: University of Illinois, 1977.

Copeland Griggs Productions. *Valuing Diversity*. Part 1: "Managing Differences." Part 2: "Diversity at Work." Part 3: "Communicating Across Cultures." Videotape. San Francisco, 1987.

Creth, Sheila. *Time Management and Conducting Effective Meetings*. Vol. 1: Instructor's Manual; vol. 2: Workbook. Chicago: ACRL, 1982.

Davis, Michael, Gary M. Gray and Harry Hallez. *Manuals That Work*. Columbia, Md.: GP Publishing, 1988.

De Bernardis, Frank, and Frank O'Connor. *Meetings*. New York: Richardson and Steirman, 1985.

Diamond, Susan Z. *Preparing Administrative Manuals*. New York: AMACOM, 1981.

Doyle, Michael, and David Straus. *How to Make Meetings Work*. New York: Jove, 1982.

Durey, Peter. "Effective Structures for the Management of Human Resources." *Australian Academic and Research Libraries* 16 (June 1985): 88-96.

Dutton, B. G. "Staff Management and Staff Participation." In *A Reader in Library Management*, edited by Ross Shimmon, 129-45. London: Bingley, 1976.

Elliott, Clifford, and David Kuhn. "Professionals in Bureaucracies: Some Emerging Areas of Conflict. *University of Michigan Business Review* 30, no. 2 (January 1978): 12-16.

Etzioni, Amitai. *A Comparative Analysis of Complex Organizations: On Power, Involvement, and Their Correlates*. Rev. and enl. New York: Free Press, 1975.

Euster, Joanne R. *Changing Patterns in Internal Communication in Large Academic Libraries*. Occasional Paper no. 6. Washington, D.C.: ARL/OMS, 1981.

Euster, Joanne R., and Peter D. Haikalis. "A Matrix Model of Organization for a Univerity Library Public Services Division." In *Academic Libraries: Myths and Realities*, edited by Suzanne C. Dodson and Gary L. Menges, 357-64. Chicago: ALA/ACRL, 1984.

Fruehling, Rosemary T., and Neild B. Oldham. *Write to the Point!* New York: McGraw-Hill, 1988.

Galvin, Thomas, and Beverly Lynch. *Priorities for Academic Libraries*. San Francisco: Jossey-Bass, 1982.

Gorman, Michael. "Reorganization at the University of Illinois – Urbana/Champaign Library: A Case Study." *Journal of Academic Librarianship* 9, no. 4 (September 1983): 223-25.

Govan, James F. "The Better Mousetrap: External Accountability and Staff Participation." *Library Trends* 26, no. 1 (Fall 1979): 255-67.

Harris, Philip R., and Robert T. Moran. *Managing Cultural Differences*. 2d ed. Houston: Gulf Press, 1988.

Harvey, John F., and Peter Spyers-Duran. *Austerity Management in Academic Libraries*. Metuchen, N.J.: Scarecrow Press, 1984.

Heyeck, John C., ed. *Managing under Austerity: [Proceedings of] A Conference for Privately Supported Academic Libraries*. Stanford, Calif: Stanford University, 1976.

Holley, Edward G. "Library Governance in Higher Education: What Is Evolving?" In *Minutes*, Association of Research Libraries, 80th meeting, May 1972, 28-33.

———. "Organization and Administration of Urban University Libraries." *College & Research Libraries* 33 (May 1972): 175-89.

International Association of Business Communicators. *Without Bias: A Guidebook for Non-Discriminatory Communication*. 2d ed. New York: Wiley, 1982.

Jay, Antony. "How to Run a Meeting." *Harvard Business Review* 54 (March-April 1976): 43-57.

———. *More Bloody Meetings*. Distributed by Video Arts, Northbrook, Ill. Videotape, 27 minutes.

Johnson, Edward R., and Stuart H. Mann. *Organization Development for Academic Libraries: An Evaluation of the Management Review and Analysis Program*. Wesport, Conn.: Greenwood Press, 1980.

Jones, Ken. *Conflict and Change in Library Organizations: People, Power and Service*. London: Bingley, 1984.

Kaplan, Louis. "The Literature of Participation: From Optimism to Realism." *College & Research Libraries* 36 (November 1975): 473-79.

Kellogg, Rebecca. "Beliefs and Realities: Libraries and Librarians from a Non-library Administrator's Point of View." *College & Research Libraries News* 47, no. 8 (September 1986): 492-96.

Kimberley, John W., and Robert H. Miles and Associates, eds. *The Organizational Life Cycle: Issues in the Creation, Transformation, and Decline of Organizations*. San Francisco: Jossey-Bass, 1980.

Kirkpatrick, Donald L. *How to Plan and Conduct Productive Business Meetings*. New York: AMACOM, 1986.

Lewis, David W. "An Organizational Paradigm for Effective Academic Libraries." *College & Research Libraries* 47, no. 4 (1986): 337-53.

Line, Maurice B. "The Survival of Academic Libraries in Hard Times: Reactions to Pressures." *British Journal of Academic Librarianship* 1, no. 1 (Spring 1986): 1-12.

Linkemer, Bobbi. *How to Run a Meeting.* New York: AMACOM, 1987.

Lynch, Beverly. "Participative Management in Relation to Library Effectiveness." *College & Research Libraries* 33 (September 1972): 382-90.

Lynch, Mary Jo. "Academic Librarian Salaries." *College & Research Libraries News* 48, no. 11 (December 1987): 674-77.

McCabe, Gerard B. *The Smaller Academic Library: A Management Handbook.* Westport, Conn.: Greenwood Press, 1988.

McCabe, Gerard B., and Constance E. Gamaluddin. "Committees with Clout: A Case for Shared Management in an Academic Library." *Library Administration and Management* 2, no. 1 (January 1988): 24-27.

Maggio, Rosalie. *The Non-Sexist Word Finder: A Dictionary of Gender-Free Usage.* Phoenix: Oryx, 1987.

Marchant, Maurice P. *Participative Management in Academic Libraries.* Westport, Conn.: Greenwood Press, 1976.

_____. "Participative Management, Job Satisfaction, and Service." *Library Journal* 107 (April 1982): 782-84.

Marquis Who's Who. *Annual Register of Grant Support.* Willmette, Ill., annual.

Martell, Charles R. *The Client-Centered Academic Library: An Organizational Model.* Westport, Conn.: Greenwood Press, 1983.

Martin, Lowell A. *Organizational Structure of Libraries.* Library Administration Series, 5. Metuchen, N.J.: Scarecrow Press, 1984.

Martin, Murray S. *Financial Planning for Libraries*. New York: Haworth, 1983. Also published as the *Journal of Library Administration* 3, nos. 3/4 (1982).

Miller, Casey, and Kate Swift. *The Handbook of Nonsexist Writing*. New York: Lippincott and Crowell, 1980.

Moffett, William A. "What Academic Librarians Want from Administrators and Faculty." *New Directions for Higher Education* 39 (September 1982): 13-24.

Munn, Robert F. "The Bottomless Pit, or the Academic Library as Viewed from the Administration Building." *College & Research Libraries* 29 (January 1968): 51-54.

Murphy, Herta A., and Herbert W. Hildebrandt. *Effective Business Communications*. 4th ed. New York: McGraw-Hill, 1984.

Neal, James G. "The Walls Came Tumblin' Down: Distributed Cataloging and the Public/Technical Services Relationship – The Public Services Perspective." State College: University of Pennsylvania, 1985. 9 pp. (Unpublished).

O'Neil, Robert M. "The University Administrator's View of the University Library." In *Priorities for Academic Libraries*, edited by Thomas J. Galvin and Beverly Lynch. San Francisco: Jossey-Bass, 1982. Also published in *New Directions for Higher Education* 39 (September 1982): 5-12.

Prentice, Ann E. *Financial Planning for Libraries*. Metuchen, N.J.: Scarecrow Press, 1983.

Reid, Marion T., et al. "The Role of the Academic Librarian in Library Governance." In *New Horizons for Academic Libraries*, proceedings of the first ACRL conference, 8-11 November 1978, edited by Robert D. Stueart and Richard D. Johnson, 123-31. New York: Saur, 1979.

Roberts, Stephen A. *Cost Management for Library and Information Services*. London: Butterworth, 1985.

Ross, Catherine, and Patricia Dewdney. *Communicating Professionally*. New York: Neal-Schuman, 1988.

Sager, Donald J. *Participatory Management in Libraries.* Metuchen, N.J.: Scarecrow Press, 1982.

St Clair, Guy, and Joan Williamson. *Managing the One-Person Library.* London: Butterworth, 1986.

Seekings, David. *How to Organize Effective Conferences and Meetings.* 3d ed. New York: Nichols, 1987.

Smith, G. Stevens. *Accounting for Librarians and Other Not-for-Profit Managers.* Chicago: American Library Association, 1983.

Smith, Kenwyn, and David N. Berg. *Paradoxes of Group Life: Understanding Conflict, Paralysis and Movement in Group Dynamics.* San Francisco: Jossey-Bass, 1987.

Sorrels, Bobby D. *The Non-Sexist Communicator.* Englewood Cliffs, N.J.: Prentice-Hall, 1983.

Spender, Dale. *Manmade Language.* London: Routledge and Kegan Paul, 1980.

Stevens, Norman D. *Communication Throughout Libraries.* Metuchen, N.J.: Scarecrow Press, 1983.

Stewart, Henry. "Staff Participation in the Management of Libraries and Its Relationship to Library Performance Characteristics." Ph.D. diss. Indiana University, 1972.

Striedieck, Suzanne. "The Walls Came Tumblin' Down: Distributed Cataloging and the Public/Technical Services Relationship – The Technical Services Perspective." State College: University of Pennsylvania, 1985. 11 pp. (Unpublished).

Talbot, Richard J. "Financing the Academic Library." In *Priorities for Academic Libraries,* edited by Thomas J. Galvin and Beverly Lynch. San Francisco: Jossey-Bass, 1982.

This, Leslie. *The Small Meeting Planner.* 2d ed. Houston: Gulf, 1979.

3M Meeting Management Team. *How to Run Better Business Meetings: A Reference Guide for Managers.* New York: McGraw-Hill, 1987.

Vasi, John. *Budget Allocation Systems for Research Libraries.* Occasional Paper no. 7. Washington, D.C.: Association of Research Libraries, Office of Management Studies, 1983.

_____. "How Academic Library Budgets Are Really Determined." In *Academic Libraries: Myths and Realities*, 343-45. Chicago: ACRL, 1984.

Vosper, Robert. "Library Administration on the Threshold of Change." In *Issues in Library Administration*, edited by Warren M. Tsuneishi et al., 37-51. New York: Columbia University Press, 1974.

Webster, Duane. "Managing the College and University Library." In *Current Concepts in Library Management*, edited by Martha Boaz, 83-95. Littleton, Colo.: Libraries Unlimited, 1979.

CHAPTER 7

Duties and Responsibilities in Librarianship

The roles of staff emerge from the institution's mission, goals, and objectives, as well as from the library's articulated program. Their development follows a logical sequence founded on the bipolar character of academic library work. Building on that foundation, administrative and professional staff codetermine what work, and what levels of work, are assigned to the various categories of employees.

ORIGINS OF DUTIES AND RESPONSIBILITIES

Librarians

The work of librarians is governed by the professional paradox, "everything is assigned and nothing is assigned."[1] Another way of looking at it is: professional work is neither assigned nor assumed, but selected through joint negotiation of librarian and administrator. Self-developed duties cannot exclusively reflect the professional's strictly personal interests, but must bear some reasonable congruence with the library's program. Similarly, no library program can be the chief librarian's simple personal preference. Joint agreement emphasizes the professionals' obligation to participate in building the library program and helps ensure that institutional mission, goals, and objectives will be met.[2] Creative and proactive professionals are eager to contribute new ways of implementing approved programs, help the library administration modify existing programs, and invent new ones.

Support Staff, Clerical Staff, and Students

Except perhaps in very small or very large libraries, support staff generally receive their assignments from middle management. A guideline from the University of Minnesota Libraries' Personnel Office is illustrative: "Job descriptions [for support staff] must be communicated vertically so that those above the unit can determine that assigned work is indeed the work necessary to reach the organization's goals."[3] With few exceptions, students' work is wholly assigned. Occasionally, a student is employed to undertake a statistical analysis or write a computer program, but overall, tasks are assigned in detail and procedures are prescribed.

Management's Responsibility to Manage

Beware of claims from classified staff that they have taken on additional responsibilities. Their duties are under the control of the professional staff and the administration. The chief administrative officer of one school made this very clear when, in the course of a budget crisis, he issued the following directive imposing a reclassification freeze on classified staff:

> . . . there is a need to advise departments that managers and supervisors, not employees, are responsible for the assignment of duties and responsibilities to positions. Further, the assignments should be based on the needs of the department and *not* the desires of the employees.

Despite this obvious fact, some library administrators are loath to exercise control when control is needed. Such loss of control over job assignments is highly visible.

A typical sign of weak, ineffective administration is the existence of a "cafeteria approach" to the distribution of duties and responsibilities. Here employees take the figurative serving trays, review duties and responsibilities, and pick and choose work that is to their liking. Self-selection of work can result in rapid upward mobility for long-term employees, while less desirable tasks are sloughed off onto newcomers or less aggressive old-timers. This type of speedy rise derives not from program change or true job development but from employee-initiated job audits. This is administration by default, a failure by management to take responsibility for program implementation.

Aside from the damage to morale, an additional impact of the cafeteria approach is its obvious encouragement of grievances. Whatever great care may have been taken to describe duties and responsibilities accurately goes to waste if management fails to implement them carefully and conscientiously. When legal arguments arise about classification, *it is always the duties actually performed – not the duties described or assigned –* that govern the outcome of a job audit or grievance hearing. The librarian-administrator is misguided indeed who fancies that duties can be distributed willy-nilly to whomever is available to carry them out. (Almost all academic personnel procedures provide for temporary redistribution of various kinds of duties; see the section below on flexibility.)

Use of Percentages to Describe Duties

Allocating percentages of effort to the various components of a person's work helps establish the significance of a responsibility and aids in measuring performance. Deciding on these percentages may be a very reasonable way to allocate the duties of those classified staff whose work is repetitive, but it is hardly appropriate for professionals whose work by definition is neither routine nor clerical, but requires the consistent exercise of independent judgment. The effort applied by professionals varies widely from responsibility to responsibility and from client to client; it cannot be metered by percentages. For certain types of work done by senior support staff, especially if they are exempt, percentages may also be inappropriate.

BUILDING STATEMENTS OF
PROFESSIONAL DUTIES AND RESPONSIBILITIES

Sometimes nonlibrary staff and line officers in the campus administration, rather than the chief librarian, are responsible for the formal personnel actions that culminate in actual hiring.[4] These officers may be bureaucratically oriented and have only the haziest notion of librarianship as an academic career. Hence, it is vital that the chief librarian meticulously review and approve job descriptions and the professional staff's statements of duties and responsibilities before any paperwork on an open position leaves the library.

To minimize mixing up the work of professionals and support staff, managers should ensure that position descriptions for professional staff are free from words that signal nonexempt work, such as "task," "job," "file," and "handle" (which imply physical rather than mental activity), or "procedure," except for contexts that clearly put the professional in charge.[5] It may also be necessary to educate staff about suitable terms. The best all-around expression for describing librarians' work is the simple but comprehensive "professional duties and responsibilities." When preparing position descriptions, detail these responsibilities with strong action verbs reflecting intellectual, supervisorial, or managerial activity. Such recommendations may not be very easy to follow in organizations that are dominated by prescribed civil service terminology. The following examples illustrate the phraseology desirable in position descriptions for professionals.

- Designs and administers college library's program of cataloging; manages three professional and eight support staff (chief cataloger or department head).

- Selects library materials and administers the library materials budget of [give number of dollars] in support of school's graduate program in earth sciences (branch librarian or head of acquisitions).

- Provides bibliographic access for faculty and students to library materials in sixteen western European languages (cataloger).

- Supervises three librarians and three clerical staff in the provision of reference and research assistance to faculty and students; supervises eight student assistants to cover service points when professional staff are off duty (head of reference).

- Administers business staff of bookkeeper and two clerks responsible for prompt, accurate payment of $675,000 annually for books, subscriptions, and other library materials from seventy-five different vendors located in over fifty countries (head of acquisitions).

Generic Duties and Responsibilities of Librarians

Because librarians perform a unique role in the academic community, it is essential to distinguish them clearly from other long-term employees (faculty and support staff). Definitions of the several ranks and specific position descriptions assist in conveying this distinction, but certain duties and responsibilities are universal and apply to every librarian. They form the foundation on which all ranks and all career development rest. If they are included in each librarian's position description, the fully professional aspects of the work receive strong emphasis, pride is enhanced, and the image of librarianship as a predominantly cerebral activity is strengthened. Inclusion of generic duties also reminds librarians that broad involvement in the entire library program is a key professional obligation.

The following generic duties and responsibilities are suggested:

1. An appreciation of academic librarianship as a life of the mind and as work of a high order of intellectual endeavor

2. Recognition and acceptance of the continuing rapid transformation occurring within the profession and within the world of library and information science

3. Acknowledgment of continuing education as a key element in the maintenance of one's capacity for problem solving

4. Acknowledgment that each librarian is accountable for expending the school's resources – personnel, space, equipment, and dollars – in the most efficient and productive manner

5. A commitment to look beyond the local environment to the profession at large, coupled to a corresponding commitment to contribute to and reach out to the profession in a variety of ways, such as publication, professional involvement, and systematic communication with colleagues in other academic libraries

6. The understanding that a librarian is foremost an analyst, designer, organizer, communicator, manager, and problem solver, not a mere operative who carries out only designated duties

7. The understanding of the organic character of the library and the role of professionals as persons who see the library as a totality, accept the institution's mission, goals, and objectives as their own, and work for the benefit of the school as a whole

We include these generic duties in the fundamental performance appraisal criteria for all ranks.

CHIEF AND DEPUTY CHIEF LIBRARIANS: DUTIES AND RESPONSIBILITIES

Chief Librarian

The chief librarian is the institution's program officer and chief executive officer. Because the full responsibility for a program cannot be delegated, it must be shared with the professional staff, but accountability is not shared and remains the chief librarian's. This individual does seek the assistance of many people and many constituencies in forming, revising, and implementing a program, however. Campus superiors (president, chancellor, provost) expect the chief librarian to be not only the architect of the library's program but also its primary advocate.

Normally, the duties and responsibilities are described very broadly, even vaguely. (A detailed listing is so uncommon that a candidate may take one as a warning that the parent institution views the position too narrowly.) The outline in Figure 7-1 might typify the position description for the purpose of explaining it to the staff. It is important to note, however, that in real life, college or university statutes might simply state, in not more than a sentence or two, that the chief librarian is responsible for administering all aspects of the library for the benefit of students and faculty.

Figure 7-1. Typical Position Description for Chief Librarian (for distribution to staff)

The chief executive officer of the Waindell College Library carries the title chief librarian and the rank of Dean. The chief librarian is appointed for an indefinite term and the position carries with it retreat rights to the rank of senior librarian. He or she is responsible for the entire college library program and reports to the Vice President for Academic Affairs. The principal duties include the following (those marked with an asterisk indicate responsibilities that may not be delegated):

- Provides library services for all of Waindell's faculty, students, and employees.

- Represents the library's specific interests on the Council of Deans and also contributes to the council's overall deliberations on the school's academic programs.*

- Represents the library before the academic senate and to all academic department heads.*

- Is ex officio secretary of the Senate Library Committee.*

- Is the voting delegate and the College's official representative to library-related membership bodies, such as the Cooperative Center for College Libraries and the Waverly/Waindell Bibliographic Network.*

- Recruits all professional staff and recommends to the Vice President for Academic Affairs candidates for appointment; recruits clerical and support staff, recommending their appointment to the director of Human Resources; carries out the library's approved performance appraisal program for all staff.

- Prepares and manages the library budget.

- Assists the development office's program to raise funds for library expansion and for the development of other college facilities.

- Within ninety days of the end of each academic year, prepares an analytic and statistical report of the previous year's achievements and a forecast of library prospects over the next five years.

The chief librarian is evaluated by the Vice President for Academic Affairs in consultation with a select committee of deans, faculty members, department heads, and librarians.

Deputy or Acting Chief Librarian

Because administration deals so much with surprises, it is a foregone conclusion that some crisis will erupt when the chief librarian is away. Whether there is a designated office of deputy chief librarian or simply an ad hoc assignment to cope with crises during the chief librarian's absence depends on library size and institutional style. Whoever is put in charge during the chief's absence should preferably be selected on the basis of capacity for prudent, rapid judgment rather than merely seniority or rank. The most senior person might be the least capable of responding creditably in a crisis, or might not even wish to assume the responsibility. Reminding staff several times a year, and on each occasion of the chief's absence, of who is in charge helps to remove uncertainty and prepare staff for coping with emergencies.

Position descriptions for deputy chief librarians are likely to be significantly more detailed than those for the chief. Some of the scope and depth of what might be expected of a deputy in a library of any size is depicted in Figure 7-2. It can easily be modified to accommodate any institution. To provide administrative flexibility, the duties and responsibilities are couched in broad, general terms appropriate to persons bearing senior administrative responsibility. Again, they are detailed in the context of explaining the position to staff, not for developing a posting for recruitment.

Figure 7-2. Typical Position Description for Deputy Librarian (for distribution to staff)

The assistant director (AD) or assistant college librarian (ACL) is a senior member of the college librarian's management team. The duties and responsibilities of ADs/ACLs are in the general areas of planning and daily management, and the administration of programs, budgets, and personnel. The scope of planning responsibility extends from day to day to long range. Positions at this level may be staff, line, or mixed. Areas in which an ACL may be assigned specific, high-level duties and responsibilities include, but are not limited to, administrative and business services, automation, collection development, personnel planning, client services, and support services. Although an individual ACL is the spokesperson for a particular area of responsibility, the sharpest focus of activity is the general welfare of the library as a whole. The ACL contributes to solving librarywide problems through discussion and analysis of broad issues and by viewing the library as a totality.

In each area, the fundamental duty and responsibility of an ACL is to support actively and fully the programs of the library as determined by the college librarian. These programs derive from many sources: the college's mission, goals and objectives; the long-range library plan approved by the president; the regular discussions and decisions of the library administrative council; decisions made by the president, board of governors, or senate; and, in some instances, the college librarian's sole decision. The ACL is expected to apply individual judgment, expertise, and experience in advising the college librarian on library programs; the college librarian must be able to depend upon the advice of the ACL and positive involvement in the decision-making process. Whatever the source or thrust of the program decision, however, support is an inherent requirement of each senior member of the management team.

Beyond the fundamental responsibility of assisting the college librarian lies a range of duties that encompass many different kinds of supportive activities, such as preparing thoroughly researched and well supported, detailed proposals originated by the ACL or assigned by the college librarian; coaching and mentoring unit heads; implementing campus personnel programs for staff development at all levels; applying critical judgment in evaluating professional staff in accordance with established criteria; and actively supporting affirmative action policies and programs;

promoting the goals and objectives of consortia and other cooperative groups to which the school and/or its library is party.

For maximum effectiveness of the library's program, the position of ACL also carries with it an expectation of active participation in major national, state/provincial, regional, school, and professional organizations, or campus committees concerned with librarianship, information processing, administration, and management, or other activity having an immediate and direct bearing upon the ACL's principal duties and responsibilities.

Any ACL may be required to take charge of the library during the college librarian's absence, or to assist temporarily in an area outside normal, day-to-day responsibilities.

The assistant college librarian reports to and is evaluated by the college librarian. A panel consisting of appropriate department heads and one person of corresponding rank from Waindell College Library assists with the evaluation by submitting analysis and recommendations to the college librarian. This is in keeping with other reciprocal arrangements designed to foster Waverly University Library's traditional, close cooperation with Waindell.

DEVELOPING STATEMENTS OF
DUTIES AND RESPONSIBILITIES FOR
SUPPORT STAFF

Dealing with Campus Personnel Offices

Job analysts in colleges and universities generally have little knowledge of the library profession and a fairly limited understanding of the levels of work in an academic library. Campus personnel analysts face several persistent obstacles in distinguishing professional from support work: (1) the invisibility of librarians' real work, (2) the fact that almost all observable, measurable activities are either clerical or have the appearance being so,[7] and (3) lack of a convenient way to distinguish professional from support staff; we have no uniforms that, say in health care, enable one to distinguish a nurse from an orderly.

Ordinary personnel terminology and the variation in labor pools available to postsecondary institutions can also get in the way of understanding appropriate distribution of duties and responsibilities. A chief librarian or library personnel officer may have to educate local personnel analysts on why differences between jobs and positions are so important to the library. A good starting point for discussion is the parallel academic status of librarians and faculty. Since faculty do not generally have job descriptions, neither should librarians. Try to stress the distinction between a profession (faculty model) and a job (industrial model). This must be done without demeaning support staff.

Sometimes the the terminology of work has been inappropriate for so long that the distinctions implicit in different terms have become lost. Other times legislation has put unsuitable terms into place. You might not be able to change the institution's use of words and terms, but you might be able to explain how terminology should be applied appropriately in an academic library.

Coping with Other Ambiguities of Job Descriptions

Control of all duties and responsibilities ultimately rests with the chief librarian. In the terminology of personnel professionals, the basic instrument for systematically delimiting work is usually the job description. Unfortunately, in labor-management parlance this term has two meanings: from the management viewpoint it is a declaration of what management wants an employee to do; from the viewpoint of personnel professionals, especially for job audit purposes, it is an employee's description of duties actually performed. It is far preferable to designate what management wants support staff to do as a job *assignment* rather than a description.

In chapter 3 we pointed out how conventional job analysis usually focuses on visible, measurable activities. Typically, a job or compensation analyst seeks out observable activities to determine what a person is actually doing for the purpose of classifying the position appropriately. This is appropriate for inherently classifiable work, which chiefly involves production and normally has outputs that are consistent and countable in terms of standardized units. Almost everything librarians do in their professional capacity is invisible, however, and while certain aspects of the work are subject to "counting" (e.g., number of reference questions answered or titles cataloged), this aspect of the work is always secondary to its intellectual content. Precisely because librarians' work is mental and intellectual, the description of their duties and responsibilities should not be encumbered with percentage of effort or similar production-related terms that only obfuscate the true character of the profession and cause others to confound librarians and support staff.

Flexibility and Change of Assignment

As positions advance from junior to senior, descriptions of duties and responsibilities should, where possible, be expressed more and more broadly. To accommodate unexpected changes in program or other condition beyond one's control, for example, legislatively mandated budget cuts, it is sound management practice to incorporate into each job a statement authorizing the assignment of appropriate additional duties germane to the library's overall program. Almost all job-classification and pay schemes, as well as collective bargaining contracts for professional and support staff, provide for some kind of flexibility on a temporary basis.[8] Contractual time guidelines must be carefully observed, however, because if an employee's incumbency in one job classification exceeds a designated period, that person may be entitled to move into the different classification permanently. It is equally important not to distribute professional work wholly among support staff in the name of flexibility, as this destroys the inherent duality of academic employment and makes it impossible to defend a position as professional.

Reasonable flexibility provides benefits all around. Management can cope with emergencies and employees acquire the opportunity to develop new skills. The University of California makes liberal use of the word "normally" in detailed descriptions of duties and responsibilities for all levels of staff. Other personnel systems conclude each position or job description with the expression, "and such other duties as may be necessitated by the program." These escape clauses facilitate short- or long-term reassignments and enable essential activities to continue with available staff until a permanent solution is found. Flexibility is of the utmost importance to the future of academic librarianship. The system of scholarly communication is undergoing very rapid development, and our profession must be able to respond as quickly as the academy changes. We can ill afford to be stuck with hard-to-change policies and procedures while the scholarly world around us changes.[9]

Change of assignment can turn into a disagreeable issue. Even in the slow-moving academic environment, programs change, and from time to time it is necessary to restructure staff duties. Just as employees cannot maintain exclusive job ownership, neither can modern management exercise change by fiat. A management decree changing duties and responsibilities without adequate explanation or selling is just as arbitrary as an employee's refusal to accept a new duty. If the library program is truly to be a flexible and cooperative enterprise, administration not only has to sell the idea of change to the staff but must be equally prepared to buy initiatives from the staff. People, especially professionals, may not have total control over their destinies, but they do like to retain reasonable control.

SUMMARY

Formation and publication of statements of employees' duties and responsibilities is a key to excellence and success in administration. Well-articulated statements not only spell out as nearly exactly as possible an institution's expectations, but also establish the employer-employee relationship as a legal contract. A clear, mutual understanding of expectations helps attract top-quality applicants to any institution and is fair to all parties. Unambiguous expectation at the outset of employment means no surprises later. A clear understanding of duties and responsibilities paves the way for successful programs, stimulating staff development, and more readily accepted performance appraisal systems. Clear distinctions between professional and support work contribute to easing the tensions caused by employment duality, an inherent characteristic of the academic library.

Notes

1. For this epigram, I am indebted to Ernest B. Ingles, University Librarian, University of Regina.

2. The responsibility of codetermination explains why professionals cannot be treated as operatives who merely carry out specifically assigned duties and responsibilities.

3. B. Doyle and G. Caldwell, "Guide to Performance Appraisal for Civil Service Employees," revised 17 March 1987 (Minneapolis: University of Minnesota Libraries Personnel Office, 1987), 3-4.

4. Appointing and hiring authority varies widely among institutions and, as often as not, even the chief librarian makes only a hiring recommendation to a higher authority, such as a provost or academic vice president. Another person, such as an Affirmative Action officer, may hold veto power.

5. In medium-size and large libraries, senior classified staff may also manage a cadre of lower-level classified staff and may even be exempt. In no case will these managers have programmatic responsibilities.

6. A somewhat different but complementary approach to the concept of generic duties may be found in José-Marie Griffiths and Donald W. King's *New Directions in Library and Information Science Education* (White Plains, N.Y.: Knowledge Industry Publications, 1986), 72-75.

7. The one tangible, vital output of professional work is the collection, but personnel analysts do not normally appreciate this product and are hardly in a position to evaluate it.

8. In a collective bargaining environment flexibility is generally lost or weakened. Unions try to minimize management flexibility by eliminating or watering down contract clauses that broaden the assignability of work.

9. The information industry is already making strong inroads on library services by promoting end-user searching and selling or leasing specialized databases on compact discs direct to scholars and/or academic departments.

Resources

Creth, Sheila, and Frederick Duda. *Personnel Administration in Libraries*. 2d ed. New York: Neal-Schuman, 1989.

Griffiths, José-Marie, and Donald W. King. *New Directions in Library and Information Science Education*. White Plains, N.Y.: Knowledge Industry Publications, 1986.

Ontario Association of Library Technicians. *Library Technician: Your First Choice*. Oakville, Ontario, 1982.

Ozaki, Hiroko. "The Role of Professional and Non-Professional Staff in Libraries, with an Emphasis on the Division of Their Duties in the Cataloging Unit: A Select Bibliography." Ottawa: National Library of Canada, Library Documentation Centre, July 1981.

"Promotion Review Program for Librarians, 1988/89." New Haven, Conn.: Yale University, 1987.

Reid, Marion T., and Walter M. High. "The Role of the Professional in Technical Services." *RTSD Newsletter* 11, no. 6 (1986): 58-60.

Stewart, Phyllis L., and Muriel G. Cantor, eds. *Varieties of Work*. New York: Sage, 1982.

Veaner, Allen B. "Continuity or Discontinuity–A Persistent Personnel Issue in Academic Librarianship." *Advances in Library Administration and Organization* 1 (1982): 1-20.

_____. "Librarians–The Next Generation." *Library Journal* 109, no. 6 (1 April 1984): 623-25.

CHAPTER 8

Recruitment

THE CENTRALITY OF PERSONNEL

The worn aphorism by Thomas Carlyle, "The true university of these days is a collection of books," was probably not true in its own day and is deplorably far from accurate as we approach the twenty-first century. When Carlyle coined it in 1841, he succeeded admirably in creating a catchy phrase, as was his wont, but the expression merely reflected his own intellectual development, founded largely on self-education from omnivorous reading.

As an aid to persuading wealthy donors to endow book funds, the adage has served librarianship well. But by placing an undue emphasis on physical objects, Carlyle may even have done some measurable harm to the development of our profession. He also said, "The history of the world is but the biography of great men," and in those words (overlooking the sexist language of his day) he may have been closer to the mark, for he was stating what modern administrators know very well: the quality of personnel, whether faculty, students, or librarians, is of much greater significance to a college or university than any collection of books or assembly of buildings. Today one might well say, "The true university these days is a gathering of top-rate faculty, highly intelligent students, and first-rate librarians."

The library director faces no greater challenge or responsibility than the identifying and recruiting of the best new people. This includes not only employing staff for current needs but also encouraging top students to enter the profession. A second-level responsibility is continually to enhance the development of further excellence within the already excellent. A third is to help motivate weak performers to acceptable levels. Fourth, and hardly less important, is the duty to slough off chronic nonperformers. Paradoxically, it is not the chief librarian's responsibility to strive for the permanent retention of the excellent. These individuals should always be encouraged to recognize their capabilities and achieve as much as they can, in the same institution or elsewhere.

FACING THE COMPETITION FOR EXCELLENCE

The economic and social changes outlined in chapter 1 have wrought colossal changes in the availability of the best possible employees. In addition, librarianship does not have the appeal it once did. Largely gone is the notion that people enter the profession solely out of ideals of public service. Top recruits in all professions now look beyond service. They seek work that will allow them to earn the livelihood highly educated people have come to expect and deserve. They also want to achieve more than a modicum of recognition. Many aggressive, energetic, and capable young people who are interested in the field can now realize their goals outside of academe, working for bibliographic utilities, book vendors, subscription agencies, or professional associations. Others, after completing graduate education find well-paid, challenging work organizing information in commerce: banks, real estate, software houses, data processing, and telecommunication.

It is imperative that academic library administrators recognize this competition and think creatively about recruiting. To attract the best candidates requires close contact with the graduate library schools, innovative approaches to salary negotiation, top-rate professional development opportunities, and even novel (for libraries) start-up packages, such as making available computerized work stations or database search budgets for new recruits. (As well, the chief librarian will have to provide similar amenities for incumbent staff who must not be disadvantaged for the sake of the newcomers.) Meeting the competition also means that academic librarians must develop and apply political skills of the highest order within the upper echelons of campus administration. Despite their appreciation of the problems of recruiting faculty, presidents, chancellors, and provosts have little experience in or knowledge of external competition in librarianship. They, like campus personnel officers, have to be convinced of its reality.

LEGAL BASIS OF
THE EMPLOYER-EMPLOYEE RELATIONSHIP

A foundation of justice in Western society is due process of law – the fundamental principle that no one's property can be arbitrarily diminished or taken away. Western tradition has recognized three kinds of property: (1) land (real estate), (2) personal belongings (tools, furnishings), and (3) intangible property (copyrights, patents). Since most work has already been transformed from actual physical labor into some form of knowledge management, Drucker argued that work itself has now become a fourth type of property, enjoying all the protection afforded to the other three.[1]

In this context, every administrator is both a de facto and a de jure actor in a legal drama that is played out every hour of every day in the workplace. This drama is a series of concurrent "performances," one for each employee. Due process, discussed in somewhat greater specificity in chapter 10, is a vital element of the drama. Just as professional theater demands honesty and conviction, sound administrative practices and procedures in the academic library require scrupulous adherence to due process. Because the legal basis of the employer-employee relationship begins with recruiting, much of what we discuss here, especially due process, applies throughout the duration of employment, and even beyond into retirement years.

The time is long past when personnel actions, especially hiring and termination, could be carried out casually, in accordance with the perceptions or whims of those involved. Within one generation the employer-employee relationship has changed from virtual employment-at-will to long-term relationships defined by contract and law.[2] The majority of personnel-related actions are governed by federal, state, or provincial legislation, and new laws crop up constantly. One is the 1986 United States Immigration Reform and Control Act (IRCA), which affects the employability of undocumented aliens and imposes verification responsibilities on employers.[3] Canada has regulated the employment of foreign workers for a long time through its Immigration Act and Regulations. Only Canadian citizens, permanent residents (landed immigrants), and persons who have obtained written authority from the Canada Employment and Immigration Commission are entitled to work in that country.[4]

The legal aspects of the employer-employee relationship are complex; dependence on experts is an absolute necessity. The campus personnel office takes care of much of the technical detail: codifying local practice in a personnel handbook, issuing bulletins and updates as laws and interpretations change, and convening meetings to alert managers of special problems or new conditions. A dependable, friendly relationship with the head of the office is an investment that will repay the chief librarian's time and energy many times over. The library administrator also can benefit from a good general knowledge of the legal basis for every major personnel action. For the United States, Yates's *Labor Law Handbook* and Hood and Hardy's *Workers' Compensation and Employee Protection Laws in a Nutshell* are excellent guides.[5]

Anything printed in a vacancy listing, policy and procedure manual, employee handbook, or application form (and even oral assurances about benefits and terms and conditions of employment) can be construed as an element of an employer-employee contract. Hence a first rule of administration is *never* to publish any personnel-related document that has not been reviewed and approved by the appropriate officer.[6] Obviously, this includes job and position postings and any library-specific personnel handbook, as well as in-house employment regulations. A second rule is that *only one* library officer should be empowered to make an offer and detail the terms and conditions of employment.

Finally, in the United States, public and private employment are clearly distinguished. Public employment is regulated by the Constitution, state and federal laws, civil service regulations, or municipal ordinances. Private employment is governed both by contracts and by applicable federal and state laws. Collective bargaining contracts may apply to either type of employment. In collective bargaining, an important distinction governs labor relations in publicly financed and privately supported institutions: state and local legislations apply to the public sector, while federal law applies to the private. Many states have laws similar to the National Labor Relations Act. More than half the states permit their public employees to bargain for wages, hours, and working conditions.[7]

Information Sources on Employment Law

In addition to the legislative record itself, several publications and database services are designed to help personnel units in educational institutions keep up with current laws and regulations.

The monthly *Management Law Newsletter* summarizes court decisions pertinent to employment and includes in each issue an appendix listing pertinent federal legislation. Of the five service publications in Commerce Clearing House's *Human Resources Management* series, *Equal Employment Opportunity* summarizes pertinent United States law and regulations. *Library Personnel News*, a quarterly publication begun in 1987 by ALA's Office for Library Personnel Resources, extensively covers major U.S. legislation affecting employment in all types of libraries. *Work-Related Abstracts (WRA)* covers current and recent historical information on the development of the labor movement in various kinds of libraries in both the United States and Canada. It is interesting to note that from 1954 through 1964 *WRA* contained no entries pertinent to libraries of any kind. From 1965 to 1970 there were one or two entries per year. In 1971 there were seven entries and by 1973 twenty-two. A new subject heading, "Librarian Unionization," was introduced in 1972.

Several organizations sponsor online information systems in labor law. The Bureau of National Affairs supports *Employment*

Guide Data Base. This service summarizes and analyzes the significance of current issues, suggests practical pointers, provides information needed for policy formulation, and in many cases, includes a sample policy statement that can be used verbatim or adapted to a specific local situation. The Bureau of National Affairs also maintains LABORLAW, an online database available through DIALOG (file no. 244); LABORLAW's coverage includes National Labor Relations Board (NLRB) decisions from 1967 on, arbitration settlement detail since 1969, Fair Employment Practice decisions from 1938, and many others. Executive Telecom System, Inc., maintains the *Human Resource Information Network (HRIN)*, covering comparisons of state laws on unemployment benefits, minimum wages, worker's compensation, temporary liability, compensation, garnishment, pay equity and comparable worth, hazards in the workplace, and child care issues. Source data are prepared by the Bureau of National Affairs, Inc., the U.S. Department of Labor, the U.S. Department of Health and Human Services, and other private and public agencies.

United States Labor Legislation

United States legislation governing contemporary employer-employee relationships goes back more than half a century, and civil rights legislation over a century. Table 8-1 highlights federal legislation, presidential orders, and court decisions applicable to employment.

Table 8-1. Overview of Decisions Affecting Employment

Year	Act
1866, 1871	Civil Rights Acts (42 USC Sections 1981, 1982, 1983, 1985).
1935	National Labor Relations Act limits employer's ability to discharge and discipline employees for union activity; establishes National Labor Relations Board to oversee collective bargaining regulations and adjudicate complaints of unfair labor practices; law applies to citizens and aliens alike, even if the latter are illegal immigrants.

1938	Fair Labor Standards Act (29 USC, Section 201 et seq.) establishes minimum wage, forty-hour week.
1939	First publication of *Dictionary of Occupational Titles*.
1963	Equal Pay Act (29 USC, Section 206(d), amends Fair Labor Standards Act to provide equal pay for equal work, regardless of sex.
1964	Civil Rights Act (42 USC, Section 2000d et seq.). Establishes Equal Employment Opportunity Commission to enforce Title VII. Prohibits discrimination based on race, sex, religion, or national origin.
1965	Executive Orders 11246 establish Affirmative Action; Executive Order 11375 amends.
1967	Age Discrimination in Employment Act (29 USC, Section 621 et seq.) protects rights of workers between ages 40 and 65 years in collective bargaining and employment agency referrals.
1970	Occupational Safety & Health Act (29 USC, Section 651 et seq.) requires employers to provide a safe working environment.[9]
	NLRB jurisdiction extended to private educational institutions.
1971	U.S. Supreme Court decision in *Griggs v. Duke Power* (401 U.S. 424 (1971)) rules out certain qualifications and tests as conditions of employment.
1973	Vocational Rehabilitation Act (29 USC, Sections 504, 701 et seq.) requires employers to establish Affirmative Action programs for the disabled; bars discrimination against handicapped and, since a court ruling in 1987, bars hiring discrimination against victims of AIDS.
	Executive Order 11758 applies the Rehabilitation Act to government contractors.

1974	Employee Retirement Income Security Act (ERISA) (20 USC, Sections 1140-1381) prohibits employers from discharging employees for the purpose of interfering with their rights to claim employee benefits; safeguards employee retirement and pension benefits; sets legal minimums on pension terms; supersedes all state laws on pensions.
1974	Federal Privacy Act (5 USC, Section 522a) limits data about individuals that government can disclose to employers.
1975	Age Discrimination Act of 1975 (42 USC, Section 6101 et seq.) prohibits age discrimination regardless of age in programs or activities receiving federal financial assistance.
1978	Mandatory Retirement Act (29 USC 631(a)).
1978	Pregnancy Discrimination Act (42 USC, 2000e(k)) forbids employers from refusing to hire pregnant women, firing those already pregnant, or forcing maternity leave.
1985	End of employment-at-will doctrine.
1986	Immigration Reform and Control Act (IRCA) (29 USC 274A) requires documentation to establish eligibility for employment and imposes verification requirements on employers.
1986	Fair Labor Standards Act, revised as PL 99-150 to cover most nonexempt state and local employees. (1986 changes dealt with compensatory time and overtime).
1987	Age Discrimination in Employment Act (PL 99-592) eliminates mandatory retirement at age 70.[10]
1988	Civil Rights Restoration Act, restores institution-wide antidiscrimination laws at schools receiving federal support under other civil rights legislation.

Canadian Labor Legislation

Although Canadian labor legislation[11] has its roots in the American Wagner Act of 1935, the two countries have developed quite different approaches to dealing with labor disputes. Both American and Canadian librarians must understand that the labor scene in the two countries differs significantly; laws and approaches to labor conditions and disputes cannot be used interchangeably. Therefore, librarians should note very carefully the source of their information and restrict its use to that specific country.

Canada has eleven different labor jurisdictions: one federal and ten provincial. For academic librarians in Ontario, the legal basis of the employer-employee relationship could fall under one of three labor acts: Federal Labour Code, Ontario Provincial Labour Relations Act, or Colleges Collective Bargaining Act. A major difference among these acts concerns whether employees have the right to strike. While in the United States most disputes are decided at the national rather than at the state level, in Canada the opposite occurs: 90 percent are determined at the provincial level.

Although labor legislation differs from province to province, arbitration rulings tend to be uniform and based on the same guiding principles. This phenomenon could be the result of the way arbitration cases are reported in Canada. The three major sources for reports and analyses of arbitration cases are: Brown and Beatty's *Canadian Labour Arbitration*,[12] Palmer's *Collective Agreement Arbitration in Canada*,[13] and Lancaster House's loose-leaf service publications.[14]

Canadian national legislation is summarized in Labour Canada's *Labour Standards in Canada*. Basic legislation affecting employer-employee relationships includes (1) the Canadian Human Rights Act, enacted in 1978, a federal law prohibiting hiring and wage discrimination based on race, religion, age, sex, marital status, disability, and other factors; and (2) the Canadian Charter of Rights and Freedoms, a federal grant of fundamental rights to citizens (incorporated in the Canadian constitution in 1982). The provinces also issue handbooks pertinent to provincial labor legislation, such as Ontario's Employment Standards Act.[15]

Volunteer and Casual Employees

A special circumstance is the volunteer. Interested laypersons, faculty spouses, retirees, and others in the community can help cope with peak loads or seasonal work that must be done even though normal labor sources have temporarily dried up. Reading the stacks and pulling books for reserve are good tasks for them. Well-educated volunteers, however, may have little or no concept of the complexity of academic librarianship and could be put off if offered menial assignments.

The greatest disadvantage of volunteers is the difficulty of scheduling them – they can be even less dependable than students at their worst. A second difficulty is endurance: volunteers sometimes do not recognize how tiring it can be to handle books for many hours. They may decide to quit shortly after you have already spent time and money to train them. A third problem relates to performance appraisal; having to get rid of a volunteer makes for poor public relations. It is best to use these people for work that is not too demanding physically, does not have tight deadlines, or does not damage the program if for any reason the project must cease.

A few other cautions should be observed before taking on what looks like free labor. Check with the school's counsel to see whether volunteers are covered by liability insurance and whether signed waivers have any legal validity. Ask the personnel department to determine whether after some years of service or a certain total number of hours worked, a volunteer is suddenly transformed into a permanent part-time employee with all the rights and privileges of that status. Such a transformation can occur within certain legislative contexts or institutional regulations.

Retired librarians paid on a casual or hourly basis can sometimes make extraordinary contributions to a library program, for example, cataloging special materials, like rare books or government documents, or processing arrears that have been around too long. Retirees from other libraries are particularly attractive. They have few social ties to the informal organization and are not jockeying for advancement. Consequently, they are likely to spend most of their time working productively.

FINDING THE BEST POSSIBLE EMPLOYEES

Attracting first-rate people to librarianship has long been recognized as a problem of broad scope throughout North America, and it affects all specialities within the profession. Library educators have long struggled with this problem. Under the auspices of a 1987 World Book/ALA Goal Award, the ALA Office for Library Personnel Resources convened an invitational conference in July 1988 to attempt an integrated approach.[16] In a conference paper devoted specifically to recruiting academic librarians, Phyllis Hudson concluded that academic librarians, both past and present, have not been very active in formal recruitment programs.[17] In her plea for better salaries and improved working conditions, Hudson put her finger on a key issue: the need to do the right political groundwork with faculty and administration, a point I make repeatedly in connection with success in any aspect of program.

In a paper prepared the previous year, Kathleen Heim argued that curriculum redesign is a necessary precondition for altering the fact that "the brightest and the best are not [in 1987] selecting librarianship" for their careers.[18]

In 1979 Taylor urged that educators and administrators change the profession by changing the kinds of people that are recruited into it:

> Instead of letting students be self-selected on a past image of libraries, we should be looking for students who are both literate and numerate, who already have a background in information technologies, economics, and research methods, and are bright, self-assured, and articulate. They are graduating from under-graduate schools, but they are not pounding on the doors of schools of librarianship. They are not seeking admission because the profession is institution-based and therefore has not begun to realize its full potential.[19]

The schools recognize their responsibility at both ends of the selection process. Stueart argued forcefully that it is important not just to identify those who should be in the profession, but also to mark those who should not, and be certain they are not admitted.[20]

In a critique of library school admission standards, Yerburgh expressed similar views:

Potential lawyers, doctors, dentists, and business administrators face much stiffer [graduate school] entrance requirements than librarians. If we're to be a truly respected (not merely respectable) profession, we must take rigorous steps to encourage the best and discourage the rest. It would be much healthier to have high standards and a shortage of librarians than to have feeble standards and a surplus.

In any event we need smaller numbers of better prepared practitioners.[21]

In the late 1950s Lyle denounced the practice of "using library posts as a dumping ground for ineffectual teachers, dependents of deceased professors, and the neurotic or frustrated."[22] We may be grateful to the beneficial bureaucracy of open recruiting for the fact that these practices have virtually disappeared.

PROBLEMS IN RECRUITING

Few things cause more anxiety in an office than hiring new or replacement staff. Budget crises come and go, but personnel may stay on. The of rank-and-file employees form a much more rigid and demanding social environment than does the company of library administrators, and they exert far greater influence on successful recruiting and librarian achievement than most of us would care to admit. They shrewdly examine every prospective addition to the staff: Will this person fit into our daily lives? What advantages does the candidate bring? What threats? Can we all get along? Will this candidate upset our equilibrium? Many other unarticulated (but real) questions are asked in subtle ways but bear little relationship to position postings and still less to mission, goals, and objectives.

Preferences for Mediocrity

Despite openly professed beliefs to the contrary, incumbent staff generally prefer mediocrity over excellence in candidates. It is much less threatening. If the search panel and interviewers gang up on a candidate, chances are the applicant is either a very poor bet or is tremendously outstanding.

Excessive Focus on Technical Ability

Transformation of the modern academic library into a new kind of institution demands new and different recruiting criteria from those of the past. The decline of departmentation, the rise of new, interactive, and more collegial management styles, the growing complexity of library and information science, and keen intrainstitutional competition for support make it evident that mere technical knowledge can no longer be a prime factor in employee selection.

Bureaucracy of Campus Personnel Office

In chapter 7 we mentioned factors limiting personnel professionals' perceptions of library work. Personnel offices on every campus are bureaucratic establishments in their own right.[23] Most of their methods are derived from business and industry; sometimes their leadership is drawn from people who have moved from business or the military into academe. Except for helping fulfill the requirements of Affirmative Action and Equal Employment Opportunity, and entering new employees onto the payroll, the personnel office's bureaucratic activity generally has little or nothing to do with recruiting faculty or librarians.

Sometimes ill-informed or prejudiced staff in campus personnel offices look on the library as the local rehabilitation center. They see it as a "calm and relaxing" backwater in the maelstrom of work. Good relationships with the campus personnel office can help assure that its staff understands the enormous stress levels in library work and the cyclical character of certain types of work, such as processing reserve books. Other problems arise from the office's mistaken notions about the simplicity of library work. Well-intentioned interviewers sometimes think the library is a great place to send trainees who can barely read or who cannot handle even the simplest arithmetic accurately.

Unsound Mental Health

Employees who are emotionally unstable or mentally ill can consume an incredibly disproportionate share of administrative time, try the patience of colleagues, and ultimately damage the library's capacity to implement its programs. But only professional medical personnel can designate the condition of a person's mental health. While librarians' amateur judgments in this sensitive area may largely be dismissed as prejudice, it is unavoidable that interviewers will generate opinions even though the risk of misjudgment is high. No methodology can rule out such applicants, and the inclusion of mental health experts on a search panel would surely empty the applicant pool instantly. Rather than venturing into a technical area where they are sure to be incompetent, interviewing librarians should focus sharply on a position's mandatory requirements and concentrate especially on interpersonal skills. The senior members of a search panel are generally seasoned professionals with dependable skills who can readily distinguish the truly capable applicants.

Motivation

It would be convenient if employees' motivation could always be congruent with management's desires, but that does not happen in the real world. If employees are unmotivated it is generally the fault of management. Managers who complain about uninspired workers are admitting that they have been unable to convince the employees to direct their energies toward fulfilling institutional goals. Lack of motivation suggests that managers fail to give challenging assignments, or do not take full advantage of the collegial, consultative aspect of academic life. They may be holding professionals on too short a tether, being too prescriptive or subjecting professional work to excessive revision.[24]

DEVELOPING STAFF-SELECTION CRITERIA

As this is not a recruiting handbook, I will not attempt an exhaustive inventory of staff selection criteria but highlight a few of the key concerns in what is at best a generally imprecise process.

Education

Despite continuing challenges, the graduate library degree (master of library science, MLS) is now regarded as an indisputable prerequisite for work in an academic library.[25] A broad liberal arts background in addition to the MLS is almost universally preferred. Certain specialized positions are demanding a second master's or doctoral degree. In connection with the MLS requirement, most institutions incorporate the word "normally" in the wording of vacancy listings to provide equal opportunity for otherwise well-qualified applicants. Blind adherence to credentials is bureaucracy at its worst and ultimately damages the profession. A flexible attitude toward educational requirements can bring in very desirable candidates who might otherwise be disqualified.[26]

Grades and Academic Achievement as Selection Criteria

The lay stereotype portrays a librarian as a person whose head is stuffed with facts, or who "likes to read." Our own stereotype holds that we work with highly complex rules and procedures. Facts can be looked up or remembered, however; rules and procedures can be documented systematically for any literate, intelligent person to apply.

We compound stereotypes when we learn in graduate school that two centuries ago Samuel Johnson divided knowledge into two kinds – personal mastery of a subject and knowing where to find information on it. Johnson overlooked a third, more important kind: knowledge as the mastery of methodology, the *how* of finding out. A fourth and still more valuable type of knowledge, perhaps less obvious in Johnson's simpler days, is how to organize and manage information for efficient retrieval and, most important, how to retrieve information even when it has not been well organized. It is the how of knowledge, not facts or procedures, that establishes the value of librarians to society. As mentioned in chapter 3, librarians' true knowledge is process knowledge – that combination of natural intelligence and problem-solving capacity that marks the worth of top professionals.

While no intelligent person denigrates the role of academic achievement, it is universally acknowledged that high grades do not necessarily correlate with a capacity for excellence in the workplace, especially in administration.[27] High grades alone do not now and probably never did suffice for real success in librarianship. If socialized to set the PhD as their ultimate goal, high achievers at the undergraduate level tend to remove themselves further and further from the realities of everyday work, possibly making themselves decreasingly suitable for administration. What is needed for all positions in modern librarianship is a combination of high intelligence, academic excellence, and outstanding human relations skills. Effective library administrators build on this base, add the requisite managerial skills, and exercise caution about elevated credentials.

Flexibility

Because of the historic centrality of cataloging and its requirement of close attention to detail, librarianship has sometimes been characterized as a rule-bound profession whose members lack flexibility. While rigidity may apply to certain persons, it surely does not hold for the profession at large. Indeed, the responsiveness of librarianship as a whole to radical change in computerized data management is remarkable in comparison with that of commercial enterprises. Sometimes catalogers are unjustly singled out negatively for their interest in ruly procedures and algorithmic processes. But the processes of librarianship closely parallel those of legal practice, and lawyers rarely find themselves accused of inflexibility or lack of imagination.[28]

Hiring personnel from widely varying economic backgrounds and geographic areas may promote flexibility. At least expanding the demographic base of employment helps to ensure that staff does not become too ingrown. Even turnover, if not excessive, has a positive impact.[29]

Risk-Taking

Risk-takers are internalizers, having a strong need to maintain the locus of control within themselves. They see their lives as under their own control, not determined by fate or luck. A centuries-long tradition of conservatism and perfectionism in bibliographic affairs, fear of failure, lack of opportunity or motivation for entrepreneurial activity, lack of funds, plus a history of discouragement by management have contributed to risk-aversiveness among librarians. Wilding of MIT commented:

> Librarians have not been particularly good at this [risk-taking] in the past and they are not taught how to take risks in their educational programs. We have not been encouraged to take them and we are not good at evaluating risk. When is the risk worth the consequence of being wrong?[30]

Operating inside an institution dedicated to the continuity and connectedness of knowledge, we have always sought people willing to work within very close financial and structural constraints. Some employees hired under this philosophy remain positively terrified of risk and uncertainty. Traditional administrators have preferred personality types who sought safety, structure, and predictability, features readily found in higher education. For two reasons, however, it is becoming easier to find risk takers. First, the profession's increased awareness is making graduate schools, library administrators, and library personnel officers more sensitive to and positive toward this characteristic in applicants. Second is simple availability: many young persons reflect the radically different outlook of the baby-boomer generation. More accepting of disorder and randomness, they are not so put off by risk.

Risk-takers require support, however, both administrative and financial, for experimentation; in recruiting we should be prepared to offer that support. We should make it clear to applicants what we mean by risk: neither disruption nor destruction, but constructive experimentation and innovation coupled to continuity with half a millennium of librarianship.

Capacity for and Interest in Administration

Research indicates that part of the reason for Lowell Martin's claim that librarians do not seem to be administration minded may lie within the psyches of library school alumni: they have not perceived their career paths as involving administration.[31] Related to this aspect is the fact that so much of the profession's actual work deals with precision, orderliness, and elaborate structure: implementing complex cataloging and classification rules, maintaining a precise arrangement of collections, obtaining accurate and exact information for clients, creating and maintaining databases, devising carefully constructed search strategies, administering different circulation rules for different users, coping with employment duality, and the like. Librarianship's traditions as a ruly profession, and its preoccupation with dependability and stability make it especially susceptible to mechanistic administrative styles and attractive to people who dislike ambiguity. In developing its own managerial and administrative personnel for the twenty-first century, the profession must deal with this inherent conflict between rigidity and flexibility far more effectively than it has in the past. It must attract a different type of student and the hiring institutions must seek candidates who welcome the challenges of administration and management and who are not afraid of uncertainty.

Experience versus Stability

Because experience plays various paradoxical roles, it can rarely be assessed at face value. It is desirable in some assignments, indispensable in others, and not required at all for entry-level positions. A long career history at one institution might mean an employee who is not especially creative. The comparatively inexperienced person could be the most energetic and imaginative. Have the years of applicable experience been in one position, or has an applicant filled a variety of responsibilities? Could loyalty mean laziness, or could it also mean that employees stay on because they are constantly challenged and constantly responding with new ideas? What is the significance of a lot of job switching? Is it better to take people who are short on commitment and long on talent? There can be no fixed answers to these questions.

Ability to Communicate with Accuracy and Tact

Writing quality among librarians varies enormously. Despite the fact that the very essence of academic librarianship is communication, startlingly large numbers of persons in the field have difficulty writing coherent, articulate prose. Some of these people are totally unaware of this deficiency. Submissions from staff frequently need considerable reworking before they can be passed on to others or incorporated into proposals and reports. In a large library, one might have an editor, secretary, or other officer to do this; in the smaller institution the chief librarian obviously has to be the editor.

Recruiting is a superb opportunity to look for applicants who can speak and write with precision and care. Both resumes and cover letters can be very revealing. It helps if each vacancy listing requires applicants to prove their communication abilities, oral and written, in language appropriate to the requirements of the position.

Technologists have often unjustly criticized library professionals as people unable to cope with technology because their life experiences have focused almost exclusively on the humanities and social sciences. The facts are otherwise: capable librarians, even some without advanced education in mathematics and engineering, have responded to the challenge of technology far more enthusiastically than many professionals in business and industry.

A capacity for fluent, tactful oral communication is indispensable in every branch of modern librarianship owing to the tremendous spread of status and power in the environment. Every employee is a front line representative of the library's public relations stance. Rude or brusque behavior to faculty, students, fellow staff, and other members of the community simply cannot be tolerated. Because no administration can afford to permit staff to damage the library's service image, the search for a consistently patient and tactful attitude among applicants forms an important part of the search panel's research and line of questioning.

Technical Knowledge and Competence

The notion that in hiring a librarian we are acquiring a kind of bibliographic mechanic and therefore require competence is surely a misplaced idea, as both White and I have suggested.[32] Developing a list of competencies that applicants must possess is not only a waste of time but also an insult to the profession. Such a list may be appropriate for support staff, implying as it does that there are certain fixed procedures, tasks, or jobs to do. Anyone can make up a list of competencies with full assurance that within a few months at most its contents will be obsolete. In the 1960s technical knowledge of library science and bibliography was probably the key criterion in selecting a librarian, just as typing ability might have been for hiring a secretary. As stated above, the profession has changed so radically that pure technical knowledge is no longer the overriding consideration it once was.

Reliance on competence reflects three obsolete ideas: (1) that a librarian has to be productive on the job virtually from the first day, (2) that technical knowledge is the prime qualification for appointment and (3) that seasoned professionals are less capable than beginners of acquiring new knowledge. In contemporary practice we hire librarians and other professionals more for their potential than for any initial capacity to produce. We hire them for their interpersonal skills and for their problem-solving capacities. It is worth repeating what we stated in chapter 3: we hire librarians not to do a job but to be and become a certain kind of person, a criterion that has very little to do with competence.

Regardless of technical knowledge, it may take up to a year for any librarian to learn enough about a school's programs, people, collections, and curriculum even to begin being creative. This is not to suggest that technical knowledge is unimportant, only that a candidate's human relations and learning skills are so important that accumulated technical knowledge takes a back seat. Long ago library schools could impart almost everything a librarian needed to know. Today, they can only hope to convey the rudiments of professional knowledge. Far more important is their capacity to recruit bright, open-minded students and teach them a philosophy of librarianship beyond mere technicalities.

Capacity to Deal with Quantification

While not every position requires knowledge of numerical and statistical methods, the growing complexity of academic librarianship increasingly demands this talent: work with database design, in-house microcomputer and minicomputer systems, the design of circulation systems and local area networks (LANs), the need to forecast workloads and transaction volumes based on probabilities and queueing theory, budget analyses, and the capacity to interact effectively with clients who apply mathematical skills to their problems. Inability to work with mathematical methods means defaulting many responsibilities to experts in other areas and ultimately implies the decline of the profession.

Specialists versus Generalists

The principle that generalists survive better than specialists is not universal but situational. Academic librarianship has to deal with the entire universe of knowledge, so to that extent, at least, the libraries of many graduate institutions must employ specialists. No reasonable person expects the chemistry librarian to take over collection development responsibility for English literature in a trice, but we do expect that librarians with graduate professional education have the capacity to apply general professional principles to a wide variety of challenges. For this reason applicants with broad liberal arts backgrounds are certainly better choices for nonspecialist positions than those whose education is solely technical or narrowly vocational. Experienced academic library administrators value the generalist, knowing that it is much easier to orient professionals with a liberal arts background to science than the reverse.

DEVELOPING POSITION DESCRIPTIONS

Developing a position description is an excellent means of building collegial spirit. Every vacancy provides an opportunity for administration and professional staff to take a fresh look at the current program, and especially to examine the previous incumbent's impact on the position. A select committee might look critically at the program and then compose draft vacancy postings for all exempt positions, even reviewing listings for highly responsible nonexempt jobs. This committee could serve as the search panel, or a separate body could be appointed. Developing the criteria gives panel members a superb opportunity to reexamine mission, goals, and objectives, distance themselves a bit from the immediate concerns of day-to-day responsibilities, and see how a position fits into the library gestalt.

Exit interviews are valuable tools for the search panel's review and understanding of a position. If a panel cannot be convened quickly enough to interview the departing employee, at least the chief librarian or personnel officer should talk to the person and record information for the position review. Were there enough of the proper type of resources at hand to do the work well? Did the supervisor have troublesome shortcomings? An employee who is not eager to talk while actively employed may, on departing, suddenly become voluble. Those who are reluctant to detail problems may be willing to talk a few months later.

While every replacement of a departing employee invites examination of the program, a more serious opportunity for review comes with the decision to create a new position. By definition a new position implies some substantially different focus. To emphasize the total professional responsibility for program, thorough and open collegial discussion should precede establishment of any new position. If a post is to be created from existing slots, wide consultation with staff at all levels is in order. Bidding for a new, separately funded position nearly always involves convincing the campus administration to put up the resources, in addition to convincing the staff at large of its need.

The chief librarian works closely with the search panel, further enhancing internal communication. The library personnel officer, if any, is usually staff to the panel, advising on technical details, such as making sure that postings for support staff state explicitly that the job is nonexempt.[33] The chief librarian reviews draft postings; if approved, they are forwarded to the affirmative action officer and others for further review before publication.

SAMPLE SELECTION CRITERIA

Selection criteria are usually a mix of mandatory and desirable requirements determined to constitute bona fide occupational qualifications (BFOQ) and complying with the *Uniform Guidelines on Employee Selection Procedures* established by the Equal Employment Opportunity Commission (EEOC).[34] Institutions, programs, and work requirements vary so widely that it is impossible to prescribe criteria common to all jobs and positions; however, an expectation of high performance ought to be built into every posting. As illustrations, we include a few examples of qualifications extracted from recent librarian postings.

1. For preservation officer: Demonstrated ability as a manager including strong communication skills, both written and oral, ability to conceptualize and organize programs, develop and direct staff, plan and monitor budgets. Ability to market statewide preservation programs and work effectively with many agencies in running the program. Success in teaching and/or training activity. Sound knowledge of preservation activities and issues desired, and/or strong background in collection development and management.

2. For a serials cataloger: Good interpersonal communication skills; aptitude for precision work and independent problem solving; ability to work effectively in a rapidly changing environment as a member of a professional team.

3. For head of an undergraduate library: Managerial experience in an academic library with demonstrated success in the areas of budgeting, planning, and staff supervision. Successful collection development and management experience. Knowledge and experience with library automation and microcomputers. A good grasp of national issues and trends facing academic libraries. Demonstrated success in working with faculty, students, and computing center staff. Excellent interpersonal and communication skills.

COMMUNICATING PERSONNEL NEEDS

Each year the American Library Association's Office for Library Personnel Resources publishes in the *Bowker Annual* a comprehensive "Guide to Library Placement Sources." This is an invaluable tool for personnel officers, search panels, chief librarians, and other administrators, and for persons seeking positions. Covering publications, library school services, state library agencies, library associations, overseas opportunities, and positions in the federal service, the guide provides valuable suggestions on the optimal use of many of the recruiting methods that follow.

Advertising

Advertising is widely used, partly because of affirmative action[35] and open recruiting requirements. Unfortunately, advertising suffers three disadvantages: slow turnaround, high cost, and less effectiveness in comparison with other methods. Many journals require such long lead times that work piles up for intolerably extended periods, and administrators begin to worry that the best candidates have already gone elsewhere. Other regular publications, such as the education supplement of the *New York Times*, may be more timely but are very expensive.

The effectiveness of advertising, especially for professional positions, is mixed. For finding minority applicants, most academic library personnel officers do not regard advertising highly. It certainly is helpful in recruiting support staff from a local labor pool, but postings on campus bulletin boards may be just as effective; a very large and competent labor pool is often waiting to be tapped. Broader use of electronic mail, bulletin boards, job hotlines, and facsimile equipment may one day overcome the costs and delays of advertising.

Employment Agencies and Civil Service

Some jurisdictions have a legal requirement to list open positions, regardless of type, with public agencies. Applicants may also be required to take civil service examinations or fill out complex forms.

Conferences

Conferences are the natural arena for meeting and sizing up applicants. Professional associations provide staffed services and facilities to bring all the parties together at their meetings. Applicants and employers also make private arrangements in advance, especially for the conferences of the American Library Association where 15,000 or more may be in attendance. A disadvantage of conferences is the difficulty of obtaining privacy, which might be desired by the institution, the applicant, or both.

Word of Mouth

Our profession has a highly developed grapevine that is far more powerful than any advertising medium. Word of mouth remains one of the most effective methods for identifying good professional applicants, especially if the word comes not from an administrator but from a colleague. It is especially valuable for recruiting people from minority groups. From time to time, however, word of mouth backfires because of unethical practices, for example, the recommendation of an unqualified or undesirable applicant by an institution wishing to get rid of the person.

Graduate Schools

Early contact with the placement officers of top library schools obviously helps ensure first pick of the best applicants for entry-level positions. A good relationship with these officers helps identify promising new graduates, perhaps before competing libraries hear about them. Increasingly, library personnel officers and chief librarians are making personal visits to schools to interview top graduates. Although the grapevine quickly transmits information on middle-level and senior positions, placement officers also routinely assist seasoned alumni wishing to relocate. Library schools are among the best resources for recruiting minority applicants.

Special Development Programs

Some libraries are exceptionally well positioned to offer special development programs for those wishing to make a career of administration in large research libraries. For example, the University of Michigan has two programs, the University Library Associates Program for entering students and the Research Library Residency Program for "graduates who are highly motivated, have demonstrated leadership potential and who have a commitment to a career in research librarianship." The former provides participants with a half-time library appointment over a two-year period and the latter involves a two-year, nonrenewable appointment at the library. Other equally distinguished academic institutions that have no library schools offer internships. This type of development opportunity is much easier to sponsor in large universities, where resources are richer and therefore more conveniently deployable than in colleges. The Council on Library Resources and the Association of Research Libraries' Office of Management Studies have each sponsored professional development programs. Despite their explicit bias toward the large research library, all these programs produce alumni that are highly sought by all types and sizes of academic libraries.

COMPOSITION OF THE SEARCH PANEL

Typically, a search panel for an entry-level professional position consists of several librarians and one or two support staff; the latter are usually recruited from operations germane to the vacant position. As the complexity and responsibility of the position increase, a faculty member may be added to the panel, especially if the position requires expertise in a particular discipline. Many administrators use search panels as staff-development experiences, frequently mixing seasoned personnel with junior staff or including individuals whose previous professional involvement has been marginal.[36]

There is enormous variation in the way these panels operate. In some libraries the department head chairs the panel, while in others this person is explicitly prohibited from any participation in the process. Some schools permit only librarians to serve on search panels for professional staff.

THE INTERVIEW AS A SELECTION TOOL

Value of Face-to-Face Contact

If high academic achievement is an unreliable indicator of the best candidates, how do we identify them? We prefer methods that test an applicant's process knowledge, a talent that no algorithm or multiple-choice test can readily uncover. In the United States, court cases and research work have both challenged the validity and reliability of qualifying examinations for many types of employment, to the point at which it has become almost impossible to administer tests even for certain types of clerical work. Factual data plus face-to-face interviews, coupled to intuition and judgment, still appear to be the best instruments for selecting personnel who excel in both process knowledge and capacity for successful public interaction with clients.[37] Interviews also produce a great deal of valuable information not necessarily elicited by questions. A good search panel can learn about candidates' attitudes toward work, detect potential for abrasiveness in human relations, and judge whether the applicants can operate successfully in the local environment.

Although most employers hold that the interview is an invaluable instrument, some social scientists, deploring the lack of research in interviewing, question its validity and reliability. In a summary of research on interviewing, Arvey and Campion complained that most popular handbooks, guidelines, workshops, and techniques derive more from intuition and hunches than from sound investigation.[38] An interview perforce focuses on externals; it cannot x-ray a personality to reveal motives, beliefs, and values. Not even the most carefully constructed one can eliminate bias.[39] In spite of these defects, few employers or applicants are willing to give up the technique. As Dewey maintaines, the interview "is and will probably remain the most important tool for the hiring decision."[40]

The Stress Interview

An employment interview is an emotional experience for all concerned; it is also unnatural and not fully rational. While most guides urge that the candidate be made to feel comfortable, some organizations deliberately exploit the interview's inherent discomfort by employing stress techniques. The object is to see how a person performs in a difficult situation within a strict time limit. Inducing stress at the interview is not surprising in the corporate culture of business and industry, and may not be altogether out of place in academe. It may be appropriate if an academic library is experiencing critical administrative problems.

Institutional conditions vary so widely that it is impossible to construct any set of stress questions. As a rule, however, the technique brings the candidate into a live discussion about problem X. The search panel informs candidates about the problem with a minute or two of advance notice, introduces them to key people, and asks them to come back in 15 minutes with an answer. Naturally, X is a very nasty, real problem.[41]

If not properly managed, purposefully stressful interviews can generate hostilities and suspicions that persist long after the candidate has joined the staff. They may put off some applicants to the point where they wonder why they ever wanted the position in the first place. These techniques may not be appropriate to every position, even for certain administrative assignments, but stress is an unavoidable part of daily administration. Whether it is induced purposely or not, search panels will and should find ways to test candidates' responsiveness to stress.

Teaching Interviewing Skills

Because interviewing is a specific skill requiring training and practice, video tools can be quite valuable. Paul C. Green, an industrial psychologist, developed *More than a Gut Feeling*, a training video that has been applied successfully in libraries and universities. It is claimed to teach techniques for developing position descriptions, controlling an interview, preparing appropriate questions, complying with Equal Employment Opportunity regulations, and using silence as an information seeking tool.[42]

Choosing Interview Questions

Interviews should always be professional and courteous, without being altogether coldly impersonal, but their tone definitely cannot resemble talk among friends and family. Many traps can be avoided if the interview purpose is kept carefully in mind, that is, business. Bingham and Moore's excellent definition is helpful: "An interview is a conversation directed to a definite purpose other than satisfaction in the conversation itself."[43]

Since the establishment of Affirmative Action, it has been universal practice to compile a uniform list of key questions for all candidates. Even if there were no legal requirement, a consistent instrument applied to all candidates would be the most sensible, rational course in recruiting, and a definite aid to minimizing bias. Despite this, from time to time a candidate is automatically assured of being hired, and the search panel merely goes through the motions, their minds (or the administration's) already made up. Not only in this practice on dangerous legal ground, it does not make sense. There is no predicting who will be best among the candidates. Researchers, interviewers, and candidates do not even agree on whether it is best to be the first person interviewed or the last. The dynamics of human interaction are so variable and so unpredictable that it makes little sense to try defining an optimum sequence of interviewing, whether from the candidates' or the search panel's viewpoint.

Specific, work-related questions naturally emerge from the posting which in turn, emerges from the library program and ultimately relates to institutional mission, goals, and objectives. To test whether candidates are doing any professional reading, some administrators ask them to identify the most provocative professional article, published within the past few months, that they have read.

It is easy to say what to avoid. Do not put applicants on the defensive (unless a stress interview is explicitly agreed to); ask close-ended questions; ask for obvious information; ask leading questions;

assume an applicant's thorough knowledge of a situation; inject personal bias; ask personal questions; or treat the process lightly. The long list of questions disallowed by the *Uniform Guidelines* includes the following: previous names of married women, height and weight (unless they are BFOQs), age, religion, race, national origin, housing arrangements, and organizational memberships that might reveal religion, sex, marital status.[44]

York University's personnel services office has compiled an excellent list of nondirective questions that are geared not to the applicant but to work dimensions.[45] This approach is especially useful for librarianship, where effectiveness is highly dependent on successful human relations. The list, covering twenty-three vital aspects of employer-employee relations, has well over a hundred questions designed to draw out a candidate's responsiveness in very broad areas. These include career ambition, ability to analyze financial data, political sensitivity, stress tolerance, management control, persuasiveness, and use of delegation. A special value of generalized, nondirectional questions is their comparative independence from any specific work situation; as guidelines, they can be tailored to almost any work environment.

Yet generality alone is only partially revealing. Paul Green recommended that interviewers formulate questions designed to elicit specific, real information about a candidate's performance in previous positions, not meaningless and vague generalities. He advocated asking the candidate to identify and detail specific instances in which notable success or egregious failure occurred.[46]

In essence, the questions developed for an interview are a mirror image of those asked in performance appraisal: they have to be specifically related to work requirements, to the reality of an individual's personality, and to the personal dynamics of a librarian's interaction with other staff. Asking the right questions and obtaining meaningful responses can spare the mutual suffering likely to ensue if the wrong person is hired. The counsel to formulate open-ended questions rather than those that hint at the desired response seems so obvious as to be hardly worth mentioning.

Organizing the Interview

The interview process should be thorough, make the most efficient use of time for both candidates and interviewers, and above all, reflect the dignity, courtesy, and hospitality appropriate to academe. Almost all institutions prepare a closely scheduled written agenda and, for candidates, a timetable. Local conditions govern many of the arrangements. Following are some of the useful considerations in preparing for interviews:

Community and School Information

It is both common sense and a courtesy to assemble an information package for candidates and send it well ahead of time. This includes a campus map and fact booklet, college catalog or register, library brochure and/or organization chart, staff list, local maps, lists of area schools and major attractions, realty listings, a sample issue of a local newspaper, names and titles of principal institutional officers and senior library staff, copies of the collective agreement, and pertinent faculty, academic, and personnel regulations.

Accommodation

Neither luxury nor midrange accommodation is appropriate, but rather a cut above the middle is the right choice. Putting up applicants in a private home has the disadvantage of stamping the visit with a personal imprint that may be inappropriate.

Interview Costs

Make sure candidates have a clear understanding of what expenses the school supports for the interview. A simple way to accomplish this is to enumerate them, for example, coach air fare, so much per diem for meals and lodging, reasonable cost of taxis and limousines. These limits can be stated in the telephone call setting up the interview and then confirmed in writing.

Picking up the Candidate

It is a pleasant and welcoming touch to meet applicants at the airport, but practical logistics sometimes intervene. Having a staff member pick up candidates at New York's Kennedy Airport or similar complex wastes an enormous amount of time, especially if there are flight delays. In large metropolitan centers it is simply better to provide detailed instructions for cabs, limousines, or helicopter.

Time for Rest

For candidates who have come a considerable distance, both the exhaustion of travel and the anxiety of the forthcoming interview require time for rest before strenuous interaction starts. Most prefer to arrive the day before to rest, and possibly several days ahead to reconnoiter.

Meals

Luncheons offer the chance for applicants to meet a broad mix of staff less formally than in interviews, while still affording a businesslike basis for talk. Dinner is rarely given over to formal questions, but still provides the search panel and others a chance to size up how candidates behave in a social situation. If time is limited, even breakfast sessions can be scheduled.

Some schools have strict regulations that make it impossible for the library to pay for everyone's meals during candidate interviews. From time to time a staff member invited to dine with an applicant may decline to do so when the library cannot reimburse the expense.

Time Alone

Occasional respite from the normally heavy interview schedule is welcomed by everyone. Provide at least two breaks each day.

Group Sessions

Open meetings to accommodate questions from any staff member give everyone a chance to see how candidates behave in public. Depending on the situation, it may be desirable to have some senior staff member present to help candidates deal with unusually sensitive issues with which they are not familiar. It goes without saying that every interview session should provide an opportunity for applicants to ask their own questions.

Escort

If the campus is large or facilities are scattered, candidates welcome assistance in getting to the right places. It is most effective if one person coordinates this. Further informal conversation en route provides opportunity for additional evaluation and mutual sizing up.

Parties and Receptions

Normally, schools schedule parties and receptions for the successful appointee, not for applicants. Institutional practice varies widely, however.

Recruitment

Individual Interviews

Within the library, the selection of individual interviewers will accord with the nature of the position. The chair of the faculty library committee, or other faculty members, may wish to see certain candidates. One or more senior officers from the campus administration will certainly want to interview applicants for chief librarian, but perhaps not for lesser positions, unless the final authority for hiring rests outside the library. In certain cases it may be desirable to schedule interviews with community interest groups, such as the Friends of the Library.

Farewell

While most candidates probably like to be met on arrival, by the time interviews conclude they are generally exhausted and no longer wish to see anyone from the school. It is a courtesy for the chair of the search panel to call a cab and see to candidates' final departure from the campus. Failing to arrange a pleasant good-bye is not only discourteous but also reveals a disorganized interview process.

Resist the impulse to send off the favorite applicant with any hint that he or she has won the position. Even if a clearly obvious winner emerges, it is better to complete the process and hear the search panel's reasoning and deliberations.

Evaluating the Interview

Applicants provide a fair amount of evidence about their own character and potential through the way they present themselves during an interview; voice, tone, dress, and demeanor speak volumes. Sometimes the signals emanating from a candidate are strong and clear, other times they are masked. Women are much better than men at reading body language and picking up on subtle signals, so an all-male search panel is definitely to be avoided.

An excellent formal procedure is to require interviewers to write down their impressions immediately after the session. This is very important if more than one candidate is seen on the same day or if considerable time elapses before the next applicant comes in. People sometimes balk at this requirement, but the losing candidate may challenge a turndown, in which case the institution must produce clear, unambiguous evidence that the person selected was the better choice. The written record then proves invaluable.

The search panel meets with the other interviewers and, if there is no clear winner, may wish to review the written notes. They will want to ask many substantive questions and also look after details, such as who controlled the interview and whether the applicant had a satisfactory explanation for gaps in employment history. Some search groups assign points to the repertoire of questions and try to rate the candidates numerically, an attempt at objectivity. The search panel presents its conclusions to the appointing authority, with or without rankings depending on its charge, and then it is up to appointing authority to act.

A vital principle of staff selection, especially for professional staff, is always to start the search again if the first cycle does not produce an acceptable candidate. *Leave a position vacant rather than fill it with a less than top-rate person.* Taking second best is a mistake everyone could regret for many years. In the tenure system, employer and employee negotiate a treaty whose terms establish a monopoly relationship: your employee "owns" both you and the library as much as you and the library "own" him or her.

The above assumes that program and positions were thoroughly analyzed and that the administration was convinced there had to be a one-for-one replacement. Failure to attract a suitable candidate after a second or third try sometimes tempts managers to redefine the work so that it can be assigned to support staff. Examine such a proposal very carefully. Such redefinition may mean permanently surrendering a professional position or diluting program content. Inability to obtain a qualified candidate might signal a need for further study of a program. A fresh look, a total reexamination, might reveal some new approach.

In striving to build a quality staff, remember the eighty-twenty rule: most of the achievement (80 percent) in an organization comes from a small number (20 percent) of outstanding people. Similarly, most of the trouble emanates from a few chronically deficient people. Try to maximize the number of first-rate hires and try either to get rid of or neutralize the defective ones.

The Lateral Move Candidate

Even in times of retrenchment you will rarely seek a candidate for whom the move is an exact lateral transfer. Organizations and their programs constantly change, and even problem employees are not totally static. Yet because most people want to expand their horizons, an applicant seeking exactly the same type and scope of work he or she had before arouses suspicion. Some people know their strengths and limitations very well, however, and may not be interested in constant upward climbing. This is a valid response as long as work quality is sustained and new learning occurs. In spite of all our talk about the best possible employees, we must concede that solid, dependable people are capable of providing quality services and they form the backbone of any staff.

Impact of Letters, Resumes, Appearance, and Work History

However much a posting stresses intellectual and achievement-related factors, it is hard to ignore an applicant's cover letter and resume or the person's appearance. An ungrammatical letter with typographical errors or strikeovers, a messy resume, or a disheveled appearance may telegraph the message that the applicant is weakly motivated or incompetent in verbal expression, or simply lacks savoir-faire. Opinion is divided on applicants' documents. Some personnel officers discount errors of style and grammar. I take the opposite view: judging the quality of application materials is an inherent part of the entire process of personnel selection. If we hire applicants who cannot express themselves clearly and accurately, what right would we have to expect them to think clearly, critically, and creatively, or to provide accurate information to clients?

If the assignment does not involve a lot of contact with the public, an argument can be made that dress and neatness are not work related. Obviously, no search committee would reject an applicant on appearance alone, but because academic librarianship is gradually being restructured to broaden individual responsibilities, it is worth weighing the significance of these surface details. Academic librarians reach out to a wider and wider circle of clients: local citizens, scholars from other institutions, government officials, and countless others. Looking professional is an asset.

Make sure candidates have credible explanations for gaps in their employment histories and satisfactory evidence that they actually possess the educational credentials they claim. Cases of non-existent or falsified credentials have occurred in academic libraries.[47]

REFERENCES

The ability to obtain references has been seriously eroded. Increasing openness of personnel files and the growth of discrimination-based litigation have made prospective references more and more reluctant to set down in writing anything that might later be drawn into a court proceeding. Increasingly the law and the courts are looking on confidential letters not seen by the subject as a form of invasion of privacy. For example, it is reported that New York state "now requires that an employee be notified of an investigation of his credit or personal background and that a copy of the report be made available to him."[48]

Even in former times, references were of questionable value. Often wishy-washy and conveying no substantial information about a prospective employee, they merely combined enough laudatory and negative material to cancel each other out, leaving the reader with no clear picture of the prospect. Many seasoned administrators feel that letters of reference are not worth the paper they are written on.

In the face of these facts, institutions are increasingly relying on oral references obtained by telephone. This method does have the advantage that people seem to open up more than they do in writing. The telephone's "invisible communication" characteristic also provides a kind of anonymity. Even so, it may still be difficult to obtain information over the phone. There is risk that the reference may be recorded, with or without the permission of the supplier. Some organizations decline to furnish reference information, even if the candidate expressly authorizes it.[49]

From whom should one solicit telephone references? Obviously it is desirable to speak to the applicant's current or immediately preceding supervisor. It may also be useful to talk with colleagues of the same rank. As for contacting subordinate staff, disagreement exists on the ethics of that practice. Some think that one obtains better quality information from subordinates, especially in the matter of how an applicant manages support staff and junior colleagues. Others feel that lower-level personnel either have an axe to grind or lack the perspective to see an applicant's potential or performance in a broad context. Some applicants who learn that subordinate staff will be consulted may withdraw their entries. On the whole, the practice of consulting lower level personnel does not seem to be worth the risks.

A special problem arises when applicants ostensibly want to protect their present positions and ask that their current supervisors not be contacted. The reasons could be otherwise. No responsible administrator wants to hire a person about whom little or nothing can be learned in advance. In such cases it is most important to obtain information from other sources whose reliability is known; another option is to reconsider whether to continue recruiting that applicant.

Some former employers decline to provide any reference information except to confirm that a person once worked there. Others, to avoid potential litigation, may provide deliberately ambiguous, ironic statements that are actually half humorous: "I enthusiastically recommend this applicant with no qualifications whatsoever; you should waste no time making an offer; you'll be fortunate to get this person to work for you."[50]

When is the best time to ask for references? When applications are first submitted? After the applications have been winnowed down to a short list? There is no best answer. Some administrators find it useful to defer acquiring references until after the interview, feeling this helps avoid the halo effect (allowing a single positive attribute unduly to influence judgment of an applicant in spite of evident weaknesses in other areas).

MAKING THE OFFER:
ETHICAL AND PRACTICAL CONSIDERATIONS

Once you have decided on the top candidate, it is usual to make an initial offer over the telephone and confirm it immediately in writing if it is accepted. Top-notch candidates are sought by others too, and a call is a good way to lock up the first choice. In general – but especially when there is very strong competition among institutions – it is essential to obtain the winner's written acceptance of the offer before any announcement is made, either in-house or to the media. Few things are more damaging to recruitment and to an administration's credibility than premature announcements of appointments that do not materialize.

In the interim between an offer and acceptance, it is equally necessary to maintain a fallback position by not dismissing other applicants until you are certain the person of choice. Even then, one can be surprised; cases have occurred in which appointees accepted positions, had moving expenses paid by the prospective employer and soon after arrival took employment elsewhere. Some colleges and universities write into their contracts a requirement that moving expenses be refunded on a pro rata basis should an employee quit before several years of successful employment. Although institutions rarely go to court to collect, be aware that the lost money might show up as a debit in the library budget.

One of the most irritating – and justifiable – complaints from applicants and candidates is lack of timely response from the hiring library. Position seekers work hard to prepare their resumes; they invest considerable time, money, and emotional energy into the process. It is good practice to acknowledge each application by return mail and decent manners to keep people posted, especially if the search is taking a long time. Applicants deserve prompt notification if they are no longer being considered. Those whose applications are rejected deserve a personal letter, *not* a form letter. It is by no means easy to compose letters of rejection. Since not every communication from an administrator can announce an award, however, consider writing personalized rejection letters as good practice for the inevitable ones denying a promotion or merit increase.

As stated earlier, it is essential to protect the library's legal position in any personnel action. Only one library officer should be empowered to make an offer, whether written or oral. No letter or offer should forecast a type of relationship that might not materialize (e.g., "long and mutually beneficial") or promise advancement, salary increase, or any benefit that is not an authorized perquisite.

Despite our best efforts to make the selection process objective and scientific, and despite the fact that we all admit that a good, defensible selection takes more than a gut feeling, the ultimate decision hinges on human judgment. It would be very difficult to gainsay Thompson and Carr's claim that ". . . what it is exactly that makes a competent librarian is still not sufficiently understood by anybody: it is not always some combination of formal training and formal qualification."[51] They then pointed to the great Panizzi, Principal Librarian of the British Museum, who possessed neither formal training nor formal qualification. Few administrators will get a chance to appoint a Panizzi, but most will consider themselves lucky if they successfully follow Wildavsky's advice: "Avoiding the worst where you can't get the best is no small accomplishment."[52]

ORIENTATION OF NEW STAFF

Do not give the new employee a breather before orientation. *The administration should use its preemptive power to socialize and orient new appointees immediately, in the very first hour of employment.* If leadership fails at this point, much of the careful effort expended on defining positions and jobs, the whole recruiting effort, and all the talk about mission, goals, and objectives will be dissipated. The new employee's peers will quickly fill in the gaps, supplying corporate history and attitudes that may be quite at variance with the messages the head office wants to convey. It is much easier to build the new person's confidence in the administration at the start than to try to undo the damage that malcontents can perpetrate. Another reason for looking after newcomers at once is to recognize how important work has become in North American society. Work is the key life experience of modern people and, as mentioned in chapter 2, the employer can ill afford to neglect the initiation ritual that unites employer and employee in the social environment. Carelessness and lack of attention at the beginning of this relationship may not only provide a setup for any subsequent dissatisfaction but also reinforce existing discontent.

In large libraries, responsibility for orientation probably falls to the library personnel officer, while the chief librarian or a senior staff person takes care of it in smaller institutions.[53] Anxiety that newcomers start producing at once can cut short their chances to achieve positive attitudes toward the library, feel some ownership in the institution's program, and perceive that the administration really cares about them. Perfunctory walks around the library or campus, plus visits to the payroll and benefits offices, are insulting and next to useless. Do not assume that new employees have received their orientation in the course of the hiring interview. Lunch with the boss and a small group of colleagues, including the new appointee's supervisor, is a great opportunity to begin the socializing process on a strong, positive note. Quickly bringing new persons into the institution's customs and allying them with key colleagues is welcoming and helps to suppress the otherwise inevitable, "we did it this way when I was at such and such."

Some administrators like to believe that newly minted librarians or those coming from other institutions need training to unlearn what they have been taught in graduate school or have acquired by experience elsewhere. They devise elaborate programs to align the new person's habits with those in force. The idea is to protect the newcomer from making mistakes. This is a proven way to demoralize new appointees and destroy any initiative or creativity they brought with them. Professionals must be permitted substantial flexibility and a modicum of mistakes as avenues to learning, innovation, and motivation. They also need time to adapt to a new situation, perhaps as much as a year before they can begin to make creative contributions. As stated in chapter 4, the main reason for hiring professionals is to generate new ideas and to guarantee that an institution can respond to change. An administration that hires such individuals to maintain the status quo is wasting its money; a library assistant can be hired to do that.

Training has a definite place within the professional work force. The difficulty lies in confounding training and continuing education.[54] Continuing education is the method professionals use to maintain and increase their broad knowledge of librarianship and their awareness of the world of higher education at large. An outcome of continuing education might be recognition that some specific training is needed, such as learning how to use a spreadsheet program in order to fulfill some programmatic responsibility.

If you make the assumption, and convey it unequivocally to newly appointed professionals (and incumbents as well), that they have been appointed to professional positions because the institution has confidence that they can cope with change, learn new techniques on their own initiative, and invent their own solutions to problems, you will have created a foundation for professional excellence and continuing acquisition of new knowledge. Throwing a difficult challenge to new appointees immediately is sure to motivate them, while starting them off by putting them into a training program will only make them feel foolish, stupid, and incompetent. Certainly, professionals have to take courses, and attend workshops and institutes to learn new things; that is not training but professional development through continuing education. If it is determined that a professional is unwilling or unable to cope with new knowledge, that can be considered in performance appraisal or career counseling.

SUMMARY

Selecting the right person for the right assignment has always been the most crucial responsibility in any organization. Recruitment and appointment in academe have become very difficult challenges owing to the proliferation of complex legal regulations, the tenure system, the increased willingness of aggrieved parties to litigate, and the huge number of people competing for a relatively small number of positions. The modern academic library especially requires top-rate professionals having both a service orientation and a strong commitment to management skills. Other sectors of the economy are competing for these same people. Well in advance of hiring, administrators must have carefully defined pictures of work requirements and qualifications, institutional performance expectations, and all rules and procedures relating to retention and other personnel actions. One and only one person must coordinate all formal, legal aspects of the employer-employee relationship and maintain a close professional connection with the campus' legal counsel to ensure that every aspect of the relationship conforms to law. In their treatment of candidates and applicants institutions should also scrupulously observe the common courtesies that help make higher education a humane and desirable workplace. Professionals should be given difficult, challenging problems as initial work assignments, not training.

Notes

1. Peter F. Drucker, "The Job as a Property Right," *Wall Street Journal*, 4 March 1980, 24. Drucker cited Japan's lifetime employment, compensation owed to the European worker for "redundancy rights," and a decision by the High Court of the European Community that a worker's claim to redundancy payments even survives a company's bankruptcy and takes precedence over all other claims on net worth except taxes.

2. Employment-at-will is discussed in some detail in chapter 10 of this volume.

3. U.S. employment law refers to two kinds of aliens: immigrant and nonimmigrant. Immigrant aliens are permanent residents and are employable in the country if they have a green card and the Department of Labor certifies that no qualified citizen is available for the work. Nonimmigrant aliens are in the country temporarily and cannot get employment unless their visas explicitly authorize it.

4. A precis of Canada's regulations on employment of foreigners may be found in the booklet, *Hiring Foreign Workers: Facts for Canadian Employers* (Ottawa: Ministry of Supply and Services Canada, 1983).

5. An excellent summary of the legal environment of library employment is Laura N. Gasaway and Barbara B. Moran's "The Legal Environment of Personnel Administration," in Sheila Creth and Frederick Duda, eds., *Personnel Administration in Libraries*, 2d ed. (New York: Neal-Schuman, 1989), 13-39. Arthur Curley's

chapter, "The Legal Framework of Personnel Administration," prepared for the first edition of Creth and Duda (New York: Neal-Schuman, 1981), continues to serve as a valuable resource for pre-1981 legislation.

6. Most schools process academic appointees through a faculty or academic office, and hire classified staff through a separate entity, usually designated the personnel office. Although it is generally safe to assume that legal counsel has reviewed academic personnel regulations and personnel office documents, it does no harm to inquire.

7. The following United States jurisdictions permit public employees to form bargaining units: Ala., Ariz., Calif., Conn., Del., D.C., Fla., Ga., Hawaii, Idaho, Ill., Ind., Iowa, Kans., Ky., Me., Md., Mass., Mich., Minn., Mo., Mont., Nebr.,Nev., N.H., N.J., N.M., N.Y., N.Dak., Ohio, Okla., Oreg., Pa., R.I., S.Dak., Tenn., Tex., Vt., Wash., Wis., Wyo.

8. Commerce Clearing House (CCH), with locations in Chicago, Ill., and Don Mills, Ontario, specializes in current information services for both U.S. and Canadian law.

9. The Occupational Safety and Health Act does not cover state or local government employees. Any covered employee may ask OSHA (the Occupational Safety and Health Administration) to inspect a workplace for hazards.

10. There is an exception for executives entitled to $44,000 per year in retirement benefits, not counting Social Security; such persons can be forced to retire at age 65 or older.

11. I am greatly indebted to Dr. Charlotte Mudge, a librarian and Canadian labor relations consultant, for supplying me with information for this section.

12. D.J.M. Brown, *Canadian Labour Arbitration*, 2d ed. (Aurora, Ontario: Canada Law Book Ltd., 1984).

13. E. E. Palmer, *Collective Agreement Arbitration in Canada*, 2d ed. (Toronto: Butterworth, 1983).

14. Among the loose-leaf service publications issued by Lancaster House, a Toronto legal publisher, are *Benefit Law Bulletin, Charter Cases/Human Rights Reporter, Contract Clauses, Health and Safety Law, Labour Arbitration News, Labour Law News, Public Service & Crown Agency Employment Law, Women's Employment Law*, and *Wrongful Dismissal Employment Law*.

15. *Employment Standards: A Guide to the Employment Standards Act* (Toronto: Ontario Ministry of Labour, Employment Standards Branch).

16. Papers commissioned for the conference appear in *Librarians for the New Millennium*, ed. William E. Moen and Kathleen M. Heim (Chicago: American Library Association, Office for Library Personnel Resources, 1988).

17. Phyllis J. Hudson, "Recruitment for Academic Librarianship," in *Librarians for the New Millennium* ed. William E. Moen and Kathleen M. Heim, (Chicago: American Library Association, Office for Library Personnel Resources, 1988), 72-82.

18. Kathleen M. Heim, "Educating the Future Information Professional," part 4 of a symposium edited by Toni Carbo Bearman, in *Library Hi Tech* 18, no. 2 (Summer 1987): 33-36.

19. Robert S. Taylor, "Reminiscing About the Future: Professional Education and the Information Environment," *Library Journal* 104 (15 September 1979): 1871-75.

20. Robert D. Stueart, "Strategies for Adapting to Constant Change," in *Changing Technology and Education for Librarianship and Information Science*, ed. Basil Stuart-Stubbs (Greenwich Conn.: JAI Press, 1985), 131.

21. Mark R. Yerburgh, "Some Unguarded Thoughts on Academic Librarianship: Vision vs. Reality," *CLIC Quarterly* 2, no. 4 (December 1983): 11-19, esp. 14-15.

22. Guy R. Lyle, *The President, the Professor and the College Library* (New York: Wilson, 1963), 62.

23. An illuminating account of the frustrations personnel offices place before applicants may be found in Lee Bowes' *No One Need*

Apply (Boston: Harvard Business School Press, 1987), chapter 3, "Personnel Departments in Private-Sector Companies," 53-74.

24. In *Motivation Series, no. 21137*, the *Harvard Business Review* has reprinted thirteen of its classic articles on motivation from 1959-1970.

25. Refusing to hear an appeal from the 8 March 1985 decision of the U.S. Court of Appeals, 5th Circuit, New Orleans, in *Glenda Merwine v. Mississippi State University* (754 F.2d 631), the U.S. Supreme Court in October 1986 upheld the MLS as "a legitimate, non-discriminatory standard for hiring academic librarians."

26. In my experience, larger, older, and more prestigious institutions demonstrate much greater flexibility in reviewing credentials than smaller, younger, less prestigious schools.

27. Evidence demonstrating the lack of correlation between grades and work performance may be found in many places. Albert Shapero's *Managing Professional People: Understanding Creative Performance* (New York: Basic Books, 1985), 27-29, cites a number of studies. J. Sterling Livingston's "The Myth of the Well-Educated Manager," *Harvard Business Review* 49, no. 1 (January-February 1971), 79-89, thoroughly analyzes this issue for the business world. In his *Inequality: A Reassessment of the Effect of Family and Schooling in America* (New York: Basic Books, 1972), Christopher Jencks pointed out that the correlation between job satisfaction and educational attainment is neglible (p. 249) and IQ has little impact on economic success (p. 76ff.).

28. Janet Swan Hill, "CCS Task Force on Education and Recruitment for Cataloging Report, June 1986," *RTSD Newsletter* 11, no. 7 (1986): 71-78, esp. 75.

29. Turnover is a technical subject requiring statistical analysis beyond the scope of this work. James G. Neal intensively studied turnover in academic librarianship; see his "The Turnover Process and the Academic Library," *Advances in Library Administration and Organization* 3 (1984):47-71.

30. Thomas Wilding, private communication, 14 October 1986.

31. Robert Swisher, Rosemary Ruhig DuMont, and Calvin J. Boyer, "The Motivation to Manage: A Study of Academic Librarians and Library Science Students," *Library Trends* 34 (Fall 1985): 219-34, esp. 230-32.

32. Herbert S. White, "Basic Competencies and the Pursuit of Equal Opportunity, Part 1," *Library Journal* 113, no. 12 (July 1988): 56-67; the same author's "Defining Basic Competencies," *American Libraries* 14 (September 1983): 519-25; Allen B. Veaner, "1985 to 1995: The Next Decade in Academic Librarianship, Part II," *College & Research Libraries* 46, no. 4 (July 1985): 298.

33. Not all support staff work is nonexempt; typically, very large libraries have several exempt senior support staff positions that do not require librarians.

34. An excellent, informative guide to EEO rules and practices is Jeniece Guy's "Equal Employment Opportunity and the College Library Administrator," in *College Librarianship*, ed. William Miller and D. Stephen Rockwood (Metuchen N.J.: Scarecrow Press, 1981), 87-96. Although Guy wrote for the college environment, she correctly pointed out that EEO rules apply to nearly all institutions of higher education.

35. Remember that Affirmative Action is really a procedure, not a recruiting method; it does not relieve you from the responsibility to exercise and defend good judgment.

36. Thomas Wilding and Roberta Fagin, "Enhancing Staff Development Through Search Committee Participation," *College & Research Libraries News* 50 no. 2 (February 1989): 130-32.

37. Despite the general agreement among library administrators that nothing beats the face-to-face interview, budget constraints have recently led several schools to experiment with telephone-only interviews. The search panel talks to the candidates by extensions or a conference call. It is too early to know how effective this technique is.

38. Richard D. Arvey and James E. Campion, "The Employment Interview: A Summary and Review of Recent Research," *Personnel*

Psychology 35 (1982): 281-322. Excerpts from this study appear in the *Journal of Library Administration* 4, no. 3 (Fall 1983): 61-90.

39. Some libraries have experimented with the "assessment center," an industry derivative, to secure greater objectivity in judging applicants and candidates; this technique is not yet widespread, however. See Nancy L. Baker and Eloise McQuown, "Assessment Centers: A Technique for Selecting Academic Library Administrators," *Journal of Academic Librarianship* 11 (March 1985): 4-7, and Henry J. DuBois, "Assessment Centers for the Development of Academic Librarians: A Foot in the Door," *Journal of Academic Librarianship* 14 (July 1988): 154-60.

40. Barbara I. Dewey, "Analytical Techniques for the Hiring Decision: A Systematic Approach." Paper presented at a program meeting of the Middle Management Discussion Group, Library Administration and Management Association, American Library Association Conference, New Orleans, La., 11 July 1988. (Unpublished.)

41. A variation on the stress technique is Andrea Dragon's proposal (see page 32 of her "Measuring Professional Performance: A Critical Examination," *Advances in Library Administration and Organization* 3 (1984): 25-46) to test a candidate's ability through actual performance under real conditions, somewhat parallel to auditioning an actor or musician: a candidate is asked to catalog materials or work the reference desk for several hours. While experts may be able to assess assess the talents of a musician or actor almost instantly, no such insight applies to librarians' work, especially in an unnatural work situation. Also, a librarian almost never does the identical work twice. We suggest this novel concept is inappropriate and unrealistic for librarians; it may also be questionable on legal grounds.

42. Available from American Media, Inc., 1454 30th St., West Des Moines, IA 50265, 1 (800) 262-2557.

43. Walter Van Dyke Bingham and Bruce Victor Moore, *How to Interview*, 4th rev. ed. (New York: Harper and Row, 1959), 3. See esp. chapter 5, "Interviewing Applicants for Employment," 97-119.

44. See the U.S. *Federal Register*, 1978, 43(166), 38308 for the full text.

45. York University, Personnel Services, "Interview Questions by Job Dimensions," typescript (Downsview, Ontario: n.d.).

46. Paul C. Green, "Behavioral Interviewing," *Performance Management* 4, no. 1 (Fall/Winter 1985): 17-18.

47. Two-thirds of the respondents to a 1986 survey of the membership of the American Society for Personnel Administration reported that they had observed misrepresentation on resumes for business positions, for example, claiming a degree where only a course or workshop was taken. With positions scarce and even systematic theft of library materials on the rise–sometimes by scholars themselves–it is no longer possible to be as trusting about credentials as we might have been a generation ago.

48. "Why References Aren't 'Available on Request,'" *New York Times*, 9 June 1985, F8-9.

49. Albert Shapero, *Managing Professional People: Understanding Creative Performance* (New York: Free Press, 1985), 15.

50. Robert Thornton has cleverly capitalized on this style of recommendation in his *The Lexicon of Intentionally Ambiguous Recommendations* (Deephaven, Minn.: Meadowbrook Press, 1988). The title words form the acronym *LIAR*.

51. James Thompson and Reg Carr, *An Introduction to University Library Administration*, 4th ed. (London: Bingley, 1987), 54.

52. Aaron Wildavsky, "The Political Economy of Efficiency: Cost-Benefit Analysis, System Analysis and Program Budgeting," *Public Administration Review* 26 (December 1966): 292-310.

53. An annotated bibliography on orientation to library facilities and services is Hannelore B. Rader's "Library Orientation and Instruction – 1987," *Reference Services Review* 16, no. 3 (1988): 57-68.

54. In British usage the word "training" does not have the same connotation as in North America; it is often equivalent to what we mean by "graduate education" in the United States and Canada.

Resources

Allison, Peter B. *Labor, Worklife, and Industrial Relations*. New York: Haworth, 1984.

American Bar Association. *Law in the Workplace*. Chicago, 1987.

American Library Association, Library Administration and Management Association, Personnel Administration Section. "A Discussion and Annotated Bibliography on the Selection Interview for Interviewers and Interviewees." Chicago, 1981.

American Library Association, Office for Library Personnel Resources. *Employee Selection and Minimum Qualifications for Librarians*. Chicago, 1984.

_____. *Hiring Library Staff*. Chicago, 1986.

_____. *Writing Library Job Descriptions*. Chicago, 1984.

American Media, Inc. *More Than a Gut Feeling*. West Des Moines, Iowa, 1984. Video. 28 minutes.

American Society for Personnel Administration. *Reference Checking Handbook*. Alexandria, Va., 1985.

Arthur, Diane. *Recruiting, Interviewing, Selecting and Orienting New Employees*. Saranac Lake, N.Y.: AMACOM, 1986.

Arvey, Richard D., and Robert Faley. *Fairness in Selecting Employees*. 2d ed. Reading, Mass.: Addison-Wesley, 1988.

Association of College and Research Libraries. "Guidelines and Procedures for Screening and Appointment of Academic Librarians." *College & Research Library News* 48, no. 8 (September 1987): 231-33. (Reprinted in *Academic Status: Statements and Resources*. Chicago: ACRL, 1988, 1-3.)

_____. "Model Statement of Criteria and Procedures for Appointment, Promotion in Academic Rank, and Tenure for College and University Librarians." *College & Research Libraries News* 35, no. 5 (May 1974): 247-54.

Association of Research Libraries. *Careers in Research Libraries*. Washington, n.d.

Association of Research Libraries, Office of Management Studies. *Recruitment and Selection Practices.* Washington, D.C., 1981.

_____. *Search Procedures for Senior Library Administrators.* Washington D.C., 1988.

Baker, Nancy L., and Eloise McQuown. "Assessment Centers: A Technique for Selecting Academic Library Administrators." *Journal of Academic Librarianship* 11 (March 1985): 4-7.

Banta, William F. *AIDS in the Workplace: Legal Questions and Practical Answers.* Lexington, Mass.: Lexington, 1988.

Bingham, Walter Van Dyke, and Bruce Victor Moore. *How to Interview.* 4th rev. ed. Prepared in collaboration with John W. Gustad. New York: Harper, 1959. See esp. chapter 5: "Interviewing Applicants for Employment," 97-119.

Bowes, Lee. *No One Need Apply: Getting and Keeping the Best Workers.* Boston: Harvard Business School Press, 1987.

Christie, Innis M. *Employment Law in Canada.* Scarborough, Ontario: Butterworth, 1980.

Cihon, Patrick J., and James O. Castagnera. *Labor and Employment Law.* Belmont Calif.: PWS-Kent, 1988.

Creth, Sheila. "Conducting an Effective Employment Interview." *Journal of Academic Librarianship* 4, no. 5 (November 1978): 356-60.

_____. *Interviewing Skills: Finding the Right Person for the Job.* Chicago: ACRL, 1984.

_____. "Recruitment: Planning for Success." *Drexel Library Quarterly* 17, no. 3 (Summer 1981): 52-74.

Curley, Arthur. "Library Personnel Administration: The Legal Framework." In *Personnel Administration in Libraries,* edited by Sheila Creth and Frederick Duda, 1-31. New York: Neal-Schuman, 1981.

Dewey, Barbara I. "Analytical Techniques for the Hiring Decision: A Systematic Approach." Paper presented at a program meeting of the Middle Management Discussion Group, Library Administration and Management Association, American Library Association Conference, New Orleans, La., 11 July 1988. (Unpublished).

_____. *Library Jobs: How to Fill Them, How to Find Them*. Phoenix, Ariz.: Oryx, 1987.

Dougherty, Richard M. "Personnel Needs for Librarianship's Uncertain Future." In *Academic Libraries by the Year 2000: Essays Honoring Jerrold Orne*, edited by Herbert Poole, 107-18. New York: Bowker, 1977.

DuBois, Henry J. "Assessment Centers for the Development of Academic Librarians: A Foot in the Door." *Journal of Academic Librarianship* 14 (July 1988): 154-60.

Engle, June L. "Guidelines for Making a Job Decision." Chicago: Library Administration and Management Association, 1978.

Farrell, Barry M. "The Art and Science of Employment Interviews." *Personnel Journal* 65 (May 1986): 91-94.

Fear, Richard A. *The Evaluation Interview*. 3d ed. New York: McGraw-Hill, 1973.

Gasaway, Laura N., and Barbara B. Moran. "The Legal Environment of Personnel Administration." In *Personnel Administration in Libraries*, 2d ed., edited by Sheila Creth and Frederick Duda. New York: Neal-Schumann, 1989.

Gorden, Raymond L. *Interviewing: Strategy, Techniques and Tactics*. 4th ed. Homewood Ill.: Dorsey, 1987.

Gherman, Paul M. "Selection Committees and the Recruitment Process." *Drexel Library Quarterly*, 17, no. 3 (Summer 1981): 14-26.

Great Way Publishing. *Management Law Newsletter*. Minneapolis, Minn. Monthly.

Green, Paul C. *Behavioral Interviewing Self-Study Program*. West Des Moines, Iowa: American Media, n.d. Six audiotapes, workbook.

Guy, Jeniece. "Equal Employment Opportunity and the College Library Administrator." In *College Librarianship*, edited by William Miller and D. Stephen Rockwood, 87-96. Metuchen, N.J.: Scarecrow Press, 1981.

Hall, Francine S., and Maryann H. Albrecht. *The Management of Affirmative Action*. Santa Monica, Calif.: Goodyear, 1979.

Heim, Kathleen M., and Leigh S. Estabrook. "Career Patterns of Librarians." *Drexel Library Quarterly* 17, no. 3 (Summer 1981): 35-51.

"Hiring the Right Person: The Dynamics of the Final Decision." An annotated bibliography distributed at a meeting of the Library Administration and Management Association, Middle Management Discussion Group, New Orleans, La., 11 July 1988.

Hite, Frederic C. *Aliens in the Workplace: An Employer's Guide to Immigration*. Boston: Immigration Information Center, 1988.

Hudson, Phyllis J. "Recruitment for Academic Librarianship." In *Librarians for the New Millennium*, edited by William E. Moen and Kathleen M. Heim, 72-82. Chicago: American Library Association, Office for Library Personnel Resources, 1988.

Hunt, James W. *Law in the Workplace: Rights of Employers and Employees*. Washington, D.C.: Bureau of National Affairs, 1985.

Jennerich, Elaine Z., comp. "Guidelines for Professional Contracts." Chicago: Library Administration and Management Association, 1978.

Kahn, Robert L., and Charles F. Cannell. *The Dynamics of Interviewing: Theory, Techniques, and Cases*. New York: Wiley, 1966.

Kahn, Steven C., et al. *Personnel Director's Legal Guide*. Boston: Warren, Gorham, and Lamont, 1984.

Karp, Rachelle Schlessinger. "Volunteers in Libraries." *Advances in Library Administration and Organization*. Greenwich, Conn.: JAI Press, 1986, 15-32..

Kelly, John G. *Canadian Recruitment Management Handbook*. Don Mills, Ontario: CCH Canadian, Ltd., 1986.

_____. *Equal Opportunity Management: Understanding Affirmative Action and Employment Equity*. Don Mills, Ontario: CCH Canadian, Ltd., 1986.

Lefkowitz, J., and M. L. Katz. "Validity of Exit Interviews." *Personnel Psychology* 22 (1969): 445-55.

Levinson, Harry. *Emotional Health in the World of Work*. Cambridge, Mass.: Levinson Institute, 1964.

Line, Maurice B. "Requirements for Library and Information Work and the Role of Library Education." *Education for Information* 1, no. 1 (March 1983): 25-37.

Lopez, Felix M. *Personnel Interviewing: Theory and Practice*. New York: McGraw-Hill, 1975.

Loretto, Vincent. "Effective Interviewing is Based on More Than Intuition." *Personnel Journal* 65, no. 12 (1986): 101-7.

Lynch, Mary Jo. "Academic Librarian Salaries." *College & Research Libraries News* 48, no. 11 (December 1987): 674-77.

Lynch, Mary Jo, and Margaret Myers. *ALA Survey of Librarian Salaries, 1988*. Chicago: American Library Association, 1988.

McGuire, Joseph W. "The Legal, Professional and Social Accountability of Administrators." Address presented to the Southern Business Administration Association, 12 November 1975.

Mika, Joseph J., and Bruce A. Shuman. "Legal Issues Affecting Libraries and Librarians." *American Libraries* 19, no. 2 (February 1988): 108-12.

_____. "Legal Issues Affecting Libraries and Librarians: Employment Law, Liability & Insurance, Contracts and Problems Patrons." *American Libraries* 19, no. 3 (March 1988): 214-17.

Mobley, William H. *Employee Turnover: Concepts, Causes, Consequences and Control.* Reading, Mass.: Addison-Wesley, 1982.

Myers, Margaret. "Guide to Library Placement Sources." A regular feature of the *Bowker Annual.* New York: R. R. Bowker.

Nelson, Mary Ann. "Emerging Legal Isues for Library Administrators: Preparing for the 1990s – A Bibliographic Essay." *Library Administration and Management* 2, no. 4 (September 1988): 188-90.

Peele, David. "Fear in the Library," *Journal of Academic Librarianship* 4, no. 5 (November 1978): 361-65.

Person, Ruth J., and George C. Newman. *Selection of the University Librarian.* Occasional paper 13. Washington, D.C.: Association of Research Libraries, Office of Management Studies.

"Personnel Recruitment and Selection in the 1980s." *Drexel Library Quarterly* 17, no. 3 (Summer 1981).

Potter, Edward E., ed. *Employee Selection, Legal and Practical Alternatives to Compliance and Litigation* Washington, D.C.: Equal Employment Advisory Council, 1983.

Price, Janet R., Alan H. Levine, and Eve Cary. *The Rights of Students: The Basic ACLU Guide to a Student's Rights.* 3d ed. Carbondale: Southern Illinois, 1988.

Rae, Leslie. *The Skills of Interviewing.* New York: Nichols, 1988.

Rothstein, Samuel. "Professional Staff in Canadian University Libraries." *Library Journal* 111, no. 18 (1 November 1986): 31-34.

Sanders, Nancy, comp. *Guidelines for Interviewing for the Entry Level Position.* Chicago: Library Administration and Management Association, 1981. (Leaflet).

Sidney, E., and M. Brown. *The Skills of Interviewing.* London: Tavistock, 1961.

Simon, Barry. "Personnel Selection Practices: Applications and Interviews." *American Libraries* 9 (March 1978): 141-43.

Simon, Paul L.S. *Employment Law: The News Basics*. Don Mills, Ontario: Commerce Clearing House, 1988.

Sovereign, Kenneth L. *Personnel Law*. Englewood Cliffs, N.J.: Prentice-Hall, 1984.

Thornton, Robert. *The Lexicon of Intentionally Ambiguous Recommendations*. Deephaven, Minn: Meadowbrook, 1988.

Trussell, Ruth C., ed. *U.S. Labor and Employment Laws*. Washington D.C.: Bureau of National Affairs, 1987.

Uris, Auren. *The Executive Interviewer's Deskbook*. Houston: Gulf Press, 1978.

_____. *88 Mistakes Interviewers Make . . . And How to Avoid Them*. New York: AMACOM, 1988.

"Using Volunteers in Libraries." *Library Personnel News* 2, no. 3 (Summer 1988): 33-37.

Volluck, Philip R. "Recruiting, Interviewing and Hiring: Staying Within the [Legal] Boundaries." *Personnel Administrator* 32, no. 5 (1987): 45-52.

Waggaman, John S. *Faculty Recruitment, Retention, and Fair Employment: Obligations and Opportunities*. ASHE Report, 83-2. Washington, D.C.: Association for the Study of Higher Education, 1983.

Wanous, John P. *Organizational Entry: Recruitment, Selection, and Socialization of Newcomers*. Reading, Mass.: Addison-Wesley, 1980.

Webreck, Susan J., and William G. Jones. "Organizational Health Screening: Reliability and Legality." *Library Journal* 113, no. 3 (15 February 1988): 134-37.

Webster, Edward C. *The Employment Interview: A Social Judgment Process*. Schomberg, Ontario, Canada: S.I.P. Publications, 1982.

White, Herbert S. *Education for Professional Librarians*. White Plains, N.Y.: Knowledge Industry Publications, 1986.

Yerburgh, Mark R. "Some Unguarded Thoughts on Academic Librarianship: Vision vs. Reality." *CLIC Quarterly* 2 no. 4 (December 1983): 11-19.

York University, Personnel Services. "Interview Questions by Job Dimensions." Downsview, Ontario: n.d. (9 pp. Typescript.)

CHAPTER 9

Performance Appraisal

... people sometimes work very hard to believe what they wish
were true.

> *—Making Performance Evaluation Work, An M/C*
> *Employee's Guide to Performance Management*

THE CHALLENGE OF EVALUATION

Performance appraisal is universally perceived as being one of the
most wrenching duties in the entire administrative process. On the
one hand, we claim that the work of professional staff is not
production work, that no two people do it the same way or even
obtain exactly the same result, and that it has nothing to do with a
fixed number of hours worked or any countable, visible output. On
the other hand, we suppose that we are wise and objective enough to
define appropriate, valid, and reliable methods and procedures to
rate this invisible product, professional service, fairly and equitably.
We have a somewhat easier but no less daunting challenge in
evaluating support staff; support work is rarely totally routine and
frequently invokes a degree of judgment. Although the gap between
our definitions of work and our evaluation methods is agonizingly

wide, it is not unbridgeable. To suppose that a professional's performance cannot be judged is to add another maxim to the folklore of academic administration.

Because evaluations evoke a wide range of strong feelings, from pride and satisfaction everywhere when the performance is outstanding, to disappointment, sadness, anxiety, and resentment when otherwise, performance appraisals are always a mixed bag, putting everyone in the organization on an emotional roller coaster for weeks or months at a time. In addition, our whole career orientation, as Stuart-Stubbs suggested, is geared to upward movement: those who can go up the ladder are said to succeed. And those who do not are said to fail. And those who go up the ladder and fall off are to be pitied. Further complicating the process are the varying perceptions of reality among evaluators and performers, and the fact that people are not socialized to accept rejection gracefully.

The abundance of literature on performance appraisal in the world of commerce and industry is in sharp contrast to its sparsity in librarianship. It is astonishing that a subject of such universal and keen interest among all sectors of the academic library community should receive such scant attention. A search of journals and indexing and abstracting services in the fields of management and labor relations reveals very meager coverage.[1] Davis and Shaw's inventory of 1,848 doctoral dissertations and masters theses in library and information science disclosed no dissertations on performance appraisal systems in any type of library.[2] An appropriate subject heading, "Employee Evaluation," did not begin to appear in *Library Literature* until 1970; a comparable separate heading did not appear in *Library and Information Science Abstracts* until 1974. Journal articles on performance appraisal still appear infrequently in our literature. According to *Library Literature*, only about ten such items are published annually; when titles dealing with public libraries and support staff are eliminated, the residue applicable to professionals in the academic library is small indeed.[3] Among recent papers, only that by Dragon raised any critical issues about the process as a whole and went deeper than the mere mechanics of administering a system.[4] Kaske, who covered the subject for the *ALA Yearbook*, pointedly stated that the basic principles of effective appraisal have always been available in the professional literature of administration. He rightly criticized librarianship for lack of will, not absence of knowledge: "What is missing in librarianship, with a few exceptions, is a strong professional commitment to implement such systems."[5]

The focus of this chapter is the professional staff. As indicated in chapter 3, which discussed the duality of library work, classified staff advance on a different basis from professional staff. The criteria, methods, and procedures for evaluating their performance are probably much more various than for professional staff because so many more agencies and jurisdictions are involved: civil service agencies, collective bargaining contracts, local campus personnel regulations, and legislation at several levels. Although policies and procedures differ, many of the same principles applicable to appraising professional staff apply equally to support staff.

In most libraries the chief librarian is reviewed by the school's principal administrative officers. Increasingly, schools are soliciting input from many constituencies, both internal and external, to evaluate the chief. The various techniques and different philosophies of appraisal are complex and rapidly changing, however. The best resource for this aspect is current literature.

DO WE NEED PERFORMANCE APPRAISAL?

Appraisal, if it was done at all a generation ago, might have consisted of calling the employee into the boss' office for a few minutes of well-deserved praise, along with news of a salary increase, or, in some cases, indications of dissatisfaction ending with the suggestion that the person might start looking elsewhere for work. Few traces of these informal, paternalistic procedures remain. Highly formal or bureaucratic systems are now almost universal. A formal system, if well designed and properly applied, protects all parties and removes much of the arbitrariness that once characterized management.

Despite the prevalence of formalized evaluation systems in North America, their necessity and effectiveness are by no means a matter of universal agreement. Our highly formalized style of appraisal is not followed in British university libraries, and it does not exist in Scandinavia.[6] Lubans, summarizing the difficulties of measuring an intangible service, the bureaucratic complexities of the process, and challenge of having faculty status plus a full work week, questioned whether the whole effort is worthwhile.[7] A survey of member libraries in the ARL indicated at least one large research library claiming that it that had no performance-appraisal system – a difficult circumstance to conceive.[8]

Whatever the sentiment in Great Britain and Scandinavia, it is clear from North American tradition that most employees not only have an emotional need for performance evaluation but also perceive the process as indicating that the employer cares about them. It is also clear from experience that employees accept appraisal that is specific, timely, appropriate to work responsibilities, and delivered in a tactful and humane manner. North American managers concede that performance appraisal does cause stress, but also agree that its absence (or inadequacy) produces even more; people prefer to know where they stand. In brief then, for North American employess, rapid and accurate feedback is the principal factor in how people perform, outweighing even the impact of salary increases. Feedback provides knowledge, reinforces excellence, and increases motivation.

It is not the purpose of this work to debate the desirability of performance appraisal systems. Within the framework of North American administrative practice, their existence and merit are considered as givens, intended to measure the extent to which employee behavior moves an organization toward its stated goals and objectives.[9] My main purpose is to describe in broad outline the principles typically invoked in good systems and to help administrators cope with the inherent complexities of the process.

The mechanics of implementing most of the suggestions in this chapter depend to some extent on organizational size. Large libraries with separate personnel offices probably invoke lengthy, complex (and likely unpopular) bureaucratic procedures of a fairly impersonal character. In smaller libraries, procedures are less formal and perhaps more personalized. Yet the principles remain the same.

SETTING THE STAGE FOR PERFORMANCE APPRAISAL

The essence of performance appraisal is communication, on a predictable cycle, of work accomplished. Despite the many protective procedures built into academic employer-employee relations, with or without contractual provisions, this is almost universally a time of anxiety on all sides. Systematic procedures for evaluation and adequate preparation help to offset the poisonous effects of these anxieties. It is easy to give praise; an evaluation process, which inevitably contains some criticism if it is to be of any use at all, must have humane, sensitive, positive ways of communicating performance that departs from the ideal. Its methods and execution must not destroy or further damage the weak performer, or build up in the good performer an exaggerated, unrealistic picture of excellence.

APPRAISAL AND REWARD: DIVIDE OR UNITE?

Bottomley divided the functions of appraisal systems into three review categories: one for allocating rewards, another for assessing performance, and a third for weighing individual potential.[10] He firmly believed the three must not only be kept separate in time but also in paperwork, procedure, and responsibility. It is simply too much to expect that one person, one procedure, and one session can accomplish the conflicting purposes of appraisal with accuracy and justice.

Prince and Lawler argued that it is wrong to outlaw salary discussion during an appraisal; they further maintained that discussion actually improves the appraisal process by improving communication and goal setting.[11] Still, an investigation indicated that some large libraries are giving serious thought to the question of these separations.[12] In all but the largest libraries, however, the practice is likely to be untenable; smaller institutions do not have enough staff to implement a divided process. The work itself could consume inordinate amounts of administrative time and create a bureaucratic monster. In larger institutions, dividing the process could invite allegations that those administering the separate parts are not sufficiently informed about an employee's work to make the required judgments. Perhaps this is another technique from large-scale business that is not easily importable into academic librarianship.

METHODS OF APPRAISAL

In his *Managing Professional People,* Shapero demonstrated how totally useless output measures (titles cataloged, reference questions answered) and personnel data (length of service, attendance, punctuality, etc.) are for professionals. I agree with his conclusion that judgment, fragile and deficient at best, is the only meaningful way to appraise professional performance. Shapero identified eight different methods that have enjoyed various levels of vogue and discredit.

Rating Scales

Scales attach some value to a series of work dimensions or personal traits. The results are used to rank employees in Sears-catalog fashion: good, better, best, or more realistically, poor, fair, satisfactory, good, excellent. Rating scales have become almost totally discredited. They operate to cluster employees around a mean (the "central tendency"), and it is nearly impossible to define traits or connect them appropriately to the work. The whole system is highly subjective and has few redeeming features, save its speed and convenience (for management). A few academic libraries still use rating scales, but they hardly seem suitable for professional work as we define it.

Behaviorally Anchored Rating Scale

The behaviorally anchored rating scale (BARS) resembles the critical incident method (see below). A group of experts assigns numerical scores to various facets of work and employee behavior. Actual incidents are monitored and associated with a score. The difficulty with BARS is that it requires extraordinary effort to design and great continuing effort to implement. A manager would have to spend so much time observing and scoring there would be little energy left for program planning or thinking ahead. Shapero called the method "expensive and tedious."[13]

A variation on BARS is BOS (behavioral observation scale). The two methods are similar but BOS employs statistical analysis instead of the judgments of expert raters to decide which incidents reflect the most significant performance aspects of the work. Also, employees' views are solicited to determine which incidents are critical to effective performance.

Checklists

Checklists resemble rating scales in that the manager applies a canned list of behaviors appropriate to the work. The method is not very responsive to work whose focus changes frequently, as is certainly the case in modern academic librarianship. Preparing the lists is time consuming, and the lists themselves are highly subjective and in the end have as much impact as elevator music.[14]

Paired or Scaled Ratings

In this system an attempt is made to balance possible favoritism by always comparing one employee with another, so that after the process everyone has been compared with everyone else. As soon as an office has more than a dozen or so people, however, the method becomes unmanageable; the number of pair combinations is over a hundred for fifteen persons. Either the time or the energy required for this method quickly exhausts the most dedicated supervisor.[15]

Essay

The essay method is extremely popular in academic libraries and in many large business firms. Its advantage is that it requires a manager to focus strongly on the achievements or problems of one individual. It explicitly avoids comparing people with each other. When combined with a self-evaluation essay written by the employee, it forms a good basis for peer review. The method is subjective, however, and takes a tremendous amount of time. To some extent its success hinges on the writing ability of the evaluator.

Critical Incident Report

In this method a supervisor keeps a notebook and records specific details of top performance incidents as well as troubling ones, and uses the data as the basis for frequent feedback interviews. Incidents are recorded as they occur, not reconstructed from memory. The report encourages prompt feedback and provides verifiable data. It forces managers to observe people very closely, so closely that employees with a lot of problems may feel they are being singled out for special attention. Critical incident reporting requires a great deal of writing and, like BARS, a huge investment in time, with the possibility that the method may be perceived as too demanding and enervating.

MBO

Management by objectives (MBO) is covered so extensively in the open literature that few specifics need be stated here. It is widely used in many types of libraries and is popular because it brings the supervisor and the employee onto common ground and can help prevent many misunderstandings. MBO has enjoyed enormous vogue since its introduction and probably it will continue for a long time. It facilitates communication in the organization and reinforces the expectation that professional staff contribute to the formation of institutional objectives.

Management by objective is not without its problems and its faults: (1) it is much easier to implement in people-centered production work where there is some countable output (e.g., sales, assembly work); (2) it is ill-suited to production work having little potential for job development or enrichment, exactly the type of work often done by some support staff in academic libraries; (3) the parties to MBO tend to set overambitious goals; and (4) it is difficult to express intangible service objectives in ways that everyone can agree to or that lend themselves to ready measurement. Levinson suggested that MBO is self-defeating because it is merely the same old reward-punishment theme in a different guise, lacks dynamism, and does not remove the hostilities inherent in the process.[16] Michalko was even more severe, suggesting that the idea that job satisfaction and job performance are in a cause-effect relationship is unsupported by research.[17]

Peer or Group Review

In academic libraries peer review is usually a prerogative of librarians having faculty or other academic status. The method is often combined with aspects of others, such as the esssay and MBO. A survey of ARL libraries indicated that almost two-thirds of respondents did not employ peer review and only some 30 percent used it regularly.[18] An interesting variation is group review, in which an employee's subordinates participate in evaluation. This method is little used, probably because, as Shapero suggested, it is too threatening to managers. In the ARL survey, however, several respondents did report their directors were evaluated by subordinate staff.

Peer review is valued for several reasons: (1) it serves to distance administration from decisions that might be construed as having an adverse effect on one individual; (2) it affords balanced judgment, as colleagues do not readily tolerate self-centered behavior when it unfairly imposes an extra workload on others or provides private advantage to any one librarian; and (3) it reduces pressures for grievances and costly litigation or arbitration. There are, however, various difficulties with peer review: prevalence of central tendency through people's inclinations to protect each other; temptation for some people to try to "get" someone else, and just the opposite, friendship operating to defeat critical judgment; enormous investment of work, time, and emotional energy for the process; and questions whether a tenured librarian of proven effectiveness should be subjected to this blistering process at every cycle. Finally, some suggest that the process is merely a cheap way for administration to get off the hook of decision making.

Researchers and practitioners have devised many other systems beyond the basic eight, but every attempt to objectify performance appraisal for professional employees has failed. As long as the work deals largely with abstract reality and intangible services nothing will relieve the supervisor from the responsibility to judge. Neither numbers nor weights nor scores will help much. A performance that

315

can be reduced solely to numbers is not professional. One might counter that the academy is a world of GPAs and SAT or GRE scores. My response is another paraphrase of Kanter: "But that is the classroom and this is the real world of work." Try as we may to escape the responsibilities of judgment, we cannot. In that context, we must recognize that the employee-supervisor interaction in performance appraisal is extremely complex and cannot be reduced to a series of mechanistic procedures.

We can only (1) acknowledge the difficulties we know about; (2) be alert for changes in the nature of professional work, whether arising from new academic programs, new technologies, or shifts in the demography of employment; (3) keep an eye on research in performance appraisal; (4) make sure that we maintain continuous training programs for in-house supervisors as the field evolves; and (5) maintain the courage and resolve necessary to implement the system of choice. In this context, we are willing, despite the risks, to apply MBO for two reasons: it fosters communication and it mixes reasonably well with peer review. Its applicability is obviously proportional to the extent of staff control over work; therefore it is best suited to professional work and least suited to the lowest levels of clerical or support work.

COMPONENTS OF A PERFORMANCE APPRAISAL SYSTEM

In her doctoral study on the effectiveness of performance appraisal, Burton cited seven purposes of the process: (1) to assist in personnel planning, (2) to provide a basis for employment decisions (i.e., promotion, termination, merit pay, demotion, etc.), (3) to guide job development, (4) to provide feedback to employees, (5) to elicit feedback from employees, (6) to serve as a basis for modifying or changing behavior, and (7) to determine the need for training and coaching.[19] Bottomley, a British writer and lecturer in administrative science, compiled a similar list: (1) to motivate staff, (2) to identify employees' potential, (3) to assist an organization in doling out promotion money with "overt fairness," (4) to help employees with individual development, (5) to discover training needs, and (6) to observe the effectiveness of personnel policies and procedures.[20]

Most administrators in North American academic libraries would regard these two inventories of purpose as reasonably valid and useful. In academe, performance-appraisal mechanisms are among an institution's most involuted procedures. Their complex rules and limitations are designed to afford a maximum of protection to academic appointees against any possibility of arbitrary or capricious behavior by administrative officers. In achieving this goal, many performance appraisal systems also achieve a negative effect: they protect the incompetent and uncreative.

To achieve the purposes outlined by Burton and Bottomley, a system has at least seven major components, all of which can be worked out into subsystems at varying levels of detail. The main components are:

A Collection of Facts

The collection of facts includes published descriptions of the work environment (for classified staff, job descriptions; for professional staff, statements of duties and responsibilities)[21] and a published inventory of institutional and departmental goals and objectives, plus written individual goals and objectives for the period under review. An essential aspect of these facts is their mutual acceptance by employee and administration. Typically, librarian and supervisor apply the MBO method to agree on a work program for the year under review. This recorded agreement is one basis of fact; another is the employee's detailed record of accomplishment during the review period.

A Set of Standards or Criteria

Normally, appraisal criteria for professional staff are established through the self-governance mechanism: collegial interaction of librarians and library administration, with a blessing from the campus administration. The approved criteria become part of the professionals' working conditions and have the force of a legal agreement. For support staff, criteria may be established by the campus personnel office in consultation with the library, or as part of the collective bargaining process. For librarians, performance expectations should be appropriate to the conduct of work that is predominantly intellectual. Quantitative criteria are associated chiefly with the work of support staff; they may even apply to certain aspects of a professional employee's duties and responsibilities, but only rarely should they constitute a major, decisive facet of a librarian's work. *The standards and expectations must be specifically articulated and communicated.* No one should have to guess about performance expectations. It is intolerable for management to withhold these from employees; it is also illegal.[22] The generic duties and responsibilities listed in chapter 7 and the general evaluative principles listed below are useful tools for establishing fundamental appraisal criteria for librarians of any rank. These must be supplemented by expectations specific to assigned professional responsibilities.

Impartial Review and Communication

These procedures occur in a fairly regular and highly regulated manner to measure performance against expectation. For professionals, they are typically created as a joint act of administration and the collegial body; procedures for support staff are generally an administrative creation of the campus personnel office, which is responsible for their legal validity. In an academic environment, self-evaluation, supervisory evaluation, community involvement (including peer review for professionals), detailed documentation, and a prescribed schedule are typical. Procedures are confined to the period under review in accordance with an established cycle.

Opinions, Judgments, and Decisions

These considerations are put into writing at various stages by officers responsible and accountable to the organization. One of the difficult aspects of performance appraisal is ensuring that supervisors distinguish intellectual from production work and recognize that different methodologies must be invoked for the two categories. Some appraisal systems attempt to quantify intellectual work by assessing quality points or other numerical indicators. Quantification, based on a desire for objectivity, is an elusive goal of questionable value in judging what goes on inside a professional's head; it should not be used to put off the judgmental responsibilities that inhere in the evaluation of academic work. Numbers are simply not appropriate for nonnumerical work.

Sets of Consequences

Consequences can take two main forms:

1. Rewards: Challenging new responsibilities in the same work area or reassignment to a new or different area, salary increases, promotions

2. Recommendations for additional training, changes in attitude and/or performance, mentoring/coaching; warnings; punishments; termination.

Planning

Planning is the systematic consideration of steps to be undertaken by employee and institution for future development and improvement: new or revised goals; list of additional resources required; inventory of additional training, workshops, or courses required.

Due Process

Due process accords with legal requirements, college and university statutes and by-laws, or any collective agreement currently in force. It is an appeal process that facilitates open discussion and rational settlement of disagreements concerning decisions and consequences.

PERFORMANCE STANDARDS AND EXPECTATIONS

The variety of standards and expectations is as manifold as the spectrum of educational institutions in North America.[23] The following four general principles might apply to the evaluation of any academic librarian anywhere. Together with generic duties and responsibilities and the specifics of particular assignment, they might be regarded as a universal, indivisible part of appraisal criteria. A dual-track approach is built in.

1. The generic duties of librarians apply to every librarian.

2. Excellence is expected of all academic librarians. Each appointee, regardless of rank, experience, or status (continuing appointment or probation), is expected to carry out duties and responsibilities with demonstrated excellence. The expectation for demonstrated excellence is the same for new appointees and for the experienced. The level of work complexity, responsibility, and achievement may differ for each appointee in accordance with assignment, experience, and education, but the expectation is that whatever is accomplished will be characterized by excellence.

3. Excellence is measured by results. The performance-appraisal process is concerned with the results obtained, not the effort applied. It is not possible to provide rewards for trying. Credits must go to achievers.

4. All librarians have the opportunity to advance to the highest academic rank, regardless of their specific career development track. As a corollary, for librarians who have chosen a non-administrative career, the criteria relating to publication, research, and professional and community service are given substantial and significantly great weight. In no case, however, does this imply diminished expectations for an appointee's performance of regular duties.

Time-in-Grade versus Merit

Organizations operating in a collective bargaining environment tend to place less emphasis on judging the merit of individual performers than those who remain nonunionized. Some private schools place particularly heavy stress on judging individual merit, even to the point of not providing automatic cost-of-living increases.

PRACTICAL PROCEDURES IN PERFORMANCE APPRAISAL

The Governor's Office of Employee Relations, state of New York, has developed a performance appraisal procedure based on the work of Marshall Sashkin, and expressly designed for exempt personnel, such as administrators, managers, and librarians.[24] The New York State Library uses this system. Because of its generic character, it can be applied in virtually any academic library, large or small. New York state employs a six-step process founded on the widely accepted principle that appraisal is a structured process best done in a private interview, out of earshot or view of other employees. The following guidelines are adapted from the New York procedures.

1. Establish an atmosphere that promotes communication. Neutral territory is best. Conducting a review in your office with you on one side of a desk and the employee on the other – the physical manifestation of authority and power – is the worst possible setting. Sitting at a conference table is not much better, especially if the supervisor occupies the head position or sits farthest from the door – another power display. Arrange informal, comfortable seating, perhaps a couple of armchairs and a low table for coffee or tea and any necessary papers. Adopting an open posture, with arms unfolded and legs uncrossed is, figuratively, throwing out the welcome mat and inviting the employee in for some real, open talk.

   Some kind of small talk or other ice-breaking technique is a good start-up ritual; few persons can go immediately into sensitive discussion. Beware of "how's the family" discussions: if there has been illness, divorce, or a financial setback, and you have bad news for an employee, you will be making it all that much worse. Small talk should be avoided if the supervisor is not skilled at it. The New York state booklet warns that an ineffective opening may make it harder still to tackle an already difficult responsibility.[25]

2. Start by encouraging the employee to open up with a self-evaluation. This provides an immediate opportunity to start a flow of communication. Most employees are generally very willing to talk about their achievements and problems. If the supervisor begins with a long monologue, that will only divert or intimidate the employee; it will not be easy to get back on track. Similarly, presenting an already filled-out evaluation form at the outset cuts off an employee's chance to start communicating.

3. Present your views of the employee's performance. After hearing out the employee, the supervisor has an opportunity to mesh management's views and evaluations with what has already been said, to build on an employee's strengths while providing encouragement and suggesting remediation in areas of weakness.

4. Draw out the employee's responses; solicit interaction. Now is the time to encourage the employee to respond, agree or rebut, explain or question. The manager should not interfere in any way with this process. This part of the session could be highly emotional; keep in mind people's propensity to make perception and fact congruent. Some employees will find the experience cathartic; others will use it to articulate previously suppressed hostilities. A false step here (e.g., denying or downgrading an employee's feelings or perceptions) can make a bad situation worse, paving the way for sullenness or grievances.

5. Summarize differences and work on their resolution. Review the areas in which management's and employee's views diverge and discuss how the differences can be reconciled. This might involve getting more information, agreeing on some specific future assignments, or obtaining any resources the lack of which might be inhibiting optimum performance. An important caution

cited by the New York handbook: "Under no circumstances should the manager allow the appraisal interview to become a negotiating session."[26] Simply stated, the appraiser must be firm and not allow the employee to talk him or her out of any soundly based findings of deficient performance.

6. Wrap up the session. It can be just as hard to conclude an appraisal session as to start. The previous step, which is based on a positive note of reconciliation, provides a suitable opening. This is the time for summarizing the discussion, settling on agreements relating to performance improvement, completing remaining business, and selecting a time for future review.

In my experience, the following ten additional principles will add to the effectiveness of the total evaluation process.

1. Maintain expertise. The field of performance appraisal is highly dynamic, with new systems evolving all the time. Managers should be prepared to invest considerable time, on a continuing basis, to training supervisors in appraisal techniques. Workshops, consultants, facilitators, videos,[27] and programs at professional conferences all help.

2. Be prepared. Although the comparison may be infelicitous, effective evaluation sessions and the theater have one thing in common: both involve intensive preparation. That is where the comparison ends. Appraisals cannot and should not be rehearsed, nor should their conduct take on a theatrical aspect. Full preparation does more to relieve a supervisor's anxiety than almost any other factor. A written outline to serve as an aide-mémoire is essential in a case of any complexity. In addition, all formal appraisal systems, good and bad, contain a confrontational element and this cannot be wished away – all the more reason for good preparation. Finally, the session may not go as you wish. Be ready to cope with unexpected responses from the interviewee.

3. Budget an adequate amount of time. Anything less than an hour is likely to convey to the employee that you are not committed to a serious purpose.

4. Be honest. People want to know where they really stand because they can cope with reality, whether pleasant or unpleasant, far more easily than with uncertainty and ambiguity. Talking around the subject, acting evasively, or failing to come to grips with the reality of poor performance breeds distrust and sets up the conditions for grievance and litigation. Maintain eye contact and firm posture. Do not permit tact to dilute directness; with preparation it is possible to be both tactful and direct at the same time, honest without being hostile.

5. Be fair. Do not confound the evaluation with hostile criticism against the doer; focus on the work, not the person. Do not ignore normal good work by being frugal with praise, or be overgenerous with criticism if poor work is infrequent. Resist the tendency for appraisal processes to focus wholly on either the negative or the positive. Critically review the administration's responsibility in instances of poor performance.

6. Stick to the facts about what has really been achieved. Do not confound an employee's capacity with actual performance. The review session is concerned chiefly with rating an employee's actual behavior, outputs, and achievements. Capacity might play a role in the discussion of future plans or remedial actions.[28] Be alert for the middle-level supervisor who, striving to focus on the positive, wants to give points for effort by emphasizing how an employee has "tried hard." It is demoralizing to star performers when low achievers are rewarded for effort rather than results.

7. Do not try bribes. Do not try to buy improved performance with the lure of a promotion or salary increase. Misstated promises can be interpreted as oral contracts.

8. Do not be the bearer of surprises. As the whole concept of effective appraisal assumes continuous communication, surprises clearly reveal failure to communicate regularly throughout the work year.

9. Schedule interviews systematically. Everyone's anxiety level rises if the exact hour of the interview is not known ahead of time. Nevertheless, it eases the pressure to pick some random method of summoning people. By random we mean a method that does not associate performance level with meeting time. Alphabetically by name or by department randomizes the performance levels you deal with.

10. Stick to established procedures. Know the authorized procedures intimately. Beware of requests for special procedures or deviations from the norm, such as an employee's asking that a witness be present or insisting on tape recording the proceedings, or introducing some totally unrelated topic for discussion or decision. None of these things will help, and they may severely hinder, if a case ever goes to grievance or court.[29]

DOCUMENTING THE APPRAISAL: FEEDBACK STYLE AND CONTENT

Feedback breeds loyalty and motivates employees to stay with the school. A verbal pat on the back during the evaluation may be appreciated at the moment given, but if it is not followed up by something more substantive, it is ultimately seen as dismissive.

A chief librarian empowered to make final decisions on promotion or salary increase should analyze and document the rationale for action so employees know exactly where they stand and why. In medium-size and large libraries, the performance appraisal may be one of the few instances where librarians receive regular, thoughtful feedback covering significant spans of professional service. Professionals who dedicate their careers to an institution deserve tailored, written analyses. Prepare an individualized letter for each librarian. Summarize the review process and explain in detail how and why a particular personnel decision was reached. These letters form a central part of the library's documentation of professional performance.

Although the need for such a response is less for support staff, it is merited for selected cases. Long-serving people who know their jobs very well and perform them dependably, year after year deserve more than a form letter. A few handwritten comments or words of thanks relieve the bureaucratic tone of appraisal. These comments should be spontaneous and factual; signing the forms without comment is better than adding a perfunctory formula.

PREPARATION OF AN EMPLOYEE'S SUBMISSIONS

Almost every performance appraisal-system requires professionals to organize and present their own supporting documentation in accordance with a specific schedule. Policies and procedures vary so much that only general guidance is provided here.

Suggested Guidelines for Self-Documentation

Although one might expect professional staff to hold to the highest standards of preparation for performance-appraisal documentation, experience indicates this is a naive assumption. Every library administrator knows that some documentation will be submitted in a form that is incomplete, late, illegible, sloppy, ungrammatical, padded with useless material, or otherwise inappropriate. Deficient documentation is a burden on those who must read it and is unfair to those who have taken the care to produce a first-class job.

People have the right to a clear idea of your expectations about performance self-appraisal. If you are implementing a new or revised system, or if you are newly appointed, one or more detailed orientation sessions will be indispensable. The following guidelines have proved useful for orienting professional staff.

1. Instructions: Please read the instructions carefully and convey to the personnel office your concerns about lack of clarity. Suggest improvements in forms and the process; they are welcome at any time. Observe the calendar and deadlines carefully.

2. Format of appraisal documentation: Place your name and the current date on each page. Use continuous pagination throughout your documentation. Prepare your documents with care for neatness and ease of reading. Avoid submission of illegible or poorly reproduced photocopies of attachments. Write and submit your material as if you were applying for a new and more responsible position. Use the same size paper throughout.

3. Contents: Be succinct. A brief statement in the active voice using the first person is much more hard-hitting than drawn out wording in the passive voice and third person. In the factual portion state only the facts of your achievements. Put your self-evaluation in the part designated for that purpose.

   If you attended a conference or participated in a professional development program, describe in detail the benefit to the library, the school, yourself. Include a short summary of the conference's major points and conclusions of the deliberations, or attach a copy of your trip report.

   Limit your statements to the period under review, except that you may include a brief historical summary of a particular program element for background information, if essential to an understanding of your current role. However, if you are applying for a promotion in rank, summarize your entire career.

   Do not encumber your packet with photocopies of letters appointing you to committees, certificates of attendance at workshops, and the like. Summarize the facts concerning your appointment, term of service, and attendance. State how your participation benefited your professional growth and the library's program.

   Letters of support from peers, colleagues, clients, or others should specifically address the evaluation criteria provided to them, rather than convey praise undocumented by example or unrelated to your professional duties and responsibilities. (The library administration provides a guideline for such letters; see below.)

Avoid forecasting the personnel action that may follow your evaluation. This could be interpreted as an attempt to influence a review panel improperly.

Suggested Guidelines for Solicited Testimonial Letters

Nonlibrary persons writing on behalf of an employee often have little understanding of internal review processes and need guidance. Give employees guidelines to pass on to the letter writers. The following general suggestions may be helpful.

1. Provide evaluative comments solely on the person being evaluated. Refrain from evaluating anyone's supervisor, subordinates, or colleagues.

2. Evaluate this candidate's performance only as you know it. Do not make recommendations or suggestions concerning possible promotion or other personnel action; this might be interpreted as an attempt to influence the review process improperly.

3. Confine your comments to the period under review. Exclude comment on performance prior to the review period.

TRAPS TO AVOID

The Equal Employment Opportunity Commission views performance appraisal as similar to tests applied in the initial selection of employees. Procedures should therefore be designed to be as objective as possible. Every performance appraisal system must (1) be work related, (2) not discriminate against any protected class, and (3) require that the supervisor understand the work requirements and have an adequate knowledge of the employee.

A pitfall to avoid is administering performance appraisal solely on a rigid annual cycle. Ideally, evaluation is a continuous process. Because it requires a considerable investment of everyone's time, however, the tendency is to do it only when policy and procedure dictate, not throughout the work year. A conference two or three times a year, even independent of the annual written procedure, helps to smooth out the process.

Ideally, performance appraisal operates as a feedback system combining the best aspects of compassion and rational analysis. The following are some of the most common pitfalls in the process.

Excessive Generality

Back up any generalities with specific evidence. Avoid empty phrases, such as "takes initiative in emergencies, makes a decision quickly, is conscientious." Looked at separately, the emptiness of each is immediately apparent: in the emergency, was the initiative taken the correct one? Was the decision quickly made a good one? Is the conscientious performance also of high quality?

Points for Effort

A supervisor wishing to be humane sometimes tries to mitigate a disastrous performance by giving credit for trying hard. These good intentions usually backfire. They mislead the employee and will not be appreciated by the genuine achievers. Giving points for effort also contributes to grade inflation. For a performance appraisal system to have any meaning, it must be oriented towards results, not effort, however conscientious.

Uncritical Appraisal, Content-Free Phrases, Playing the Seer

The appraisal process is most useful if it includes critical analysis and judgment. Critical judgment should be open, not something that is undisclosed or an item in a "hidden agenda." Of course, the term "critical" is easily misunderstood, with some staff mistakenly thinking it involves a mandate for negative, destructive criticism. Documents or orientation talks alluding to "critical" appraisal can usefully include the definition from *Webster's Ninth New Collegiate*

Dictionary: "exercising or involving careful judgment or judicious evaluation."

Some supervisors are expert wordsmiths in compiling content-free statements, another factor in grade inflation. Some feel they cannot appraise a performance without including some element of praise, if only minimal, but it is possible to go overboard. Avoid obvious exaggerations, nonspecific expressions, speculations, or items unrelated to assigned responsibilities. Some examples of unsuitable comments are:

- ". . . totally successful reference librarian" (no evidence attached).

- ". . . keen ability to analyze problems in their totality" (no examples provided).

- ". . . learned to deal with all the managerial and political problems concerned with an academic department" (no detail included).

- ". . . miraculous performance. I visualize a very creditable, if not distinguished, future" (clear hyperbole plus prediction).

- ". . . cheerfully does an honest day's work without complaining" (content-free statement).[30]

Avoid forecasting the candidate's future – an evaluation is an appraisal of past performance, not a prediction. It is unfair and unrealistic to set up employees for expectations (especially promotions) that may not be deliverable by reason of budget, or organizational or other constraint.

Skewed Talent Model

Although our professionals like to think of themselves as the self-selected best, experience in the field does not bear out the theory. As in other large groups, the distribution of knowledge, talent, skills, and abilities is not grossly skewed but follows a bell-shaped curve. Yet no incumbent concedes to performing on a level less than superior or outstanding. The staff of an academic library is much like the staff of any other large organization: it has its due share of brilliance and stupidity, energy and laziness, equanimity and tension.

Overwhelmed by Numbers

Critics of librarianship state that the profession has a history of paying too little attention to statistics. The opposite extreme, preoccupation with quantity, can distract from the need to judge quality. Numbers of titles cataloged or reference questions answered tell little or nothing about work quality or workload complexity.

Trapped by Dishonesty

Supervisors who wish to avoid friction and practice evasiveness or lavish unwarranted praise on employees ensnare themselves hopelessly. Acceptance of an employee's given level of performance guarantees management's satisfaction with that level. That level, in effect, becomes part of the terms and conditions of that employee's continued employment. Indicating that an employee's performance is better than is actually the case, or including promises of advancement or retention, lays the groundwork for future litigation if termination for cause is subsequently invoked.

UNACCEPTABLE BEHAVIOR AND DISCIPLINARY ACTION

Grounds for disciplinary action in colleges and universities normally are specified in collective agreements, school statutes and regulations, or law. Disciplinary action is usually administered for behavior not warranting dismissal. Examples include chronic tardiness, failure to show up for work, and willful damage to school property.

Despite the generally refined and humane behavior in academe, gross misbehavior (including sexual harassment) is not unknown; egregious examples among faculty sometimes receive wide publicity. Librarians too can be overbearing about their professional status and seriously impair library unity by unduly distancing themselves from support staff. Unwarranted self-importance or mistreatment of support staff, clients, or fellow workers deserves appraisal and, depending on severity and persistence, is grounds for some form of disciplinary action.

Disciplinary measures follow a graded scale beginning with oral warnings. The next step is the written warning, usually cosigned by the employee as evidence of having read the document. A stronger written warning is the formal reprimand. Beyond these can come a written warning with stipulations, suspension with or without pay, disciplinary transfer, demotion, and discharge.

A FINAL WORD

A hiring action occurs only once per person, but because some form of appraisal goes on as long as the person is employed, appraisal exerts a cumulative emotional impact on the administrator. Appraisal quickly leaves the terra firma of easily established facts for the uncertain realms of value judgment: resources efficiently administered, organizational problems perceived and forestalled, new systems and procedures designed, personality clashes prevented, faculty crises intercepted and resolved, and so forth. Further complicating the appraisal procedure are increasing numbers of court cases that are calling into question vague criteria and wholly subjective judgments. Appraisal is the one critical area of academic library administration where we have far more questions than answers. Dragon's critical examination of current philosophies and practices demonstrated the many pitfalls in the process, invokes new analytic concepts in understanding it, and forms a valuable research agenda.[31]

Administrators tend to resist systems of upward evaluation on a variety of grounds, chiefly on the notion that subordinates are in no position to see the overall picture and are therefore incapable of rendering appropriate judgment. The real reason for the lack of bidirectional evaluation must be that administrators find the process too threatening and prefer to argue it away. Yet common sense indicates that some aspects of subordinate feedback must be better than the judgment of superiors: subordinates see how the boss responds to everyday reality, both adversity and success. Upward evaluation has its traps, however. For example, the need for anonymity makes it difficult to administer. Subordinates easily become cynical about the process, fearing that they may be punished if found out, or that results may be ignored. Yet if performance appraisal is to be meaningful, it must involve two-way discussion. A report from the ARL Office of Management Studies indicated that libraries are showing increasing interest in having the chief librarian evaluated by staff.[32]

SUMMARY

Although formal performance appraisal is virtually universal among North American academic libraries, affection for the process is minimal. Most procedures are complex, time consuming, nerve-wracking, confrontational, and beset with traps and difficulties. All have legal implications for retention, promotion, compensation, and other personnel actions, and all judgments short of superior performance have potential for grievance and litigation. The employee-supervisor interaction in performance appraisal is an extremely complex phenomenon that cannot be reduced to a series of simple, mechanistic procedures. No one has devised a truly satisfactory, thoroughly acceptable substitute for the judgment call as a method of evaluating the performance of professional staff. Despite manifold disadvantages in academe, MBO and similar systems do provide essential feedback between the parties and, when adequately implemented, foster good internal communication and help to build and maintain staff morale and quality. Still, there is a hazard to fixing on any one appraisal system and treating it as the only way. Far more research is required on performance appraisal in the academic environment.

Notes

1. See, for example, *Personnel Management Abstracts* or *Work Related Abstracts*.

2. Charles H. Davis and Debora Shaw, eds., *Library & Information Science: A Catalog of Selected Doctoral Dissertation Research* (Ann Arbor: University Microfilms, 1986). (Covers the period 1970-85.) Davis and Shaw did list one master's thesis done in 1979 for a degree in Business Administration: Karen Eloise

Stoudenmier, *An Examination and Evaluation of the Performance Appraisal System for Library Employees in an Academic Library* (Lamar University, Beaumont, Texas, 1979).

3. *Library Literature* indicates the following number of entries on performance appraisal for a recent ten year period: 1978, 8; 1979, 10; 1980, 10; 1981, 11; 1982, 6; 1983, 11; 1984, 8; 1985, 9; 1986, 7; and 1987, 11. The literature of performance appraisal in other sectors of the nonprofit institution is similarly meager: a 600-page book on the management of nonprofit organizations devotes only 15 pages to performance appraisal.

4. Andrea C. Dragon, "Measuring Professional Performance: A Critical Examination," in *Advances in Library Administration and Organization* 3 (1984): 25-26.

5. Neal K. Kaske, "Personnel and Employment: Performance Appraisal," *ALA Yearbook* 6 (1981): 223.

6. G. Edward Evans, "Another Look at Performance Appraisal in Libraries," *Journal of Library Administration* 3, no. 2 (Summer 1982): 61-69.

7. John Lubans, "Performance Evaluation: Worth the Cost?" *North Carolina Libraries* 42, no. 1 (Spring 1984): 15-17.

8. Association of Research Libraries, Office of Management Studies, *Performance Appraisal in Research Libraries* (Washington, D.C., 1988). SPEC Kit no. 140.

9. Performance appraisal is a required element of administration in many collective agreements.

10. Bottomley, *Personnel Management,* 108-10.

11. J. Bruce Prince and Edward E. Lawler III, "Does Salary Discussion Hurt the Developmental Performance Appraisal? *Organizational Behavior and Human Decision Processes* 37 (1986): 357-75.

12. Association of Research Libraries, Office of Management Studies, *Performance Appraisal in Research Libraries.*

13. Shapero, *Managing Professional People,* 105.

14. In the preface to *Making Performance Evaluation Work*, Marshall Sashkin provides a long table of humorous interpretations to show what checklist entries have come to "really" mean to many employees: forceful and aggressive = argumentative; often spends extra hours on the job = miserable home life, etc.

15. The method is explained in some detail in two articles by J. Peter Graves, "Let's Put Appraisal Back in Performance Appraisal," *Personnel Journal* 61 (November 1982): 844-49, and 61 (December 1982): 918-23.

16. Harry Levinson, "Management by Whose Objectives?" *Harvard Business Review* 48 (July-August 1970): 125-34.

17. James Michalko, "Management by Objectives and the Academic Library: A Critical Overview," *Library Quarterly* 45 (July 1975): 235-52.

18. Association of Research Libraries, Office of Management Studies, *Performance Appraisal in Research Libraries*.

19. Eileen Burton, "Measuring the Effectiveness of a Performance Appraisal System," Ph.D. diss., University of Washington, 1979. See page 9. (Cited in Stanley P. Hodge, "Performance Appraisals: Developing a Sound Legal and Managerial System," *College & Research Libraries* 44, no. 4 (July 1983): 235. The Hodge paper deals with classified staff, not professionals, and is in a context of United States legislation; it has little direct applicability to Canada.)

20. Michael H. Bottomley, *Personnel Management* (Plymouth: Macdonald and Evans, 1983), 108ff.

21. An outline of generic duties and responsibilities applicable to academic librarians of any rank is in chapter 7.

22. Cf. Dragon, "Measuring Professional Performance," 42-44.

23. For samples of performance appraisal documentation among members of the Association of Research Libraries, see "Performance Appraisal," referred to in note 8. Many of the definitions, principles, and procedures used in large research libraries can apply to or be adapted to any academic library.

24. The original work is Marshall Sashkin's *A Manager's Guide to Performance Management* (New York: American Management Association, 1986). The New York State derivative is "Making Performance Evaluation Work, An M/C Employee's Guide to Performance Management," (Albany N.Y.: Governor's Office of Employee Relations, 1986). Note: M/C = Management/Confidential. I am indebted to Jerome Yavarkovsky, New York state librarian, for bringing these guidelines to my attention in a personal communication, 28 April 1987.

25. "Making Performance Evaluation Work," 36.

26. Ibid., 39.

27. Several training films are available to help supervisors maintain currency. ALA distributes *At the Interview*, a 20-minute videotape designed to help supervisors deal with staff in "potentially awkward situations." American Media, Inc., West Des Moines, Iowa, publishes two: *The Human Touch Performance Appraisal*, and *Who Wants to Play God?*, each a 30-minute training aid.

28. Some performance appraisal systems have built into their procedures an evaluation of an employee's potential. Obviously, this must be taken into account. Even so, the prime focus of evaluation is past performance, a factor that cannot be ignored by appeals to potential and capacities.

29. You can partially prepare yourself for the unexpected by seeking the counsel of a respected, experienced colleague.

30. I always looked for–but never found–the mirror-image claim for the employee who "grudgingly does a top quality, bang-up job."

31. Dragon, "Measuring Professional Performance."

32. Association of Research Libraries, Office of Management Studies, Systems and Procedures Exchange Center, *Performance Appraisal in Research Libraries* (Washington, D.C.: , 1988).

Resources

Alexander Hamilton Institute. "Will Your Next Performance Appraisal Land You in Court?" *Management Studies* 31, no. 7 (July 1986): 5-9.

Allan, Ann, and Kathy J. Reynolds. "Performance Problems: A Model for Analysis and Resolution." *Journal of Academic Librarianship* 9 (May 1983): 83-88.

American Library Association. *At the Interview.* Chicago, 1988. Videotape, twenty minutes.

American Library Association, Office for Personnel Resources. *Managing Employee Performance.* Chicago, 1988.

American Media, Inc. *The Human Touch Performance Apraisal.* West Des Moines, Iowa, n.d. Videotape, thirty minutes.

_____. *Who Wants to Play God?.* West Des Moines, Iowa, n.d. Videotape, thirty minutes.

Association of College and Research Libraries. "Model Statement of Criteria and Procedures for Appointment, Promotion in Academic Rank, and Tenure for College and University Librarians." Rev. *College & Research Libraries News* 48, no. 5 (May 1987): 247-54.

Association of Research Libraries, Office of Management Studies. *Staff Performance Evaluation Program at the McGill University Libraries: A Program Description of a Goals-Based Performance Evaluation Process.* Washington, D.C., 1976.

Association of Research Libraries, Office of Management Studies. *Performance Appraisal in Research Libraries.* Washington, D.C., 1988.

_____. *Performance Evaluation in Reference Services.* Washington, D.C., 1987.

Baer, Walter E. *Grievance Handling: 101 Guides for Supervisors.* New York: American Management Association, 1970.

Berkner, Dimity S. "Library Staff Development Through Performance Appraisal." *College & Research Libraries* 40 (July 1979): 335-44.

Bottomley, Michael H. "Performance Appraisal." In *Personnel Management*, 106-15. Plymouth, England: Macdonald and Evans, 1983.

Cascio, Wayne F., and H. John Bernardin. "Implications of Performance Appraisal Litigation for Personnel Decisions." *Personnel Psychology* 34, no. 2 (1981): 211-26.

Creth, Sheila. *Performance Evaluation: A Goals-Based Approach.* Chicago: ACRL, 1984.

DeProspo, Ernest R. "Personnel Evaluation as an Impetus to Growth." *Library Trends* 20 (July 1971): 60-70.

Dragon, Andrea C. "Measuring Professional Performance: A Critical Examination." *Advances in Library Administration and Organization* 3 (1984): 25-26.

Fear, Richard A. *The Evaluation Interview.* 3d ed. New York: McGraw-Hill, 1973.

Frank, Donald G. "Utilization of Total Staff Participation in the Development of and Implementation of a Performance Evaluation System for Academic Librarians." In *Issues in Academic Librarianship: Views and Case Studies for the 1980s and 1990s*, edited by Peter Spyers-Duran and Thomas W. Mann, Jr., 138-60. Westport, Conn.: Greenwood Press, 1985.

Gibbs, Sally E. "Staff Appraisal." In *Handbook of Library Training Practice*, edited by Ray Prytherch, 61-81. Brookfield, Vt.: Gower, 1986.

Ginzberg, Eli. *Understanding Human Resources.* Lanham, Md.: University Press of America, 1985.

Governor's Office of Employee Relations. *Making Performance Evaluation Work, An M/C Employee's Guide to Performance Management.* Albany, N.Y., 1986.

Grothe, Mardy, and Peter Wylie. *Problem Bosses: Who They Are and How to Deal with Them*. New York: Facts on File, 1987.

Hilton, Robert C. "Performance Evaluation of Library Personnel." *Special Libraries* 69 (November 1978):429-34.

Hodge, Stanley P. "Performance Appraisals: Developing a Sound Legal and Managerial System." *College & Research Libraries* 44 (July 1983): 235-44.

Hodgson, Philip. *A Practical Guide to Successful Interviewing*. New York: McGraw-Hill, 1988.

Horn, Judy. "Peer Review for Librarians and Its Application in ARL Libraries." In *Academic Libraries: Myths and Realities*, edited by Suzanne C. Dodson and Gary L. Menges, 135-40. Chicago: ACRL, 1984.

Imundo, Louis V. *Employee Discipline: How to Do It Right*. Belmont, Calif.: Wadsworth, 1985.

Johnson, Marjorie. "Performance Appraisal of Librarians: A Survey." *College & Research Libraries* 33 (September 1972): 359-67.

Kanter, Rosabeth M. "From Status to Contribution: Some Organizational Implications of the Changing Basis for Pay." *Personnel* 64, no. 1 (January 1987): 12-37.

Kaske, Neal K. "Personnel and Employment: Performance Appraisal." In six successive volumes of the *ALA Yearbook*: 6 (1981): 223; 5 (1985): 236-37; 4 (1979): 203-4; 3 (1978): 229-30; 2 (1977): 239-40; 1 (1976): 260.

King, Patricia. *Performance Planning and Appraisal: A How-To Book for Managers*. New York: Mc-Graw-Hill, 1984.

Kirkpatrick, Donald L. *How to Improve Performance through Appraisal and Coaching*. New York: AMACOM, 1982.

Kleiman, Lawrence S., and Richard L. Durham. "Performance Appraisal, Promotion and the Courts: A Critical Review." *Personnel Psychology* 34 (1981): 103-21.

Kroll, Rebecca. "Beyond Evaluation: Performance Appraisal as a Planning and Motivational Tool in Libraries." *Journal of Academic Librarianship* 9 (March 1983): 27-32.

Levinson, Harry. "Appraisal of What Performance?" *Harvard Business Review* 54, no. 4 (1976): 30-36. Reprinted in *On Human Relations*, New York: Harper and Row, 1979.

_____. "Emotional Health in the World of Work." In *Management by Guilt*, 267-91. New York: Harper and Row, 1964.

_____. "Management by Whose Objectives?" *Harvard Business Review* 48 (July-August 1970): 125-34.

Library Administration and Management Association. *Problem Employees: Improving Their Performance*. LAMA Program, Dallas ALA Conference, 1984. Chicago: ALA, 1984. Two cassettes.

Library Administration and Management Association, Personnel Administration Section, Staff Development Committee. *Personnel Performance Appraisal: A Guide for Libraries*. Chicago: 1979.

Lindsey, Jonathan A. "The Human Dimension in Performance Appraisal." *North Carolina Libraries* 42, no. 1 (Spring 1984): 5-7.

_____. *Performance Evaluation: A Management Basic for Librarians*. Phoenix, Ariz.: Oryx, 1987.

Lubans, John. "Performance Evaluation: Worth the Cost?" *North Carolina Libraries* 42, no. 1 (Spring 1984): 15-17.

McConkey, Dale D. *MBO for Nonprofit Organizations*. New York: AMACOM, 1975.

McGregor, Douglas. "An Uneasy Look at Performance Appraisal." *Harvard Business Review* 35 (May-June 1957): 89-94; reprinted 50 (September-October 1972): 133-38. Reprinted in the author's *Leadership and Motivation*, 184-97 (Cambridge: MIT Press, 1966).

Mager, Robert F., and Peter Pipe. *Analyzing Performance Problems, or: You Really Oughta Wanna.* 2d ed. Belmont, Calif.: Wadsworth, 1987.

Maier, Norman R. F. *The Appraisal Interview.* Revised. San Diego, Calif.: University Associates, 1976.

Michalko, James. "Management by Objectives and the Academic Library: A Critical Overview," *Library Quarterly* 45 (July 1975): 235-52.

Neal, James E., Jr. *Effective Phrases for Performance Appraisals.* 5th ed. Perrysburg, Ohio: Neal Publications, 1988.

Patten, Thomas H. *A Manager's Guide to Performance Appraisal.* New York: Free Press, 1982.

Performance Appraisal. Chicago: ACRL, 1980.

Peskin, Dean B. *Human Behavior and Employment Interviewing.* New York: American Management Association, 1971.

Pinzelik, Barbara P. "A Library Middle Manager Looks at Performance Appraisal." In *Energies for Transition, Proceedings of the Fourth National Conference of the ACRL,* edited by Danuta A. Nitecki, 141-45. Chicago: ACRL, 1986.

Plumlee, Lynnette B., A. E. Machemehl, and Robert F. Utter. *Improving Performance Evaluation Procedures: A Content Validation Guide.* New York: AMACOM, 1983.

Rader, Jennette, comp. *Performance Evaluation: A Selected Bibliography.* Chicago: ALA/OLPR, 1977.

Rae, Leslie. *The Skills of Interviewing.* New York: Nichols, 1988.

Reifler, Henrietta. "Peer Evaluation at Washington State University Libraries: A Two-Year Experiment." *Journal of Academic Librarianship* 4 (Summer 1983): 51-73.

Reneker, Maxine H.. "Performance Appraisal in Libraries: Purpose and Techniques." In *Personnel Administration in Libraries,* edited by Sheila Creth and Frederick Duda, 227-89. New York: Neal-Schuman, 1981.

341

Rice, B. "Performance Appraisal: The Job Nobody Likes." *Psychology Today* 19 (September 1985): 30-36.

Rooks, Dana C. *Motivating Today's Library Staff: A Management Guide.* Phoenix, Ariz.: Oryx, 1988.

Rohrer, Randi Matchik. "Performance Appraisal Decisions: A Process Approach to Organizational Evaluations." Thesis. California State University at Long Beach, 1987.

Roth, Laurie Michael. *A Critical Examination of the Dual Ladder Approach to Career Advancement.* New York: Center for Career Research, 1982.

Rothstein, Samuel. "Professional Staff in Canadian University Libraries." *Library Journal* 111, no. 18 (1 November 1986): 31-34.

Sashkin, Marshall. "Appraising Appraisal: Ten Lessons from Research for Practice." *Organizational Dynamics* 9, no. 3 (Winter 1981): 37-50.

_____. *Assessing Performance Appraisal.* San Diego, Calif.: University Associates, 1981.

_____. *A Manager's Guide to Performance Management.* New York: American Management Association, 1986.

Schlessinger, Bernard S., and June H. Schlessinger. "Management." *Texas Library Journal* 61 (Spring 1985):18-19. Discusses conducting a performance appraisal interview.

Seldin, Peter. *Evaluating and Developing Administrative Performance.* San Francisco: Jossey-Bass, 1988.

Shrock, Sharon A., et al. "Merit Evaluation: A Proposed Model." In *Academic Libraries: Myths and Realities,* edited by Suzanne C. Dodson and Gary L. Menges, 155-62. Chicago: ACRL, 1984.

Smith, Karen F., and Gemma DeVinney. "Peer Review for Academic Librarians." *Journal of Academic Librarianship* 10, no. 2 (May 1984): 87-91.

Stuart-Stubbs, Basil. "Levels of Incompetence: The Peter Principle Applied to Libraries." *IPLO Quarterly* 12 (October 1970): 43-56.

Stueart, Robert D., and Barbara B. Moran, *Library Management*. 3d ed. Littleton Colo.: Libraries Unlimited, 1987, 114-28.

Sullivan, Maureen. *Improving Job Performance: Strategies for Supervisors*. ACRL Continuing Education Program CE 112. Chicago: ACRL, 1985.

Trotta, Maurice S. *Handling Grievances: A Guide for Management and Labor*. Washington, D.C.: Bureau of National Affairs, 1976.

_____. *Supervisor's Handbook on Insubordination*. Washington D.C.: Bureau of National Affairs, 1967.

Vincelette, J. P. "Improving Performance Appraisal in Libraries." *Library and Information Science Research* 6 (April 1984): 191-203.

Wallace, Patricia M. "Performance Evaluation: The Use of a Single Instrument for University Librarians and Teaching Faculty." *Journal of Academic Librarianship* 12, no. 5 (1986): 284-90.

Weber, David C., and Tina Kass. "Comparable Rewards: The Case for Equal Compensation for Non-Administrative Expertise." *Library Journal* 103 (15 April 1978): 824-27.

Wylie, Peter, and Mardy Grothe. *Problem Employees: How to Improve Their Performance*. Belmont, Calif.: Pitman Management and Training, 1981.

Yarbrough, Larry N. "Performance Appraisal in Academic and Research Libraries." *ARL Management Supplement* 3 (May 1975): 1-6.

CHAPTER 10

Termination

WHY FOCUS ON TERMINATION?

Termination is a dreaded subject. People so much dislike talking about it that they willingly use amazingly inventive euphemisms: unfund, dehire, derecruit, outplace, outcounsel, select out, RIF, separate, surplus, not retain, not renew a contract, not reappoint. The word termination is condemningly negative, even though in professional personnel practice it covers the severance of the employer-employee relationship for any reason whatever.

Employer-employee relationships in North America are generally contractual. Except for persons explicitly hired on term appointment, the normal assumption is that once employees have passed an established trial period, they are employed for the indefinite future, gain a property interest in their work, and are subject to dismissal only for reasonable cause and with reasonable notice. An employer who dismisses an employee without reasonable notice is judged to have breached the contract and may be required to provide compensation in lieu of notice. Beyond this, courts have held that employees may sue for wrongful dismissal and seek punitive damages for mental stress, loss of prestige, and other emotional factors.[1] Since the virtual demise of the employment-at-will doctrine (see below), it no longer matters whether an employer and an employee have a written contract; the fact of employment itself suffices to establish a contractual relationship, especially if there was a clear intention to hire for an unlimited time and if, in fact, the employee has served for a long period. It is for this reason, in part, that institutions now take great care in deciding who may make an offer of employment or describe to candidates the actual terms and conditions of employment.[2]

Employment-at-Will and Termination for Cause

Employment-at-will is the concept that an employer can discharge an employee without due process, or that an employee can leave an employer without notice. Until overthrown in 1959, it was the prevailing doctrine in United States for over a century. The first recorded case was *Blaisdell v. Lewis, 32 Me. 515 (1851).* After the publication of Judge Horace G. Wood's *A Treatise on the Law of Master and Servant* in 1877, the doctrine became known popularly as "Wood's rule."[3]

For over a century, and especially in private educational institutions, employment-at-will generally governed the terms and conditions of employment of both management staff – persons who are often described as working "at the pleasure of" the boss – and rank-and-file employees. A 1959 California court decision, *Petermann v. International Brotherhood of Teamsters, 174 Cal. App. 2d 184, P.2d 25 (159),* marked the beginning of the end of the system. Since 1980, court decisions in twenty-five states, as well as congressional legislation, have all but done away with it.[4] *Richard M. Woolley v. Hoffman-La Roche,* decided by New Jersey's highest court in 1985, marked the end of Wood's rule, and virtually established work as a kind of property right.

Nowadays even the most casual employer-employee relationships, including oral promises, are regarded as having the force of an implicit contract. Where no such relationship is mutually desired, the parties often prepare and sign a contract stating explicitly that no relationship exists. Yet even such arrangements are now increasingly suspect and the risk of an unenforceable contract great. Steiner and Dabrow suggested that a prearranged employment-at-will contract, even if signed by the employee, has no legal standing and does not give the employer relief from a wrongful discharge suit. Their concluding advice, while excellent, may not be very comforting to administrators who inherit staff hired long ago: hire the right people in the first place and you will not have to contend with wrongful discharge litigation.

Termination of Casual Employees

Casual and temporary employees typically do not have the same contractual rights as permanent appointees. Institutions often have explicit rules designed to maintain the casual status of such employment. If the rules governing it are not carefully followed, administrators may find that casual employees have suddenly been converted into permanent ones, with all the attendant rights and prerogatives. Among the cautions to observe (aside from knowing institutional rules thoroughly) are the number of regular hours casual employees are allowed to work and the maximum allowable term of their tenure. Allowing a casual employee to work for some long period can create an expectation of continuing employment, and the courts may hold such expectations to be valid.

Termination for Cause

As stated in chapter 2, the academic workplace is a natural environment for overstability, inviting people to put down deep roots. The most tenacious are not always the best performers, however. Simple incumbency is an obvious obstacle to excellence: a large number of tenured slots are held by people of widely varying abilities.

Just as it is an administrator's duty to hire only the best possible employees it is even more a duty to release the poor performers. Fayol rightfully called the elimination of the incompetent an "imperative duty."[5] Wherever incumbents are locked into position by tenure or collective bargaining, it may be difficult, but it is not impossible, to dislodge them. A decision to terminate always means a long series of unpleasant tasks done with due care for proper procedure: face-to-face evaluation sessions in which facts are presented unemotionally and incorporated into the written performance appraisal, regular and continuing documentation of the alleged poor performance, issuing warning letters, standing up against the inevitable grievances that will be filed, issuing the termination notice, and finally, facing the potential of a court challenge.

Because the required actions appear formidable and are not easy to implement, some administrators fail to perceive termination of the chronically deficient as a powerful weapon for upgrading both program and staff. Its use requires recognition that chronically deficient employees are likely to remain just that. Of course, there are other possible outcomes: under pressure to perform, the employees may quit or actually improve to the point where retention is not only desirable but well deserved.

Sometimes a new administrator is hired with the specific mandate to terminate a chronically nonproductive employee. Although not every candidate for the chief librarian's post will relish such a challenge, some may be willing if the possibility of success greatly outweighs the risk of failure. If an unquestionably bad condition has long been festering and if the campus administration is willing to back the candidate 100 percent, the impact of success can give the winner an enormous deposit in the bank account of credibility. Some will want to take this chance; others, not wishing to play hatchet man, will shy away. In such cases, the cliché "time is of the essence" rules; without immediate commencement of termination-related actions, the initiative will be lost and the effectiveness of the new regime dissipated.

Institutions do not lightly commence action to terminate for cause. Tolerance for less than outstanding performance is high; the sense of duty toward the institution is frequently tempered by keen knowledge of employees' obligations or length of service. Eventually, however, the administrator is obliged to choose between these conflicting forces.

GROUNDS FOR TERMINATION FOR CAUSE

Managers unfamiliar with employment law and court cases may hold naive ideas about justifiable cause. Therefore, before discussing grounds, let us inventory a few of the factors that cannot be invoked. These even include behavior that falls into the vague area of general dissatisfaction: personality conflict, lack of initiative, lack of commitment, deficiencies in oral or written communication, misjudgment in decisions, even disruptive behavior. In the United States disabilities such as addiction to alcohol or tobacco are not grounds for dismissal because they are within the range of normal human behavior. Reasons more likely to stand up include (1) unmitigated, persistent failure to fulfill duties and responsibilities out of neglect, incompetence, or failure to respond to training and/or warnings; (2) criminal misconduct (stealing, defrauding, falsification of records and documents); (3) deliberate, willful, and malicious sabotage, dishonesty, or disloyalty, (4) persistent disobedience, insolence, or insubordination; (5) persistent verbal abuse or physical violence; and (6) permanent illness that renders the employee incapable of performing. The burden of proof is, of course, on the employer. In all cases demonstrable proof–not conjecture, is required.

Of these possibilities, the first constitutes the most frequent and legitimate motive for terminating employees for cause. To avoid a wrongful dismissal suit, termination must clearly be just and based on a preponderance of objective, demonstrable data.

Except by reason of sudden ill health, no employee's performance declines so precipitously that it falls from acceptable to unacceptable. Years of so-so performance, if accepted by the institution, argue for continued retention, although not necessarily in the same position. Even moving a person to a different position can be challenged, however. Therefore honest, forthright performance appraisal is absolutely vital.

DUE PROCESS AND DOCUMENTATION

While it may not be difficult to recognize incompetence, doing something about it is aggravating, expensive, and time consuming.

The procedures involved require thoroughly objective investigation, meticulous documentation, and careful observance of due process. For three reasons the last may be the best starting point for discussion: (1) ignoring due process dooms the proposed action to failure, and (2) termination for cause requires an in-depth understanding of its legal ramifications,[6] and (3) a fundamental aspect of Western legal tradition is that one cannot arbitrarily deprive people of rights or property.

There are eight minimal requirements are for due process:

1. A *clear, preexisting articulation of what performance level is acceptable*

2. Prompt, appropriate documentation of the unacceptable performance; preferably several evaluations at different times by more than one person

3. Evidence that the employee has received performance-appraisal information and is aware of the potential consequences of failure to perform

4. An understanding that an employee's rights of free speech, association, and academic freedom must be respected

5. Ample, explicit prior warnings of unacceptable behavior and clear notice that its continuation will not be tolerated

6. Notice appropriate to the employee's seniority and potential reemployability, except in cases of criminal action where, almost universally, an employee forfeits the right to notice

7. Codified, published procedures applicable to all personnel actions, including the right to hearings[7]

8. The right of appeal in accordance with established procedures, including timely notice of hearings; opportunity to prepare responses, confront and cross-examine witnesses; the opportunity to present oral and written evidence on one's own behalf; the right to retain an attorney

Regardless of the institution's size, it is essential that the manager seek expert legal advice at the earliest stages of terminating an employee. This is no task for amateur lawyers. Normally, advice is readily available from staff legal counsel.

When published performance expectations are well articulated and a system of appraisal is in place, the next element of due process is a series of warnings. After initial investigation has established that a problem exists, a rehabilitation program for the problem employee provides reasonable opportunity for improvement. Normally, the time limits for improvement will be established by local procedures or contract terms.

Terminating employees during an initial trial period requires special care. The trial period usually includes the time for notice. Thus if regulations require thirty days' notice of termination, a nominal six-month trial may really only be five months.

Documentation of evidence for terminating an employee for cause is crucial. It accomplishes three things: (1) it helps to affirm the facts claimed by the administration, (2) it establishes that agreed on procedures were followed, and (3) it provides a foundation for confident response to cross-examination in a hearing. Failure in any one of these areas virtually eliminates the case. Pertinent material must be in writing; without written records the case for dismissal does not exist. Ample and satisfactory documentation – sometimes called "preventive law" – means that decisions are documented in such a way that they will withstand the scrutiny of judicial examination. To make sure that this requirement is satisfied, both the decision-making process and the decisions themselves are often developed by staff legal counsel, an arrangement that contributes to putting arbitrary decision making far from the deciders.

The golden rule of documentation is always to be specific and factual. In difficult cases, it is better to have too much documentation than too little. Every step along the way, including statements of the problem and progress of any rehabilitation program, must be specified with date, time, place, and a summary of what was said to the employee. The cost of starting and maintaining all of these data is staggering. It must be weighed against the cost of doing nothing, which will only worsen any bad situation, or doing a bare minimum, which will likely backfire by ensuring failure. The following suggestions may be useful: (1) take notes immediately after each documentable event, (2) be sure that the notes are well written and accurately reflect the exact circumstances, and (3) record time, date, place, and the names of witnesses. Check with staff legal counsel whether it is required to give a copy of each documented item to the affected employee.

A special sign of need for management to make careful documentation of its own views is indication that employees are making their own notes. If an administration fails to perceive these signals, a case can easily be lost by default through lack of any counterview when a case comes to a hearing. Unusually assertive employees sometimes prepare notes or minutes of their own understanding of a transaction, send you a copy and inform you that unless they hear otherwise from you, their notes constitute an official or semiofficial record of events or statements. To avoid a contretemps, it is best not to allow individualized, adversarial proceedings but simply to affirm in principle that any such notes represent solely that writer's own views.

Beware of weak supervisors who, acting on a misguided principle of parsimony, urge minimal documentation. Even though they are willing to bring their complaints to you, they may be reluctant to face the troubling facts about a case and even more reluctant to set their judgments down in writing. It may take a long time but it will be worth your effort to help your supervisors understand the necessity of proceeding against a chronically deficient employee. In the end, you may have to change supervisors to discharge an employee whose chronic incompetence is dragging down organizational performance and staff morale.

To help strengthen a weak supervisor, point out that control in the work relationship has passed from the supervisor to the employee and that failure to act will have to be taken into acount when that supervisor's own performance appraisal is prepared. Emphasize that as time passes people acquire a property right in their work and corresponding rights in their work habits and that courts generally interpret long-established sufferance as normal employer policy.

Despite determination and a good case, the road to a successful discharge is long and arduous. It might takes years to develop a case and bring it to a successful conclusion. Increasingly, modern legislation and court decisions at the federal, state, and provincial levels are protecting employees from arbitrary or capricious action, such as a discharge based merely on personality clash. Such laws and rulings benefit the entire organization, because they require that action be taken only with due process, on the basis of provable fact, and through the application of objective, observable, and verifiable criteria.

FISCAL AND OTHER OBLIGATIONS OF TERMINATION

Statute and school regulations govern most of the financial and other obligations connected with termination. A formula allocating the costs of hearings and transcripts is normally built into personnel policy and procedure, whether or not there is a collective agreement. In almost every case the administrator should expect the usual financial obligations – severance pay, vacation accrual, opportunity for limited continuation of benefits such as health insurance – to be debited against the library budget. In unusual cases it may be possible to negotiate additional special costs (e.g., outplacement fees, removal expenses, or in exceptional cases, buy-off fees).

In the case of buy-off fees, it is typical to require departing employees to sign irrevocable agreeements waiving any right to sue the school in connection with termination action. A usual condition of settlements is that their terms remain confidential, a protection for both ex-employees and institutions. Staff legal counsel normally is responsible for preparing the agreement, which the parties may negotiate out of court. An unfriendly termination can have a severe impact, with some risk of inflicting economic damage to the library's program if the library is required to pay the full cost of a settlement.

AVOIDANCE OF SECRECY

When recording documentation that could lead to dismissal, it is essential to avoid secret files. Inquire of staff legal counsel whether you should give the persons involved copies of pertinent documents. If employees are denied access to such documents, they will probably obtain the papers anyhow in the legal process of discovery.[8] The defense then may claim that the administration was secretly conspiring to rid itself of an employee without just cause and without due process. A requirement for open communication of warnings, appraisals, and related documentation is usually built into bargaining contracts or academic procedure manuals.

Few things are more embarrassing or hazardous at a hearing than a witness who is unable to recollect particulars. Since memory for detail often fades quickly after the event, notes can be invaluable. You should ensure that your notes do not contradict written documentation or contain anything that might weaken or overturn your case. If they are the sole source of a case, however, you have no case. In the event of hearings, notes can be used only as an aide-mémoire, not as principal documents.

OBSTACLES TO TERMINATION FOR CAUSE

A principal enemy of termination for cause is inaction over a long period. Employees whose bad habits have been tolerated for many years have earned the right to continue the level of performance that has clearly justified their retention. Sometimes a change of administration is the only really effective method of removing long-time non-performers.

Unlike other major industrial countries, the United States has virtually no federal legislation explicitly preventing termination without good cause.[9] Despite this, in forty-six states workers can sue for wrongful discharge.[10] Although employees in many sectors now enjoy considerable job security, there is no de jure lifetime incumbency anywhere. Even tenured faculty have been removed, sometimes as a disciplinary measure and sometimes owing to financial constraints. Despite institutional tendencies toward inertia, seriously deficient performers can be terminated for cause.

A final obstacle to termination action is fear of reprisal or countersuit. There is no real answer to this threat, although liability insurance might help. Most institutions carry their own liability insurance or are self-insured. If a school officer is sued for wrongful dismissal the school normally defends the suit if the action was approved at all steps and all procedures properly followed. Even a successful institutional defense does not, however, protect anyone from a private lawsuit.[11]

Challenges to termination for cause can be based on considerations such as the following:

1. Constructive dismissal: Demoting an employee to a junior position that has just been vacated

2. Employee's actions were simple misjudgment, not gross incompetence

3. Demotion, including a cut in pay, benefits, and responsibilities

4. Shift downward in the reporting structure, usually accompanied by a loss of prestige

5. A unilaterally implemented change in responsibilities (this might include "kicking someone upstairs")

6. A forced transfer or reassignment

7. Employer misconduct: (a) deliberately making a person's work situation intolerable, tantamount to forced resignation, (b) termination without justifiable cause or proper notice

EMOTIONAL IMPACTS OF TERMINATION

A common initial reaction to termination for cause is employee confusion and disbelief. This may be followed by shock, physical and mental pain, outrage, shame, grief, or even anomie. The emotions are real, intense, and enduring. The worker's daily routine is disrupted: gone is the pattern of getting up, having breakfast, going to work, and coming home at the end of the day. The worker who once "belonged," is now alone. Emotional trauma may prevent the former employee from using newly found surplus time for leisure or any constructive purpose.

Once chronically deficient employees perceive that the administration means business, however, resignation without a fight is a possible – but unlikely – response. Other, less agreeable responses are more probable, for the threat of termination can be an exceedingly powerful motivator and energizer. Employees facing termination can summon seemingly inexhaustible energies to build a case for retention, manufacture a surprisingly wide range of interpretations of regulations or challenges to the credibility of witnesses' and supervisors' testimony, or threaten to "blow the whistle" on other employees, especially anyone in administration.

There are negative impacts on administrators, too: guilt over an action that hurts others, guilt over the exercise of power and authority, shame at failure to rehabilitate those in decline, disappointment that so much administrative time had to be diverted from the library's programmatic affairs. No amount of practice or role playing can prepare a manager for the difficulties of terminating an employee for cause, and no administrative action makes more demands on a leader's emotional health. Except possibly for the institution, there is never a real "winner" in termination cases. Every closely involved individual pays dearly; only the currencies differ among the parties.

TERMINATION FOR REASONS OTHER THAN CAUSE

Employee-initiated terminations typically progress through a series of administrative steps provided in most institutions' canons of personnel practice. Actions on termination for lack of work, lack of funds, or abandonment of a program, however, rarely proceed in accordance with predetermined steps. Such actions are often challenged by individuals, informal pressure groups, or unions.

When a school closes a program, academic librarians can hardly claim that it should be maintained to ensure continuation of their employment. Unless an entire institution goes bankrupt, programs almost never close instantaneously. When they do shrink and staff are released, the jargon in personnel practice is RIF (reduction in force), a term invented by government employees. Typically, admissions are cut off beyond a certain date, students in the pipeline are permitted to complete their degrees, and library purchasing specific to the program is discontinued. Faculty and specialized librarians may be offered the options of early retirement or outplacement assistance. Even the most specialized librarians have enough generalist capacity to move into a different assignment, however, and if they perform well they ought to have the chance to find another job in the profession. Here is where librarianship has it all over the professoriate, since the transformation of a physics professor into an African studies specialist is a most unlikely prospect.

Early retirement is widely used in industry as a means of "downsizing" large companies and realizing huge salary savings. Such a technique would be totally counterproductive in an academic library: it is precisely the long-term employees who have the greatest fund of process knowledge so indispensable to the library's functioning. The only long-term employees for whom one might encourage early retirement are those who have become totally unproductive. Even then, a much better alternative is to invest in some rescue program to retrain or restimulate them.

Attrition is hardly ever program related but often serves as an expedient to meet budget cut targets. The use of attrition to regulate staff size implies a capacity for flexibility and reassignment; otherwise it can inflict long-term damage to the program.

ADMINISTRATIVE ASPECTS OF TERMINATION

Four vital aspects of termination are where to do it, when to do it, how much time to take, and what documents should be given to the fired employee. It is best not to call employees into your own office to fire them. Use neutral territory because you will undoubtedly wish to leave that space immediately after the action. Earlier in the week is better than later because it gives former employees an opportunity to come to grips with the situation. Friday is a poor choice; not only does it damage the weekend but it also sends a person's family life into a nosedive. Some experts suggest noon as a good time because many will already have gone for lunch and the terminated individuals are spared from having to confront their colleagues. It is brutal to terminate anyone in a five minute session, but it is equally painful to prolong the agony beyond fifteen or twenty minutes. Naturally, the session must cover the effective date plus details of the severance package, and duration of benefits (e.g., health insurance). Finally, each terminated employee should be given a letter summarizing what has been covered in the final interview. It goes without saying that no such document can be presented without prior approval by the institution's staff legal counsel.

When management personnel are terminated, arrange for others to take over the appropriate responsibilities at once, and simultaneously announce the new arrangements. Prompt action ensures that your announcement will not go through the grapevine.

It is also necessary to obtain keys, identification badge, credit cards, and parking permits; require return of computer diskettes, documentation, library-owned hardware (e.g., portable computer, dictation machine), and files that are library property. Debit any unexpended business expense advances against accrued salary or vacation. Cancel or change telephone and other credit card numbers. Arrange for payroll to deduct from accrued vacation or severance pay any applicable taxes. Have employees sign waivers prepared by staff legal counsel plus other regular separation papers. Arrange a non-embarrassing opportunity for the discharged employee to remove personal property from the office, but bear in mind that it may not be wise to allow that person to be completely alone in the office. In a few extreme cases it may be necessary to rekey locks.

OUTPLACEMENT

Outplacement, a comparatively new word in the vocabulary of personnel administration, is a form of employee assistance provided by firms specializing in helping those laid off or terminated. The services may include permission to use an office and limited access to telephone, secretarial, and photocopy services, plus career assessment sessions with a professional relocation counselor. Sometimes, as part of the termination settlement, the institution pays for outplacement, even if an employee has been terminated for cause, as a humanitarian gesture, or simply to avoid embarrassment. Occasionally an outplacement service is called in ahead of time to help plan the services to be provided for the terminated employee.

Owing to the general shrinkage of management throughout North American business, outplacement has become a major service industry. No full-time outplacement business has yet developed for librarianship, however.

SUMMARY

While selection and appointment are the most critical responsibilities at one end of the personnel spectrum, termination of the chronically deficient is an equally heavy burden. Severing the employer-employee relationship, however, is far more complex than establishing it. Law and contract provide generous protection to employees, putting the burden of proof and due process on the inherently more powerful institution. It is virtually impossible to terminate employees without expensive, time-consuming consultations with staff legal counsel, and compilation of exhaustive documentation. The uniform advice of termination experts is to hire the right people in the first place, but academic library administrators have that opportunity comparatively infrequently. Leave positions vacant in preference to hiring applicants who do not meet the requirements. A vacancy is merely a temporary inconvenience; a chronically deficient employee could be a permanent one.

Notes

1. In *Foley v. Interactive Data Corporation,* a 1988 California Supreme Court decision sharply limited an employee's rights in the matter of wrongful dismissal. The court ruled that the dismissed employee could sue only on the basis of breach of employment contract, thus severely curtailing the right to sue for punitive damages under tort law. It will be essential to watch carefully as law develops in this area.

2. Certain large corporations now attach disclaimers to personnel handbooks, and even to employment application forms, explicitly stating that those documents are not part of the employment contract.

3. *Payne v. Western & A.R.R.,* 81 Tenn. 507 (1884), the most frequently cited "first" case is actually the first based on Wood's Rule.

4. Don A. Zimmerman and Jane Howard-Martin, "The National Labor Relations Act and Employment-at-Will: The Federal Preemption Doctrine Revisited," *Labor Law Journal* 37, no. 4 (April 1986): 223-34.

5. Fayol, *General and Industrial Management*, 98.

6. Disclaimer: The author's recommendations pertinent to the employer-employee relationship are intended solely as the suggestions of an informed layperson, not as legal advice. Every administrator contemplating or involved in termination for cause must obtain legal advice from a lawyer and/or the institution's staff legal counsel, or both.

7. In *Perry v. Sindermann* (402 US 593 (1972)), the Supreme Court ruled that the dismissal of Sindermann, a college professor, violated the U.S. Constitution's Fourteenth Amendment because the school had failed to grant him a hearing before declining to renew his contract.

8. In civil procedures in the United States, opposing counsel has the right to demand copies of any pertinent evidential material. Only privileged material is immune (i.e., communications between client and attorney). Discovery is designed to give all parties equal access to the facts of a case and to prevent surprise revelations at a hearing or trial. Thus, almost any documentary material pertinent to an employee's dismissal may be subject to examination.

9. As of 1987 only Montana had such legislation.

10. In Canada, unionized workers cannot sue over wrongful dismissal, but they may invoke their grievance procedures. If the grievance outcome is not to their satisfaction, the final step is arbitration.

11. Joseph J. Mika and Bruce A. Shuman, "Legal Issues Affecting Libraries and Librarians," *American Libraries* 19, no. 2 (February 1988): 108-12. See also Nasri, William, "Professional Liability" *Journal of Library Administration* 7, no. 4 (Summer 1986): 141-45.

Resources

Allen, Jeffrey G. *The Employee Termination Handbook*. New York: Wiley, 1986.

American Library Association, Office for Library Personnel Resources. *Administering Staff Cutbacks; Planning and Implementing a Reduction in Force*. Chicago, 1983.

Barbash, Joseph, John D. Feerick, and Jerome B. Kauff. *Unjust Dismissal and At Will Employment*. New York: Practising Law Institute, 1982.

Brown, F. "Limiting Yours Risks in the New Russian Roulette – Discharging Employees." *Employment Relations Law Review* 18 (1983): 380-406.

Canada Law Book. *Dismissal and Employment Law Digest*. Aurora, Ontario, nine issues per year.

Canadian Manufacturers' Association. *Termination of Employment – Wrongful Dismissal*. Toronto, 1982.

Coulson, Robert. *The Termination Handbook*. New York: Free Press, 1986.

"Due Process in Decisions Relating to Tenure in Higher Education." *Journal of College and University Law* 11, no. 3 (Winter 1984): 323-44.

The Economist. *Managing Redundancy*. London, 1985.

Grosman, Brian A. *The Executive Firing Line: Wrongful Dismissal and the Law*. Toronto: Methuen, 1984.

_____. *Fire Power*. Toronto: Penguin, 1985.

Harris, Richard. *Wrongful Dismissal*. Don Mills, Ontario: Richard de Boo, Ltd. (Loose-leaf service.)

Hendrickson, Robert M., and Barbara A. Lee. *Academic Employment and Retrenchment: Judicial Review and Administrative Action*. ASHE Report, 83-8. Washington, D.C.: Association for the Study of Higher Education, 1983.

Holloway, William J., and Michael J. Leech. *Employment Termination: Rights and Remedies*. Washington, D.C.: BNA, 1985.

Imundo, Louis V. *Employee Discipline: How to Do It Right*. Belmont, Calif.: Wadsworth, 1985.

"Interview with a Fired Librarian." *Illinois Libraries* 59 (March 1977): 224-28.

"It's Getting Harder to Make a Firing Stick." *Business Week*, 27 June 1983, 104-5.

Jeffries, John A. "Employment at Will: When Can an Employee be Terminated?" *Public Libraries* 22, no. 4 (Winter 1983): 150-51.

Kauff, Jerome B. *Employment Problems in the Workplace*. New York: Practising Law Institute, 1986.

Kauff, Jerome B., and Maureen E. McClain. *Unjust Dismissal Update 1985: How to Evaluate, Litigate, Settle, and Avoid Claims*. New York: Practising Law Institute, 1985.

Kelly, John G. *Human Resources Management and Government Regulation*. Don Mills, Ontario: CCH Canada, 1987.

LaNoue, George R., and Barbara A. Lee. *Academics in Court: The Consequences of Faculty Discrimination Litigation*. Ann Arbor: University of Michigan Press, 1987.

Larson, Lex K., and Philip Borowsky. *Unjust Dismissal*. New York: Bender, 1985. (Loose-leaf service.)

Latack, Janina C., and Janelle B. Dozier. "After the Ax Falls: Job Loss as a Career Transition." *Academy of Management Review* 11, no. 2 (1986): 375-92.

Levitt, Howard A. *The Law of Dismissal in Canada*. Aurora, Ontario: Canada Law Book, 1985.

Library Administration and Management Association. *Guidelines on Job Termination for Librarians and Their Employees*. Chicago, n.d. (Leaflet.)

McEwen, Joan I., et al. *Wrongful Dismissmal*. Vancouver, B.C.: Continuing Legal Education, 1986.

Mika, Joseph J., and Bruce A. Shuman. "Legal Issues Affecting Libraries and Librarians." *American Libraries* 19, no. 2 (February 1988): 108-12.

____. "Legal Issues Affecting Libraries and Librarians: Employment Law, Liability and Insurance, Contracts and Problems Patrons." *American Libraries* 19, no. 3 (March 1988): 214-17.

Oliver, Anthony T., and Bruce D. May. "Wrongful Termination Law: Replacing Employment-at-Will." In *The Employee Termination Handbook*, edited by Jeffrey G. Allen, 1-40. New York: Wiley, 1986.

Roberds, Darryel Lee. *Small Companies and the Employment at Will Doctrine: Discipline and Discharge Dispute Resolution, Personnel Procedures and Practices, and Unfair Dismissal Lawsuits and Their Outcomes in Small, Nonunion Companies*. Ph.D. diss., University of Mississippi, 1987.

Saxe, Stuart. *Ontario Employment Law Handbook: An Employer's Guide*. Rev. ed. Scarborough, Ontario: Butterworth, 1986.

Simon, Barry. "Developing Termination Policies and Procedures." *American Libraries* 4 (January 1973): 45-47.

Steiner, Julius M., and Allan M. Dabrow. "The Questionable Value of the Inclusion of Language Confirming Employment-at-Will Status in Company Personnel Documents." *Labor Law Journal* 37, no. 9 (1986): 639-45.

Stumpf, Warren W. "Liability Insurance for Library Directors and Officers." *Library & Archival Security* 7, no. 2 (Summer 1985): 33-37.

Walker, Susan O., and Margaret N. Newborg. "Termination: A Manager's Toughest Job." In *The Handbook of Executive Communication*, edited by John Louis DiGaetani, 699-709. Homewood, Ill.: Dow Jones-Irwin, 1986.

Weeks, Kent M. "Dismissal for Cause." *AGB Reports* 21, no. 3 (May-June 1979): 8-22.

Yerburgh, Mark R. "Some Unguarded Thoughts on Academic Librarianship: Vision vs. Reality," *CLIC Quarterly* 2, no. 4 (December 1983): 11-19.

Youngblood, Stuart A., and Gary L. Tidwell. "Termination at Will: Some Changes in the Wind." *Personnel* 58, no. 3 (May-June 1981): 22-33.

Zimmerman, Don A., and Jane Howard-Martin. "The National Labor Relations Act and Employment-at-Will: The Federal Preemption Doctrine Revisited." *Labor Law Journal* 37, no. 4 (April 1986): 223-34.

CHAPTER 11

Staff Development

Upper-echelon administrators are ex officio in a permanent staff development program. A privileged few, they enjoy every conceivable development perk: rich channels of communication, travel, authority, highly flexible work schedules that are often of their own making, stimulating mental challenges, and generously supportive human, material, and technical resources. Enlightened administrative practice, social science research, and common sense all suggest that this historically narrow focus of staff development is no longer tenable. In a competitive atmosphere, would-be recruits at all levels are eager for development opportunities.

Active leaders and professional staff exemplify the best type of staff development by attending conferences and workshops, producing high-quality initiatives, keeping up with, sharing, and contributing to professional literature, conducting research, and maintaining contact with colleagues. Not all employees want to have their talents developed, however. While there is no sense trying to jam development activities down the throats of uninterested people, administrations do not have the option of offering development opportunities only to the proactive; they must provide equally to all.

A program that really works, however, is so stimulating that hardly anyone refuses a development opportunity.

For a long time rank-and-file professional staff have benefitted from modest but continuing development programs. In contrast, the general situation of highly educated support staff in academic libraries--mostly baby boomers--exemplifies what Bardwick calls "structural plateauing," for no others have greater limitations placed on their career development potential.[1] The strongly vertical layering of academe itself and the exempt/nonexempt labor distinction combine to put a tight lid on advancement possibilities for these individuals. They present the greatest and most difficult challenge to staff development.

In brief, a mix of age, attitude, expectation, legal status, and rapid technological change has disrupted the former steadiness of library work, displacing the stable conditions of a time when all workers "knew their places" and a unit's time budget could be regarded as comparatively fixed. Staff development implies a complete reordering of a library's time budget; it is the primary institutional response to this relatively new social instability in the academic library workplace.

WHAT IS STAFF DEVELOPMENT?

Staff development is no single thing, nor is its main purpose the development of individual qua individual. No program can be justified solely on the basis of individual benefit, but must bear demonstrable connection to a school's academic community. Staff development is that corpus of activity that focuses on enhancing human capacities in communication, knowledge and work expertise. By fostering community values, successful staff development contributes to employees' self-realization, self-fulfillment, and self-respect in ways that are less self-centered, less self-conscious, and more community oriented than the generation of the 1960s would have expected. Through staff development programs, people realize they are working in and for a community.

Promotion

Earlier we stated that many library workers, both professional and support staff, conceive of promotion into a management position as the ultimate step in staff development. Academic librarians used to complain, with considerable justification, that salaries were geared almost entirely to their level of administrative responsibilities, a practice that undervalued academic and intellectual achievement and undermined morale. The custom of rewarding administrative responsibilities also attracted to management some people who had little interest in or talent for its challenges. To resolve this problem the dual track system was devised: as in the professoriate, librarians could advance to the highest rank whether or not they held administrative assignments.[2]

Dual track can be used whether or not librarians have faculty status. In solving one problem, however, it creates another: librarians who take their administrative responsibilities seriously quickly see their nonmanagerial colleagues rising in rank and pay at practically identical rates, but at significantly lower stress levels. In some schools this problem is partially solved by paying a modest stipend to those bearing administrative responsibilities, or by limiting the terms of administrators. Even this solution is far from satisfactory: making the stipend substantial defeats the dual track concept. The real merit of dual track is that it rewards outstanding performers without moving them into management. This is a tremendous advantage precisely because it enables people not suited to management to apply their skills in areas where they are most capable and valuable. Research laboratories have this same problem: the best scientists often have the least patience with administrative detail; promoting such a scientist to a manager is a disaster. Dual track systems enable first-rate librarians to choose their own style of development--unit manager or state-of-the-art librarian.

Staff Development to Help the Locked-In Classified Staff

For support staff, job classification and employee development programs form a system in constant tension. They work against each other because support work does not have development automatically built in, as professional work does: the job, not the person, is classified. The effect is to put a classified employee's development opportunities on hold until a slot opens up, a program is changed, a job is reconstituted, or its duties reallocated. As technological development continues, it remains a management responsibility to encourage these employees to take other posts, even in the face of resistance. Fortunately, people seem to be fairly willing to make the necessary moves, but once they learn some basic computer skills, opportunities for further development and advancement may lie outside the library.

LIBRARY PERSONNEL OFFICERS AND STAFF DEVELOPMENT

The chief librarian and the library personnel officer (LPO) play key roles in staff development. Regardless of size, every library has someone filling that position even if it is only the chief librarian.

In libraries that have not previously had personnel officers, staff sometimes respond negatively to the proposal for such a position. If the LPO position does not exist, the chief librarian will have to convince at least two constituencies that it is needed: local staff and the professional staff of the campus personnel office. The latter may see establishment of an in-house LPO as a threat to its own turf, while the former may consider it to be a disruption of familiar, informal ways. Skepticism comes partly from a perceived threat of this new and unknown power in the administration and partly from line managers' tendency to see another slot "wasted" in unproductive overhead.

In an important review article, Webb pointed out that while everyone expects to find an LPO in large libraries, increasingly the position is showing up in middle-size organizations.[3] She correctly identified a shift from collections to services and human resources--

and the major programmatic changes consequent to this shift--as the principal forces behind growth of the LPO position in academic libraries. As the library consciously turns into an environment for lifelong learning, the library personnel officer becomes a vital added value consultative position in the academic library. Webb's inventory of duties and functions for the LPO is informative:

1. Recruiting officer

2. Designer and manager of personnel records system

3. Custodian of campus policy and procedures manual (as it affects personnel administration)

4. Developer and conductor of orientation, training, and staff-development programs

5. Spokesperson for Affirmative Action, Equal Employment Opportunity, and other legal requirements in connection with recruiting and employment

6. Counselor of individual employees on personal and career problems; helper in resolving conflicts in professionals' different interpretations of what is important to the library program

In an increasingly complex and litigious world, the LPO is the internal consultant and facilitator who researches issues and provides a menu of options prior to personnel actions. He or she understands legal issues or knows where and how to acquire the knowledge of such issues. In small to medium-size libraries, the LPO might be responsible for both the legal aspects of personnel administration and for staff development; obviously, no one person could do both in large libraries. Conventionally, this person is staff rather than line, but this handy distinction is not always a good fit to administrative reality. The LPO plays vital line roles in implementing staff-development programs and helping to redesign work.

COMPONENTS OF A STAFF-DEVELOPMENT PROGRAM

There are two interlocking aspects of a staff-development program. First, every program component must contribute to continuous learning. Second, and inextricably tied up with the first, no employee should be permitted to wither away, year after year, in a series of unchanging responsibilities. In short, successful staff development means change. The specific content of staff the programs is limited by available resources, and also by the imagination of its planners and how they have ranked local program and planning priorities.

Conferences and Continuing Education Workshops/Institutes

The benefits of external professional involvements are often available independently of conference program quality and in spite of association bureaucracy: (1) the face-to-face social and intellectual contact with colleagues and the collegiality this builds, (2) the broadening of outlook and the changed perspective afforded by seeing what is done elsewhere and how others approach problems, (3) the reduction of the effects of isolation from the mainstream, (4) the opportunity to stimulate and be stimulated, and (5) the stimulus provided by contact with vendors' new technology at exhibits. In short, the best aspect of conferences and workshops is not necessarily their formal content but rather the opportunity to meet new people, exchange ideas, and in general, receive stimulus from other professionals.

Librarians who attend professional meetings and conferences tend to be a highly skewed, self-selected sample of the profession. Despite the impressive attendance figures at ALA meetings in recent years, the vast majority of librarians rarely or never attend such meetings. Rothstein pointed out how overstability of staff contributes to stagnation in the Canadian academic library community, an observation that is equally valid for the United States.[4] When resources were abundant and educational institutions were expanding rapidly and continuously, new appointees, staff turnover, and a constant infusion of fresh funds stimulated innovation. Now that resources are scarce, the need for outside stimulus is even more important.

The Association of College and Research Libraries (ACRL) is an excellent source of high-quality, modestly priced continuing education institutes and workshops. In recent years, ACRL has provided continuing education both at conferences and on site at schools throughout North America. Topics include interviewing, managing student workers, performance evaluation, strategic planning, supervision, survey research methods, basic statistics, time management, Affirmative Action, personnel management, written communication, using business literature effectively, writing and publishing, and the role of the library within the college or university. National ACRL conferences bring together leading academic librarians in a national forum; their published proceedings form a valuable research record. The Association of Research Libraries' Office of Management Studies (ARL/OMS) maintains a program in organizational training and staff development in management skills. The group also provides consulting services for libraries wishing to developing their own programs. (Almost every ARL/OMS program is open to non-ARL libraries for a fee.)

Take advantage of the tremendous ferment and change in modern academic libraries to convene local or regional meetings to share the results of new approaches and new methodologies. A conference opens up the library to others and helps to inhibit isolationism. Planning and managing its organizational complexities are also good administrative experiences for junior staff. Acting as local arrangements liaison for a national or regional conference in the local area is another development opportunity.

Active Membership in Nonlibrary Professional Associations

Participation in the work of nonlibrary professional associations is especially valuable. In a study of 150 managers from fifteen different kinds of libraries employing 50 or more professionals, Person discovered that only two subjects belonged to nonlibrary management associations and that few even belonged to management groups within library associations. Person concluded, "A rather insular view of library management may develop if personal sources of definition are largely confined to the same type of library setting or to the organization itself."[5]

Travel and Site Visits

The map of higher education in North America shows many schools located far from large urban centers. Support for conference attendance is much more important for remote institutions than for those in large metropolitan areas. Because a professional's external involvement is an investment in career development, not a frill, when resources are scarce, the investment is critical. It is the chief librarian's responsibility to secure support for professional participation to complement the program. Unlike business, higher education never has and probably never will provide full support for participation. Professional commitment will continue to mean personal commitment.[6]

At one time traveling librarians were limited to a small coterie of active members of the major North American library associations and directors of the very large member libraries of the Association of Research Libraries. The computer revolution has radically changed the exclusivist character of travel. Library programs now demand interaction with many persons and organizations outside the library, both local and distant. Merely to keep up with the technology it is essential for librarians to attend a variety of professional conferences, and most especially for network participants to attend committee meetings and continuing education workshops to maximize the profit of network services for their institutions.[7]

If you administer a small library, you can probably get away with allocating travel funds informally, perhaps personally by reviewing and approving a submission. As soon as the span of direct control is reduced by establishment of departmentation or subject specialist groups, some bureaucratic process must be implemented. Peer review is an excellent, collegial way of allocating travel support, provided that you have something to allocate. The professional staff will be eager to participate in a process of immediate benefit to themselves and will gladly draft a review procedure. You must establish firm guidelines for them to work with, however, or the results may not be acceptable. Indicate in your guidelines that you expect simplicity and directness in the proposal.

The question arises as to whether the administration should maintain veto power over the recommendations of a staff travel review body. As the chief librarian is the person ultimately responsible for all resource allocation decisions, it could be argued that that person should have final review rights. On the other hand, there is little point in having a collegial review process if it is not going to be implemented. There can be no sure answer to this question. If resources are generous, one can afford to give the review body real spending authority and let pass some recommendations that the administration might regard as questionable. When resources are tight, staff would probably find it acceptable if the travel committee were disbanded and any pretense removed from the start. When the institution at large faces a budget crunch, a higher-level decision often preempts all library policy. This frequently happens in state institutions when a distant bureaucrat decides that a lot of money can be saved simply by banning all out-of-state travel.

It is a mistake to suppose that travel by professionals is always more important than travel by support staff. As libraries computerize more and more bibliographic processes, it is increasingly important that key support staff travel for both training and educational purposes. The need is especially critical for those who supervise vital data entry and maintenance operations. Seeing similar work being done elsewhere--perhaps quite differently--is especially beneficial to long-term, loyal support staff who generally lack the developmental opportunities accorded to librarians. Organized visits with specific learning objectives can have a dramatic and exhilarating impact on support staff, broadening their outlook, increasing their respect for professionals, and helping them perceive themselves as part of a group with a unified purpose.

Travel for support staff is typically on a need-to-go basis and is approved by the administration on recommendation from appropriate professional staff. The distinction between professional and support staff emerges clearly in the two styles of financing their travel: normally, professional travel is based on proposals originated by professionals in fulfillment of academic responsibilities, while for support staff it is usually based on professional analysis of program needs, recommendation, and administrative judgment.

Campus Lectures and Courses

Overrigid administration of the privilege of attending campus lectures can be counterproductive. Some administrators require that the lectures be work related if they are scheduled during working hours. This is not such an easy decision when dealing with professional staff whose interests range widely. It is probably better to be more generous than less and rely more on good judgment than on a prescription.

In addition, because courses extend over a considerable period, one must consider the return on investment. In this sense, courses are like travel: the applicant should prepare a proposal for review by a committee of peers who could judge the benefit to the individual and the institution.

Colloquia and Special Guests

Regardless of a school's location, it is generally possible to persuade an accomplished librarian or other distinguished person from another institution to spend a day interacting with staff. Colloquia are especially beneficial to libraries off the beaten track or whose budgets do not permit generous travel support. A meeting with a librarian, dean, or association leader at the state, provincial, or national level can be tremendously stimulating to staff.

Training

Some libraries meet part of the staff development challenge by requiring that new employees' training programs be prepared (and approved by unit manager and library personnel officer) well in advance of the start of employment. Creth prepared a complete monograph on staff training.[8] (As stated in chapter 8, we associate the word "training" with repetitive, task-oriented work, and therefore believe the term is generally inappropriate for professional staff. The reader is cautioned that in British usage, "training" is frequently equivalent to our "graduate education.")

Instruction; Research Assistance

Development, design, and implementation of courses in bibliographic instruction or teaching in any other field for which the librarian is qualified provide variety, stimulus, and broad public contact. Extensions include the development of video training aids, advising on theses for graduate students, and for undergraduates, term paper clinics.

Requests for Proposals

Because distributed computing is now so cheap, in-house bibliographic systems are becoming widely available. The development of functional and performance specifications for local systems, and eventually a request for proposals (RFP) is a major development opportunity for all levels of staff. These major undertakings are only the beginning of opportunity: through them professional staff can begin to develop their own proposals for realizing some heretofore unfulfilled aspect of the library program. Peer group administration of a local development fund can enhance the sense of system ownership.

Development of an RFP requires exceptionally careful, closely detailed planning. If librarians have little experience with proposal writing, some guidance from the administration will be helpful, especially in proposed design and budget preparation. For specifying performance criteria, it may be necessary to call in consultants or other technical experts. Where experience is lacking, a professionally conducted workshop on proposal preparation is of value.

Split Assignments and Exchanges

The view that an employee should "stick to the knitting" might be valid in some low-level manufacturing or industrial jobs, but it is inappropriate at any level in an academic library. Split assignments and exchanges enhance everyone's technical knowledge and help people see how their work is related to the entire program. Work sharing is especially beneficial to classified staff because they do not have the same development opportunities as professionals.

Always encourage staff to prepare proposals for an exchange of professional responsibilities. Preparation of the proposal itself develops planning and writing skills, which can be further enhanced by requiring a final written report. An exchange also opens up an opportunity for public presentation on campus or at a conference, and as a follow-up, publication. Exchanges can be extended to other institutions and even those abroad. Work permits, immigration regulations, and tax liability complicate the planning of foreign exchanges.[9]

The effect of any short-term exchange is transient and, as with job enlargement, there can be a letdown when the exchange is over. Bardwick suggested that lateral transfers and exchanges should be normal administrative practice and should be on some regular cycle; she suggested a five-year cycle.[10] As libraries move more toward integrated styles of operation, work requirements become more variable and it is easier to assign a wider variety of duties to staff and thus keep the work environment fresh. Bargaining contracts sometimes inhibit exchanges or limit them to periods so short they are practically useless; this too may change as labor unions increasingly perceive the benefits of flexibility.

Job Enrichment

Job enrichment can build up expectations of permanent reclassification or continuing advancement that might not be deliverable. At its best, it encourages staff to seek better positions in the library or elsewhere. But not everyone is interested in mobility, and there is nothing wrong with that as long as everyone is informed about the risks of immobility. Finally, not all jobs can be enriched.

Reorganization

Of all staff-development opportunities, reorganization is the most comprehensive because it is impossible to omit any unit or person from the process. Normally, reorganization appears as a threat because it is perceived as changing the informal social and power structures that coexist in every formal bureaucracy. If a leader has vision and can sell it convincingly to employees, it is a superior opportunity.

Community Service/Outreach

These functions include service in some library-related capacity to a civic organization: becoming a public library board member or trustee, acting as library liaison to a school's PTA, volunteering in a church, mosque, or synagogue library. Community service helps to broaden vistas and increases community respect for librarianship.

Exhibits and Public Relations

See chapter 6, where this topic is discussed.

Editorship of Library Publications; Graphics

Opportunities for persons with good writing skills are numerous: editing in-house library bulletins or newsletters for faculty; drafting news releases for the media; writing training and procedure manuals; and designing book marks, stack guides, and informational leaflets, and so forth. Artistic talent can be tapped for logos, mastheads, and signs.

Librarian Career Opportunities for Classified Staff

Many fine professionals emerge from the ranks of classified staff who have been encouraged to enroll in graduate programs of library and information science. Lack of immediate local openings for the new graduates can, however, have a significant, though normally temporary, negative impact, while some successful graduates may be reluctant to leave the area for work elsewhere. It is important that classified staff studying for the M.L.S. understand that they cannot be guaranteed positions at the sponsoring institutions but must compete in the open market. They also need to appreciate that the best professional opportunities may exist at another library.

Service on Search Panels

Assisting the recruiting process is a good antidote to narrow views.[11] By serving on search panels all ranks and classifications of staff can contribute importantly to the total library program. In some libraries, however, membership on such panels is restricted to professionals or academic appointees.

Study and Research Leaves

Leaves of absence for research and publication can be highly productive for both librarians and the campus at large if a clear professional goal or institutional need is identified. Some institutions require that projects be of direct or indirect benefit to the school or library. Flexibility, availability, and a supportive climate are desirable. Leaves will be most stimulating and productive if the research topic originates with the researcher rather than comes as an assignment. Professional staff should enjoy wide discretion in choice of research topics and leaves should be granted liberally.

Where librarians have faculty or academic status, leaves may be a built-in perquisite, or may be provided in the terms of a collective agreement. Collegial discussion or peer review of leave applications may result in an improved proposal. Librarians applying for leave should be willing to have both their projects and their final reports subjected to academic review. Depending upon campus regulation or contract terms, the chief librarian may be empowered to grant or deny applications. Of course, such programs require active support from the administration: services (photocopying and secretarial support), materials, supplies and postage, equipment (PCs), and time to prepare.

A major problem with leaves is covering the absentee's responsibilities. A leave financed by a grant provides the opportunity to hire a temporary replacement, in itself a possible source of fresh ideas. In larger research libraries, staff can take advantage of the ARL/OMS Collaborative Research/Writing Program.[12]

Advanced Degree Programs

In supporting work and advanced degree programs concurrently, administrators normally put institutional needs ahead of personal development opportunity. As with courses, it is desirable to support as liberally as possible employees' desires for continuing learning throughout their working lives, although program obligations do not always permit such generosity.[13] The Council on Library Resources' Advanced Study Program is especially designed to help librarians increase their knowledge in a scholarly field. Usually this is worked out in connection with a paid leave of absence from work.

Learning New Software and Hardware

People with a special affinity for software enjoy the challenge, can teach its use to others, and provide heretofore unavailable benefits to the entire library. The opportunity to learn new microcomputer techniques is an unbeatable chance to stake out some new professional turf and invent new products and services. Offering software training requires management. It is best to select employees who would make good teachers and who are unlikely to get "hooked" to the point where interest in software overtakes their sense of responsibility for their primary work.

Developing a Video for Training or Orientation

The VCR is a superb adjunct to training and orientation. North Americans are so socialized to visual images that some people readily give more attention to canned presentations than to live ones. Modern video technology has changed the expectations of viewers to the point where only professional-quality videos are worth presenting. As has already occurred with complex graphics, software for video development is reaching the point where homemade videos can approach professional quality.

Mentoring Relationships

Many successful administrators have begun their careers by working under a mentor. Academic librarianship provides several opportunities to work with mentors: the Academic Library Management Intern Program, sponsored since 1973 by the Council on Library Resources; the ARL/OMS Academic Library Program; programs offered by individual libraries, such as those at the University of California (at Santa Barbara), Chicago, Columbia, Georgia, Illinois, Michigan, Missouri (at Columbia), Northwestern, and Yale. Most of the programs in this last category are designed for recent graduates and have received their initial support from the Council on Library Resources.

There are hazards in any mentoring relationship: a tendency for the junior person to attribute superhuman wisdom to the mentor; a possibility that the mentor might take advantage of the relationship to offload routine work or use the protege as a kind of "gofer"; a risk that the relationship could shift from professional to personal or simply go sour because of personality differences. Another inherent risk lies in the general uncertainty that characterizes all top administrative positions: if the boss is fired, resigns, or falls into disfavor, what happens to the protege's relationships with co-workers? No matter how democratic or impersonal the selection process, the protege must contend with jealous reactions, even from trusted colleagues. The relationship can become too comfortable, with potential future administrators reaching a plateau even before their careers are launched. Thus, a mentor/protege setup should probably have some fixed, nonrenewable term, perhaps a year or eighteen months at the outside. A term of only a few months is not likely to be of much value to anyone. Despite these problems, a mentor/protege relationship has more benefits than risks, especially if the mentor is truly willing to share information and power.[14]

Individual Study

Professionals have to spend many hours on site reading numerous types of materials. The question arises whether they should use company time simply to stay current with literature. This depends on an individual's responsibilities and work habits, the status of current work, and ultimately, on personal integrity. It is doubtful whether anyone can form an acceptable policy on this issue. If a person does a lot of reading at work but accomplishes little else, that fact will show quickly.

PROBLEMS IN FUNDING

Unlike business and many other professions, librarianship has not been notable for providing development incentives. We have no widely available mechanisms to give financial rewards to promote excellence or to stimulate research. The few opportunities that do exist help only a few dozens or hundreds of people each year. What we have is mostly controlled by library administrations, not by the profession itself.

A weakness of institution-controlled development grants is that they do not emerge from the profession itself. As there is no formal profit sharing in academe, development funds and cost-avoidance savings do not flow back to a professional group as a reward for some successful new product or service. Because they are controlled by the local administration, their focus is necessarily on projects that the director judges to be most important. A superior arrangement would be to set aside development funds each year for deposit into an account administered by the professional staff itself. Given the number of professionals, the proactive attitudes we expect, and the principle of codetermination, it is not reasonable that the administration control every resource. A fund controlled by professionals could be a powerful motivator for the staff to undertake original research and development emerging from needs perceived at the working level.

CAREER LIFE CYCLES

Staff development is closely connected to employees' time lines, that is, their ages and where they are in their careers. Wright and Hamilton discussed three theories of career cycles.[15] The first is "cohort" theory, which suggests that people move in cohorts according to their generational position: older employees with a Depression-based attitude, younger ones with a "me-generation" orientation. A second hypothesis suggests that, regardless of generation, everyone's expectations decline with age, especially in bureaucratic organizations where opportunity for advancement is limited. The third rejects both these themes and asserts that professionals' careers go through a more or less fixed life cycle.

Dalton hypothesized four distinctive career phases: (1) apprenticeship, during which the professional finds a niche; (2) mastery, when the professional becomes a specialist and makes a creative contribution to the organization; (3) mentorship, a stage when the professional can begin to guide newcomers; and (4) sponsor, a senior role of preeminent leadership.[16] In a review of these various theories, Raelin boiled them down to three stages not so tied to age or cohort: (1) finding a niche, learning, developing, looking for a challenge; (2) digging in, placing a strong emphasis on professional performance and not wishing to be bothered overmuch by bureaucratic detail; and (3) entrenching, showing some loss of aspiration but stability and dependability.[17] The word with bad connotations, "entrenching," ignores the fact that in librarianship, a service profession, the older, more senior professionals have typically amassed an enormous and valuable fund of knowledge and experience. The middle stage, digging in (another unfortunate expression) and wishing to evade supervisory work is not congruent with the realities of modern academic librarianship, where supervisorial and administrative responsibilities increasingly form an essential aspect of work for people in midcareer.

Raelin's tripartite model was derived from studies of lawyers, financial professionals and scientists; its transferability to librarianship is questionable. The same can be said of the others. All are valuable, however, for helping to sensitize academic library administrators to the human needs of their professionals at various stages in their careers.

A factor often ignored in life-cycle studies is the stage at which a person enters academic librarianship. Many incumbents and some new recruits have come to librarianship by way of another profession. We do our profession a disservice when we associate a late career choice with failure or disillusionment. In an age of serial careers and of willingness to experiment, latecomers' choices are often the result of mature reflection and sound judgment. These are the people who have at last found a career to which they can fully dedicate their creative energies. Their development needs cannot be the same as anyone else's.

SUMMARY

Coping with rapid change, both in technology and in the structure of society, is a prime motivating factor in staff development. Even independent of such change, staff development is a humane and sensible program, beneficial to all. Yet personnel overstability can mean low or reduced motivation, which is a considerable challenge to leadership. Staff development has more community emphasis than private focus. Perhaps the biggest pluses are that people can get credit for activities beyond their regular duties and responsibilities and begin to see where their contributions fit into the total picture. While development opportunities are virtually unlimited, the budget is not, and cost is the main obstacle. Development of human resources and regular program obligations compete with each other, leaving the administration with the difficult task of choosing between them.

Notes

1. Judith Bardwick, *The Plateauing Trap* (New York: Bantam, 1988), 30-46.

2. David C. Weber and Tina Kass, "Comparable Rewards: The Case for Equal Compensation for Non-Administrative Expertise." *Library Journal* 103 (15 April 1978): 824-27.

3. Gisela Webb, "Personnel Officers: How Do You Know When You Need Them?" *Wilson Library Bulletin* 62, no. 3 (November 1987): 25-27.

4. Samuel Rothstein, "Professional Staff in Canadian University Libraries," *Library Journal* 111, no. 18 (1 November 1986): 31-34.

5. Ruth J. Person, "The Third Culture: Managerial Socialization in the Library Setting," *Advances in Library Administration and Organization* (JAI Press) 4 (1985): 1-24.

6. We observe that in academe 100 percent institutional support for professional development is almost never possible. Many professionals contribute extensively of their own time and resources for their career development, precisely because they view the contribution as a key investment in their own future.

7. In a comparative study of CLR senior fellows and a control group, Dorothy Anderson found that the fellows were three times more active professionally, held three times as many leadership positions in professional organizations, and moved twice as often. See her "Comparative Career Profiles of Academic Librarians: Are Leaders Different?" *Journal of Academic Librarianship* 10, no. 6 (January 1985): 326-32.

8. Sheila D. Creth, *Effective On-the-Job Training: Developing Library Human Resources* (Chicago: American Library Association, 1986).

9. See Linda Eileen Williamson, *Going International: Librarians' Preparation Guide for a Work Experience/Job Exchange Abroad* (Chicago: ALA, 1988), and Hannelore B. Rader, "International Personnel Exchanges for Librarians," *Bowker Annual of Library and Book Trade Information*, 33d ed. (1988), 146-51.

10. Judith Bardwick, *The Plateauing Trap*, 138.

11. Thomas Wilding and Roberta Fagin, "Enhancing Staff Development Through Search Committee Participation," *College & Research Libraries News* 50, no. 2 (February 1989): 130-32.

12. This program is described each year in the *Annual Report* issued by the Office of Management Studies, Association of Research Libraries. Several ARL/OMS programs are open to small academic libraries that are not members of ARL.

13. When a full-time employee with some key responsibility chooses to drop back to half-time for an extended period, administrations usually hire replacement staff and do not permit automatic reversion to full-time status.

14. In 1988 Ajaye Bloomstone prepared an extensive bibliography, *Mentor/Protégée: Librarians Helping Librarians* (Chicago: Li-

brary Administration and Management Association, Women Administrators Discussion Group, 1988).

15. James D. Wright and Richard F. Hamilton, "Work Satisfaction and Age: Some Evidence for 'Job Change' Hypothesis," *Social Forces* 56, no. 4 (1978): 1140-58.

16. Gene W. Dalton et al., "The Four Stages of Professional Careers," in *Managing Career Development* ed. M. A. Morgan (New York: Van Nostrand, 1980), 43-60.

17. Joseph A. Raelin, "Work Patterns in the Professional Life-Cycle," *Journal of Organizational Psychology* 58 (1985): 177-87. Raelin's triad closely resembles Towill's three stages of employment--socialization (a few months), innovation (up to and including the third year), and adaptation (fourth year and beyond)--cited by Bardwick, *The Plateauing Trap*, 75-77.

Resources

Alley, Brian, and Jennifer Cargill. *Librarian in Search of a Publisher: How to Get Published*. Phoenix, Ariz.: Oryx, 1986.

Arthur, Michael B., et al. *Working with Careers*. New York: Center for Career Research, 1983.

Association of College and Research Libraries. *Travel Policies of Twenty-one College & University Libraries*. Chicago, 1980.

Association of College and Research Libraries, Northern California Chapter. *Management and Staff Development*. Proceedings of a 1979 workshop. Chicago.

Association of Research Libraries, Office of Management Studies. *Internships and Job Exchanges*. Washington, D.C., 1981.

_____. *Library Publications Programs*. Washington, D.C., 1988.

Automation and the Workplace: Selected Labor, Education, and Training Issues, A Technical Memorandum. Washington, D.C.: Government Printing Office, 1983.

Buck, Paul. "The Recruitment and Training of Professional Librarians." In *Libraries and Universities: Addresses and Reports,* edited by Paul Buck, 107-10. Cambridge, Mass.: Harvard University Press, 1964.

Collins, Eliza G. C., and Patricia Scott. "Everyone Who Makes It Has a Mentor." *Harvard Business Review* 56, no. 4 (July-August 1978): 89-110.

Creth, Sheila. *Effective On-the-Job Training: Developing Library Human Resources.* Chicago: American Library Association, 1986.

Creth, Sheila. *Job Training: Developing Training Plans for Your Staff.* Chicago: ACRL, 1984.

_____. "Staff Development and Continuing Education." In *Personnel Administration for Libraries,* edited by Sheila Creth and Frederick Duda, 189-225. New York: Neal-Schuman, 1981.

Employee Assistance Programs: A Positive Approach to the Problem Employee. Tape recording of LAMA/OLPR program from the 1987 ALA Conference. Available from ACTS, Inc., 1025 E. Clayton Road, Ballwin, MO 63011.

Euster, Joanne R. *Changing Patterns of Internal Communication in Large Academic Libraries.* Washington, D.C.: Association of Research Libraries, Office of Management Studies, 1981.

Gwinn, Nancy E. "CLR Academic Library Management Intern Program: A Symposium: The First Two Years." *Journal of Academic Librarianship* 6 (September 1980): 196-97.

Hoffmann, Ellen. "Institutional Responses to Career Plateaus." In *Building on the First Century: Proceedings of the Association of College and Research Libraries Fifth National Conference, Cincinnati, Ohio, 5-8 April 1989,* edited by Janice C. Fennell. Chicago: American Library Association, 1989.

Hunt, Suellyn. "Staff Development: Your Number One Investment in the Future." *Library Personnel News* 1, no. 1 (1987): 5-6.

Kohl, David, F., ed. *Library Education and Professional Issues.* Santa Barbara, Calif.: ABC-CLIO, 1986

Library Administration and Management Association. *Staff Development in Libraries: Bibliography*. Chicago, 1983.

Linsley, Laurie F. "The Dual Job Assignment: How It Enhances Job Satisfaction." In *Academic Libraries: Myths and Realities*, 146-50. Chicago: Association of College and Research Libraries, 1984.

Lipow, Ann Grodzins. *Staff Development: A Practical Guide*. Chicago: Library Administration and Management Association, 1988.

Masi, Dale E. *Designing Employee Assistance Programs*. New York: AMACOM, 1984.

Nadler, Leonard, and Garland D. Wiggs. *Managing Human Resource Development*. San Francisco: Jossey-Bass, 1986.

Nofsinger, Mary M., and Mary Gilles. "A Faculty Retreat: Coping with Challenges." *College and Research Libraries News* 50, no. 6 (June 1989): 484-85.

Rader, Hannelore B. "International Personnel Exchanges for Librarians" In *Bowker Annual of Library and Book Trade Information*, 33d ed. New York: R. R. Bowker Co., 1988, 146-51.

_____. "Library Orientation and Instruction, 1987." *Reference Services Review* 16, no. 3 (1988): 57-68. (An annotated bibliography.)

Rae, Leslie. *How to Measure Training Effectiveness*. New York: Nichols, 1986.

Sellen, Betty-Carol. *Librarian/Author: A Practical Guide on How to Get Published*. New York: Neal-Schuman, 1985.

Shaughnessy, Thomas W. "Staff Development in Libraries: Why It Frequently Doesn't Take." *Journal of Library Administration* 9, no. 2 (1988): 5-12.

Shea, Gordon F. *The New Employee: Developing a Productive Human Resource*. Reading, Mass.: Addison-Wesley, 1981.

Skitt, John. "Setting Up a Staff Development Scheme; Staff Appraisal and Training Needs." In *Management Issues in*

Academic Libraries edited by Tim Lomas, 67-77. London: Rossendale, 1986.

Standing Conference of National and University Libraries. "Education and Training." In *Issues Facing Academic Libraries: A Review*, 7-10. London, 1985.

Stine, Diane, Judith Bernstein, and Janet Frederick. "The Personnel Officer in the Medium-Sized Academic Library." *Journal of Library Administration* 5, no. 3 (Fall 1984): 23-42.

Sullivan, Maureen. *Resource Notebook on Staff Development.* Washington, D.C.: Association of Research Libraries, 1983.

Van Til, William. *Writing for Professional Publication.* 2d ed. Boston: Allyn and Bacon, 1986.

Webb, Gisela. "Personnel Officers: How Do You Know When You Need Them?" *Wilson Library Bulletin* 62, no. 3 (November 1987): 25-27.

Weber, David C. "The Dynamics of the Library Environment for Professional Staff Growth." *College & Research Libraries* 35, no. 4 (1974): 259-87.

Weber, David C., and Tina Kass. "Comparable Rewards: The Case for Equal Compensation for Non-Administrative Expertise." *Library Journal* 103 (15 April 1978): 824-27.

Williamson, Linda E. *Going International: Librarians' Preparation Guide for a Work Experience/Job Exchange Abroad.* Chicago: ALA, 1988.

CHAPTER 12

Entering and Departing
the Administrative Suite

POSITION AVAILABILITY VERSUS CAREER GOALS

Except for the executive directorship of a consortium, network, bibliographic utility, or association, chief librarian is generally the highest achievable status in the profession. The number of top positions is limited, however, and because higher education is no longer a rapid growth industry, new positions are rare. Nothing demonstrates the inherently hierarchical character of academe more obviously than the search for major administrative positions.

Whether an executive post is in general college or university administration or in librarianship, as positions rise in rank availability decreases and, correspondingly, as the rank falls the number of posts increases. Persons seeking administrative work quickly recognize that the opportunity for increasing advancement diminishes at a rapidly accelerating rate. Aspiring chief administrators may have to wait until an incumbent quits, dies, or is fired. The pattern of a hundred or more well-qualified applicants for one position is now as common in librarianship as in the professoriate. No wonder that many intermediate-level administrators prefer to extend their tenure where they are and never reach for advancement.

Establishing an explicit career goal to become chief librarian at a medium-sized or large library can be an exercise in frustration. Frequently the window of opportunity does not coincide with individual readiness or vice versa. Inside one institution, advancement in administration may be limited if the boss is firmly established, so that one remains on a plateau not because of any innate deficiency. Advancement is not necessarily associated with constant upward movement from one tier of institution to another. One can make important career progress by "trading down," that is, taking a challenging position at a less prestigious college or university.

PREREQUISITE ATTITUDES AND SKILLS

Because leadership is idiosyncratic and highly resistant to analysis, identifying administrative skills is controversial. Whether such skills are inborn or acquired is a never-ending argument. Obviously, every successful administrator needs both types of abilities.

In 1955 Katz published a survey of the effective administrator's skills, but when he reviewed his paper nearly twenty years later he found he had shifted away from the traits concept toward a more dynamic, flexible viewpoint.[1] His original concept postulated three basic skills--human, conceptual, and technical--and his views on all three changed in two decades. In 1974 Katz shifted from the view that conceptual skills could be imparted by training to the idea that they were innate. If a manager did not exhibit conceptual skills early in life, probably he could not be trained to them later. In the technical area, he observed that managers in small companies needed greater technical skill than those in large, a point that makes great sense in libraries. In human relations skills, Katz's revised opinion placed greater emphasis on intragroup skills with peer managers and intergroup skills within higher levels of management. This too makes good sense in librarianship, since the academic library administrator must be able to interrelate effectively with peer administrators on campus. A completely different set of skills is required for relating to larger units outside the library.

Dedication to self-actualization does not indicate good potential for management according to John W. Hunt, professor of human relations at the London Business School. Hunt suggested that the self-actualizers are basically separatists who are too impatient and too self-centered to commit themselves to an organization. In fact, these persons have a strong aversion to management control concepts. They are the creators, but they do not make very good bosses.[2]

Even though controversy and imprecision surround the topic of skills, beliefs, and attitudes, we still have to know what characteristics are required or preferred for administrators, if only to compose meaningful vacancy postings and interview candidates. Thus, with both limitations and requirements in mind, a few basics can be identified, some old and obvious, others made necessary by modern technology. Good administrators should:

- Have a never-empty fount of optimism.

- Be proactive.

- Be good listeners.

- Be confident, articulate speakers.

- Keep their cool.

- Be active in professional associations.

- Look beyond the profession.

- Welcome complexity and not be put off by uncertainty.

- Desire and seek public recognition.

- Be unembarrassed by failure and willing to fail.

- Be willing to delegate both authority and responsibility.

- Be able to observe pattern in a broad mass of detail.

- Be spontaneous in expression and have a good sense of humor.

- Be strategists: take a long-range view.

- Be capable of accepting criticism.

- Be decisive but not imperious, impulsive, or stubborn.

- Be convincing and persuasive at many levels: campus administrators, peers and subordinates.

- Be goal and achievement oriented.

- Be willing and eager to develop careers of subordinates.

- Be honest and not dissembling.

- Be technically competent.

Thompson and Carr cited a similar list of nineteen executive virtues developed by Patmore.[3] Because of the scarcity of paragons, it is almost an embarrassment to read any kind of list, but such listings may serve to remind administrators how far from perfect they are.

Acquiring Administrative Skills

There are many roads to the acquisition of administrative skills.[4] Additional degrees in business or public administration are helpful, although expensive and time consuming. All four major North American professional associations, ACRL, ALA, CLA, and SLA (and their subunits), offer a wide variety of continuing education courses, mostly in the form of preconferences or special institutes. (Contact the organizations for full information.) Library schools and business schools often conduct special workshops on various aspects of library administration. Two of these are long-established and especially notable: (1) the University of Maryland's Library Administrators Development Program, which in 1988 was in its twenty-second year, and (2) Miami University's Middle and Advanced Management Programs for Library Administrators. The possibilities of self-development by means of a mentoring relationship were mentioned in chapter 11.

The Council on Library Resources (CLR) has long pioneered programs to help librarians acquire administrative skills. The most notable CLR activity is the Academic Library Management Intern Program, begun in 1973. The internships and a startup grant for the ARL's Office of Management Studies are CLR's most visible contributions. Other vital aids include the CLR Fellowship Program (begun in 1968), the Professional Education and Training for Research Librarianship (PETREL) program (dating from 1981), and the Institutes for Library Educators. The role of the Council on Library Resources in promoting management excellence in academic libraries cannot be overestimated; outside the professional associations, no single agency has done more over an extended period to enhance academic librarians' management skills.

Developing Listening Skills

Good listening habits are indispensable for successful administration, especially in performance appraisal, interviewing, employee counseling, program planning, and fund raising. Needless to say, the most important listening skill is comprehending what the boss is saying.

Listening and hearing are quite different concepts. Hearing is physical, passive, and automatic. Listening takes mental effort. The enemies of effective listening include interrupting other speakers, ignoring what they are saying, concentrating on what you want to say, showing impatience, losing eye contact, and doing something distracting such as doodling. If your mind is already made up on some issue, further discussion is probably a waste of time. Your ear may hear what a colleague is saying but your brain will not process it. For administrators, who are accustomed to being listened to, one of the hardest aspects of listening is giving up their normal center-of-attention position.

Listening skills are so important to higher education that campus administrations commonly offer courses or workshops in their development. Mostly these are designed for new people in junior supervisory positions and are run by the campus personnel office. A course in listening skills is a good part of any library's supervisors' orientation or staff development program.[5]

Accepting the Management Concept

Entry into management provides benefits but exacts costs. The benefits are fairly obvious: usually an increase in salary, prestige, influence, span of control, and responsibility. These do not come free, however. Their price is loyalty that is expected to override personal preferences. Administration differs from academic instruction, research, and service in that it involves a different kind of commitment: your personal outlook and preferences are secondary to the institution's, even if its views, policies, and decisions are at variance with your value system or professional judgment. Of course, part of the fun and challenge of administration is convincing others that your vision does indeed encompass everyone else's best interests as well as those of the school.

We stressed in chapter 4 that an administrator should not try to build rank-and-file staff, especially the professionals, into a team, but rather develop cooperative independence. This constraint is not true of management and administration, which by definition are team concepts. Once a basic policy decision is made, all management personnel are expected to support the decision fully because managers are agents of the institution. While the management team concept does not imply blind, uncritical loyalty, it nevertheless does require loyalty. Persons who prefer not to be agents of an institution cannot and should not be managers.[6] If your own views do not accord with the institution's mission, goals and objectives, or its politics, it is unlikely that you will be a good agent.

Managers who work against authorized, higher-level management decisions by unilaterally undermining them behind the scenes are playing a very dangerous game of power politics. If their strategy fails, they may justifiably be subject to severe disciplinary action.[7] Although one sometimes hears the defense of intellectual freedom or freedom of speech invoked as a justification for these actions, the argument does not hold: the corporate culture of administration, including academe, requires one to differentiate institutional mission, goals, and objectives from personal beliefs, outlooks, and preferences.

THE POLITICS OF FINDING A POSITION

Despite the recruiting changes wrought by Affirmative Action, Equal Employment Opportunity, and related legislation, the invisible college, "old grads' network," or personal network is still functional in at least one respect: early communication of desirable openings to favored protégés of mentors, colleagues, and friends. Scanning position announcements in the usual places (e.g., *Chronicle of Higher Education,* the *New York Times,* library journals) is certainly valuable, but availability of the most highly desired posts will be known through the grapevine long in advance of print. Here, some caution is advisable: jumping the gun, forwarding an application too soon, especially before a position has been publicly announced, can be damaging.

Merit and achievement are extremely useful in support of an application, but the value of good references and good luck should not be underestimated. The recommendations of respected colleagues, especially high achievers and those associated with prestigious schools, carry great weight with search panels.

The safeguards now built into recruiting all but eliminate appointment of the unqualified or those whose candidacy, for one reason or another, appears to be based solely on favoritism. Although favoritism can never be completely discounted, today the probabilities are high that reasonably well-qualified applicants will at least get onto a long list, if not the short list, and earn a preliminary hearing.

The mutual review by appointer and potential appointee is the work of two experts, each hoping to get a good deal. The hunt for an administrative post is not for the thin-skinned: you must have patience, tenacity, and the ability to maintain self-assurance and balance while you open one letter of rejection after another. A contender may have to apply for administrative positions ten, twenty, thirty, or more times before being invited even for an interview.

A few final words on the nature of the administrative position itself: most are appointments, not the outcomes of elections. There are two reasons for this: (1) appointment status makes it easy for the school to dismiss an incompetent manager immediately, and (2) many governing bodies and school officers believe that an elected administration virtually guarantees weak leadership, as there would be little motivation to change the system.[8]

SCOUTING OUT THE LAND

Institutions are quite shameless about touting their virtues and they recruit top-level administrative staff much as they recruit students–by conveying images of success, progressiveness, and opportunity for further career development. The savvy position hunter sees through these façades and learns as much or more from information the institution declines to share openly. Some institutions are quite straightforward in explaining, even in detail, issues the successful candidate is likely to face; nonetheless, while outright lying is rare, people find ways to manage information. Others may try to disguise their deepest, most serious difficulties. Regrettably, in some cases institutional officers are so uninformed about the library's problems that they can neither share nor withhold information. Candidates must learn to delve, probe, and ferret out enough accurate information to learn whether the appointment offers potential for real career development.

It is up to candidates to develop their own lists of concerns and priorities that must be satisfied before they are willing to dedicate several years of their lives to a leadership position. Below are selected key questions to which applicants or candidates might want answers, along with other topics worth investigating in the course of a site visit or interview. Of course, seasoned job seekers add many more questions specific to an institution and their own experience.

1. Tell me about the circumstances of the previous director's departure. (Vital if the predecessor was fired.)

2. Who exercises control over budget savings? Do they revert to a central pool administered at a higher level?

3. Is the chief librarian a member of the Council of Deans or similar body?

4. How does the chief librarian contribute to or learn about academic program changes that affect library budgets and services?

5. Does grant or gift money mean that an equivalent sum is taken away from the budget allocation?

6. Describe the informal campus power structure; who calls the shots when decisions are made?

7. What is the informal power structure in the library? Who are the natural leaders? Who is held in high esteem by staff and who in low?

8. Who has final authority over promotions and the decision to award security of employment?

9. What are the methods of terminating nonperformers? Have they been effective?

10. Are any employees currently grieving or litigating against the institution?

11. How does the institution typically cope with budgetary crises? Across-the-board cuts? Selective trims? Program discontinuations?

12. What specific, articulated satisfactions and dissatisfactions with the library have reached the upper levels of administration? From what constituencies do these reports arise and how much political power do they represent?

13. Where does the institution see itself five years hence?

Some judgment must be exercised concerning whom to ask such questions. The immediate predecessor may not be the best one to ask about problem areas, especially if there is evidence of administrative failure. Nearly everyone will have some axe to grind, so you must measure the responses.

Additional key steps in candidates' research include arming yourself with up-to-date biographical information on chief campus officers, deans, department heads, members of the search panel, and professional staff. Study the school's bulletin and its entry in the appropriate *Peterson's* guide.

Examine the staff's record on participation in the work of professional associations at the regional and national levels. Do they attend conferences? Do they serve on association committees? To what extent do they publish? Minimal participation may be evidence of insularity, a low level of professional commitment, or lack of support for travel, all challenges the successful candidate will have to face.

Find out how much turnover there has been in professional positions. When was the last time a new face appeared? Is there evidence of stagnation? Signs of staff trouble to look for include (1) people who consume grossly disproportionate amounts of administrative time through formal or informal complaints, (2) professionals who need excessively specific guidance in the work situation, (3) individuals who routinely launch a series of continuing appeals to higher authority, and (4) excessive memo writing. You should find out how extensive and how acute these conditions are. Naturally, you must not expect to find perfection, but you have to gauge the extent of any trouble potential.

Ask for the privilege of reviewing performance appraisal documentation before you make any commitment. Documentation that is excessively laudatory, or records steady, unchallenged promotions over a long period may reveal weak administration and problems lying ahead. A preview gives you the chance to pinpoint potential causes and identify troublemakers; then if you decide to accept an appointment, you can at least plan counterstrategies.

You must be in a strong position to attend professional meetings and retreats wholly or partially at institutional expense. Find out the extent to which the school supports travel by peer administrators or academic department heads, and what rules pertain.

Determine the power relationships and the magnitude and direction of political forces on the campus before you show keen interest in the position. You have no say in how these forces are arrayed, and if they are not to your liking during the interview, they will be even less appealing if you are appointed. Recognize also that the power base can change rapidly and significantly in the academy, just as it can in business or politics.

Determine whether administrators are eligible for retreat rights (appointment with tenure to a nonadministrative position). Compare the library's physical facilities and condition with other campus buildings. If the library is in much poorer shape, find out why and inquire about prospects for improvement.

Try to find out what kind of image the position projects. Is the chief librarian's position seen as mainly symbolic or ceremonial? An image as a flunky conveys expectation of weak leadership. How the chief librarian's authority, duties, and responsibilities are construed by the various campus constituencies is a key piece of information that sharp candidates will sift out by cogent questioning very early in the job interview process.

Sniff out the areas in which the school provides special privileges or financial "sweeteners" to those whom it is courting, such as swing loans for mortgages, outright purchase and reselling of vacated homes, and generous moving allowance. Determine the tax liabilities imposed by the new jurisdiction.

PREPARING YOUR RESUME

Those already in administration should be well qualified to prepare their own resumes. If you are just getting into administration and have not seen many, some of the popular books on the subject may offer slight assistance. Most commercial resume books are business oriented, however, and have little to do with the academic marketplace. Two very useful items are the Library Administration and Management Association's "Guidelines for Writing an Effective Resume,"[9] and Henry M. Wilbur's "On Getting A Job," a chapter in *The Academic's Handbook*.[10] The following specific suggestions and cautions may be helpful.

1. Use hard-hitting, action-oriented verbs to describe your accomplishments: administered, planned, directed, analyzed, implemented, organized, saved (money), reallocated, originated, convinced, coordinated, strengthened, established, abolished, conceived, managed, systematized, developed, negotiated, appointed, presented.

2. If you have an extensive publication list or a detailed outline of how you solved a particularly challenging problem, incorporate that material in appendixes, to keep your resume from bulking up. To lead your readers to the supplementary material, make strong, brief statements in the resume (and selectively in your cover letter) about the

problems you solved, especially if they relate to what the hiring institution is looking for. Reviewers do not read attachments if the initial career summary does not catch their attention.

3. Be wary of commercial agencies that use laser printers to produce canned resumes with very high-quality graphics and a typeset appearance. At this early stage in the use of laser printers, beautiful graphics may be counterproductive, conveying an impression that form is more important than content, or that you make a profession of applying for positions.[11] A resume should be neat but contain no distractions from the content; it is not a work of art but a document designed to focus on your accomplishments and qualifications.

4. Grammatical and spelling errors stick out. They communicate the message that you are not a good communicator. If you think you have problems in this area, seek competent help.

5. In the cover letter, some applicants make the mistake of emphasizing how the desired position meets their career goals. The institution has little interest in these except as they may serve local needs and priorities. Focus on how your qualifications meet the institution's goals as stated in the posting.

HEADHUNTERS

To fill top business positions, companies and executives often use professional recruiting agencies. Our profession has such a well-established grapevine for communicating open positions that an aspirant probably need not consider a headhunting agency. Sometimes a hiring institution decides that a professional agency offers greater objectivity than is normally available or assures that Equal Employment Opportunity and Affirmative Action guidelines will be followed objectively. Whatever the merits of professional recruitment, this method of filling executive positions is still a comparative rarity in academic librarianship.[12] Few business-oriented recruiting firms understand the academic world well enough to be of much help. A work by Taylor describes in detail what may be expected when dealing with business-oriented executive search firms.[13]

THE INTERVIEW PROCESS

In a superb account of the total interview process from the viewpoint of both institution and applicant, Biggs and Naslund offered an excellent list of questions together with advice on how to adopt a proactive stance in the interview.[14] They described the interview as "a candidate's prime opportunity to demonstrate marketing skills. . . ." They also illustrated the value of an appropriate balance between an excess of self-promotion and undue modesty, either of which is harmful to one's prospects.

Administrators spend considerable time interviewing candidates for jobs they control. It is uncomfortable when the shoe is on the other foot. Although most of the pitfalls are obvious, special attention might be paid to the following points.

1. Appearance and body language add up to a personal image and convey a critical, immediate impact that survives long after a candidate has left campus. Anywhere in Canada or the United States conservative dress will serve you better than trendy apparel.[15]

2. Try not to take over and dominate the interview process by focusing too much on your own abilities and achievements; spend your time learning what the institution wants.

3. Firm handshakes, direct eye contact, erect (but relaxed) posture--all contribute to the image of candidates in charge of themselves, a prerequisite for those who would be in charge of others.

4. The hiring institution has called you in to see if you can meet its needs. Just as with the cover letter, it is wise not to push too hard on how the opportunity fits into your career development plans.

The first interview is your opportunity to outline your vision of the library's future. If subsequently it appears that you may be the candidate of choice, tactfully start laying out any major adjustments to the library's mission, goals, and objectives that you perceive require full backing from the central administration. It does no good after arrival to try to convince your boss that you really do need several tens or hundreds of thousand of dollars to implement a local integrated system or set up daily van service to support a cooperative of neighboring academic libraries that you plan to form. If your self-marketing effort is successful and you receive an offer or are asked for a follow-up interview, pursue your initiatives vigorously and try to get the principal officers to reach closure on your own vision of the library's future before you leave that day. Then try to have that commitment put in writing as you work out the details of the final offer.

COMPETENCE, MEDIOCRITY, DISAPPOINTMENT

A frustration in the search for an administrative position is the unfortunately inaccurate assumption that an institution always seeks the best possible candidate. We are strongly socialized to the concept that the very best people always become the winners; it comes as a shock to learn that competence is sometimes punished. In reality, some schools merely want a low-key caretaker, not a highly ambitious mover and shaker. This gives credence to some of the administrative folklore described in chapter 3. Regardless of public declarations, enormous inertia pervades academe; some high-level academic officers see their library directors merely as shepherds charged to keep the flocks quiet. Faculty frequently prefer their programs and procedures to continue in the same familiar direction. Thus schools may avoid candidates whose program vision seems aberrant, expensive, challenging, threateningly rivalrous, or highly distinctive.

In short, the final choice for an administrative position may be a lesser candidate who best meets the unwritten criteria of compromise that govern every local power structure. Candidates who present themselves too strongly, evince too great an independence, appear to be too demanding, or show signs of charisma might actually be disqualifying themselves.

The elitist structure of the academy builds disappointment into many personnel processes. Of the hundreds who apply for a desirable position, perhaps a dozen will make it through the preliminary sifting and maybe half that number to the final list. Be realistic about the loss of what seemed like an irresistible opportunity at the moment. Other chances will present themselves and life itself is filled with unexpected turns. In addition, through the process of seeking a position, someone who has set top-level administration as a major career goal might also discover that, in reality, another career direction, or even remaining at one's current post, is actually the better choice.

NEGOTIATING YOUR PERKS

If the hiring institution is dangling an offer before you, you can probably negotiate some perks before you send in your written acceptance. The campus administration expects you to be reasonably demanding about perquisites. If you make few demands, you may be perceived as weak. The institution is eager to please at the time of hiring, and that is when your chips have the highest value. Determine what is really important to you and try to secure it before you accept the offer. Above we stated that institutions can be wary of candidates who are too demanding and now we are stating that too little demand signifies weakness. How much demand is correct? This question, whose answer is irreducible to a formula, revolves entirely about face-to-face human interaction, personal chemistry, and judgment.

The perks available from a private institution will be much more flexible and likely more generous than those offered by publicly financed schools. Expect them to be proportional to the seniority of the position. Almost all schools, except possibly the impoverished, provide all or a substantial part of moving expenses, including moving household goods and automobile, as well as personal transportation for you and your family. Some are willing to arrange loans so that you can buy a new house before your former residence is sold. Others might even agree to buy your old house and sell it on your behalf through a realtor. Schools may finance mortgages, or offer on-campus housing for selected faculty and administrators. If you do not wish to move your children to the new location in the middle of a school year, you may be able to negotiate financing for dual living arrangements for some limited transition period. Determine whether the school is willing to engage the services of relocation professionals to help your spouse find an appropriate position. If they want you enough, they will take care of you and not perceive these demands as unreasonable.

To ensure uninterrupted protection, check whether institutionally supported benefits, such as life insurance and health coverage, can continue during your transition to a new position. See if you can secure protection before actually being on the payroll, even if it means arranging for a temporary appointment without pay. Most institutions offer standard benefits packages. Consult appropriate reference works to study typical benefits offerings.[17]

Position titles are usually set by tradition or administrative directive and are rarely subject to negotiation. Most institutions prefer not to disturb the comparative tranquillity of status afforded by conventional, established titles. To campus peers a new title may suggest new powers or imply threats of trespass upon someone else's turf. When the parent institution does expressly create a new title, it is often because the authorities are bent on redistributing political power. This is evident in recent title changes reflecting the administrative union of libraries and computer facilities.

Parking and business cards are two minor areas deserving brief comment. Because parking space is critically short at every college and university, you should bid for the highest privileges you can negotiate, remembering that you may need your car for off-campus responsibilities. Be sure that your business cards are produced to the highest typographic standards, so that outside the library they adequately reflect the significance of your position.

Finally, salary is almost always subject to some negotiation, though you may have to trade off a portion of it for other perquisites. It is useful to consult trusted colleagues and thoroughly analyze published salary surveys. (A list of published surveys is appended to the end of this chapter.)

SELF-DEVELOPMENT

Few business-oriented self-help publications are useful for career development in academic librarianship, as most are not oriented to collegial operating styles or self-governance. The ALA's Library Administration and Management Association (LAMA) issues many high-quality publications designed to help administrators with self-development.[18] The Special Libraries Association has published an annotated bibliography that is useful to any position seeker.[19] The SLA guide lists articles on virtually every topic of importance to those aspiring to careers in administration: time management and productivity, decision making, stress, public speaking and making presentations, career and life planning, resume writing, interviews, communication skills, intuition, and creativity.

WHEN IS IT TIME TO LEAVE?

The position of chief administrator has a life cycle, with only a small number of unusually capable and highly successful leaders remaining in their positions for very long periods. An administrator's effectiveness runs anywhere from three to perhaps five years, though in a few cases it is beyond that. It is important to understand that this cycle has comparatively little to do with your personal talents and abilities. It is built into the bureaucratic system.

Part of the art of administration is not simply sensing when you should leave but sensing it before your superiors or constituents do. Naturally departure at or near one's peak performance capacity is much better than during a decline. The achievement of one truly major accomplishment, and possibly a series of lesser ones, permits one to think about moving on to a new challenge. Savvy administrators develop their own early warning systems to detect the time when declining effectiveness is approaching the danger point. The signals vary so greatly from one situation to another that it is almost impossible to give any guidelines, but the following examples illustrate.[20] It is time to think about moving on when:

- You observe that you are invited less and less to participate in key decision-making meetings with the powerful and the influential.

- You find it increasingly difficult to get an appointment with your boss.

- The initiatives emerging from your office become fewer, narrower in scope, and less innovative.

- Your actions become reactive and you become enmeshed in the bureaucratic maze of the school's policy and procedure manual.

- You find yourself consistently referring to "my library."

- You find it a chore to get up in the morning to go to work, and you have settled into a dull routine that seems the same every day, or you become so absorbed in the work that you no longer have free time for yourself or your family.

Some messages have double meanings and it can be hard to decode their significance. One of these double-edged signals is feedback from staff whenever your decisions turn out to be unpopular. Remind yourself occasionally that you are not in your position principally to make people love you but to look out for the institution's best interests. Sometimes these interests are congruent with those of one or more constituencies and sometimes not. A general rule is that a negative reaction is less effective in the earliest stages of your tenure. Another obvious trouble sign is an increase in the severity and frequency of dissatisfied comments after you have been on the job several years.

Institutions change. If their policies, goals, and resources lose congruence with your own vision, consider whether you have reached your walkaway point. You will not work effectively in an environment where you can accomplish little or nothing. In addition, recognize that your position is finite. Bureaucracies and institutions are exceedingly unforgiving of administrators who develop and start to believe fantasies about their own self-importance, durability, or indispensability.

Naturally, there are other reasons for leaving a position. You may feel that you have learned enough and are ready to take on a still more difficult challenge. If you are fortunate enough to have had a string of successes and your failures were not very noticeable, your upward climb is probably assured. Because modern leadership is cyclic, however, one constant duty is always to have the way prepared for your successor. A well-organized office and a well-documented program will earn you points that follow you throughout your career. Do not count on leaving a permanent, personal imprint on an institution. Perhaps long ago there were giants in this field – Justin Winsor, Louis Round Wilson, Keyes D. Metcalf, to name a few. Today's leaders are quickly forgotten once they leave their posts.

Unlike business, librarianship has no formal mechanisms for helping administrators find new positions. College and university administrations normally have few appropriate contacts to help library administrators relocate. Your colleagues are your best assistance.

SUMMARY

Administrators tend to be more mobile than persons who have decided to dedicate their careers to craft or service work. Movement from one institution to another and increases in responsibility take a toll on emotional and family life. Moving into administration is a bit of a one-way street; a return years later to the craft or service side might be very difficult. The technology of the field will have advanced to the point where the erstwhile administrator has not only lost his or her expertise, but also has fallen so far behind that catching up is nearly impossible or unappealing. Unless one wishes merely to try administration for a short time, the commitment tends to be unidirectional. Not many libraries are eager to foster administration by trial.

Therefore, persons seeking administrative positions should have clearly formulated career goals and a clear perception of their fitness for work that offers substantial ambiguity, unpredictability, and frequent discomfort. Individuals who place a high value on the craft aspect of librarianship (e.g., preparing a first-rate bibliographic record) or its service aspect (e.g., tracking down a difficult reference) may be disappointed to find that once committed to administration, they must virtually abandon other aspects of the profession.

Once the goal has been set, finding an administrative position requires tremendous persistence plus a high capacity for rejection, since the number of top and intermediate slots is fairly limited. Aspirants must make extensive and careful preparations, secure dependable references, maintain good network contacts, and develop a certain penchant for theatrics. The taxing interview process is a great test of investigative and negotiating powers on all sides. Regular participation in professional conferences is an important aspect of personal development, but in general, many of the opportunities for self-development must be self-financed. Despite advances in the availability of major administrative positions for women, general administration in higher education, including academic librarianship, is still strongly male dominated, and females continue to face both overt and covert discrimination.

Administration is closely tied to the human life cycle and there are seasons in people's lives. A few high achievers seem to be able to carry on almost indefinitely, successfully filling only a small number of major positions throughout their professional lives. Others move about at varying rates, some rising, some falling, some always seeming to make lateral moves. Yet there is something for everyone in administration. Knowing when to stop reaching for the next position is itself a valuable skill, and those who have settled into positions of creditable, dependable performance have much to be proud of.

Notes

1. Robert L. Katz, "Skills of an Effective Administrator," *Harvard Business Review* 33, no. 1 (January-February 1955): 33-42. Katz's retrospective analysis follows a reprint of the original article and appears in the *Harvard Business Review* for September-October 1974.

2. John W. Hunt, *Managing People at Work: A Manager's Guide to Behaviour in Organizations* (London: McGraw-Hill, 1979), 14-15.

3. James Thompson and Reg Carr, *An Introduction to University Library Administration*, 4th ed. (London: Bingley, 1987), 54-55. The

original citation is S. J. Patmore, "The Qualities Required for Good Management," in Association of Assistant Librarians, South East Division, *Management for Librarians* (London: 1968).

4. An informative precis of available management training methods is in Deanna B. Marcum's "Management Training for Research Librarianship," *Advances in Library Administration and Organization* 2 (1983): 1-19.

5. Excellent, brief and practical recommendations on the use of listening skills to counsel employees is in Judith Bardwick's *The Plateauing Trap* (New York: Bantam, 1988), 149-51.

6. It is for this reason that managers are generally excluded from membership in bargaining units.

7. Of course, there is always the possibility of success, so that a "palace revolution" brings in a totally new administration and a completely different environment, which might be better--or worse.

8. An informative outline of the North American style of appointing rather than electing academic leaders is Henry Rosovsky's "Highest Education," *New Republic*, combined issue, nos. 3782, 3783 (13, 20 July 1987), 13-14.

9. Library Administration and Management Association, "Guidelines for Writing an Effective Resume" (Chicago, n.d.). This leaflet is also available from ALA's Office of Library Personnel Resources.

10. Henry M. Wilbur, "On Getting A Job," in *The Academic's Handbook*, ed. A. Leigh Deneef et al. (Durham: Duke University Press, 1988), 63-76.

11. Perhaps a few years hence when lasers supplant typewriters and impact printers altogether, things will be different.

12. A personnel agency specializing in librarianship is Gossage Regan Associates, 15 W. 44th St., New York NY 10036, (212) 869-3348.

13. A. Robert Taylor, *How to Select and Use an Executive Search Firm* (New York: McGraw-Hill, 1984.)

14. Debra R. Biggs and Cheryl T. Naslund, "Proactive Interviewing," *College & Research Libraries News* 48, no. 1 (January 1987): 13-17. This article also contains excellent, pertinent citations to recent articles from the literature of personnel administration.

15. An extraordinarily informative treatise on dress is Allison Lurie's *The Language of Clothes* (New York: Vintage Press, 1983).

16. Well-known relocation firms include Price Waterhouse, Merrill Lynch Relocation Management, Inc., Homequity, Inc.

17. *Corporate Benefit Plans, 1987* (Brookfield, Wis.: International Foundation of Employee Benefit Plans, 1988).

18. A complete catalog of LAMA publications is available from ALA headquarters.

19. Valerie Noble, *Guide to Individual Development: An Annotated Bibliography* (Washington, D.C.: Special Libraries Association, 1986).

20. In *The Plateauing Trap* (New York: Bantam, 1988), 193-96, Judith Bardwick lists forty self-analysis questions for people who are plateaued at work and an additional thirty-five for those plateaued in their lives. Her book also provides a valuable checklist of symptoms of plateauing (197-200). Academic library administrators can use many of Bardwick's questions, as well as the checklist.

Resources

"ACRL List of Materials Available." Complete checklist of ACRL publications in print. *College & Research Libraries News* 49, no. 2 (February 1988): 97-102.

American Library Association. *Handbook of Organization and Membership Directory*. Chicago, annual.

Association of Research Libraries, Office of Management Studies. *Search Procedures for Senior Library Administrators*. Washington, D.C., 1988.

Bardwick, Judith M. *The Plateauing Trap: How to Avoid Today's #1 Career Dilemma*. New York: Bantam, 1988.

Biggs, Debra R., and Cheryl T. Naslund. "Proactive Interviewing." *College & Research Libraries News* 48, no. 1 (January 1987): 13-17.

Braunagel, Judith S. "Job Mobility of Men and Women Librarians and How It Affects Career Advancement." *American Libraries* 10 (December 1979): 643-47.

Bridges, William. *Transitions: Making Sense of Life's Changes.* Reading, Mass.: Addison-Wesley, 1980.

Canadian Library Association. *Directory of Members.* Ottawa, annual.

Cargill, Jennifer. "Career Development: It's Your Option." *College & Research Libraries News* 49, no. 8 (September 1988): 513-17.

Deneef, A. Leigh, et al. *The Academic's Handbook* Durham: Duke University Press, 1988.

Directory of Executive Recruiters. Fitzwilliam, N.H.: Consultant News.

International Foundation of Employee Benefit Plans. *Resources in Employee Benefits: 1988.* Brookfield, Wis., 1988. Bibliography.

Levinson, Daniel J., et al. *The Seasons of a Man's Life.* New York: Knopf, 1978.

Levinson, Harry, ed. *Designing and Managing Your Career: Advice from the Harvard Business Review.* Boston: Harvard Business School Press, 1988.

Library Administration and Management Association. "Guidelines for Writing an Effective Resume." Chicago, n.d. (Leaflet.)

Lurie, Allison. *The Language of Clothes.* New York: Vintage, 1983.

Lynch, Mary Jo. "Academic Librarian Salaries." *College & Research Libraries News* 48, no. 11 (December 1987): 674-77.

McAnally, Arthur M., and Robert B. Downs. "The Changing Role of Directors of University Libraries." *College & Research Libraries* 34 (March 1973): 103-25.

McDade, Sharon A. *Higher Education Leadership: Enhancing Skills through Professional Development Programs.* Washington, D.C.: Association for the Study of Higher Education, 1987.

Marcum, Deanna B. "Management Training for Research Librarianship." *Advances in Library Administration and Organization* 2 (1983): 1-19.

Medley, H. A. *Sweaty Palms: The Neglected Art of Being Interviewed.* Berkeley, Calif.: Ten Speed Press, 1984.

Metz, Paul. "Administrative Succession in the Academic Library." *College & Research Libraries* 39 (September 1978): 358-64.

Molyneux, Robert E., comp. *ACRL University Library Statistics 1985-1986 & 1986 "100 Libraries" Statistical Survey.* Chicago: ACRL, 1987.

Moran, Barbara B. "A Reexamination of the Career Patterns of Academic Library Administrators." In *Building on the First Century,* Proceedings of the Fifth National Conference of the Association of College and Research Libraries, Cincinnati, Ohio, 8-11 April 1989, edited by Janice C. Fennell, 276-80. Chicago: ACRL, 1989.

Myers, Margaret. "Guide to Library Placement Sources." New York: R. R. Bowker Co. (A regular feature of the *Bowker Annual.*)

Person, Ruth J., and George C. Newman. *Selection of the University Librarian.* Washington, D.C.: Association of Research Libraries, Office of Management Studies, 1988.

Peskin, Dean B. *A Job Loss Survival Manual.* New York: AMACOM, 1981.

Sheehy, Gail. *Passages: Predictable Crises of Adult Life.* New York: Dutton, 1976.

White, Herbert S. "Oh, Where Have All the Leaders Gone?" *Library Journal* 112, no. 16 (1 October 1987): 68-69.

Salary Surveys

Annual Salary Survey. Washington, D.C.: Association of Research Libraries. (Covers only the ARL member libraries; excludes a few private institutions that do not disclose salary information.)

Bowker Annual of Library and Book Trade Information. New York: R. R. Bowker. (Each volume contains a survey of current salaries and placements; covers all types of libraries.)

Canadian Library Yearbook. Toronto: Micromedia Ltd. (Covers all types of libraries in Canada; figures in Canadian dollars.)

Lynch, Mary Jo. "Academic Librarian Salaries." *College & Research Libraries News* 48, no. 11 (December 1987): 674-77.

_____. "Academic Librarian Salaries: 1987-1988." *College & Research Libraries News* 50, no. 2 (February 1989): 120-24. (Reported data came from a 1986-87 survey conducted by the College and University Personnel Association.)

Lynch, Mary Jo, and Margaret Myers. *ALA Survey of Librarian Salaries.* Chicago: American Library Association, 1988. (Covers all types of libraries.)

SLA Triennial Salary Survey. Washington, D.C.: Special Libraries Association.

CHAPTER 13

The Self:
Time, Privacy, and Stress

"One cannot rent, hire, buy, or otherwise obtain more time."

– Peter F. Drucker,
The Effective Executive

MANAGING YOUR TIME

You will find innumerable handbooks, workshops, models and other aids designed or purporting to help you master one of your scarcest resources: time. While the value of external helps should not be underrated, bear four facts in mind: (1) your own history, habits, and predilections are the chief determinants of how well or how poorly you manage time; (2) no system of time management will prevent the eruption of critical, random events that require your immediate attention; (3) no matter how efficient you are with time, as the organization increases in size, your effectiveness is in direct proportion to the efficiency and effectiveness of the immediate subordinates to whom you must delegate work details you cannot possibly perform yourself; and (4) unlike ditch digging or factory assembly, knowledge work cannot be broken down into small increments; a substantial block of uninterrupted time is absolutely essential for any creative administrative work.

Organizational structure is one key determinant of how your time is consumed. Oncken identified three sources of demand for business time: the boss, subordinates, and oneself.[1] Academic librarianship has a fourth category: the client or constituency. Bosses and clients are disposed of easily: you have no control over them. When the vice president or vice chancellor makes a demand, it automatically goes to top of your list. When an upset faculty member calls or a student delegation marches into your office, you drop what you are doing. You have control only over subordinates and yourself, and even there control is somewhat limited by your own habits and personality.

Additional difficulties with time include reluctance to delegate, tendency to workaholic behavior, and the ease with which you can be manipulated by upward delegation. The last deserves special discussion.

Subordinates Demands on Time: Upward Delegation

Subordinates make two kinds of demands on time, each influenced by the mechanism of upward delegation. One type is desirable and the other most definitely is not. Desirable upward delegation occurs when subordinates regularly communicate with you and inform you of the resources they must have to accomplish their work. It is up to them to implement the program elements you and they have codeveloped, but it is your job to obtain the necessary resources.

The undesirable kind of upward delegation occurs when you start doing what is really the responsibility of your subordinates. Oncken suggested that these workers have learned to manage you so well that you actually do double duty. Usually, but not always, this kind of upward delegation happens by default--the subordinate fails to do the job, but your cooperation is required. If your subordinates work forty hours a week and have restful, relaxing weekends while you work far into each night as well as the weekends, it might pay to examine whether this type of upward delegation is operating.

Some employees are so skilled at managing their superiors that they can successfully orchestrate work habits--theirs and yours--without your noticing it.[2] A typical indicator is when a subordinate says, "We have a problem, boss." In plain English this means he has a problem, one he is trying to dump on you. Return it with the suggestion or directive that the employee bring you not one but several proposals for solving it.

An administrator faced with many such crises might take a critical look at the intermediate and lower management levels and consider some rearrangements. If this is not done, the habitual response, or lack of response, at lower levels merely perpetuates itself. Management's time will constantly be eroded and the real work of administration, planning, and decision making at the global level will quickly and permanently become paralyzed. The administrator's best aid to time management is confidence that capable, responsive, and responsible middle managers are part of the administrative team. Such persons should be willing to do their own staff work and be able to make whatever tough decisions are appropriate. If this is not the case, intermediate responsibilities inevitably drift upward. A chief administrator in such cases will always be putting out fires, never initiating new programs.

Constituents' Demands on Time

Scheduling work by the day, week, or month is a valuable exercise but often remains just that--an exercise. Administrative work in a human-centered organization cannot be neatly planned as if it were an industrial operation. The academic library has no system to ensure that essential resources are brought into play precisely at the moment of need. You can make lists and schedule all you want, but they may be in shambles minutes after you arrive at your office. You can plan everything except the priorities that your constituents are planning for you. Every constituency in the academic world complains that the institution seems to have no systematic management methods, that everything is handled by crisis management. Academic administration, in the library or elsewhere, is one of the least deterministic and least predictable lines of work. Be prepared to respond to crises that break out without notice. If certainty and predictability are what you seek, look into another line of work.

Subordinates' and clients' demands on time also arise from a leader's ceremonial duties: presenting service awards, attending fund-raising affairs, entertaining potential donors, and representing the school at civic events. These unavoidable activities, while not directly productive, support morale even though they contribute little to the solution of immediate crises. In no case can they be called time wasters, although they may have that appearance.

Your Own Work Schedule

It would be ridiculous for administrators to force themselves into keeping the same regular hours as everyone else when irregularity is built into their work. It is a mistake to explain or apologize for irregular comings and goings. Simply regard flexibility as a mix of perks, penalties, and privileges that go with responsibility, and make the best of your own time. Recognize, of course, that under the best conditions you will always have to make yourself available in accordance with the preferences of certain other people. If your boss is a morning person, you will find yourself coming in early. When a committee invites you to attend its proceedings, it is you, not the committee, who must make a schedule adjustment.

Aside from realizing that you can control neither your boss's nor your constituents' demands on time, you may consider the following suggestions to help you control your own time. Once you move into administration, leave behind the vocational aspects of your former responsibilities. Do not try to "do a little cataloging" to "keep up with the code" or maintain your craft skills. Liberally but selectively say no to invitations to speak, consult, run for office, or contribute chapters to books or articles to journals. Try to do the most difficult things first instead of the opposite. Try block scheduling, setting aside one or two hours not subject to interruption. Be sure you have an absolutely first-class secretary or administrative assistant.

Analyze how you use your time. Before microcomputers came into common use, administrators kept diaries to record and keep track of their use of time by the hour. While maintaining a diary is not very laborious, analyzing it is burdensome. A diary in combination with a spreadsheet program eases the burden. Five to ten minutes spent each day recording time usage in a diary and then transferring it to a spreadsheet makes an invaluable tool for serious library administrators who wonder where their time goes. Analysis can help identify work that might be delegated to others.

Keeping in Touch with Your Work Schedule

No matter that your secretary or administrative assistant maintains your appointment book at the office, you will have to keep a lot of data on your person. Several pocket diaries are available to help keep appointments straight and record important items for which you have a recurring need. Portable electronic appointment reminder systems store telephone numbers and brief memos, display calendars, and even beep to alert you of upcoming meetings. Still in the developmental stage, they have a limited capacity for notes, telephone numbers, and other items; their keyboard design makes data entry slow and cumbersome. When they commonly reach the stage where data can be loaded and maintained from an office or home microcomputer, they will be far more useful. If you are out of the office a great deal and need or wish to be within easy telephone reach, a pager or beeper is advisable. As their prices have come down dramatically, they should no longer be considered pretentious luxuries.

USING MODERN OFFICE TOOLS

Recording and Transmitting Your Ideas

Supplementing the traditional notepad and dictating machines are laptop computers, with which you can easily upload your notes into the office computer for further refinement without the need for wasteful rekeying. A built-in or accessory modem can communicate text to and from home or office. Like other executives, academic library managers will also find portable and laptop computers (with modems) increasingly necessary for keeping in touch while on the road. Pocket-sized dictation machines are so cheap that it is possible to keep separate units in car, night table, and the briefcase or suitcase at the ready for business travel. Facsimile (fax) transceivers are becoming as commonplace as photocopiers, and even personal computers can support fax service by accessory boards and scanners.

Making Computers and Software Work for You

Unlike typewriters, the personal computer is not just another office tool. It is quickly becoming the universal office machine and management communication tool. It links into complete systems for document generation, control, filing, copying, communication, data analysis, and data management. Even personnel administration can be managed with it.

While comprehensive office automation is not yet here, it is clearly on the way. If you lack basic computer skills you may soon be unable to check files of correspondence, locate important documents, receive electronic mail, develop or obtain statistical data for decision making, or communicate with colleagues. You should not only learn the fundamentals but maintain your skills to ensure that you are not helpless in the event of staff sickness, strikes, equipment malfunctions, or other disruptions. All administrators looking toward the future should acquire their own equipment, and link into local network services and national electronic mail systems.

PRIVACY AND SELF-DEVELOPMENT

Philosophies of human resources management have advanced enormously in the past few decades. Most of the beneficiaries of this new enlightenment deservedly have been staff. Working in a bureaucracy is hard on leaders too, and it is easy for organizations and administrations to overlook the health and personal concerns of managers. Three areas of importance to all administrators are private life, personal development, and response to stress.

Maintaining Your Privacy

The personal life of any boss is a subject of great curiosity among employees, and television has conveyed to the general public a pervasive sense of entitlement to know the personal affairs of leaders.[3] Some staff are cheeky enough to ask, quite directly, intensely personal questions ranging from your favorite Italian restaurant to your sexual preference. Some innocuous questions are merely part of the small talk that goes on in any social situation, but others may contain hidden agendas that are not easily decoded. Be prepared for the questions of the curious and consider in advance a measured response to ward off anything intrusive. Above all, do not be caught off guard by presumptuous inquiry.

Community size powerfully influences one's privacy. Obviously, it is easy to be anonymous and invisible in a big city, whereas in a small town your comings and goings will be widely known and quickly communicated. Your preferences for privacy will naturally influence your choices when it comes to seeking positions.

Personal and Professional Development: Finding Time to Think

The most important matters, the long-range problems, are never in your in-basket. While you struggle with the bureaucratic tangle of administration--forms, reports, procedures, statistical analyses, proposals--the urgent drives out the important. You may be failing to delegate appropriately or allowing your time to fall into the many sinkholes that await it.

Aside from the usual time-management methods, some of which are described above, it may be helpful deliberately to schedule time away from the office, at random intervals. Some people also find that coming to the office very early or staying long after everyone else has left provides essential time to work undisturbed, to read or think.

Support Groups

Support groups and networks, essential for all administrators, are easily available in large metropolitan centers. College librarians in small cities who do not have a personal support group of peers can get a great deal of help from colleagues by liberal use of the telephone. Many support groups for administrators are available within the professional associations.[4]

STRESS AND BURNOUT IN LIBRARY ADMINISTRATION

Preoccupation with lofty missions can lead inexperienced or junior administrators to fail to grapple with the reality that administrative work is often mundane, almost always exhausting, and frequently frustrating.[5] Chapter 5 described how easy it is to become caught up in the stereotype of the administrator as a powerful person. Equally tempting is the view that the administrator can afford to be "laid back" most of the time. Compare and contrast administration with the supposed academic life: the academic lifestyle is often imagined by lay people as one of comparative ease, an image enhanced by the media's portrayal of professorial types. Those who participate in academic life, however, are keenly aware of its bitter rivalries, intense competition and stress levels, which can surpass anything in the world of commerce, sports, or politics.[6] Students may face final examinations with trepidation several times a year and junior faculty, mindful of the "up or out" tenure decision lying ahead, may look nervously at the stacks of papers that must be graded. But administrators face a kind of final examination virtually every day and homework almost every night. In addition, they live under the constant sword of Damocles of serving "at the pleasure of" a vice president, provost, or other superior. Whether appointed for an indefinite period or elected for a term, chief librarians can be removed whenever campus administration deems necessary.

Living and working with ever-present uncertainty breeds anxiety and makes administrators susceptible to stress, burnout, or emotional anxiety. In discussing burnout among executives, Harry Levinson focused on the immense difficulties and unending stress that a manager faces:

> The manager must cope with the least capable among employees, with the depressed, the suspicious, the rivalrous, the self-centered, and the generally unhappy. The manager must balance these conflicting personalities and create from them a motivated work group. He or she must define group purposes and organize people around that, must resolve conflicts, establish priorities, make decisions about other people, accept and deflect their hostility, and deal with the frustration that arises out of that continuing interaction. Managing people is the most difficult administrative task, and it has built-in frustration.[7]

Since the 1970s a great deal of research has gone into stress and burnout. It is well known that stress, when properly managed, is not altogether evil and can contribute positively to motivation. It can also be addictive, and this is a real and present danger to administrators, especially for those who are highly competitive and not satisfied unless they are facing a challenge. The thrill of pressure becomes self-feeding, so that like a parasite, stress eventually consumes its host. It also causes other illnesses that destroy a person's effectiveness. In excessive amounts, it can immobilize an ambitious, eager employee, and lead to behavior that is indecisive on the one hand, impulsive on the other. The burnout syndrome, widespread in the helping professions, demonstrates a mix of very unpleasant symptoms: increased emotional exhaustion, chronic tiredness, accumulating negative attitudes toward clients, a feeling of being put upon by the organization, loss of feeling of accomplishment from work, and a short fuse in relationships with colleagues. Victims become disengaged from their sense of professional commitment and duty.

In the teaching profession, research indicates that males suffer from burnout and stress far more deeply than females, and younger people sustain worse symptoms than their more experienced colleagues.[8] The difference in sex-based response may be attributable to the nurturing role to which females have traditionally been socialized. As for age, it is possible that younger professionals tolerate stress less well than their older colleagues because they grew up on a continuous upward swing in the economy and are unaccustomed to deprivation. One research team concluded that the chief cause of stress and burnout was lack of preparation for the realities of work.[9] This conclusion might also help explain the reasons for Lowell Martin's contention that "as a group librarians have not been administration minded."[10] Observation of stress in other professions suggests that the burnout syndrome is esentially identical for librarians, teachers, mental health professionals, and nurses.

Nauratil suggested the main causes of librarian burnout are insufficient autonomy in judgment, lack of opportunity to exercise professional skills independently, rigidly bureaucratic work constraints, and not enough say in the formation of goals.[11]

Counterposed to these valuable criticisms of bad administrative practice is the reluctance of some professionals to be sufficiently proactive. Both factors, in negative synergism and mutual discord, reinforce each other, result in stasis, and deprive the profession of promising leaders.

Innumerable techniques and a multitude of self-help books are aimed at helping people combat and control stress. Almost anything that produces a sharp change of pace helps, such as sports or quiet relaxation. The most difficult aspect of coping with stress is that whatever your preferred technique, that particular method may not be available or practical at the time of greatest need.

SUMMARY

Academic managers do not field their human resources the way a general marshalls the troops and, as stated earlier, cannot mold a diverse work force into a unified team, as in sales or sports. Because uncertainty and the unexpected dominate academic library administration so powerfully, stress is inherent and it is nearly impossible to "plan" a day's work. Only the strictest personal discipline can impose a modicum of control onto a schedule that is by nature disorderly. An important element of that discipline is effective delegation--but that works well only given extraordinarily competent and loyal subordinates. Time management methods from commerce are generally much more adaptable to academe than other business techniques. Certain new technologies, such as cellular telephones, portable computers, and electronic mail, help maintain better control over administrative communication, but they also increase the communication workload, add stress, and make it difficult to have time alone for thinking, planning, or relaxing. The new technologies can be invasive, opening up segments of time that were previously private. In the face of these changes, it takes strenuous effort and a certain toughness and determination to preserve one's privacy.

Notes

1. William Oncken, *Managing Management Time* (Englewood Cliffs, N.J.: Prentice-Hall, 1984).

2. A highly instructive, semihumorous presentation on this topic is William Oncken and Donald L. Wass's article, "Management Time: Who's Got the Monkey?" *Harvard Business Review* 52 (November-December 1974): 75-80.

3. Meyrowitz, *No Sense of Place,* 62-67, 271, 315-17.

4. American Library Association support groups, especially those within ACRL and LAMA, are identified in the annually issued ALA *Handbook of Organization.*

5. James G. March, *How We Talk and How We Act: Administrative Theory and Administrative Life* (Urbana: University of Illinois, 1980).

6. If at this point in this work, you are still in doubt of this, reread "The Faculty and Its Politics," chapter 3 of Van Cleve Morris's *Deaning* (Urbana: University of Illinois, 1981).

7. Harry Levinson, "When Executives Burn Out," *Harvard Business Review* 59 (May-June 1981): 72-81. Reprinted in *The Executive Dilemma* (New York: Wiley, 1985), 61-71, esp. 65.

8. Kamal Dawani, "Teacher Burnout and Its Relation to Sex, Age, and Years of Experience," *National Forum of Educational Administration and Supervision Journal* 4, no. 3 (1987/88): 99-110.

9. Cary Cherniss, E. Egnatios and S. Wacker, "Job Stress and Career Development in New Public Professionals," *Professional Psychology* 7, no. 4 (1976): 428-36.

10. Lowell Martin, *Organizational Structure of Libraries* (Metuchen, N.J.: Scarecrow Press, 1984), 134.

11. Marcia J. Nauratil, "Librarian Burnout and Alienation," *Canadian Library Journal* 44, no. 6 (December 1987): 385-89.

Resources

Adair, John. *Effective Time Management.* London, Pan Books, 1988.

American Media, Inc. *The Time Trap.* West Des Moines, Iowa, n.d. Videotape. 28 minutes.

Baltus, Rita K. *Personal Psychology for Life and Work.* 3d ed. New York: McGraw-Hill, 1987.

Bartolome, Fernando. "Executives as Human Beings." *Harvard Business Review* 50, no. 6 (November-December 1972): 62ff.

Bates, Jefferson D. *Dictating Effectively: A Time Saving Manual.* Washington, D.C.: Acropolis, 1980.

Bates, Jefferson D., and Stuart Crump, Jr. *The Portable Office: Take Your Office on the Road.* Washington, D.C.: Acropolis, 1987.

Braudy, Leo. *The Frenzy of Renown: Fame and Its History.* New York: Oxford University Press, 1986.

Bruemmer, Alice, ed. *Library Management in Review.* New York: Special Libraries Association, 1981.

Creth, Sheila. *Time Management and Conducting Effective Meetings.* 2 vols. Vol. 1, Instructor's Manual; vol. 2, Workbook. Chicago: ACRL, 1982.

Dawis, Rene V., Rosemary T. Fruehling, and Neild B. Oldham. *Psychology Applied to Human Relations and Work.* 7th ed. New York: McGraw-Hill, 1988.

Drucker, Peter F. *The Effective Executive.* New York: Harper and Row, 1985.

Freudenberger, Herbert J., and Gail North. *Women's Burnout.* Garden City, N.Y.: Doubleday, 1985.

Freudenberger, Herbert J., with Geraldine Richelson. *Burn-Out: The High Cost of High Achievement.* Garden City, N.Y.: Doubleday, 1980.

Goldberg, P. *Executive Health.* New York: McGraw-Hill, 1978.

Gothberg, Helen M., and Donald E. Riggs. "Time Management in Academic Libraries." *College & Research Libraries* 49, no. 2 (March 1988): 131-40.

Labier, Douglas. *Modern Madness: The Emotional Fallout of Success.* Reading, Mass.: Addison-Wesley, 1986.

Leach, Ronald G. "Finding Time You Never Knew You Had." *Journal of Academic Librarianship* 6, no. 1 (March 1980): 4-8.

Levinson, Harry. *Executive Stress.* New York: New American Library, 1985.

Mackenzie, R. Alec. *The Time Trap.* Toronto: McGraw-Hill Ryerson, 1975.

Nauratil, Marcia J. *The Alienated Librarian.* Westport, Conn.: Greenwood Press, 1989.

Oncken, William. *Managing Management Time.* Englewood Cliffs, N.J.: Prentice-Hall, 1984.

Oncken, William, and Donald L. Wass. "Management Time: Who's Got the Monkey?" *Harvard Business Review* 52 (November-December 1974): 75-80.

Servan-Schreiber, Jean-Louis. *The Art of Time.* Reading, Mass.: Addison-Wesley, 1988.

Spaniol, LeRoy, and Jennifer J. Caputo. *Professional Burn-Out: A Personal Survival Kit.* Lexington Mass.: Human Services Associates, 1979.

Special Libraries Association. *Time Management in the Small Library.* Washington, D.C., 1988. (A self-instructional course available in two formats: a programmed learning workbook and a microcomputer-oriented diskette.)

Taylor, Harold L. *Delegate: The Key to Successful Management.* New York: Beaufort Books, 1984.

_____. *Making Time Work for You.* Toronto: Stoddart, 1986.

CHAPTER 14

2000 and Beyond:
New Trends, Problems, Questions, and Challenges

Any process of change is a lifetime's job.

> – Aldous Huxley,
> *Eyeless in Gaza*

The more things change, the more they will never be the same.

> – Cover of *Datamation,*
> 15 November 1978

We have lived and participated in an extremely productive, historic era. Academic librarianship has changed more within the past several decades than in its entire previous history. Manorial structures and systems, some predating the nineteenth century, and industrial methods dominated librarianship even into the 1960s. Our durable old ways perforce kept librarians occupied with volumes, titles, cards, files, materials, and procedures, with the focus on facilities, materials, and clerical work rather than cerebral activity and transactions with clients. We treated our quantitative output as if it were a gross national bibliographic product. Large-scale computerization and new management tools give us the power to transform our profession and the potential to restore its former glory as a life of the mind. Librarianship has absorbed radical, technology-driven changes with remarkable efficiency but at high human cost; many problems remain to be solved before a transformation can be fully realized. In this concluding chapter we review the challenges, some clear, some dim, that future administrators must face if academic librarianship is to effectively employ new digital communication technology in the service of scholarship.

WORK IN THE FUTURE:
THE LIMITATIONS OF FORECASTS

Futurists and specialists in the sociology of work have pondered the nature of work and hypothesized changes that might be wrought by new developments in automation, robotics, and microchip technology.[1] The rapid evolution of computers persuades us that a cornucopia of technical devices will sweep away the traditional stratification of the academic library and all the essential labor-intensive work that has nurtured it for centuries.

We may rightfully ask, however, whether such innovations might actually accentuate the academy's well-developed hierarchy and exacerbate the pecking order among the staff levels. Technology may squeeze the pyramid higher still, narrowing its base and increasing the prestige of the haves who work with clients, while lowering the status of the have-nots who perform warehouse duties with lifeless objects, such as checking in journal issues with bar code wands. Just as new technology has failed to save money for the library, it is doubtful that it will relieve academic librarianship from continuing reliance upon existing media or from the considerable manual labor required for their physical management.

Until robotic stack maintenance is available, libraries will continue to require human beings to perform the boring, disagreeable, unstimulating–and indispensable–work of marking, shelving, fetching, sorting, and reshelving. As long as the professoriate maintains a reward system tied to publication in hard copy, materials handling will continue. Even if the reward system should be altered to accept some form of digital publication, libraries would still have to buy, install, house, and repair the hardware, and they would have to staff the work stations with professionals to ensure an optimal educational return on this huge investment.

Would access to comprehensive retrospective catalogs in digital form relieve libraries from manual activity? Long after the major retrospective bibliographic records have been keyboarded and put onto laser disks, and long after the faculty's universal adoption of digital publication, the disks themselves will have to be checked in when they arrive from a vendor and manually loaded into a carousel or playback unit. Someone will have to determine that the delivered disks are actually the correct ones for that library or data service center, exactly as is done now for books and journals.[2] Libraries will still have to process materials that have no ISBNs or bar codes, that cannot be recognized by scanners, or that cannot be economically converted to published digital form; other data will still have to be keyed into terminals. Even voice-recognition technology has a long distance to go before it can cope with the incredible ambiguity of words and the multitude of languages and accents heard in the world of higher education.

Exciting and dramatic new techniques now in their infancy may mature to the point where they become economical and reliable, as has already occurred with personal computers. Some of these technologies will eventually reduce the amount of drudgery that someone must do in academic libraries. But the glamour of the new should not be permitted to distract administrators from limitations that will likely continue to govern library operations, at least through the remainder of this century.

Work-Related Ergonomic Limitations

Despite remarkable rapid advances in screen display technology, the evolution of multiple-window systems for text comparison, and ever higher computing speeds, the fleeting image still cannot rival the convenience and naturalness of work with paper and print on a large table for study and research. Human hand-eye-brain connections developed over millennia still make up a wonderfully integrated, powerful system of thought processing that will not easily be displaced by fifty or sixty square inches of a cathode ray tube plus a mouse. Computerized text and bibliographic processing are best viewed as strong support systems for research, not techniques that will replace traditional methods.[3]

Social and Emotional Limitations

Automation, originally seen as a means of saving labor (or creating a threat of unemployment), has in practice demonstrated a demand for a different and more expensive kind of labor than the industry-like work done in academic librarianship during the manorial and industrial eras. In fact, the successful development of automation has conclusively proved Shaw's contention that librarians formerly performed very large amounts of mindless clerical work: searching uncumulated bibliographies, typing, sorting, proofreading, and filing.[4] This clerical work produced its own stresses of boredom, fatigue, alienation, and dissatisfaction. While automation has eliminated these sources of stress in the modern academic library, an unexpected side effect has erupted: the former deliberateness and slowness to change demanded by conservative systems have given way to ceaseless innovation, which in turn creates technology-induced stress for long-term employees. It appears that one type of stress has been exchanged for another.[5]

Social and emotional constraints are powerful inhibitors to change. It may take decades to change users' attitudes and employees' work habits. Comparatively little progress has been made in discovering ways to speed up human adaptation to change. With microcomputers and network systems, users must invest herculean mental and emotional effort, and large blocks of time, to master the mounting collections of software documentation. Today's systems are never complete. All employees, professional and support staff, must learn anew each revised version of the software; they must also reconcile themselves to ever-changing hardware. The coming generation will be at ease with these systems and with change in general, but in this transitional era libraries must be administered with the staff on hand.

Despite thirty years of research and experimentation in information retrieval, there is little evidence that information-based work and knowledge industries, like the library, will soon be based entirely on mysterious machines functioning with little or no human intervention.[6] It has taken almost a generation to develop the first, fairly rigid, application-specific artificial intelligence (AI) systems suitable for science, business, and medicine. Even these are really idiot savant systems that can deal only with knowledge that is easy to define, stable, and sufficiently narrow in scope so that the whole process can be worked into an algorithm. In the world of abstract, original thought, artificial intelligence in its current state may be a misnomer; "computerized research assistance" is a more accurate term.[7] While AI remains a field of intense research interest and development, its immediate impact on academic librarians' employment potential is negligible. On the other hand, expert systems might eliminate certain low- or middle-level tasks, promote enforcement of standards, assist professional staff with extraordinary challenges, and reduce the time required for limited types of repetitive inquiries.[8]

THE PROMISE OF TELECOMMUTING

Some futurists paint yet another rosy picture: work at home, or telework.[9] This concept, they claim, will end the intrigues and pressures of the institutionalized office environment, emancipate workers from the confines of fixed space and comparatively inflexible hours, eliminate the need for close supervision, and solve the problems of child care. If access to all future library activity is to be via machines, then indeed few workers may be needed onsite. Are we to imagine an army of people working in a cottage industry to convert retrospective collections to digital form, or another army of telecommuters providing remote reference service to off-campus faculty and nonresidential students? These are most unlikely prospects if any kind of quality control over educational outcomes and work performance is to be exercised, and if the essential social intercourse between students and faculty, clients and librarians/consultants is not to be eliminated. These visions also suggest that today's colleges and universities will assume some totally new shape overnight–an unlikely prospect for institutions so slow to change.

Still another futuristic outlook posits students, faculty, workers, and databases all interconnected by the wizardry of fiber optics, satellites, digital networks, and cheap computers: a decentralized academic community using technology to build a "distributed university." This fantasy is viable only until the bills for telecommunication and the invoices for access fees begin to arrive, and until its proponents realize that, unlike library service, database access is not to be given away without transaction charges.

Work at home is not enthusiastically endorsed by everyone. Olson concluded that for professional employees, telecommuting "is not a significant phenomenon."[10] As long ago as 1976 Maccoby asked, "Who would want to stay at home all day doing his work, when in fact one of the most enjoyable aspects of work for many people is the chance to meet people and socialize?"[11] Telework is meaningless for academics whose work is interactive, transactional, and occurs in real time.

Work at home, and its academic counterpart, study at home, are unlikely to play major roles in the immediate future of the academic library. Both concepts challenge the foundation of higher education as a social experience, one that is essential to the preparation of youth for careers based on continuing social interaction with clients and people in all walks of life. If implemented on a large scale, work at home and study at home would demolish a thousand years of college and university life and would desocialize higher education. What technology might give us, and what we desperately need in the institutional workplace, is greater organizational decentralization to enhance opportunities for staff development at all levels. Improvement in the quality of work in the workplace will benefit the academic library far more than any amount of work at home. Personal computers and large databases on laser disks are already providing a basis for this change.

AN ACADEMIC LIBRARY PERSPECTIVE ON THE FUTURE

A fault of technology-based forecasts is simply that they are technology based; they confound expertise and wisdom. Often the products of technological minds working in feverish enthusiasm and in virtual isolation from the user community, such forecasts can go awry even in the heat of development.[12] What will our future look like? Can we protect ourselves from misguided prediction? A generation ago, before the common expectation of constantly accelerating technological advance, forecasting was often based on simple linear extrapolation. In academic librarianship, perhaps the most familiar extrapolation is Fremont Rider's dramatic but incorrect exponential growth model for research libraries, published in 1944.[13] One-third of a century later, Holley looked ahead from a perspective advantageously closer to modern technological development.[14] For academic librarianship, there is no more accurate or comprehensive overview of the future than Holley's.

The general quality of library forecasting is necessarily tied to that of higher education. There, the situation has been erratic at best: in the expansionist mid-1960s it was suggested that 100,000 librarians were needed, a bubble that burst quickly. In the mid-1970s the U.S. Office of Education trimmed its projected growth rate of college enrollment from an earlier 3.9 percent to only 1.3 percent. Yet in the United States today there are 175 more private and public colleges than there were in 1980, and students are pounding on the doors so desperately that admissions officers are bewildered. When society changes so erratically and so much technical fantasy turns into fact, predicting the future of any institution is a chancy business. The number of known variables, let alone the unknown, is far too great for modeling. As Daniel Bell pointed out, society is not a closed system or instrumentality whose phenomena can be treated algorithmically or deterministically.[15] Consequently, the reader may find in this concluding chapter many more questions than answers.

For academic librarianship, new technology promises capabilities whose educational consequences can hardly be guessed at: broadband optical-digital networks capable of moving huge quantities of data with great speed, the document microphone (facsimile), universal connectivity among networks, full-presence communication via live videophone, voice command, computerized rendering of speech into text, automatic translation, and a host of Memex-like services not even dreamed of by Vannevar Bush.[16] Designating these developmental systems the "knowledge navigators" of the future, vendors claim they will free the mind from burdensome house-keeping chores, make possible virtually instantaneous retrieval and communication, establish a paperless society, and enable scholarship to flourish as if in a new renaissance.

Can these promises be fulfilled? As indicated in chapter 1, the record of pure technology applied to human problems is not impressive. It is a mistake to focus so much attention on the technology, to look for a technological quick fix for problems that are primarily social and human. The enduring problems are neither material nor technical, but emotional and spiritual. As long as people work in libraries, we foresee continuing human challenges. A partial list might include self-identification and professionalism, recruiting, graduate education, staffing, motivation, the possibly changing academic reward system, response to continuous technological change, response to challenges from the information industry, the fate of middle management, the growing impact of collective bargaining in higher education, tenure, compensation, industrial-style democracy, redesign of library work and library organizations, demographic change, and service to users. In general, the list also includes the capacity to respond to political challenge, the professional's need to come to terms with general administration, and the profession's need to reinvent library administration as well as the library itself. Let us examine a few of these items in detail.

AN ACTION AGENDA FOR THE NEXT DECADE

Self-Identification

Self-understanding is a prerequisite for defining our social role to the general public. As indicated in chapter 3, many problems of professional status and duality in librarianship stem from the profession's inability to define its role clearly to its own membership, let alone to constituencies and jurisdictions, a point made at length by Shiflett and to some extent by Reeves and Bennett.[17] In the workplace, some librarians remain confused about the responsibilities appropriate to professionals and support staff and seem not to comprehend the risks to which this unclarity exposes them.[18]

Many feel the profession is threatened by the sale or lease of information resources. Unlike law, medicine, and engineering, which have always provided services for a fee and which through licensure maintain an exclusive grip upon their members' expertise, librarianship is one of the most giving of professions. Giving, not selling, is our stock in trade.[19] When all that librarians had to give was their time, energy, and dedication, self-identification was relatively easy. But to do their work effectively, modern librarians must invoke very expensive collateral systems and services. Providing these new capabilities imposes new fiscal management responsibilities and requires a new image for the profession.

Upgrading Librarians' Professionalism

As professionals, librarians are different from faculty and researchers. Our principal domain is service, and we do not have the leisure of faculty and researchers to keep up with literature while we work. But we have not designed our work to help our professionals remain current. In fact, some library administrators are known to complain when librarians read at work. In restructuring our profession, we might follow the faculty-researcher models more closely. We should offload every facet of production work onto support staff and budget the time academic librarians need to carry out the full range of work consistent with a professional life of service: work with clients, collection development, cataloging, management and administration, system design, study, research, and publication.

Recruiting

Intelligence is a necessary but not a sufficient prerequisite for effective professionalism. The main challenge in recruiting is not only to attract the best employees but to ensure that those highly intelligent students who do enter the field (1) perceive academic librarianship as a people-centered service profession, (2) appreciate technology as a tool, not as an end in itself, and (3) understand their roles and responsibilities as resource managers in a total process of scholarly communication that comprehends teaching, administration, research, and publication. Fundamental to these assumptions is acceptance of, indeed enthusiasm for, the essentially elitist character of higher education. Academic institutions are ideally great islands of equal opportunity for the most talented minds, but they can never be democratic places where every member of the community is on the same level and has an equal voice. Failure to come to terms with the stratified character of academe and the profession's need for managers may have impaired our capacity to recruit and retain the most effective people. Clearly, understanding the relationship of the library and library services to the academic community as a whole is a key element in ending this failure.

Graduate Education

The general ferment in the Association for Library and Information Science Education (ALISE) makes it evident that graduate schools have perceived both the management crisis in the profession and their own crises in the realm of institutional politics.[20] Faculty and curriculum renewal, a heightened political consciousness, and improved recruiting may produce a generation of leaders that will be management minded. Rayward, however, maintained that the problem of adequate preparation is complicated by the lack of clear agreement among the stakeholders on the appropriate distribution of educational responsibilities: with limited time the schools cannot do everything, cannot prepare students for "day one" and also for their lifetime career needs.[21] Thompson and Carr, chief librarians at British universities, agreed: "Professional education is here to stay, of course, but students cannot be taught how to be librarians in the classroom: only the practice of librarianship can do that."[22] Clearly, the responsibilities for creating the mature librarian are conjoint; library schools and libraries are interdependent. If this fact is acknowledged, each party can cease to point the finger at the other and allege deficiencies.

Staffing: Professionalism, The Dilemma of Appropriate Use of Human Resources and Technological Advances

The historically bifurcate model of personnel administration emerges directly from the structure of higher education itself and from the related dualities inherent in the industrialization of the West. It has dominated librarianship for more than half a century. There is no question that the dual system impairs organizational unity and fosters adversarial relationships. This condition is exacerbated by a large, highly educated labor pool whose members are powerfully attracted to academe's superb working conditions. In administering two employment levels, some librarian-administrators sense they are not making optimal use of human resources. Certainly the current split pleases no one: well-educated library assistants are singularly frustrated by the limits to their career development, while professionals see their positions threatened by displacement from below. Jurisdictions and funders, especially in public librarianship, are taking a hard look at duality and seeing it as an opportunity for cost reduction: why employ a librarian when someone who can "do the same work" is available at half the cost?[23] This challenge from the public library sector makes it all the more important that academic librarianship portray itself accurately to its constituencies and carry out the necessary politicking effectively.

What is the future of duality? The current tensions between professional and support staff might recede if technology continues to radically change the nature of library work. There is no logical reason why this should not occur. Clearly, technology does not simplify mental work. Rather, it eliminates simpler, menial work, replaces it with more work that is mentally more demanding and acts to transfer some work to lower levels in the staff hierarchy. These work shifts occur because new technology does not merely displace older methods but stimulates management to devise new programs and encourages clients to make new demands. Because of continuing technical advance, the work load that technology can support becomes self-amplifying. In a sense, the future of information-based work is unlimited, or is limited only by the technical capacity to support its exploitation and the economic capacity to pay. The past generation's dissatisfactions with the relationship between professionals and support staff could fade as information-based work becomes ever more sophisticated and demands the very talents that the highly educated, exempt or nonexempt, possess. If and when that happens, some totally new structuring of the labor force will be required in the higher-education sector. After all, the exempt-nonexempt dichotomy is simply the product of a manufacturing economy grafted onto higher education. Like many other industry-based paradigms, it is a poor fit to higher education's social and managerial needs in an era of increasingly complex information processing.

That is the logic of the situation; but where politics is pervasive–and it is hard to imagine a more political environment than higher education–logic does not always prevail. The techno-logical and social forces that might erode duality and the rigid caste system of academe have been on a collision course since the 1960s.[24] How will higher education, among the most conservative of all institutions, respond? The professoriate will certainly not give up its privileges any more willingly than a politician surrenders power. Colleges and universities will not become apolitical institutions overnight. But there are other possibilities. Resnikoff suggested that major advances in educational technology might one day transfer higher education to the private sector.[25] Viewed from a strictly in-strumental perspective of higher education, such a change might be beneficial. What then of the humanities and social sciences? What happens to a thousand years of tradition? What about accreditation and the credibility of research? We cannot answer these questions; but they surely have personnel implications for the future adminis-tration of academic libraries–whether they are called libraries, in-formation centers, knowledge laboratories, or something else.

Motivation Problems

Although the work of the human relations school has not been altogether discredited, it has certainly been vigorously challenged by knowledgeable critics such as Maccoby, Michalko, De Gennaro, and Savall. No one suggests that humane styles of administration be abandoned. Yet it is clear that human interaction in the workplace is infinitely more complex than once supposed. The approach to motivation requires more fundamental research so that we may avoid simplistic solutions. This may be an excellent joint research opportunity for the library and social science communities.

It is well known that salary is not the chief motivator of employees. In a study by Sheppard and Herrick, the highest ranked desiderata among employees, regardless of age, were interesting work, opportunity to develop one's special abilities, and the chance for promotion.[26] For support staff, the bifurcate system might deliver the second item but offer little hope for the first and third. As for the professional staff, of whom we increasingly demand administrative responsibilities, a study by Swisher, DuMont, and Boyer reveals the disturbing finding that "both men and women select librarianship as a career because a large majority do not want to be managers."[27] In view of the profession's clear-cut need for management-minded personnel, this finding has implications for both student recruiting and curriculum design.

Response to Technological Change

Publication Growth and the Academic Reward System

Librarians point to the high costs of publishing, distributing, cataloging, and making available scholarly communications; specifically, they attack publishers and distributors for their high prices. The publishers' retort is that they are only fulfilling a role created by the academic community itself. Could technology, by the year 2000, permanently alter the academic reward system and thereby change forever the archival and service functions of the academic library? What would happen to traditional librarianship if economic factors force the whole reward system of higher education (the professoriate, libraries, scholarly publishers, and learned societies) into a new pattern, perhaps a national or international digital network running from central data banks, maybe even operated by the for-profit sector?

Encroachment of the For-Profit Sector in Information

The view of the library as a special preserve, protected from the rough-and-tumble of the business world, is fast disappearing. Scarcity of funds, demands for fiscal accountability, plus expensive, ever-newer technology-based products and services essential to teaching and research increasingly prompt some to question aspects of the academic library's raison d'être. Increasingly, those in charge of public policy see traditional libraries and information centers consuming expensive resources whose costs must be brought under control. Might computer centers, in combination with national database and communication services, supplant libraries for all but archival functions? Could the entire apparatus and system of an academic library be contracted out to a commercial firm, as Resnikoff suggested?[28] Would a private service be cheaper and better than a publicly financed system? There is no reason why the "make or buy" question, long since settled in the matter of acquiring and distributing bibliographic data, cannot be asked of the entire library system. An aggressive, growing information industry sees immense profit potential in the business of knowledge heretofore perceived as higher education's exclusive realm.

Potential Displacement of Professionals by Software

Library technicians and other support staff are not the only threats to professionals. What if expert systems, artificial intelligence, and neural networks achieve grand success and begin replacing the support academic librarians now provide to students and faculty? Would clients come to rely more and more on electronic and mechanical systems? The vendors certainly hope so. It is much too early in the history of these developing technologies to forecast their ultimate impact. Michael Georgeff, director of the Australian Artificial Intelligence Institute, dismissed the notion that by the twenty-first century we will have a computer that behaves like HAL in Arthur Clarke's *2001: A Space Odyssey*.[29] Although nineteenth-century utopian visions of a mechanistic future did not fully materialize, history demonstrates that it can be dangerous to dismiss new ideas. Today's vision of a computer-based utopia will have to be monitored carefully.

The Fate of Middle Management

Social scientists and computer development experts studying business and industry voice continuing frustration over the low growth in white-collar productivity. As technology makes it possible for management information (and its analysis) to flow upward with ease, some have forecast that middle management will greatly diminish, if not altogether disappear.

For middle management to decline in higher education, two preconditions must be met: (1) the hierarchical, elitist structure of colleges and universities would have to change radically and (2) upper-level administrators would have to use computers themselves (rather than delegate responsibility to subordinate staff) to analyze data for decision making. There is no evidence that either change is in sight; academic administration is far too political and complex for top administrators to base their decisions strictly on data analysis. As long as academic librarianship's major service remains custom-tailored intellectual work, never the same from day to day, its need for middle management is not likely to diminish. Only in mass production operations can computers carry out the data collection and analysis traditionally done by middle management. Indeed, arguments can be made that middle management in higher education needs strengthening: the enormous complexity of computerization, the ever-changing hardware and software, the nonrepetitive nature of cerebral work, the staggering challenges of preservation, the huge influx of new students from nontraditional backgrounds, the tremendous burden of continual training and reeducation, and the general conservatism of higher education in its administrative affairs. All factors point to a continuing need for strong, competent, proactive middle management.

With the demise of the expert bookman as chief librarian, the management function may have to be completely redesigned. Cronin suggested that the need for managerial expertise will far outweigh technical and professional competence as the principal criterion for selecting a library manager: "By the 1990s we may have a three-tier profession, with a managerial elite controlling the most influential positions within the LIS [library and information science] community."[30]

Increased Impact of Collective Bargaining

Both professional and support staff show increased interest in collective bargaining, the former perhaps out of disillusionment with faculty status, and the latter out of frustration with duality and the lack of any real opportunity to influence program. Harvard University's support staff vote to affiliate with a union will likely have an enormous impact on higher education throughout the United States, increasing the bitterness and resentments already inherent in the caste system.[31] It is ironic that at the very time when academic libraries are emerging from their manorial systems, into modern, computerized service agencies able to take advantage of the infinite flexibility of computers, they face the comparative inflexibility and adversarial nature of collective bargaining. This is but another indication that it is the human element, rarely the technology per se, that is at the heart of the administrative process.

Tenure versus Renewal

Young recruits are enthusiastic about changing the profession and creative administrators are eager to support them. The spirit of intrapreneurship has grown, and librarians keen to use computers have been recruited from disciplines beyond the usual. Cooperatives and bibliographic utilities have caused isolationism to decline. An undercurrent of resistance to change continues to flow among some long-tenured staff who are marking time basically, neither going nor wishing to go anyplace. Such stagnancy impairs an institution's capacity for spiritual and intellectual renewal. Tenure and budget constraints put a brake on renewal. It is very difficult to finance renewal if high salaries are tied up in deadwood, a point made in chapter 10. A day of reckoning is coming with respect to institutions' ability to bear the continuing costs of tenured library staff who have found for themselves a comfortable niche in a protected enclave. In Britain, reform of higher education eliminated tenure for professors appointed or promoted after November 1987.[32] As we move into the twenty-first century, higher education in North America may similarly probe the concept of tenure, for both faculty and librarians, even in the face of disappearing mandatory retirement.

Renewal is required at the top administrative levels, too. While some schools appoint or elect chief or deputy chief librarians for a term, most appoint high-level administrators for an indefinite period. Yet top leaders can go stale just as easily as rank and file librarians. By keeping people in leadership posts for long periods, schools trade off creativity for stability. Top academic administrators prefer a steady-state library with highly reliable services over one that shows many ups and downs, a preference that coincides with that of the highly successful library leaders. Yet such arrangements are not necessarily in anyone's best interests. Both people and institutions need change in the form of regular, controlled intervention. Perhaps the future will see more schools appointing or electing top library leadership for specific terms, in spite of Rosovsky's well-articulated reservations about such schemes.[33]

How Do We Reward Innovators?

Business and industry normally find quick, generous ways to reward innovators. As a conservative, slow-moving institution, the academic library has not been a hotbed of innovation in the areas of reward. Most of the library's new technology or market-driven methods have been imported from the outside. Although during the 1980s microcomputer technology enabled us to begin taking charge of our own changes, the system for rewarding successful innovators has not kept pace. Few colleges and universities have devised meaningful incentive systems to motivate or reward the innovators.

Compensation and Performance

In a 1987 study, Berger and Ochsner, two executives of the Hay Management Group foresaw radical changes in the compensation patterns for professionals.[34] They predicted two innovations in compensation: (1) systems that reward top performance rather than seniority or tenure and (2) nontraditional reward techniques such as skill-based pay and lump-sum payments for special merit. Perhaps their forecast, geared to the for-profit sector, has elements of novelty for the business world, but the first technique has been used by private colleges and universities for a very long time, and elements of the second (e.g., the higher-than-usual pay scale for systems analysts and programmers) began to appear in all types of schools almost a generation ago. The main consideration in library administration is not really the compensation methodology but the fact that, with very few exceptions, pay scales for professionals are totally inadequate. To attack this problem, the profession must project a much-improved image to those who make public policy. On this topic the Special Libraries Association published a preliminary report that deserves long-term research and further action by the entire profession, not just special librarianship.[35]

Can Industrial Democracy Be Grafted onto Librarianship?

North American industry is coming around to the very academic view that real capital is not machinery and production lines but personnel, knowledge, and information. To implement this new philosophy, progressive businesses are restructuring–developing more democracy in the workplace, evolving semiautonomous work groups dedicated to immediate problem solving and responsibility for a total product, eliminating the red tape of bureaucratic procedure, encouraging participatory management, reducing the number and levels of supervisors, and collaborating with unions to reduce the number of job classifications and permit greater flexibility of assignment.

Experience proves that these techniques can work, both in manufacturing and in large, office-intensive operations, such as credit agencies, insurance companies, and high-volume retailing.[36] There, semiautonomous worker teams ". . . manage themselves without first-line supervisors, determine their own work pace within parameters set by management, schedule their own vacations, and have a voice in hiring and firing team members and deciding when they qualify for raises."[37]

But how can these arrangements work in higher education's service sector, where so much of the social structure is based on historical elitism and the output is largely intangible? When library employees have been accustomed to departmentation for many years, how could they be motivated to move to a team model? Unlike factory employees, almost all regular academic employees hold permanent positions, a right enjoyed by contract, tenure, sufferance, tradition, legislation, or other protective device; they cannot be moved about like pieces on a gameboard. It is relatively easy for industry to dismiss inefficient or redundant employees, even to get a fresh start by closing a plant and opening up a new one in a different location. The academic community cannot terminate staff and bring in replacements, and relocation of the physical plant is virtually impossible. Besides, academic staff may represent, in the aggregate, hundreds of years of highly specialized intellect, education, training, experience, and historical knowledge. Even if all members are not operating at an optimum level, it is impossible to replace their expertise in the same way as industry can hire new hands. Nor is it possible to quickly resocialize the established power groups of a self-governing entity to form a team.

Fundamentally, team structures spell the redistribution of power in an organization. In the strongly elitist and highly stratified microcosm of academe, however, all members of the group are not peers. It is quite impossible to give everyone an equal voice in programmatic affairs. As stated in chapter 4, an academic community cannot and should not be turned into a team; the concept implies a degree of unity and intimate cooperation that is not attainable in academe. The stratified groupings in an academic library have their own informal structures, separate agendas, group and individual goals, all of which are more in conflict than in congruence. To claim that such diversity can be welded into a team is more than wishful thinking, it is nonsense. Within this arena of conflict, management is an integrating force acting to assure the achievement of institutional mission, goals, and objectives in spite of all these differences. Managers are expected to find or invent ways to get different groups of employees to work together as a coordinated group. Among other things, management is paid to do exactly that.

Redesigning Academic Library Work

The contemporary image of large cadres of operators working at CRTs bears an uncanny resemblance to photographs of nineteenth-century employees, mostly female, tending spindles in textile mills. Given the choice of bending work or the worker, the logical choice is the former; since the industrial revolution, however, business has nearly always picked the latter. There is little point in applying modern technology to recreate a nineteenth-century environment, what Barbara Garson calls the "electronic sweatshop."[38] Flexible scheduling and flexible work assignments are essential to morale and productivity and are far more effective than attempts to convey obviously hollow images of big happy families or work teams.

The first generation of personal computers is being superseded by new machines, operating systems, and software. Where among these changes is the recognition that technology alone, unaided by redirected human energies, cannot solve everything and even creates new problems of its own? Every new tool increases productivity, but the increase may be limited if the new tool is directed largely at solving old problems. Putting microcomputers into the hands of the staff does not merely facilitate work restructuring but demands it. The really effective use of microcomputers requires redefinition and redesign of the work to be accomplished and, ultimately, restructuring of the entire organization.

Redesigning the Organization

A new structural paradigm is needed to lead academic libraries into the twenty-first century. Caution should be invoked in designing it, however, lest expectation exceed realization. The dissolution or alteration of departmentation does not imply the substitution of an organizational style that is infinitely flexible, highly participatory at all decision-making levels, or thoroughly democratic. It would be self-deceptive to believe that in the future hierarchies will be so flattened that they virtually disappear or the collegiality typical of the small college will be scaled up to medium-size and large university libraries.

Complex bureaucracies come into being precisely because unfettered individual autonomy and an institution's overall mission are in perpetual conflict. Acting without coordination, independent professionals cannot produce results in ways that are efficient, timely, or economical. The funders, however, are not requesting but demanding reasonable efficiency. As Michalko emphasized, the effectiveness of a library depends on staff coordination, not staff independence.[39] Like other organizations, libraries require stability to achieve consistency and efficiency; this is why, as Lynch maintained, they tend to "make tasks routine, reduce uncertainty, increase predictability, and centralize authority."[40] We concur with Lynch's bald conclusion that libraries are likely to remain bureaucracies,[41] but they need not and must not remain Fayol-style machine bureaucracies. The library organization of the future will likely be quite dynamic, changing constantly to meet new requirements.

A Matrix Approach to Redesign

For decades the profession at large has suffered from double fragmentation: duality on the personnel side and the enduring public services/technical services rift on the organizational side. To combat hierarchical rigidity, matrix structures have been explored in academic librarianship.[42] A matrix structure combines a functional specialty (e.g., cataloger, reference librarian) with generic duties and responsibilities that range over the entire library. Such a construct is inherently group centered, with group membership changing in accordance with the problem; a matrix arrangement helps to combat the narrowing effects of departmentation.

Matrix structures originated in the aerospace industry, emerging from the unsuitability of conventional organizational styles to realize complex, pioneering development work within budget and schedule. A matrix is inherently fuzzy and diffuse, seemingly unstructured and lacking in focus; it is the very opposite of the "ruly" organizational styles prevalent in the precomputer era of librarianship. It takes many years, a high tolerance for error, and some managerial turnover to install an effective matrix system.[43] Academic libraries have a record of highly successful group efforts in a matrix-like environment: virtually every major automation system implemented in the 1970s and 1980s was the outcome of dedicated teamwork, often superimposed, matrix-fashion, on an established hierarchical framework. But it is important to understand that these successes occurred in project-oriented environments, after years of arduous, often frustrating work, amidst conditions of conflict with traditional views. Now, academic library work itself has changed radically and permanently, having shifted from a comparatively steady-state existence to virtually nonstop project development.

An organization whose work style has changed this radically cannot maintain its old organizational structure. A matrix arrangement tests an entire organization's capacity to deal with uncertainty, lack of structure, constant change, and perpetual conflict–features of organizational life to which librarianship has historically not been accustomed. Further complicating adoption of a matrix structure are a firmly established employment duality and the generally poor fit of business practices in the not-for-profit service sector. Academic librarians will likely need to experiment cautiously with the matrix style, bearing in mind that an academic library is not an aerospace endeavor.

Making Adaptation to Change a Permanent Feature

An institution whose entire history is founded on comparative lack of change and on the preservation of the past does not easily shift its orientation. But the dependable and familiar workplace of the pre-1960 library is gone, and we must assume that the library of the year 2000 will be virtually unrecognizable from today's vantage point. For this reason top management must orchestrate change according to the human capacity to absorb it. Daily, or even weekly, unpredictability is unbearable. Each morning people ought to be 99 percent confident that their work will be much like it was the day before. A week later, they might be prepared for 98 percent congruence with the preceding week. In six months 95 percent, and within a year perhaps down to 90 percent. Within five years, the probability that employees will do then what they actually did five years earlier might be down to 50 percent or less. People can cope with an intelligently planned pace of change; they cannot cope with chaos. The entire staff should be motivated to see the library not as it is but as it can be; therefore, it would be wise to incorporate a schedule for deliberate change into the library's statement of mission, goals, and objectives.

Coping with Demographic Change: Work Force, Enrollment, Social Stress, and Lifestyle Expectations

As the baby-boom generation matures, older people will dominate the work force. These people will compete for limited employment opportunity with the children of rapidly multiplying minorities. By the year 2000 the student population is expected to be older, more ethnically diverse, and more international.[44] More students will return to college as adults to explore several career options throughout their lifetimes. One report suggested that by the 1990s three-quarters of all new hires will be women or minorities; it also claimed that at the end of 1987, "72 percent of women with children between the ages of six and seventeen were [already] in the work force."[45] These figures have profound implications for child-care needs. Still, except for people of oriental extraction, minority enrollment in higher education continues to decline, a fact that raises the unpleasant prospect of a permanent underclass, limited in literacy and low in the complex skills required in a technological society. The academic workplace does not enjoy any exemption from the emotional stresses and demands for benefits that social and technical change has imposed on business and industry – day care, alternative work schedules, parental leave for both sexes, the health impact of video terminals, commuting marriages, care for the elderly, care for sick children, and pay equity issues. Nor can academe be immune from the impact of increasingly unequal education within the white and nonwhite populations.

The Users

Freed from the traditional academic library's information monopoly, future users will be much less tolerant of any surviving bureaucracy that comes between them and their educational or research needs. After the arrival of the Xerox 914 photocopier in the early 1960s, it took users only a few years to build up new delivery expectations in the area of photocopy service. A few decades later, the various networks' computerized interlibrary loan services built up further expectations. As technology continues to accelerate, we may look forward to a rapid buildup of further new services and a significant change in user attitudes. Direct, immediate access to computer power is already perceived as a new entitlement: access to campus, national, and international mainframes is becoming routine. Personal microcomputers and minicomputers are becoming the ordinary accoutrements of scholarship. In contrast, traditional library services and facilities appear static, immobile. In the light of new developments, all academic library users will become more demanding, more vociferous, less patient, and more willing to turn to the commercial sector if the local institution is perceived as unresponsive. To remain responsive, the academic library must become a new kind of institution, with a stronger marketing orientation to cope with the competition for limited resources.

Reinventing Administration

Traditional administration, especially that fashioned after departmentation, has tended to be reactive and retrospectively oriented. Out of existing administrative structures come problems that are sometimes the symptoms of a system that is already unstable. Research and experimentation are needed to develop improved models that detect and anticipate organizational instability so that we can respond before damage occurs. Few groups of human beings care to be the subjects of social experimentation, however, and the technique for accomplishing such change is not clear. Perhaps some experiments in matrix (or other) styles of reorganization are yet another area for joint research among librarians and social scientists. Most important is to understand that an experiment is an experiment; we must not be seduced into viewing every new scheme as a panacea, as in the past.

Like a well-built bridge, a healthy institution is a balanced combination of stiffness and resilience – sturdy enough to resist the static force of its own dead weight and flexible enough to bend under highly variable dynamic loads. If leadership is unimaginative, stiffness gains ascendance over resilience, making it possible for external change to bring the whole organization crashing down with catastrophic suddenness. The administrator's responsibility is to protect the institution's health by maintaining its stability, while at the same time designing and implementing changes that enhance its capacity to respond to external developments, a paradox elegantly expressed by Kanter.[46] The departmental (Kanter's term is "segmental") structure of typical medium and large academic libraries ensures that few units ever see the complete picture. This traditional pattern fosters a fortress mentality, encourages territoriality, and is a throw-back to the manorial-industrial style. Departmentation is inimical to administrators' capacity to "sell" change to the community at all levels.

Reinventing the Library and Reunifying the Profession

The first batch computer systems of the 1960s reinforced a well-entrenched nineteenth-century pattern of scientific management and functional departmentation. The online systems of the 1970s encouraged some redesign in the structure of the library, particularly in the reallocation of work among professionals and support staff, and brought in the stimulating influence of programmers and systems analysts. The arrival of distributed computing and the personal workstation in the 1980s completed a cycle of technological change that enables librarianship to reintegrate itself. At last librarians have a powerful tool to help them implement *their* ideas.

Yet in many libraries traditional organizational structures and obsolete attitudes, remnants of the profession's industrial era, are still in place. Functionally specialized, fragmented structures are more than simply obsolete; they are hazardous to survival. In a society marked by extremely rapid development and communication, narrow work specialization ultimately becomes dysfunctional, no longer contributing to an institution's capacity to competitively deliver the products and services demanded by the modern academic world. In reviewing the impact of new forces on the profession, James G. Neal, dean of libraries at Indiana University, saw six important benefits: (1) new people, new skills, and new ideas in the profession; (2) new organizational structures; (3) new management responsibilities; (4) new work behaviors and work patterns; (5) new relationships among the various strata of employees; and (6) new career opportunities.[47]

The library of the future will not be a place but an agency servicing distributed resources.[48] Supported by telecommunications, academic librarians will constitute a national and international resource. With the help of tools such as databases on CD ROM, the OCLC/Carnegie Mellon Mercury Project, and the Research Libraries Group's Conspectus method of collection analysis, the profession will extend its own invisible college far beyond institutional walls. Through the major bibliographic utilities and the Linked Systems Project, subject specialists and other professionals will work closely together, even if they are in different institutions or countries.

Concisely summarizing how radically librarianship's milieu has changed within a few years, Charles Lowry, director of libraries at the University of Texas, Arlington, urged professionals to recognize that the library has shifted from a labor-intensive craft workshop to a capital-intensive, high-technology, light industry.[49] As part of this shift, no form of librarianship operates in a stable environment. To cope with turbulent change, academic librarianship has to surrender any remaining disconnectedness, laissez-faire autonomy, and dedication to ownership of materials. Higher education now has the opportunity and the tools to transform the library into a people-centered outreach agency with powerful interinstitutional linkages. This transformation is not only proper but essential; if it fails to materialize, the way is open for other agencies to seize the library's domain, as has already occurred in some graduate schools of library and information science.

SUMMARY AND EPILOGUE

Like the airlines, librarianship has entered an era of deregulation. The academic library is no longer a campus information monopoly. The nonlibrary information world is not resting comfortably on its technological achievements. Proponents of these new technologies see them as worthy competition for the university library in the role of key academic information center. For us merely to use new technology to maintain our positions is no longer enough; if academic librarianship is accorded only a maintenance level of support, and if its key professional staff are content with only maintaining existing systems, it cannot survive. Strong leadership is required, and leadership can be developed only by reaching beyond librarianship as we know it today.

The focus of past administration has been on warehouse functions (collections, buildings, facilities), on policy and procedures (rules and regulations, cataloging codes, authority files), and on transaction systems (circulation, networks, database building and maintenance). To restore and regain its preeminence in the pursuit of the life of the mind, a transformed academic librarianship must focus not solely on hardware and systems but on intellectual activity and on people (both staff and clients). Artificial intelligence, expert systems, knowledge navigation systems, and high-capacity digital telecommunication systems ought to be recognized as revolutionary, transformational, and preemptive of established methods, but they do not displace the human element. Like other libraries, the academic library is and will continue to be people serving people. But its survival depends on librarians who are fully empowered proactive professionals, knowledgeable in management science, expert in subject areas, agile and analytical of mind, and masterful of bibliography and its computerized support systems.

By examining the sequential application of new administrative styles, we can easily trace the evolution of management theory in academic libraries from Taylor and Fayol, through the behavioralists, and the still newer theories described by Rehman. Every generation rediscovers and reinvents management and administration. That in itself holds more good than bad, demonstrating flexibility and willingness to change. But if anything negative can be said of recent administrative practice in our profession it is this: both theory and practice have been too slavishly imitative of styles derived from business, too uncritically accepting of apparel tailored for a quite different body. We have searched for techniques rather than principles. The academic world is not the world of commerce and is not the world of democratic politics. We must be more original and less imitative, less trendy and more oriented toward the long range.

Administration is creative and exciting because it deals with the most variable and mercurial of all academic resources–human beings. The human mind is fertile and inventive, human behavior highly variable and adaptive; that is why employees will always be more than a match for any canned approach to administration. Our language and our imagination show a vividness and creativity beyond formula and often beyond analysis.[50] Herman Kahn's comment on history illuminates the enigma of administration equally: "History has a habit of being richer and more ingenious than the limited imaginations of most scholars or laymen."[51] The richness, variability, and unpredictability of human behavior, coupled to rapid, worldwide economic and social change, create ever new challenges to administration and make it a stimulating field.

It is the mind's capacity to deal with uncertainty and ambiguity–precisely the strength of the human spirit–that we require to lead our libraries into the unknowns of the twenty-first century. The beacon of human judgment outshines the brightness of any formula or vogue methodology, however attractive at the moment. As librarianship advances into that realm of high-technology light industry, Shapero's second law may become recognized as the foremost principle of effective, flexible administration: "No matter how you design a system, humans make it work anyway.[52]

Notes

1. Guenter Friedrichs and Adam Schaff, eds., *Microelectronics and Society: A Report to the Club of Rome* (New York: Mentor, 1983).

2. One could easily postulate direct transmission of databases via digital networks to local write-once-read-many times (WORM) compact disks, but a human being would still have to verify the correctness of the delivered material.

3. Three articles challenging the "paperless" view are Maurice B. Line's "The Paperless Society: Do We Want It? Do We Need It?" *Technicalities* 1, no. 12 (November 1981): 2-3; Line's "The Death of

Procrustes? Structure, Style, and Sense," *Scholarly Publishing* 17 (July 1986); 291-301; and Allen B. Veaner's "Into the Fourth Century," *Drexel Library Quarterly* 21, no. 1 (Winter 1985): 4-28, esp. 17-21.

4. Ralph R. Shaw, "Mechanical Storage, Handling, Retrieval and Supply of Information," *Libri* 8, no. 1 (1958): 38.

5. See Shoshana Zuboff's *In the Age of the Smart Machine: The Future of Work and Power* (New York: Basic Books, 1987) and Barbara Garson's *The Electronic Sweatshop: How Computers Are Transforming the Office of the Future into the Factory of the Past* (New York: Simon and Schuster, 1988), for an overview of how computerized work methods are drastically changing conditions of employment.

6. Gerard Salton, "Historical Note: The Past Thirty Years in Information Retrieval," *JASIS* 38, no. 5 (1987): 375-80; Don R. Swanson, "Historical Note: Information Retrieval and the Future of an Illusion," *JASIS* 39, no. 2 (March 1988): 92-98.

7. For an excellent, brief critique of artificial intelligence, see Heinz R. Pagels, *The Dreams of Reason: The Computer and the Rise of the Sciences of Complexity* (New York: Simon and Schuster, 1988), 91-94.

8. There is some evidence that expert systems have the potential for contributing to high-level work, too. Two examples may be cited. With the aid of MITINET, a bibliographic expert system, it is now possible for an operator with little or no technical knowledge to create catalog records in the MARC format; the Pro-Cite system, developed by Personal Bibliographic Software, permits both librarians and scholars to put citations into a variety of authorized forms and relieves them of a burdensome nuisance.

9. An international conference, Telework: Present Situation and Future Development of a New Form of Work Organization, was held in Bonn, 18-20 March 1987. Proceedings are to be published by North-Holland.

10. Margarethe H. Olson, "An Investigation of the Impacts of Remote Work Environments and Supporting Technology," (New

York: New York University, Graduate School of Business Administration, Center for Research on Information Systems, August 1987). See chapter 7, p. 16.

11. Michael Maccoby, *The Gamesman* (New York: Simon and Schuster, 1976), 134.

12. A superbly documented analysis of technology forecasting gone wrong is Bruce C. Klopfenstein's "Forecasting Consumer Adoption of Information Technology and Services–Lessons from Home Video Forecasting," *Journal of the American Society for Information Science* 40, no. 1 (January 1989): 17-26.

13. Fremont Rider, *The Scholar and the Future of the Research Library* (New York: Hadham Press, 1944). Rider overlooked the fact that exponential growth systems are self-limiting, ultimately ending when the raw materials of growth are exhausted or another factor intervenes.

14. Edward G. Holley, "What Lies Ahead for Academic Libraries?" in *Academic Libraries by the Year 2000: Essays Honoring Jerrold Orne*, ed. Herbert Poole (New York: Bowker, 1977), 7-33.

15. Remarks by Daniel Bell at the Special Libraries Association conference, New York City, 12 June 1984.

16. This list is adapted from a presentation by Arno Penzias before the Special Libraries Association Conference, Anaheim, Calif., 8 June 1987.

17. Shiflett, *Origins of American Academic Librarianship*; William Joseph Reeves, *Librarians as Professionals* (Lexington, Mass.: D. C. Heath, 1980), 7. See also George E. Bennett, *Librarians in Search of Science and Identity: The Elusive Profession* (Metuchen, N.J.: Scarecrow Press, 1988).

18. See Richard M. Dougherty, "Personnel Needs for Librarianship's Uncertain Future," *Academic Libraries by the Year 2000*, ed. Poole, 107-118; see esp. 112-13.

19. The giving nature of librarianship may explain, in part, why librarians are not administration minded, have resisted quantification of their work, and have been slow to accept fiscal responsibility

for their programs. We have resisted fees for services, looked askance at the commercial sale of information services, and worried that new technologies might mean a bipolar distribution of access to information – quick and easy access for the well-to-do and prohibitively expensive access for the poor.

20. Richard K. Gardner, ed., *Education of Library and Information Professionals: Present and Future Prospects* (Littleton, Colo.: Libraries Unlimited, 1987); Marion Paris, *Library School Closings: Four Case Studies* (Metuchen, N.J.: Scarecrow Press, 1988); Basil Stuart-Stubbs, ed., *Changing Technology and Education for Librarianship and Information Science* (Greenwich, Conn.: JAI Press, 1985); Sajjad ur Rehman, *Management Theory and Library Education* (New York: Greenwood Press, 1987).

21. W. Boyd Rayward, "Academic Librarianship: The Role of Library Schools," in *Issues in Academic Librarianship: Views and Case Studies for the 1980s and 1990s*, ed. Peter Spyers-Duran and Thomas W. Mann, Jr. (Westport, Conn.: Greenwood Press, 1985), 100-114.

22. James Thompson and Reg Carr, *An Introduction to University Library Administration*, 4th ed. (London: Bingley, 1987), 56.

23. Cf. Richard M. Dougherty, "Personnel Needs for Librarianship's Uncertain Future," 113.

24. See Joshua Meyrowitz, *No Sense of Place* (New York: Oxford University Press, 1985) chapter 15, 307-329.

25. Howard Resnikoff, in *Universities, Information Technology, and Academic Libraries: The Next Twenty Years*, ed. Robert M. Hayes (Norwood, N.J.: Ablex, 1986), 77-133.

26. Harold L. Sheppard and Neal Q. Herrick, *Where Have All the Robots Gone? Worker Dissatisfaction in the 70s* (New York: Free Press, 1972), 118.

27. Robert Swisher, Rosemary Ruhig DuMont, and Calvin J. Boyer, "The Motivation to Manage; A Study of Academic Librarians and Library Science Students," *Library Trends* 34 (Fall 1985): 219-34, esp. 230-32.

28. Howard Resnikoff, in *Universities, Information Technology, and Academic Libraries,* 77-133.

29. Michael Georgeff, quoted in "Don't Expect a Real HAL by 2001," *In Future* (July 1988): 4.

30. Blaise Cronin, "Disjointed Incrementalism and 1990," *ASLIB Proceedings* 37, nos. 11/12 (November/December 1985): 421-36; see esp. 432.

31. Unionization of professional and clerical employees has been long established in Canadian universities.

32. "British Parliament Votes to End Tenure for New Faculty Members at Universities," *Chronicle of Higher Education* 34 (3 August 1988): A1, A32.

33. Henry Rosovsky, "Highest Education," *The New Republic,* nos. 3782-3783 (13, 20 July 1987): 13-14.

34. Lance A. Berger and Robert C. Ochsner, *Compensation in the 90s: A Diagnostic Approach to Customization* (n.p.: Hay Management Consultants, 1987).

35. President's Task Force on the Value of the Information Professional, *Final Report, Preliminary Study* (Washington, D.C.: Special Libraries Association, 1987).

36. Even so, these new techniques are not free from problems. Traditional middle managers typically find team structures threatening and adapt uneasily. Unions continue to view labor-management relations as basically adversarial and see team setups as a possible deterrent to unionization; thus they are slow to give up their rights. The new paradigm's highest rates of success occur in new plants or offices where semicollegial team structures can be installed without the agonies of trying to resocialize an established middle management and/or persuade unions to surrender some power.

37. "Management Discovers the Human Side of Automation." *Business Week,* 29 September 1986, 70-74, 79. See also "The Plant of Tomorrow Is in Texas Today," *Business Week,* 28 July 1986, 76, an article recounting the experience of the Westinghouse Corporation

at College Station, Texas. There, teams of eight-twelve employees often work out their own solutions to production problems. Incentive pay is available for developed, work-related skills; peer pressure encourages quality output. Turnover has been cut from 22 percent to 4 percent. Perhaps the most interesting aspect of the Westinghouse experience is that the company has been forced "to seek a new kind of employee. Applicants must submit to interviews and tests that measure initiative, ability to take advice, creativity, and skills. Only about 5 percent are hired."

38. Barbara Garson, *The Electronic Sweatshop: How Computers Are Transforming the Office of the Future into the Factory of the Past* (New York: Simon and Schuster, 1988).

39. James Michalko, "Management by Objectives and the Academic Library: A Critical Overview," *Library Quarterly* 45 (July 1975): 297.

40. Beverly Lynch, "Libraries as Bureaucracies," *Library Trends* 27 (Winter 1979): 259-67, esp. 266-67.

41. Ibid., 267.

42. Joanne R. Euster and Peter D. Haikalis, "A Matrix Model of Organization for a University Library Public Services Division," in *Academic Libraries: Myths and Realities*, ed. Suzanne C. Dodson and Gary L. Menges (Chicago: ALA/ACRL, 1984), 357-64; Hugh F. Cline and Loraine T. Sinnott, *The Electronic Library: The Impact of Automation on Academic Libraries* (Lexington, Mass.: D.C. Heath, 1983), 130-32, 174.

43. In describing the complexities and problems of matrix-style organization, one of Kanter's interviewees estimated that it can take from three to five years for a manager to learn to work within a matrix system. See Rosabeth M. Kanter, *The Change Masters*, (New York: Simon and Schuster, 1984), 147; see also 138-42, 146-48, for further detail on both the problems and potential of the matrix style.

44. William Schaefer, "Students in the Year 2000: How Many of the Goodly Creatures Are There Here?" in *Universities, Information Technology and Academic Libraries: The Next Twenty Years*, ed. Robert M. Hayes (Norwood, N.J.: Ablex, 1986), 47-55.

45. From a promotional piece on *The National Report on Work & Family* (Washington, D.C.: Buraff Publications, 1988).

46. Kanter, *The Change Masters*, 122ff.

47. James G. Neal, "Where We Stand Today on the Issue of Merging Public and Technical Services," presented to the North Carolina Library Association, Resources and Technical Services Section, Southern Pines, N.C., 29 September 1988. (Published version in press). See also Anna E. Altmann, "The Academic Library of Tomorrow: Who Will Do What?" *Canadian Library Journal* 45 (June 1988): 147-52.

48. Allen B. Veaner, "Progress Towards Goals: Response," in *Library Resource Sharing, Proceedings of the 1976 Conference on Resource Sharing in Libraries*, ed. Allen Kent and Thomas J. Galvin (New York: Dekker, 1977), 105-106.

49. Charles B. Lowry, "A Convergence of Technologies: How Will Libraries Adapt?" *Library Administration and Management* 2, no. 2 (March 1988):77-84. A seminal article.

50. Jeremy Campbell, *Grammatical Man: Information, Entropy, Language, and Life* (New York: Simon and Schuster, 1982), esp. chapter 9, "Jumping the Complexity Barrier," 99-111. Additional related material may be found in Pagels, *The Dreams of Reason*, esp. chapter 3, "Life Can Be So Nonlinear," 71-87.

51. Herman Kahn, *On Thermonuclear War*, 2d ed. (Princeton: Princeton University Press, 1961), 137.

52. Albert Shapero, *Managing Professional People; Understanding Creative Performance* (New York: Free Press, 1985), xvi, 196.

Resources

Adams, John D., ed. *Transforming Work: A Collection of Organizational Transformation Readings*. Alexandria, Va.: Miles River Press, 1984.

Amara, Roy. *Toward Understanding the Social Impact of Computers*. Menlo Park, Calif.: Institute for the Future, 1974.

_____. *Twelve Emerging Technologies for the 1990s.* Menlo Park, Calif.: Institute for the Future, 1986.

Asheim, Lester. *Library School Preparation for Academic and Research Librarianship.* Washington, D.C.: Council on Library Resources, 1983.

Automation and the Workplace: Selected Labor, Education, and Training Issues, A Technical Memorandum. Washington, D.C.: U.S. Government Printing Office, 1983.

Bailey, Martin Neil, and Alok K. Chakrabarti. *Innovation and the Productivity Crisis.* Washington, D.C.: Brookings Institution, 1988.

Bezold, Clement, et al. *The Future of Work and Health.* Dover, Mass.: Auburn House, 1986.

Blyton, Paul. "New Technology and Future Work Patterns." In *The Management Implications of New Information Technology*, edited by Nigel Piercy, 122-39. New York: Nichols, 1984.

Boaz, Martha. *Strategies for Meeting the Information Needs of Society in the Year 2000.* Littleton, Colo.: Libraries Unlimited, 1981.

Boyce, Michael T. "Can Quality Circles be Applied in the Public Sector?" *Journal of Collective Negotiations* 14, no. 1 (1985): 67-75.

Breivik, Patricia S., and E. Gordon Gee. *Information Literacy: Revolution in the Library.* New York: Macmillian, 1989.

Capra, F. *The Turning Point: Science, Society and the Rising Culture.* London: Wildwood House, 1982.

Carnegie Commission on Policy Studies in Higher Education. *Three Thousand Futures: The Next Twenty Years for Higher Education.* San Francisco, Calif.: Jossey-Bass, 1980.

Chiara, Lynn A., and Dan Lacey, eds. *Work in the 21st Century.* Alexandria, Va.: American Society of Personnel Administrators, 1984.

Cline, Hugh F., and Loraine T. Sinnott. *The Electronic Library.* Lexington, Mass.: Lexington, 1983.

Cordell, Arthur J. "Work in the Information Age." *Futurist* 19, no. 6 (December 1985): 12-14.

Cornfield, Daniel B. *Workers, Managers, and Technological Change: Emerging Patterns of Labor Relations.* New York: Plenum, 1987.

Cross, Thomas B., and Marjorie Raizman. *Telecommuting: Work Strategies for the Information Organization.* Homewood, Ill.: Dow Jones-Irwin, 1986.

Davinson, Donald. *Academic Libraries in the Enterprise Culture.* London: Library Association, 1989.

Davis, Louis E., and Albert B. Cherns, eds. *The Quality of Working Life: Cases and Commentary.* 2 vols. Vol. 1, *Problems, Prospects and the State of the Art*, vol. 2, *Cases and Commentary.* New York: Free Press, 1975.

Deken, Joseph. *The Electronic Cottage.* New York: Bantam, 1981.

Dobson, Cynthia, Paula Morrow, and Dilys Morris. "The Impact of Changes in Office Environment on Productivity and Work Attitudes." Presented at a poster session, Association of College and Research Libraries Fifth National Conference, Cincinnati, Ohio, April 1989.

Drucker, Peter F. "The Coming of the New Organization." *Harvard Business Review* 66, no. 1 (January/February 1988): 45-53.

Eder, Peter F. "Telecommuters: the Stay-at-Home Work Force of the Future." *The Futurist* 17, no. 3 (June 1983): 30-35.

Enzer, Selwyn. *Working Our Way to the Twenty-First Century.* Report, F60. Los Angeles: Center for Futures Research, 1985.

Epstein, Hank. "Technological Trends in Information Services to the 21st Century." Paper prepared for the Urban Library Management Institute, Milwaukee Wis., October 1988. (Unpublished.)

Euster, Joanne R., and Peter D. Haikalis. "A Matrix Model of Organization for a University Public Services Division." In *Academic Libraries: Myths and Realities*, edited by Suzanne C. Dodson and Gary L. Menges, 357-64. Chicago: Association of College & Research Libraries, 1984.

Evans, G. Edward. "Research Libraries in 2010." In *Research Libraries: The Past 25 Years, The Next 25 Years*, edited by Taylor E. Hubbard, 77-94. Boulder, Colo.: Colorado Associated University Press, 1986.

Fennell, Janice C., ed. *Building on the First Century: Proceedings of the Fifth National Conference of the Association of College and Research Libraries*. Chicago: American Library Association, 1989.

Garson, Barbara. *All the Livelong Day: The Meaning and Demeaning of Routine Work*. Harmondsworth: Penguin, 1983.

_____. *The Electronic Sweatshop: How Computers Are Transforming the Office of the Future into the Factory of the Past*. New York: Simon and Schuster, 1988.

Gould, Leroy C., et al. *Perceptions of Technological Risks and Benefits*. New York: Russell Sage Foundation, 1988.

Govan, James. "The Creeping Invisible Hand: Entrepreneurial Librarianship." *Library Journal* 113, no. 1 (January 1988): 35-38.

Hayes, Robert M., ed. *Universities, Information Technology, and Academic Libraries*. Norwood, N.J.: Ablex, 1986.

Heron, Alexander R. *Why Men Work*. Stanford: Stanford University Press, 1948.

Hirschhorn, Larry. *Beyond Mechanization: Work and Technology in a Post-Industrial Age*. Cambridge: MIT Press, 1986.

Hirshon, Arnold. "Vision, Focus, and Technology in Academic Research Libraries: 1971 to 2001." *Advances in Library Automation and Networking* 2 (1988): 215-57.

Holley, Edward G. "What Lies Ahead for Academic Libraries?" In *Academic Libraries by the Year 2000: Essays Honoring Jerrold Orne*, edited by Herbert Poole, 7-33. New York: Bowker, 1977.

Horny, Karen L. "New Turns for a New Century: Library Services in an Information Age." *Library Resources & Technical Services* 31 (January/March 1987): 6-11.

Hunt, H. Allan. "Technological Change and Employment; Fears and Reality." *Looking Ahead* 10, no. 1 (Summer 1987): 1-5.

Hunt, H. Allan, and Timothy L. Hunt. *Clerical Employment and Technological Change*. Kalamazoo, Mich.: W. E. Upjohn Institute for Employment Research, 1986.

Inderscience Enterprises. *Future Development in Technology: The Year 2000*. Proceedings of a conference held in London, 4-6 April 1984. Geneva, 1988.

Johnston, William B., and Arnold E. Packer. *Workforce 2000: Work and Workers for the 21st Century*. Indianapolis: Hudson Institute, 1987.

Jones, Barry. "Information, Education and Human Resources Development: The Information Explosion and Its Threats." C. A. Housden Lecture. Supplement to the *Australian School Librarian* 18, no. 4 (Summer 1981): i-xv.

_____. *Sleepers, Wake! Technology and the Future of Work*. 2d ed. New York: Oxford University Press, 1985.

Kanter, Rosabeth M. "Work in a New America." *Daedalus* 107 (Winter 1978): 47-78.

Keane, John G. "Our Cities: Trends and Times." Address to the U.S. Conference of Mayors, Anchorage, Alaska, 18 June 1985. Washington, D.C.: Bureau of the Census, 1985.

Kent, Allen, and Thomas J. Galvin, eds. *Information Technology: Critical Choices for Library Decision-Makers*. New York: Dekker, 1982.

Kimberley, John W., and Robert H. Miles and Associates, eds. *The Organizational Life Cycle: Issues in the Creation, Transformation, and Decline of Organizations*. San Francisco, Calif.: Jossey-Bass, 1980.

Lancaster, F. Wilfrid. "Future Librarianship: Preparing for an Unconventional Career." *Wilson Library Bulletin* 57 (May 1983): 747-53.

_____. *Libraries and Librarians in an Age of Electronics*. Arlington, Va.: Information Resources Press, 1982.

Lapham, Lewis, ed. *High Technology and Human Freedom*. Washington, D.C.: Smithsonian Institution, 1985.

Leontief, Wassily, and Faye Duchin. *The Future Impact of Automation on Workers*. London: Oxford University Press, 1986.

Levitan, Sar A. "Beyond 'Trendy' Forecasts: The Next Ten Years for Work." *Futurist* 21, no. 6 (November-December 1987): 28-32.

Lewis, David W. "An Organizational Paradigm for Effective Academic Libraries." *College & Research Libraries* 47, no. 4 (July 1986): 337-53.

Lieberman, Ernest D. *Unfit to Manage!* New York: McGraw-Hill, 1988.

Leonhardt, Thomas W. "Cataloger/Reference Librarian – The Way to Go?" *RTSD Newsletter* 9, no. 3 (1984): 27-29.

Line, Maurice B. "Librarianship as It Is Practised: A Failure of Intellect, Imagination and Initiative." In *A Little Off Line*, 39-50. Huntingdon, Cambs: ELM Publications, 1988.

_____. "Libraries and Information Services in a Post-Technological Society." *Journal of Library Automation* 14, no. 4 (December 1981): 252-67.

_____. "The Research Library in the Enterprise Society." *LSE Quarterly* 2, no. 4 (Winter 1988): 361-78.

Lipson, Joseph I., and Kathleen M. Fisher. "Technologies of the Future." *Education and Computing* 1, no. 1 (January 1985): 11-23.

London, Keith. *The People Side of Systems*. London: McGraw-Hill, 1976.

Lowry, Charles B. "A Convergence of Technologies: How Will Libraries Adapt?" *Library Administration and Management* 2, no. 2 (March 1988): 77-84.

Lucas, Barbara. *Electronic Information Services*. Menlo Park, Calif.: Institute for the Future, 1986.

Lynch, Beverly, ed. *The Academic Library in Transition: Planning for the 1990s*. New York: Neal-Schuman, 1989.

MacCrimmon, Kenneth R., and Donald A. Ehrenburg. *Taking Risks: The Management of Uncertainty*. New York: Free Press, 1988.

Marcum, Deanna B. "Management Training for Research Librarianship." *Advances in Library Administration and Organization* 2 (1983): 1-19.

Marks, Mitchell Lee. "The Question of Quality Circles." *Psychology Today*, March 1986, 36-46.

Martin, Susan K. "The Immovable Force and the Irresistible Object." *Library Trends* 37, no. 3 (Winter 1989): 374-82.

Mathews, Anne J., ed. *Rethinking the Library in the Information Age*. 3 vols. Washington, D.C.: Office of Educational Research and Improvement, U.S. Department of Education, 1988.

Moran, Barbara B. "Academic Libraries: Meeting the Challenges of the Electronic University." *Library Times International* 6, no. 1 (July 1989): 1, 3.

Neal, James G. "The Walls Came Tumblin' Down: Distributed Cataloging and the Public/Technical Services Relationship – The Public Services Perspective." State College, University of Pennsylvania, 1985. (Unpublished.)

"A New Era for Management." *Business Week*, 25 April 1983, 50-86.

O'Neil, Robert M. "Academic Libraries and the Future: A President's View." *College & Research Libraries* 45 (May 1984): 184-88.

Osterman, Paul. *Employment Futures; Reorganization, Dislocation and Public Policy.* New York: Oxford University Press, 1988.

Pagels, Heinz R. *The Dreams of Reason: The Computer and the Rise of the Sciences of Complexity.* New York: Simon and Schuster, 1988.

"The Plant of Tomorrow Is in Texas Today," *Business Week*, 28 July 1986, 76.

Porter, Alan. "Work in the New Information Age." *The Futurist* 20 (September-October 1986): 9-14.

Provenzo, Eugene F., Jr. *Beyond the Gutenberg Galaxy.* New York: Teachers College Press, 1986.

Reeves, William Joseph. *Librarians as Professionals.* Lexington, Mass.: D.C. Heath, 1980.

Reneker, Maxine H. "The Matheson-Cooper Report: Transforming the Capabilities of Academic Research Libraries." In *Library Lectures*, no. 53, edited by Jane P. Kleiner, 1-16. Baton Rouge, La.: Louisiana State University, 1987.

Richardson, John. "Expert Systems for Reference Service." *Bulletin of the American Society for Information Science* 14, no. 6 (August/September 1988): 19-20.

Riggs, Donald E., and Gordon A. Sabine. *Libraries in the '90s: What the Leaders Expect.* Phoenix, Ariz.: Oryx, 1988.

Rochell, Carlton. "Changing Technology and the Personnel Requirements of Research Libraries." In *Changing Technology and Education for Librarianship and Information Science*, edited by Basil Stuart-Stubbs, 23-37. Greenwich, Conn.: JAI Press, 1985.

Rogers, Everett M. *Diffusion of Innovations.* 3d ed. New York: Free Press, 1983.

Shaiken, Harley. *Work Transformed: Automation and Labor in the Computer Age.* New York: Holt, Rinehart and Winston, 1985.

Shaughnessy, Thomas W. "Technology and the Structure of Libraries." *Libri* 32 (1982): 144-55.

Sheldon, Brooke E. "On Beyond Management: Leadership and the Information Professional." *ALA Yearbook* 13 (1988): 8-10.

Standing Conference of National and University Libraries. "Information Technology as It Affects Access to Materials Over the Next 5-10 Years." In *Issues Facing Academic Libraries: A Review*, 33-44. London, 1985.

Strassman, Paul A. *Information Payoff: The Transformation of Work in the Electronic Age*. New York: Free Press, 1985.

Striedieck, Suzanne. "The Walls Came Tumblin' Down: Distributed Cataloging and the Public/Technical Services Relationship – The Technical Services Perspective." State College, University of Pennsylvania, 1985. (Unpublished.)

Stuart-Stubbs, Basil, ed. *Changing Technology and Education for Librarianship and Information Science*. Greenwich, Conn.: JAI Press, 1985.

Terkel, Studs. *The Great Divide: Second Thoughts on the American Dream*. New York: Pantheon, 1988.

Thompson, James. *The End of Libraries*. London: Bingley, 1982.

"Trends in Professional Employment." *CLR Reports* 2, no. 1 (February 1988): 1, 3.

U.S. Congress, Office of Technology Assessment. *The Electronic Supervisor: New Technology, New Tensions.* Washington, D.C.: U.S. Government Printing Office, 1987.

_____. *Informing the Nation: Federal Information Dissemination in an Electronic Age.* Washington, D.C.: U.S. Government Printing Office, 1988.

_____. *Technology and the American Economic Transition.* Washington, D.C.: U.S. Government Printing Office, 1988.

Von Oech, Roger. *A Whack on the Side of the Head*. New York: Warner, 1983.

Vosper, Robert. "Library Administration on the Threshold of Change." In *Issues in Library Administration*, edited by Warren M. Tsuneishi et al., 37-51. New York: Columbia University Press, 1974.

Webb, Gisela M. "Implementing Team Management at the Texas Tech University Libraries." *Library Personnel News* 1, no. 4 (Fall 1987): 39-40.

Weisbord, Marvin R. *Productive Workplaces: Organizing and Managing for Dignity, Meaning, and Community*. San Francisco, Calif.: Jossey-Bass, 1987.

Westin, Alan F., et al. *The Changing Workplace: A Guide to Managing People: Organizational and Regulatory Aspects of Office Technology*. White Plains, N.Y.: Knowledge Industry Publications, 1985.

White, Herbert S. *Librarians and the Awakening from Innocence*. Boston: G.K. Hall, 1989.

_____. "Managing Libraries and the Societal Moral Good." *Library Journal* 113, no. 7 (15 April 1988): 60-61.

Wilensky, Harold L. *Organizational Intelligence*. New York: Basic Books, 1967.

_____. "Work, Careers, and Leisure Styles." In *Harvard University Program on Technology and Society, 1964-1972, A Final Review*, 140-44. Cambridge, Mass., Harvard University, 1972.

Work in America. Report of a Special Task Force to the Secretary of Health, Education, and Welfare. Prepared under the auspices of the W. E. Upjohn Institute for Employment Research. Cambridge, Mass.: MIT Press, 1973.

Yerburgh, Mark R. "Some Unguarded Thoughts on Academic Librarianship: Vision vs Reality." *CLIC Quarterly* 2, no. 4 (December 1983): 11-19.

Yngstrom, Louise, et al. *Can Information Technology Result in Benevolent Bureaucracies?* Amsterdam: North-Holland, 1985.

Zuboff, Shoshana. *In the Age of the Smart Machine: The Future of Work and Power*. New York: Basic Books, 1987.

Appendix

Resources in Library Administration

For the reader's convenience, the principal English-language monographs that are pertinent to academic library administration and within the scope of this volume are listed below. Many of these titles have already been cited throughout the text.

In recent years several important new types of reference material for management and administration have appeared: audio cassettes, videos, software. New materials in electronic format are proliferating so rapidly that it is impossible to provide an up-to-date listing in a work such as this. Refer to professional journals for current electronic media.

Boaz, Martha, ed. *Current Concepts in Library Management*. Littleton, Colo.: Libraries Unlimited, 1979.

Buck, Paul. *Libraries and Universities: Addresses and Reports*. Cambridge: Harvard University Press, 1964.

Cargill, Jennifer, and Gisela Webb. *Managing Libraries in Transition*. Phoenix, Ariz.: Oryx, 1987.

Creth, Sheila, and Frederick Duda. *Personnel Administration in Libraries*. 2d ed. New York: Neal-Schuman, 1989.

De Gennaro, Richard. *Libraries, Technology, and the Information Marketplace.* Boston: G.K. Hall, 1987. (Reprints of De Gennaro's most noted articles.)

Dougherty, Richard M., and Fred J. Heinritz. *Scientific Management of Library Operations.* 2d ed. Metuchen, N.J.: Scarecrow Press, 1982.

Durey, Peter. *Staff Management in University and College Libraries.* Oxford: Pergamon Press, 1976.

Evans, G. Edward. *Management Techniques for Librarians.* 2d ed. New York: Academic Press, 1983.

Farber, Evan Ira, and Ruth Walling, eds. *The Academic Library: Essays in Honor of Guy R. Lyle.* Metuchen, N.J.: Scarecrow Press, 1974.

Foster, Donald L. *Managing the Cataloging Department.* Metuchen, N.J.: Scarecrow Press, 1987.

Galvin, Thomas J., and Beverly Lynch, eds. *Priorities for Academic Libraries.* San Francisco, Calif.: Jossey-Bass, 1982.

Georgi, Charlotte, and Robert Bellanti, eds. *Excellence in Library Management.* New York: Haworth, 1985.

Godden, Irene P. *Library Technical Services: Operations and Management.* Orlando, Fla.: Academic Press, 1984.

Issues Facing Academic Libraries: A Review. London: Standing Conference of National and University Libraries, 1985.

Kohl, David F. *Handbooks for Library Management.* 6 vols. Santa Barbara, Calif.: ABC-Clio Information Services, 1985.

Kreissman, Bernard, and Gerard McCabe, eds. *Advances in Library Administration and Organization.* Greenwich, Conn.: JAI Press, annual.

Kusack, James M. *Unions for Academic Library Support Staff: Impact on Workers and the Workplace.* Westport, Conn.: Greenwood Press, 1986.

Line, Maurice B. *Academic Library Management.* London: Library Association, 1990.

Lomas, Tim. *Management Issues in Academic Libraries*. London: Rossendale, 1986.

Lyle, Guy R. *The Administration of the College Library*. 4th ed. New York: H. W. Wilson, 1974.

Lynch, Beverly, ed. *The Academic Library in Transition: Planning for the 1990s*. New York: Neal-Schuman, 1989.

_____. *Management Strategies for Libraries: A Basic Reader*. New York: Neal-Schuman, 1985.

McCabe, Gerard B., ed. *The Smaller Academic Library: A Management Handbook*. Westport, Conn.: Greenwood Press, 1988.

McClure, Charles R. *Information for Academic Library Decision Making: The Case for Organizational Information Management*. Westport, Conn.: Greenwood Press, 1980.

_____, ed. *Planning for Library Services: A Guide to Utilizing Planning Methods for Library Management*. New York: Haworth, 1982.

McElroy, A. Rennie. *College Librarianship*. Phoenix, Ariz.: Oryx, 1984.

Marchant, Maurice P. *Participative Management in Academic Libraries*. Westport, Conn.: Greenwood Press, 1976.

Martell, Charles. *The Client-Centered Academic Library: An Organizational Model*. Westport, Conn.: Greenwood Press, 1983.

Martin, Lowell A. *Organizational Structure of Libraries*. Metuchen, N.J.: Scarecrow Press, 1984.

Martin, Murray S. *Budgetary Control in Academic Libraries*. Greenwich, Conn.: JAI Press, 1978.

_____. *Issues in Personnel Management in Academic Libraries*. Greenwich, Conn.: JAI Press, 1981.

_____, ed. *Financial Planning for Libraries*. New York: Haworth, 1983.

Metcalfe, Keyes D. *Planning Academic and Research Library Buildings.* Rev. by Philip D. Leighton and David C. Weber. Chicago: ALA, 1986.

Miller, William, and D. Stephen Rockwood, eds. *College Librarianship.* Metuchen, N.J.: Scarecrow Press, 1981.

Moran, Barbara B. *Academic Libraries: The Changing Knowledge Centers of Colleges and Universities.* Washington, D.C.: Association for Study of Higher Education, 1984.

Pack, Peter, and Marian Pack. *Colleges, Learning, and Libraries.* London: Bingley, 1989.

Person, Ruth. *The Management Process: A Selection of Readings for Librarians.* Chicago: American Library Association, 1983.

The Personnel Manual: An Outline for Libraries. Chicago: American Library Association, 1977.

Poole, Herbert, ed. *Academic Libraries by the Year 2000: Essays Honoring Jerrold Orne.* New York: Bowker, 1977.

Prentice, Ann E. *Financial Planning for Libraries.* Metuchen, N.J.: Scarecrow Press, 1983.

Rawles, Beverly A. *Human Resources Management in Small Libraries.* Hamden Conn.: Shoe String Press, 1982.

Rizzo, John R. *Management for Librarians: Fundamentals and Issues.* Westport, Conn.: Greenwood Press, 1980.

Rogers, Rutherford D., and David C. Weber. *University Library Administration.* New York: Wilson, 1971.

Rooks, Dana C. *Motivating Today's Library Staff: A Management Guide.* Phoenix, Ariz.: Oryx, 1988.

St. Clair, Guy, and Joan Williamson. *Managing the One-Person Library.* London: Butterworths, 1986.

Shimmon, Ross, ed. *A Reader in Library Management.* London: Bingley, 1976.

Stebbins, Kathleen, and Foster E. Mohrhardt. *Personnel Administration in Libraries*. 2d ed. Metuchen, N.J.: Scarecrow Press, 1966.

Stevens, Norman D. *Communication Throughout Libraries*. Metuchen, N.J.: Scarecrow Press, 1983.

Stirling, John F., ed. *University Librarianship*. London: Library Association, 1981.

Stueart, Robert D., ed. *Academic Librarianship: Yesterday, Today, Tomorrow*. New York: Neal-Schuman, 1982.

Stueart, Robert D., and Barbara B. Moran. *Library Management*. 3d ed. Littleton, Colo.: Libraries Unlimited, 1987.

Thompson, James. *The End of Libraries*. London: Bingley, 1982.

Thompson, James, and Reg Carr. *An Introduction to University Library Administration*. 4th ed. London: Bingley, 1987.

Wasserman, Paul, and Mary Lee Bundy, eds. *Reader in Library Administration*. Washington, D.C.: Microcard Editions, 1968.

White, Herbert S. *Librarians and the Awakening from Innocence*. Boston: G.K. Hall, 1989.

_____. *Library Personnel Management*. White Plains, N.Y.: Knowledge Industry Publications, 1985.

Wilson, Louis Round, and Maurice F. Tauber. *The University Library: The Organization, Administration, and Functions of Academic Libraries*. 2d ed. New York: Columbia University Press, 1956. (Chiefly of historic interest.)

Woodsworth, Anne, and Barbara A. von Wahlde, eds. *Leadership for Research Libraries: A Festschrift for Robert M. Hayes*. Metuchen, N.J.: Scarecrow Press, 1988.

INDEX

Compiled by Susan Klement

This index indicates only the first full bibliographic reference to a cited work.

and program, 167, 168-69
and recruitment, 263
and travel, 372-73
Collins, Eliza G.C., 91, 386
colloquia and special guests, 374
Columbia University, 380
Commerce Clearing House, 255, 293
committee participation, 65
committees, 181-82, 418 *see also* faculty library committee; search panels
  and decision making, 127, 199
  to draft vacancy postings, 272
  and exhibits, 217
  friends groups, 214
  and new administrator, 97
committees (campus), participation, 199, 200
communication, 184-95, 218, 273, 366, 405, 424, 435, 436 *see also* confidentiality and secrecy
  and all-staff meetings, 190
  and cultural diversity, 194-95, 222-23
  and decision making, 184-85
  and delegation, 129
  deterioration of skills in, 13
  and exhibits, 217
  expense of, 185-86
  and the faculty club, 213
  and the grapevine, 191
  and hierarchical structure, 184
  and management by objectives, 316
  meetings, 191-93
  and morale, 186
  and new positions, 272
  and performance appraisal, 311, 318, 321-25, 333
  and personal regimes, 136, 138
  and power, 184
  public speaking, 108

and support staff, 185-86
  telephone, for employee references, 286
  and termination, 354
  written, 185-86, 193-94, 222, 269, 273, 371 *see also* memos; reports
  and budgeting, 205-6, 209
  and discipline, 332
  excessive, 194
  performance appraisal, 325-26
  and termination, 348, 349-53, 357-58
community service, 320, 377
compensation *see also* pay
  in lieu of notice, 345
compensatory time, 87, 258
competence and incompetence, 262, 270, 317, 349, 352, 355, 402
computer programming professionals, 171, 273, 446, 453
computers, xix, 273, 419-20, 424, 430, 431-34, 443, 448, 452, 453, 457
  and education of workers, 34
  impact, 372, 373
    on budgeting, 205
    on productivity, 13-14, 15
  librarians and, 16, 266
  and library work, xvi, 75, 442
  and professional development, 379
  and recruitment, 253
conferences *see* professional conferences
confidentiality and secrecy, 185, 221 *see also* communication
  and cabinet reports, 188
  and litigation, 221
  and mail, 111
  necessity for, 187
  and program review, 177
  and termination, 353-54
Conflict Clinic, Inc., The, 132

Odiorne, George S., 152, 160
O'Donnell, Cyril, 118
office equipment and tools, 178, 418, 419-20, 424
Office for Library Personnel Resources, 153, 255, 261, 274, 299, 337, 361
Office of Management Studies *see* Association of Research Libraries, Office of Management Studies
office productivity, 13-14
office routines, 110-11
O'Hare, Patrick, 157
Oldham, Neild B., 228, 426
Oliver, Anthony T., 363
Olson, Margarethe H., 434, 457-58
OMS *see* Association of Research Libraries – Office of Management Studies
Oncken, William, 416, 424, 425
one-person libraries, 79
O'Neil, Robert M., 44, 231, 469
Ong, Walter, 25
Online Computer Library Center (OCLC), 141, 151, 180, 454
Ontario Association of Library Technicians, 249
Ontario Colleges Collective Bargaining Act, 259
Ontario Employment Standards Act, 259
Ontario Provincial Labour Relations Act, 259
Oram, Robert, 214
orchestra versus a library, 133, 166
organization charts, 6, 51, 144
organizational structure, 55-58, 166, 184, 416, 448-49, 453-54
matrix structure, 449-50, 452, 461
orientation, 289-91, 298, 326, 369
videos, 379
Orne, Jerrold, 44, 46
Osgood, Charles, 118

OSHA (Occupational Safety and Health Administration), 293
Osterman, Paul, 469
outplacement, 353, 356, 358-59
outreach, 377
outside commitments, 137-39
overtime, 71, 72, 86, 87, 258
Ozaki, Hiroko, 92

P

Pack, Marian, 476
Pack, Peter, 476
Packer, Arnold E., 466
Pagels, Heinz R., 457
Palmer, E.E., 259, 293
Panizzi, Sir Anthony, 289
paradox
of academe, 202
of administration, 52, 139, 453
professional, 235, 247
paraprofessionals *see* support staff
Paris, Marion, 199, 223
part-time work, 384
paternalism, 145-46, 169, 309
Patmore, S.J., 392, 409
Patten, Thomas H., 341
pay, 11, 255, 436
academic, 39
and administrative responsibilities, 367
and collective bargaining, 181
and confidentiality, 185
discrimination, 259
and Equal Pay Act of 1963, 67-68
equal pay for equal work, 257
exempt versus nonexempt staff, 54
and flexibility of position descriptions, 246
and Hay system, 78
increase, in job offer, 289
increases, demand for, 202

ABOUT THE AUTHOR

Allen B. Veaner is the principal of Allen B. Veaner Associates, a Toronto consulting firm specializing in academic libraries. An alumnus of the Simmons College Graduate School of Library and Information Science, he began his career as a cataloger in Harvard University's Widener Library. Applying his background in physics, he became head of Harvard's Microreproduction Library, serving other libraries and scholars worldwide. In 1964, he moved to Stanford University Libraries as chief of acquisitions and later served as Stanford's assistant director for automation and technical services. From 1977 to 1983, he was university librarian at the University of California, Santa Barbara, where he introduced both the OCLC and RLIN systems. He established his consulting business in Toronto when he married Susan Klement, a Canadian library consultant.

Throughout his career, Veaner has been in the forefront of promoting new technologies in the service of academic librarianship. He has served on numerous committees within major U.S. professional associations (ACRL, ALA, ARL, ASIS, and SLA) and has consulted for academic, public, and special libraries, the Library of Congress, and national libraries abroad. Veaner has been particularly supportive of bibliographic standards through his work in international librarianship in North America, Europe, and Asia. He has lectured and taught at library schools throughout North America and has actively participated in the accreditation of graduate library programs under the auspices of ALA's Committee on Accreditation.

In 1981 the Simmons College GSLIS Alumni Association honored him with its Alumni Achievement Award, and in 1988 the Special Libraries Association presented him with its President's Award for Exceptional Service.